THE UNOFFICIAL GUIDE

TO

ETHNIC CUISINE

AND

DINING IN AMERICA

Also available from Macmillan Travel

The Unofficial Guide to Atlanta, by Fred Brown and Bob Sehlinger
The Unofficial Guide to Disneyland, by Bob Sehlinger
The Unofficial Guide to Euro Disneyland, by Bob Sehlinger
The Unofficial Guide to Las Vegas, by Bob Sehlinger
The Unofficial Guide to Miami and the Keys,
        by Bob Sehlinger and Joe Surkiewicz
The Unofficial Guide to the Great Smoky and Blue Ridge Mountains,
        by Bob Sehlinger and Joe Surkiewicz
The Unofficial Guide to Walt Disney World, by Bob Sehlinger
The Unofficial Guide to Washington, D.C.,
        by Bob Sehlinger and Joe Surkiewicz
The Unofficial Guide to Dining in Atlanta, by Terrell Vermont
The Unofficial Guide to Dining in Chicago, by Camille Stagg
The Unofficial Guide to Dining in Miami and Southeastern Florida,
        by Lucy Cooper
The Unofficial Guide to Dining in Washington, D.C., by Eve Zibart

THE UNOFFICIAL GUIDE

TO

ETHNIC CUISINE

AND

DINING IN AMERICA

Eve Zibart
Muriel Stevens
Terrell Vermont

MACMILLAN • USA

Macmillan Travel
A Prentice Hall Macmillan Company
15 Columbus Circle
New York, New York 10023

Produced by Menasha Ridge Press
Interior book design by Suzanne H. Holt, *B. Williams & Associates*
Decorative borders by Mary Holt, *TexStyles*

Macmillan is a registered trademark of Macmillan, Inc.
The Unofficial Guide is a registered trademark of Robert W. Sehlinger

ISBN 0-02-860067-3

Library of Congress Catalog Card Number: 94-73806

Manufactured in the United States of America

10 9 8 7 6 5 4 3 2 1

First Edition

PREFACE

It is one of the most fascinating paradoxes of modern American life that we are obsessed with food, inundated with advertising, bombarded with advice, and offered thousands of varieties of consumables from all over the world—and yet we have forgotten the most vital truths about *eating*. Preparing food, serving it, and sitting down with friends or family is more than a physical necessity or social exercise; it's a ceremony, a re-exploration not just of our own short and visible history but of thousands of years of barter and translation and conquest and commerce and marriage and migration and famine. It encodes genealogies, tribal allegiances, taboos, languages, prescriptions, fears of pollution, and hopes of resurrection. Within a single menu item—lamb curry, for instance—are written whole romances: how the spices of Indonesia, the rice of China, the flatbreads of Mesopotamia, the compotes of Persia, and the meat of the conquering Mongols came to be lumped together under the casually mistranslated title bestowed by imperial Britain.

Centuries before refrigeration, before marked roads or sea routes, peoples and foods moved across continents: rice from China to India to the Middle East, to Egypt to Greece to Portugal to South America to South Carolina to Africa. Corn from Peru to Spain to Morocco to Turkey to Italy, chilies from Mexico to Malaysia to Thailand; tempura from Portugal to India to Japan, sauerkraut from China to Rome to Germany. When we enter a restaurant, therefore—when we become a guest in another culture and participate in its traditions—we ought to appreciate the intricate piecing together of peoples that a nation represents.

Satisfaction is another thing we have forgotten with regard to food. A social meal should absorb us: capture our eyes with color, fascinate us with flavor and texture and aroma, feed our sense of wonder as well as the others. Nutrition, "diet," and convenience are all important considerations, but companionship, conversation (or the contemplation of a good book, even), and full sensual enjoyment of a meal are just as vital to our well-being.

This, then, is more than a restaurant guide, and less than an encyclopedia. It's an armchair traveler's companion to ethnic dining, a gazetteer to the overlapping cultures and waves of civilizations and discoveries that have framed our world. It's designed to make dining in an ethnic restaurant less intimidating, more illuminating, and more familiar, like a return to a favorite destination or even a childhood story remembered. To that end, it looks back to each cuisine's history, its natural limitations, its borrowed or impressed additions, its techniques and tools.

This guide also encourages you to reexamine some of the cultural assumptions our society makes about others. We'd like you to try dining in the traditional manner of each region, which is a way not only to be respectful but also to lose a lot of prejudices. Western European cultures have a tendency to look down on societies that eat with their fingers, although they themselves only gave up the habit—reluctantly—a handful of generations ago. We feel clumsy wielding chopsticks or rolling lettuce leaves or tortillas, a discomfort we confuse with a lack of sophistication. But eating with the hands slows you down, makes you concentrate on and enjoy your food more, so you actually eat less (tastes great, more fulfilling).

Eating by hand restores the human touch in metaphorical fashion as well: The proliferation of serving utensils, a particularly conspicuous form of consumption designed by the wealthy few, implicitly required the expansion of the servant class and a distancing of the kitchen labor from the privileged diner. This way you receive the food the way it is prepared.

Considering the history of a cuisine is another way to shake off some biases. If there is a great unsung hero of international cooking, it is the Persians, whose cuisine is not only maintained in so many countries today, from the Middle East to Afghanistan, but was also integral to the development of Mediterranean, Indian, and Indonesian foods as well. Yet

Persian restaurants (many of which owned by Iranians or Iraqis and suffer a sort of guilt by association with political events back home) are given short shrift by many critics.

The phrase "Middle East" itself recalls another assumption—that Europe was the center of the world. China was the Far East or the Orient, and Lebanon and Syria and so on were just halfway between here and there. Unfortunately, although we have managed to lose the "Oriental" habit, there isn't a real alternative to "Middle Eastern." Similarly, although we realize that the date markers "B.C." and "A.D." are ethnocentric, the alternatives B.C.E. (Before the Common Era) and C.E. (Common Era) are still confusing to many readers, we have reluctantly used the common style.

We have taken note, in a general way, of the various nutritional strengths and drawbacks of each cuisine. We have mentioned various religious taboos, too, but we pass no moral judgments on any diet, other than the classic "moderation in all things." However, you will probably notice that few other cultures overwhelm their plates with meat, which is not only a dietary issue but an economic one as well. Here in the United States, where meat is cheap and plentiful, we have a tendency to eat more than we need—more, arguably, than our share—just because we can. (In fact, one of the problematical accommodations cooks from other nations often make in restaurants here is to our inflated expectations of meat.) You may also find you like more kinds of seafood than you did when it only came frozen. Dining as others do may alter your tastes as well as your outlook.

One last thing to consider: cuisine as class distinction. When, in the unspoken etiquette of American society, does "immigrant food" become "ethnic cuisine"? What makes one country's food fashionable and another merely fast? Is it a matter of political alliance, cultural chic, Hollywood romance, novelty? All these have some impact, of course: Jamaican and West African foods are gathering places for the emerging urban black entrepreneurial class; *Jewel in the Crown* and *A Passage to India* prompted a rush for Indian fashions; and the craze for hot chilies has made any number of otherwise unrelated cuisines, from Thai to Ethiopian to Tex-Mex, good investment bets.

But on a much more serious level, the answer is that we the consumers decide. We choose what styles evolve, not just by selecting a particular restaurant to dine in or talk about but also by the respect we afford a particular ethnic group. The quality and variety of a foreign cuisine doesn't reflect the sophistication of that culture—an assumption too many people make—but only the economic stability that immigrant community has achieved in our society.

The first members of an immigrant society are rarely prosperous. They are far more likely to be refugees from war or oppression, poverty or political upheaval—and of that group, only a very few are apt to have any real cooking experience. (Most countries in the world do not even have a restaurant tradition, since it requires a successful middle class, those with some disposable income but not full-time servants, as customers.) Even those immigrants who do have some history as cooks will have limited access to the ingredients they are used to, and little money to spend on them anyway. Being able to afford to rent restaurant space, much less buy it, is usually years away.

So the first generation of immigrants traditionally recreates the simplest food they know—street food, in effect. Once they save up enough money or the community itself grows more stable, you begin to see mom-and-pop establishments serving family-style food; not for some time do you find "real" restaurants that offer more formal cuisine (with more expensive ingredients). Consequently, we should not assume that a particular ethnic group has only cheap food; rather, we should look at it in context. After all, you wouldn't want someone from another country to think the food at a truck stop was American haute cuisine.

These are difficult issues, and you can relax—there is little preaching in the text that follows. These are just impressions that took hold in the writing of this book, and you may hear echoes of them in your own mind as time goes on. But the main purpose of this book is for you to eat and to enjoy. We want you to have fun from here on. This is the first time we'll wish you "Bon appetit!" The next time, you'll be on your own.

—Eve Zibart

Contents

LIST OF ILLUSTRATIONS

SCANDINA

GERMAN
AUSTR

FRANCE/
BELGIUM

SPAIN/
PORTUGAL

NORTH
AFRICA

**PART II:
AFRICA**

WEST
AFRICA

NORTH
PACIFIC
OCEAN

NORTH
ATLANTIC
OCEAN

MEXICO

THE
CARIBBEAN

CENTRAL
AMERICA

**PART VI:
THE AMERICAS**

SOUTH
AMERICA

SOUTH
PACIFIC
OCEAN

SOUTH
ATLANTIC
OCEAN

REGIONS OF THE WORLD COVERED IN
**THE UNOFFICIAL GUIDE TO
ETHNIC CUISINE AND
DINING IN AMERICA**

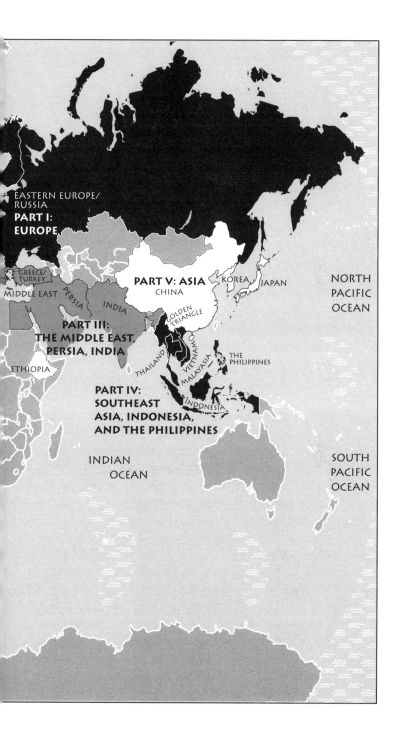

EASTERN EUROPE/
RUSSIA
PART I:
EUROPE

GREECE/
TURKEY

MIDDLE EAST

PERSIA

INDIA

PART V: ASIA
CHINA

KOREA

JAPAN

GOLDEN
TRIANGLE

PART III:
THE MIDDLE EAST,
PERSIA, INDIA

ETHIOPIA

THAILAND

VIETNAM

MALAYSIA

THE
PHILIPPINES

PART IV:
SOUTHEAST
ASIA, INDONESIA,
AND THE PHILIPPINES

INDONESIA

NORTH
PACIFIC
OCEAN

INDIAN
OCEAN

SOUTH
PACIFIC
OCEAN

Acknowledgments

We would like to thank the following people for their help in compiling the appendix of suggested ethnic restaurants: Molly Abraham, Detroit, MI; Betsy Amster, Los Angeles, CA; Eileen Bailey, Phoenix, AZ; Jane Berkowitz, Kansas City, MO; Jeffrey Beutner, Milwaukee, WI; Lilia F. Brady, Cincinnati, OH; Karen Brooks, Portland, OR; Lucy Cooper, Miami, FL; Kelly Estes, Charlotte, NC; John Garganigo, Saint Louis, MO; Linda Giuca, Hartford, CT; Judyth Hill, Santa Fe and Albuquerque, NM; Eddie Hogan, Charleston, SC; Suzanne A. Holloway, Tulsa, OK; Scott Joseph, Orlando, FL; Frederic Koeppel, Memphis, TN; Shannon Landry, San Antonio, TX; Terry Libby, Columbus, OH; Mary Malouf, Dallas, TX; Karl Okamoto, Philadelphia, PA; Scott Perry, Salt Lake City, UT; Sarah Riehl, Cleveland, OH; Patty Ryan, Tampa, FL; Bill St. John, Denver, CO; Rob Sangster, Memphis, TN; Donna Segal, Indianapolis, IN; Camille Stagg, Chicago, IL; Mei-Yen Teo, Toronto, Canada; Margo True, Houston, TX; Kathleen Walker, Ottawa, Ontario; Holly Wallace, Raleigh / Durham and Chapel Hill, NC; Bob Weber, Vail, CO; Jennifer Weglarz, Minneapolis / St. Paul, MN; Mark Zanger, Boston, MA.

Author's Note

Although only Terrell Vermont and Muriel Stevens directly provided research for this book, there were many whose affection and support sweetened the writing of it: Francis Reed and Anna Giacomo and Alice, Robert, Page, and Nancy, who gave fresh meaning to the phrase "soul kitchen"; the members of the LWGLCC, who stirred the pitchers; the Tako/Kanpai crew, who kept my protein levels high; Peter Gamba, who kept my fat ratio low; and Bob Sehlinger, Molly Burns, and Barbara Williams, who grinned and bore those slipped deadlines.

And for D., who, as always, had faith.

—E. Z.

INTRODUCTION

As the boom in food magazines and television cooking shows attests, Americans have never been more fascinated by food, or more adventuresome in their dining habits. The great melting pot has suddenly become the world's most eclectic kettle as well.

Cuisines almost unheard of until recently, or confined to the larger urban centers such as New York and Miami, are working their way into the heartland; many, such as the Middle Eastern and Southeast Asian styles, have acquired new prominence as second- and third-generation Americans, now firmly established in this country, take time to rediscover their cultural roots. More familiar ethnic cuisines that had been cruelly homogenized in deference to American tastes (whether actual or assumed)—particularly Chinese and Indian—are reemerging in far more authentic and satisfying forms. The explosion of Pacific Rim trade and cultural exchange has produced pidgin cuisines that owe as much to American as to Asian traditions. The emergence of a black entrepreneurial class in the United States and West Africa has inspired a restaurant tradition that is new to both cultures.

Hence our embarrassment of riches. No longer is dining out a choice between French and Italian, or carryout a toss-up between pizza and kung pao chicken. Nowadays, picking a restaurant for dinner more often recalls the method by which Dr. Doolittle chose his destinations: closing his eyes, letting the gazetteer fall open on the table, and stabbing downward with his finger.

And picking a restaurant is more and more frequently the answer to "What's for dinner?" The major shifts of the baby boom generation—the increase in two-career families, the decline of self-contained small towns, and the shift toward bedroom communities and rush-hour gridlock—have combined to strip the kitchen of its longtime role as the center of family life. At the same time, the disappearance of the domestic servant and the need to bring social partners together from across larger urban areas has made restaurant entertaining standard practice. Business meetings among residents of different countries is now commonplace; and since more and more Americans have friends and coworkers from other countries, they are even more likely to be invited to a restaurant that serves ethnic food.

That's the "riches" part: So many cuisines, so little time. We want you to try them all. But we also understand that you may feel overwhelmed by the choices as well as perplexed by the novelties. What is Ethiopian food? How much of it is raw? How should you handle it? If you have vegetarian friends, kosher friends, squeamish friends, where should you go (or not)? How do you eat hard-shell crabs in spicy black bean sauce? What are the lettuce leaves for at the Vietnamese restaurant? How can you keep from dropping the fish into the soy sauce at the sushi bar? What's the difference between Hunan and Szechwan, Indian red curries and Thai green curries, samosas and sambusas, a bellini and a blini? And how *do* you master chopsticks?

Read on. In this book you'll find a short history of any style of ethnic cooking you're apt to find in any restaurant in the United States, with a smattering of social and political history (why a certain region produces spicier food, or emphasizes shellfish, or emulates a colonial power), key ingredients and staple menu items, and suggestions for ordering a complete meal. We'll tell you how certain dishes are eaten (if you don't like to eat with your fingers, you'll know which cuisines to avoid in advance) and, perhaps even more important, how they're not eaten—how not to offend your hosts unintentionally. We'll try to give you an idea of the relative expense of various cuisines, although of course that will vary depending on what city you're dining in and the formality of the particular restaurant.

And although this is not primarily a cookbook, we hope you'll find a few cuisines you really like, so we've included a few simple recipes you can reproduce or even preview at home. There are few better ways to get to know other people, or to appreciate their taste and the choices they make, than to go step by step through their recipe map. If the way to someone's heart is through the stomach, the way to their homes is through the kitchen. (Each recipe feeds four to six people unless otherwise stated.)

Finally, since exploring restaurants is one of the best parts about taking vacations (and one of the inescapable elements of traveling on business), we've included the names of some of the best established restaurants of each style in cities you might be likely to visit or need to entertain in.

Notice we said some of the best restaurants in each cuisine, not necessarily the most authentic. While cooking techniques may be traditional and staple ingredients essential, one of the first things an immigrant cuisine must do is adapt to the available food supply. In the case of cuisines transplanted to the United States, this has been an advantage as often as a barrier, not merely because of the variety of foods available—and the increasing demand for more ethnic foods has certainly increased the quantity and interest of foods at chain as well as specialty groceries—but because in many countries, storage and refrigeration are extremely problematical. The vastly greater supply of meat and poultry in even the most pedestrian American pantry is an obvious difference, but the uniformly high quality of fruits and vegetables has also produced more vigorous interpretations of many traditional dishes from other countries.

Notice, too, that not every country in the world is specifically discussed. That's because we're talking about restaurant dining, specifically; and although there are, for example, chains of "Australian steakhouses," their ethnicity is generally limited to Aussie-ized item names and brands of beer. Though there are great restaurants in Vancouver and Quebec—and plenty of Canadian chefs working in the United States—there are no "Canadian" restaurants here. There are plenty of "Irish pubs," but Irish stew (authentic or not) scarcely needs translating. South Africa may have a "cuisine," but it certainly hasn't been exported.

We also discuss some cuisines in combination, covering several Middle Eastern or Central American countries together, because the styles are so closely related and are frequently prepared interchangeably in the United States; as the regional styles become more prominent, they will be profiled more fully.

On the other hand, we do include some cuisines many people may already be familiar with, particularly if they live in larger cities. Even so, you may find tips, terms, and titles you hadn't known—and you might well discover that your neighborhood "Szechwan" restaurant isn't Szechwan at all but Taiwanese or even Korean. And that the "international" market down the street is just as all-American as the mega-grocery in the mall.

Reading this book is one way to begin to notice underlying similarities among apparently untranslatable cuisines and to feel more confident about trying new ones. Nearly every continent has stumbled upon such basics as the hot grill (the Tex-Mex fajita skillet, the European griddle, the Italian pizza stone, the Japanese teppanyaki, the Mongolian barbecue, the Chinese "sizzling platter"), the stuffed noodle (the wonton, the aushak, the ravioli, the piroshki), and the fried egg. Pasta, one of the staple foods even in cafeterias, is being rediscovered not only in finer Italian forms but in its "original" Asian varieties: Chinese, Japanese, and especially Vietnamese *pho* restaurants are tossing whole racks of noodles. Long, fat, flat, curly, stringy, springy, spicy—they're like rock musicals in menu form.

Even batting champ Wade Boggs, who refused to eat anything but chicken every game night in a decade of baseball seasons, could order comfortably in almost any ethnic restaurant in the world. He could have it Southern fried, Cajun blackened, South American grilled, or Jamaican jerked; he could order African stew with peanuts, French coq au vin, Italian cacciatore, German Black Forest stew with cherries, Hungarian paprikash, spinach and feta–stuffed Greek chicken breast, chicken Kiev, Chinese kung pao chicken, Japanese teriyaki, Vietnamese hen stuffed with pork, Thai drumsticks fried inside out, and Korean tabletop barbecue without even needing a translator.

So come, explore, eat—*Mange! Kin khao! Bon appetit!* The world is waiting. The old saw has it that to understand another person, you need to walk a mile in their shoes. We think there's a better way to get to know another culture: Spend an hour at their table. It's a lot more fun.

No, we didn't forget those chopsticks. Here's the trick: Snuggle one down in the fold between your thumb and index finger, with one-third extending out the back side of your hand—the thicker end, or it may be the square end as opposed to the round part—and the longer section facing your palm. (Remember learning about levers in school? Let the chopsticks do the work, not your hand.) Curve your ring finger in and brace the chopstick against its first knuckle.

Now take the other stick and grasp it with your thumb and first two fingers just as you would a pen or pencil, and wiggle it. When you pick up food, you "write" up and down with the upper stick; the lower one just stays put—the base of your thumb becomes the fulcrum, to finish that comparison—and you pinch the food between the two sticks. Got it?

If not, don't worry. Just smile and ask for a fork. After all, this is America.

PART I

EUROPE

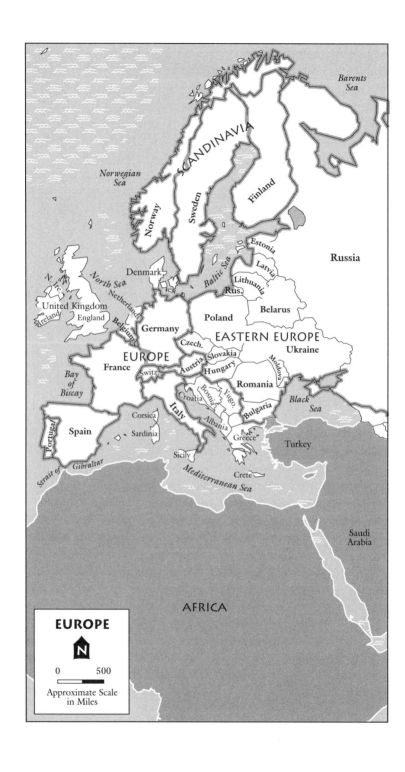

FRANCE AND BELGIUM

BASIC CUISINE

STYLE:
Rich, refined, precise

KEY FLAVORS:
Cream, fine herbs, wine, wild mushrooms, garlic

EATING UTENSILS:
Forks and knives

DISTINCTIVE FOODS:
Foie gras, champagne, truffles, escargot, cheeses

UNIFORMITY OF MENUS:
Very good

NUTRITIONAL INDEX:
High fat, high cholesterol, high sodium

COST:
Moderate to expensive

"THANK YOU":
"Merci"

It's no mere coincidence—in fact, it's a masterstroke of cultural gamesmanship—that the phrase commonly used to describe fine cooking, "haute cuisine," is in French. Most Americans have grown up taking for granted that French chefs and French restaurants were the finest; we've even been taking France's word for it, using the Michelin Guide ratings as the international standard.

There are a couple of twists to this legendary sophistication, however. First, very little of the French cuisine served in American restaurants qualifies as "haute." Just the opposite, in fact: Translated into English, the names of many dishes reveal their working-class origins, such as *bouillabaisse*, the "bubble and settle" soup made from the fisherman's leftovers, and shellfish *marinière*, cooked the way the barge workers did (with fish stock). Chicken *bonne femme* or *fermière* just means from the farmwife's recipe—good old home cooking—and fish *a la meunière* is the way the miller's wife makes it—i.e., coated with flour (and cooked in butter).

Second, many other French favorites are only French in name: hors d'oeuvre (foods "outside of the task") were lifted almost entirely from the Russians *zakouskis*; the spices and citrus sauces (the famous duck *a l'orange*, for instance) were introduced by the Arabs; the tomato and the sauces based on it came from Spain; and an astonishing number of recipes—pastas and noodles, meat flourings, pastries and creams—were introduced by Italian chefs at the French court. These sweeping adaptations led many white-linen restaurants in the United States to describe their menus as "Continental cuisine," covering the whole of Europe.

Third, French cuisine as we know and admire it is more nearly modern than classic; it began to take shape in about the seventeenth century but was mainly formulated in the eighteenth and nineteenth centuries. Compared to the other so-called great cuisines—those of China and India—*all* French food is nouvelle cuisine.

The truth is that when it comes to cooking, the French were never the most imaginative, the most adventuresome, or the most flexible. They were just the most obsessively perfectionistic. They knew what they liked (they bought so much Phoenician wine that by the seventh century B.C. there was a dedicated port at Marseilles) and they always believed that whatever anyone else could do, or brew, they could do better.

So they became the greatest technicians, and the greatest salesmen, of Western culinary civilization. It was the French who made the craft of cooking into what Julia Child and company could honestly call an "art"; they made it sound like one of the anchors of Western civilization. ("Gourmandism is one of the chief links uniting society," Brillat-Savarin pronounced.)

It was also the French who made the profession of cooking into a viable business. French culinary arbiters laid down elaborate and often intimidating rules for making sauces, serving banquets, and selecting wines. It was even a pair of French restaurateurs, the Troisgros brothers of Rouen, who in the 1970s decided that serving the portions in the kitchen and then "presenting" plates was more practical, and more profitable, than carving to order at the table. With their rules, their schools, their toques, and their wine tastings, the French succeeded in molding most ambitious restaurants in the United States, French or not, into their own image.

Which brings us to the fourth irony: Haute cuisine may be an endangered species.

Diners in the United States and Europe are becoming much more diet-conscious and wary of the cholesterol- and calorie-packed cream sauces; and they eat out far more often, meaning that they are less likely to want every restaurant meal to be extravagant and more likely to seek variety in flavor. The 1994 edition Michelin Guide eliminated nearly 50 previously ranked French restaurants and downgraded several more. The editors warned that "the cuisine of our country must adjust to a new behavior of its customers, use less sophisticated products and shoot for lighter additions without giving up the traditional quality."

French chefs are under pressure not only at home but, in a historical turnabout, from the United States, where classically trained but more eclectically minded chefs are exploring low-fat cuisine or applying French techniques to American and Asian ingredients.

So after 200 years of following every prescribed step of the recipes enunciated by Careme or Escoffier, French chefs have spent the past 20 years reinventing them. They are now finding ways to replace the rich cream sauces that were their signature and giving up the more elaborate Parisian fare in favor of the provincial specialties (especially those that, not coincidentally, are more closely related to the southern Italian dishes so popular in the United States).

Because of this shifting state of affairs, and because so much of the mystery about a French restaurant is in the language, this chapter will focus more on preparations and provincial styles than on specific ingredients. And although Belgium is an independent nation, its cuisine is so closely related—and most of the Belgian-owned restaurants in the United States describe themselves, for simplicity's sake, as French or even German—Belgian cuisine will be described in the section on provincial cuisine.

THE COUNTRIES

France is the leading agricultural nation in Europe—57 percent of its land is devoted to agriculture and viticulture—and so diverse in its climate, soil quality, and topography that different regions produce widely varying crops. Physically, France resembles a rather dumpy starfish with its most prominent "ray" sticking out to the west. It's bordered on the east by the Ural Mountains and Rhine River, running beside Italy, Germany, Switzerland, Luxembourg, and Belgium. On the north it is washed by the English Channel and on the west by the Atlantic Ocean. The Pyrenees and Spain lie to the south, and the rest of the southern "corner" opens onto the Mediterranean.

Rivers cover the country like palm lines. The eastern crescent— Champagne, Burgundy, and the Rhône River and Loire River valleys— encompasses the great wine-growing regions, along with the area around Bordeaux on the west coast. Except for a few tropical crops, such as coffee, France is fully self-sufficient. For more on regional agriculture, see the "Provincial Cuisines" section on page 15.

Belgium, which has historically been tugged between France and the Netherlands, has an appropriately divided population: Dutch, who speak Flemish, and Walloons, who speak French. Their food follows the patterns: abundant fresh seafood on the coast, bountiful German-style meats and sausages in the west, and in the middle, fields of grains—oats, rye, wheat, and barley—as well as beets, potatoes, and the famous endive (also known as chicory, *chicon*, or *witloof*). They also grow a large quantity of hops, with which they make some of the world's most potent beers. They're so potent, in fact, that they're often referred to as "the Burgundies of Belgium."

THE HISTORY

Although there are extremely ancient archeological artifacts in France, very little is actually known about the people who inhabited the region before the Romans took over in the first century, but it was already a crazy-quilt of "provincials."

France, which faces the Atlantic and Bay of Biscay along one side and the Mediterranean on the other, repeatedly absorbed invaders and refugees from both. The Gauls of Julius Caesar's famous "veni, vidi, vici" campaign were actually Celtic; the Pyrenees were dotted with Basques (see the chapter on Spain); Brittany was populated by Britons driven out by the Anglo-Saxons; there were Greeks and Middle Easterners along the Mediterranean coast; and there were Germanic tribes in the east, including the Franks (actually Belgians), who gave their name to the region. Attila's Huns poked around in the fourth century, leaving behind the horse (and perhaps yogurt). The Saracens invaded in the eighth century, leaving behind pockets of Arab settlements along the Mediterranean and Spanish borders.

Not surprisingly, although the great majority of people speak French, there are still many other languages heard in France: The Basques speak Euskera, the Bretons have a Celtic dialect, the Alsatians speak a German dialect, the Corsicans speak Italian, and the residents of the districts near Belgium speak Flemish. And since the Franks ruled the Low Countries, western Germany, Austria, Switzerland, and northern Italy, there are family resemblances to all these countries in French regional recipes.

THE CUISINE

Early Frenchmen ate pretty much as their Roman and Greek predecessors had, depending heavily on fish, wild game, and fowl, boiled, roasted, or grilled and flavored with vinegar as often as oil. Winter meats had to be salted or dried, so spices and marinades were highly prized. The India-Constantinople trade supplied cumin, pepper, coriander, and caraway, to which the early French added green herbs such as dill, marjoram, and lovage. The Romans had mixed powdered thyme into soft cheese; the French experimented with fennel seeds. An early recipe for duck involved reducing the cooking liquid, already full of spices, and then adding wine, honey, vinegar, and more herbs and thickening the gravy with starch.

Fireplaces were huge, open affairs, with large spits and a few hooks to hang pots on. Although early records suggest that Frankish banquets were lavish, they were still largely matters of roasts or joints and small whole fowl; vegetables were almost always boiled and even stews were pretty much unknown until the twelfth and thirteenth centuries, when ovens appeared. Then smaller pans—including saucepans—became practicable, and a greater variety of dishes were possible.

By the Middle Ages, the French had gaped at the abundance and variety of Middle Eastern cuisine—it's estimated that fully half the French knights alive between 1100 and 1130 marched either to Spain or the Levant—and their banquets had become elaborate affairs, at least in terms of presentation. Feudal lords were served pheasants and whole calves and pigs, and peacocks with gilded bills, and swans that were baked and then re-feathered; but these meats were still basically either roasted or boiled—and they were still all being served at once, so they inevitably congealed and hardened. Rice was sometimes used as a thickener, as was bread; and the almonds introduced by the Arabs were now a staple. Eggs and cheese were used more widely, and cream sauces were now fairly common.

Not until the mid-sixteenth century, when Catherine de Medici, daughter of the Duke of Urbino, married Henry II and brought along her whole cooking staff, did the French look past their first joints, so to speak. Catharine imported butchers, pastry chefs, pasta makers—even forks (although she was signally unsuccessful in persuading people to use them). Both Catherine and her Tuscan cousin Marie, who married Henry IV in 1600 and brought along a new generation of Italian chefs, insisted that France take its place among the most sophisticated societies of the day.

So food became fashionable, and France suddenly became the party capital of the world. A seventeenth-century banquet menu for Louis XIV listed 168 entrees and accompaniments in the first five courses alone. Talleyrand, the great diplomat and gastronome, once remarked that "in England there are three sauces and 260 religions; in France there are three religions and 360 sauces." This is even more remarkable, when you consider they were still eating with three fingers and the point of a knife.

After this point, however, the French obsession with exactitude took hold. Once established, recipes became immutable. No matter how far the French empires reached into Africa or Asia, they rarely adopted any new culinary techniques or ingredients—even though the same regions had contributed to Mediterranean cuisines so long ago.

THE RISE OF WESTERN CULINARY CIVILIZATION

The relatively abrupt evolution of French cuisine also reflects much broader changes in the day-to-day life of nearly all medieval Europeans and deserves a moment's digression. Game and fish had always been relatively plentiful, and that was most of what early Europeans expected or desired. Consequently, farmers planted the same few crops for centuries, gradually leaching the nutrients out so that produce became progressively poorer, and the people who lived off them both poorer and weaker.

(The Crusades thinned the men, and the plague culled out all but the strongest of both sexes.)

But in the fifteenth and sixteenth centuries, as the advantages of crop rotation were discovered, a wider range of foodstuffs, and more nutritious ones, became available. The larger supply of food meant less had to be preserved by salting or smoking, so that individual flavors became more apparent and people could afford to express preferences. As there was more food, there was more surplus—more to sell as well as subsist on—so the markets began to increase in size.

The improved quality of grain crops also improved the quality of the farm animals: As cattle became more productive, beef became as common as mutton. As horses became stronger, farmers began to use them for transport as well as labor, taking their products to more distant, larger markets.

Finally, Europeans began to have easier access to imported spices. Whole regions of France and Spain, particularly along the Mediterranean coast and Rhône River, had been depopulated by Mongol and Moorish invaders; as these areas were gradually resettled, shipments that had previously zigzagged from East to West—Indonesia to Baghdad to Byzantium to Venice, then over the Alps and up the Rhine—could now be steered more directly. Thus they also became more affordable—one of the major inspirations for the development of a fine cuisine.

Just Right

Nutritionally, exploring French cuisine is a little like Goldilocks tasting the Three Bears' dinners: Haute cuisine can be too big and rich; cuisine minceur can be too little and too light; and most people find nouvelle cuisine just about right. The differences are, as always, in the sauces: Classic cuisine uses the greatest number of cream- and butter-based sauces, usually poured over an already butter-sautéed fish or meat, and sometimes requires wrapping the whole thing in pastry doughs that are also heavily larded with butter.

Cuisine minceur, which borrowed from classic Japanese cuisine the idea of visual extravagance and severe simplicity of ingredients, is composed of many tiny courses of small portions and often ornate garnishes. Sauces and pastry may still be involved, but in tiny quantities. Nouvelle, which simply means "new," French cuisine (and also what is sometimes calls "new Continental" cuisine) tries to provide rich flavors but in lower-fat dishes, frequently by poaching or steaming foods instead of sautéeing them and by using reductions of stock, vegetable purees or crême fraîche to thicken dishes instead of creams or roux.

If you're concerned about avoiding fat, you'll have to either memorize the basic sauces or learn to look perfectly comfortable asking for your hollandaise on the side; but there are a few dishes that you can just expect to break your cholesterol bank on. Anything *en croute* is wrapped in pastry; anything with *crême* probably refers to heavy cream. Almost anything from Normandy will have cream in it, so titled or not. *Confit* is game, usually duck or goose or rabbit, cooked and stored in its own rendered fat; *blanquettes* are white stews thickened with cream and butter and eggs. Any dish described as *Milanaise* or *Velleroi* is coated and fried.

Ironically, the Italians now found themselves effectively priced-out of the imported spice market and had to learn to do with fewer; so just as French cuisine became richer, Italian cuisine became simpler.

GETTING THROUGH THE MENU

Navigating a French menu isn't hard once you crack the code—the "a la" syndrome, so to speak. In fact, some dishes seem to lose more than their mystery when the veil of language is pierced: Everyone who's ever had the experience of being offered caviar and asking, "What's that?," will remember how unappetizing the answer "fish eggs" sounded. "Pâté" just means "paste"; "soufflé" means "puffed up." Worst of all, probably, "foie gras" means "fat liver," which is exactly what that silken delicacy is—the livers of geese force-fed into gross immobility.

Most dishes are named either for the sauce they are served with or for the major ingredient in the recipe; and when that ingredient is often the prize product of a particular region, it is often called by the name of the province itself. Chicken *Dijonnaise*, for instance, means the poultry is served in a sauce honoring Dijon's most famous product, mustard. Calvados, the name of a province that produces fine apples and apple brandy, also refers to a dish containing either or both of those specialities. (There are also various recipes named for famous people or events, usually having been so called by the chef to curry favor with a rich patron; you'll just have to memorize those.)

Of course, those sauces named for other countries, such as *indienne* or *grecque* (or *americaine*), don't reproduce other cuisines; they just represent the French image of Indian or Greek food.

The sauces may be applied to *bouef* (beef), *veau* (veal), *venaison* (venison), *agneau* (lamb), *mouton* (mutton), *lapin* (rabbit), *porc* (pork) or *jambon* (ham), *volaille* or *poulet* (chicken), *caille* (quail), *canard* (duck), *oie* (goose), *poisson* (fish), *crevette* (shrimp), *ecrevisse* (crawfish), *homard* (lobster), or *huitres* (oysters), just to get you started.

The following is a glossary of some of the major a la's you are apt to see on a French menu and a practical, if not purist, pronunciation guide. Just remember that even the most classic of sauces is under revisionary scrutiny these days, and adventuresome chefs may be experimenting with their own versions. The most important provincial and regional styles, in which a whole restaurant menu might be prepared, are described a little more fully in the next section.

Allemande (all mond): "German," but in reference to its pale color rather than its actual origin; *sauce allemande* is a basic white sauce, but the use of the word may imply horseradish or vinegar or sour cream in the recipe.

Alsacienne (all saw syen): Also Alsatian. From the Alsace region (see page 15).

Amandine (ah mon deen): Cooked with almonds.

Americaine (ah mare ee ken): Shellfish with tomatoes. A Parisian specialty, oddly; it's common to have lobster *americaine* in Paris.

Ancienne (ahn syen): "Ancient," or in the old style. Typically, ancienne recipes are cooked for a long time—braised or stewed—and sometimes served in pastry. They often use the more delicate sections (sweetbreads or kidneys) or rarities such as truffles and wild mushrooms as garnish.

Anglaise (ahn glez): "English," implying rather plain fare, usually boiled or fried and without garnish.

Anna (ah nah): Specifically, a dish of sliced potatoes, seasoned with butter and layered in a casserole; but also any dish served with them.

Ardennaise (ahr den nez): Refers to the Ardennes mountains. Usually applied to fowl or game birds, but sometimes to meat, and characteristically flavored with juniper berries (or the juniper-based gin).

Au jus (oh zhoo): With juice—that is, pan juices or stock.

Aurore (oh roar): A tomato-flavored sauce, hence pink-tinged and named for Aurora, the goddess of the dawn.

Ballonttine (bal on teen): Meat or poultry boned, stuffed, and rolled, then braised. A galantine is similar but usually served in aspic.

Basquaise (boss kez): Basque-style, after the indigenous peoples of the Pyrenees. Basquaise cuisine is similar to Provençal cuisine (see page 19) but with a stronger Spanish (Mexican) influence. Typically it involves tomatoes, olive oil and olives, garlic, and hot peppers. *Espagnole* is very similar. *Bayonnaise* food is closely related but implies pork; *catalane* is also similar but more garlicky.

Bearnaise (bare nez): One of the primary sauces, a butter emulsion flavored with a reduction of wine, vinegar, shallots, and herbs, particularly tarragon. *Bearnaise* cuisine in general is somewhat similar to *basquaise*.

Béchamel (beh shaw mel): One of the most basic white sauces, made of flour, butter, and milk.

Bercy (bare see): Generally means a dish finished with wine.

Blanc (blonk): Literally, "white"—a dish with white sauce or just white by nature.

Bordelaise (bor deh lez): From Bordeaux, most often referring to a brown sauce flavored with red Bordeaux wine but sometimes meaning garnished with artichokes.

Bourgeoise (boorzh waz): Middle-class, i.e., *not* haute cuisine; generally refers to hearty but relatively simple, chunky-cut stews.

Bourguignonne (boor geen yon): Made with Burgundy wine; also refers to a provincial style (see page 17).

Bretonne (breh tuhn): From Brittany (see page 17); made with white beans.

Bruxelloise (bruk sell waz): From Brussels; Belgian food (see page 16). Similarly, *flamande* (flah mond) refers to Flemish cooking.

Champenoise (sham pen waz): Made with champagne. Similarly, *porto* means flavored with port wine, *madere* with Madeira, and *Xeres* with sherry.

Chasseur (shaw syer) or *chasseuse* (shaw soose): "Hunter style," usually meats or game fowl with hearty sauces, but any dish with a brown tomato and mushroom sauce; livers are often used as flavoring. A *civet* is a related stew characteristically flavored with blood.

Dauphine (dough feen): Like Anna, refers either to a potato dish (a sort of croquette) or to a meat served with it. *Duchesse* is similar, too, but the potatoes are mashed and treated with cream and eggs.

Diable (dee a bluh): "Devil"; a dish with a hot and spicy sauce made either with cayenne or mustard.

Farci (far sea): Stuffed.

Florentine (flor ann teen): Refers to the city of Florence; a dish (fish, chicken, omelet, etc.) served on a bed of spinach and topped with mornay sauce.

Gratin (grah tan): A dish topped with grated cheese or bread crumbs and butter and browned to a crust.

Grecque (greck): Greek, using a lot of olive oil, tomatoes, onions, and lemon juice.

Hollandaise (all ahn dez): "Dutch," but refers particularly to what many people consider the queen of sauces, a lemon-flavored butter and egg emulsion.

Indienne (ann dee en): "Indian"; curry-flavored.

Jardinière (zhar dee nair): From the garden; a dish garnished with turned, or trimmed to bite-sized, vegetables.

Lyonnaise (lee ahn nez): From the province of Lyonnais or the city of Lyon (see page 19); but typically implies the use of vinegar.

Maitre d'hôtel (may truh dough tel): Refers to the restaurant host, of course, but in a recipe means a dish flavored with a seasoned butter.

Milanaise (mee law nez): From the city of Milan; any dish coated in cheese and bread crumbs and then sautéed.

Mornay (more nay): One of the great sauces, a white cream sauce with cheese (frequently Parmesan) and any dish served with it.

Mousseline (moose ah leen): Any puree lightened or stiffened with egg whites or whipped cream.

Nage (naj): "Swimming"; shellfish served in its own poaching liquid.

Nantua (nawn too ah): A city famous for crawfish, hence, a dish with crawfish.

Niçoise (neece was): From the city of Nice on the Riviera, a Mediterranean style with olive oil, tomatoes, garlic, and also potatoes (as in the famous *salade Niçoise*). *Parmentier* also means that potatoes are involved.

Normande (nor mond): From the province settled by Norman (Norwegian) invaders, who went on to conquer England as well. Characterized by the use of apples or oysters (see page 19).

Papiotte (on poppy oat): Paper or parchment (or nowadays foil). A fish cooked *en papiotte* is seasoned, sealed in parchment, and baked in its own juices.

Parisienne (pair easy en): From Paris, and thus not provincial—a fairly light and generally "white" style.

Perigourdine (pair eh goor deen): From Périgord (see page 18), where truffles and foie gras are specialties, hence, dishes garnished or stuffed with them.

Poivre (pwov ruh): Pepper (peppercorns, not chilies).

Provençale (pro van sahl): From Provence (see page 19); and one of the styles most influential in the current renaissance of French (and Mediterranean) food.

Savoyarde (sah voh yard): From Savoy (see page 19); two specific dishes: one an omelet filled with potatoes and Gruyère cheese, the other potatoes and Gruyère served in a crock.

Supreme (sue prem): A chicken recipe, specifically one involving the breast and wing.

Vigneronne (veen yair own): From the vine grower, hence, a dish with grapes. *Veronique* is similar.

PROVINCIAL CUISINES

It used to be that even those French restaurants in the United States that advertised provincial rather than haute cuisine tended to mix and match their menus, preparing an Alsatian-style choucroute along with a Provençal bouillabaisse. Some of them, rather than specializing in a true regional cuisine, even used the term "provincial" to mean bourgeois or home-style food. However, many celebrated French chefs in the United States, having proved their proficiency at classical cuisine, are recreating more and more of their own regional specialties. (You may also see more restaurant reviews mentioning provincial styles.)

Again, technique and detail are the hallmarks of French cooking, and despite regional differences, once a recipe is established it can be reliably ordered anywhere—one benefit of those rote recipes. There are some broad distinctions to take note of, however: For instance, in the colder regions, the cooking fat is butter; in the temperate zones, duck and goose fat or lard; and in the south, olive oil. It is also true that there is much less dependence on cream sauces, and more on garlic, in the south, where the cuisine is clearly Mediterranean; and that the regions bordering Germany, particularly Alsace, show a strong German influence, involving cheeses, rich sausages, and pastries.

Here is a shorthand guide to some of the provincial styles you are apt to see more of in the next few years:

ALSACE AND LORRAINE This is one of the most fertile regions of France, with a broad variety of fruits, corn, hops, grains, and root vegetables. Not surprisingly, since the region borders Germany, the cuisine is strong on German-style *spaeztle* (dumplings) and sausages, blood puddings, civets (blood-thickened game stews), and pastry-wrapped hams; but they also specialize in poultry. The Alsatian foie gras is among the most highly prized, in fact; and Alsatian restaurants are apt to show it off gloriously, using it to top or even stuff game. The *choucroutes* of Strasbourg (hearty winter-warmer casseroles of white beans, goose or duck confit, sausages, smoked pork, sauerkraut or, even more authentically, fermented turnips) are considered the apogee of the dish. This region is also the home of powerful Limbourger cheese. Alsace is famous for its spring asparagus, which is consumed in vast quantities. The quiche Lorraine is a nonsweet tart of cream, eggs, and bacon, which sparked its own culinary revolution in the United States—did real men eat it or not? But no such question would have attended the version called *tourte a la Lorraine*, which has both veal and pork in it. Like Alsace, Lorraine produces good foie gras, boudin (blood sausages), and potted meats; it is also known for its macaroons and the *madeleines* that sent Proust to his pen. Alsace is famous for its fruity white wines, particularly Riesling (which can stand up to both fish and sauerkraut) and Gewürztraminer; and its sweet Muscat. Lorraine produces highly ranked reds, whites, and rosés; the best-known example here is Moselle.

ANJOU AND TOURAINE   Bordered by the Loire River, Anjou is rich in freshwater fish, including pike, shad, salmon, and bream; one of its specialties is *bouilleture*, a mixed fish stew with eels. Other common dishes are chicken or cabbage fricassees. The region is partial to fruits, particularly pears and prunes, which are often cooked with fish or game (a touch of the Arab influence). Anjou's soft cream cheeses are extremely popular. Characteristic flavorings include sorrel and walnut oil. Anjou produces fine, generally dry white wines and spicy cabernets. Touraine is also particularly rich in game.

ARTOIS AND BOULOGNE   This region, which borders Belgium, is seafood central; its ports are filled with lorries of turbot, mullet, bass, sole, and skate, but most important are the mackerel and herring that have represented its major industry since the ninth century. Its dishes, not surprisingly, feature primarily seafood—"bloaters," which are slightly salted and smoked herring, the salted kippers so dear to the English across the Channel, Danish-style herring in white wine and oil, and so forth. It also has plentiful supplies of river trout, salmon, eel, and mussels, and produces good pork and sausages.

BELGIUM   Belgian food has the same cheerfully hybrid style as the country as a whole: French techniques are applied to North Sea ingredients and served in German portions. However, unlike the French, the Belgians prefer to customize recipes to individual tastes. Sea bass may be topped with grilled foie gras; sea urchin is combined with oysters, artichokes, and asparagus; local baby shrimp or oysters are poached in Vouvray wine; and grilled fish and rabbit are typically dressed with coarse mustard. One-pot and casserole dishes are common: *Waterzooi* is a rich hotpot, usually of chicken but sometimes of rabbit or even eels or fish. *Carbonnades* are beef stews that use beer. Belgian endive is particularly popular wrapped with ham and covered with a cheese sauce. In cooler weather, the Belgians enjoy farmer's-style sausage platters or long, slow-cooked stews called *hutsepots*, which may be pork, beef, or game, usually with cream and sometimes varied by the use of dried fruits, such as prunes, and the dark, spicy beers of the region. Here rooty, earthy vegetables are not just tolerated but are in fact preferred, most notably cabbages, leeks, turnips, carrots, and cauliflower.

BORDEAUX Although it produces particularly fine lamb, cheese, and foie gras, Bordeaux has been known since the fourth century as the wine-growing heart of France, source of the great Medocs (Margaux, Saint-Julien, and Pauillac), Graves, Sauternes, Saint-Emilions, and Pomerols. It is rich in both freshwater and saltwater fish, and crayfish and eels are favorites. As in the other southern regions, Bordelaise cuisine emphasizes olive oil and garlic over cream, butter, and shallots.

BRITTANY The sharpest ray on France's profile juts out into the Atlantic Ocean close to Great Britain; in fact, the region is named for the Britons who escaped back to France after the Anglo-Saxons took over in the fifth century. Its Celtic-rooted cuisine shows a family relationship to Welsh fare but with an even heavier emphasis on seafood: clams, oysters, cockles, scallops, spiny lobsters, crabs, sardines, salmon, eels, sole, mackerel, pike, turbot, herring, and shad. *Cotriade* is an eel soup or stew, and salt-meadow lamb served with beans is a Bretonne specialty; this meat is said to have a particular tang from the salt water that floods the meadows. Brittany is well-stocked with duck (Nantes ducks are famous) and turkey, mutton and pork, and its cauliflowers, artichokes, strawberries, and apples are considered premium. It also produces Muscadet wine.

BURGUNDY Burgundy is to food as Bordeaux is to wine. Its poultry, including many smaller fowl such as squab, woodcock, and dove, is so good that even other Frenchmen admire it; the Charolais beef cattle is prime; the escargots are considered to be the finest; and the wines, including Chablis, Côte de Nuit, Pouilly-Fuisse, Macon-Village, and Montrachet—are big-bodied enough to go along. Wild mushrooms, currants (used for making Cassis), bleu and goat cheeses, Dijon ham, *coq au chambertin* (the original chicken braised in red wine), beef and rabbit *a la bourguignonne* (stewed in red wine), pike *quenelles* (poached "dumplings" made of fish mousse), and escargots, the legendary first course of snails in garlic butter, are quintessential Burgundian dishes. Cooking emphasizes not the four food groups but the four indulgences: wine, cream, lard, and pastry. No wonder they talk about "hearty Burgundies."

CORSICA   This Mediterranean island abounds in fish and seafood (and bouillabaisses), but it also has an abundance of game, including blackbirds, which are considered a delicacy. It also produces a large variety of fruits and vegetables, most importantly almonds, figs, chestnuts, and olives. Typical dishes include beef braised with juniper berries, and a sort of tripe deluxe called *tripa*, stuffed with spinach, beets, and herbs. Corsica has been Italian as well as French (and Byzantine, Arab, a Papal state, and briefly British), and many dishes and dialects recall the Italian connection: sun-dried goat or roast kid; prisuttu (prosciutto, Italian-style raw ham); polenta, the corn-meal mush; and stuffed leg of lamb. Corsicans also make fine pastries, flavored with almonds, vanilla, aniseed, chestnuts, and pine nuts.

GASCONY   On the Atlantic coast just over the Pyrenees from Spain, Gascony is probably most revered for its Armagnac region, which produces the brandy that bears its name; but it also has fine oysters and truffles, goose, and duck (foie gras and confits). Ham here is often served "raw," meaning unsalted.

GUYENNE   In this province is Périgord, mecca for truffle-lovers; the region also produces Roquefort cheese and is famous for pâtés, confits, tripe, eels, oyster sausages, jugged heart, roast wood pigeon, and partridge and trout a la meunière.

LANGUEDOC   Named *langue d'oc*, language of the Westerners— as opposed to the *langue d'oil*, the Parisian dialect—this Mediterranean coastal region still shows strong Roman and Arab influences: Its most famous creations include *cassoulet*, the Roman-era mutton ragout with white beans; ragout of veal or duck with olives; and tripe with saffron and roast suckling pig; and to be cooked *a la languedocienne* means to be garnished with cèpes, eggplant, and tomatoes. (Further demonstrating its ties to old Mediterranean cooking, Languedoc dishes are often described as *a la catalone*, referring to the nearby coastal region of Spain.) Typical Languedoc menus highlight soups, particularly *pot-au-feus*, or hotpots; fish and shellfish stews (including a bouillabaisse entirely unlike the Marseilles version); and hearty vegetable soups made of garlic and cabbage. Egg dishes are unusually popular, especially omelets; and the many fine fowl as well as meats are made into sausages. Languedoc is also the source of the Côte du Rhône wines.

LYONNAIS   This is primarily an industrial region but does produce high-quality potatoes; fish, particularly pike; and pork, including organ meats and offal such as tripe, chitterlings, and sausages. Lyonnais produces Beaujolais and Gamay red wines.

NORMANDY   One of the most famous provincial cuisines, it richly deserves its reputation, so to speak—it's very proud of its butter and cream, which are obvious in almost all its dishes. Many Normandy dishes are even cooked in a special fat called *graisse normande*, which is a clarified pork fat and suet with herbs and vegetables. Normandy is also the home of many rich cheeses, including Camembert and the creamy Neufchatel. Like Brittany, it has vast apple orchards (which produce Calvados, the great apple brandy), as well as meadows of salt-water grass that flavor its mutton and beef. The shellfish from the region are highly prized, especially the giant mussels, the prawns, and the small sweet lobsters called *demoiselles*, or "young girls."

PROVENCE   While it is certainly true that garlic (or *aioli*, a garlic mayonnaise) is the number one ingredient of this quintessentially Mediterranean cuisine, it's also true that their garlic is much sweeter than what we are used to in the United States. However, there's no way of knowing what a particular chef is using. Other famous dishes include *pistou*, a typically Mediterranean dish of white beans, tomatoes, and vermicelli; bouillabaisse; *bourride*, a similar stew with white fish only and no saffron; *tapenades*, the savory spreads and tarts and breads with black olives and anchovies; grilled fish with fennel or swiss chard; and dried salt cod. Other typically Midi ingredients include chickpeas, artichokes, tomatoes, grilled peppers, and citrus condiments. The most important wine of the region is Chateauneuf-du-Pape.

SAVOY   This northeasterly province, which adjoins Switzerland and Germany, is mountainous, but its slopes provide fine pasture and orchard space, and its dairy produce, beehives, fruit and nut trees, and game are famous. Its cooking can be generously characterized as hearty: Its specialties include *civet*, a hare and pork stew with a rich blood, spice, and cream sauce; gratins in general, and gratin of cabbage in particular; and cabbages stuffed with potatoes, bacon, and lamb. Dishes featuring veal and lamb offal (sweetbreads, brains, and livers) are extremely popular. *Matafans* are cornmeal pancakes often served rolled around meat or poultry, something like an Alpine blini. The region has fine fish, which is often batter-fried or floured a la meunière. The influence of its neighbors can be seen in its fondues and especially its desserts, particularly *bonbons au miel des Alpes* (honied Alpine sweets), nougats, pastries, and chocolates.

HOW TO ORDER AND EAT LIKE A NATIVE

As mentioned in the chapter on Russian cuisine, the manner in which dinners are now served—in courses, with all diners served simultaneously, and ideally at tables of no more than eight—was the Russian mode and replaced the French (and generally European) system of three mega-courses. The "correct" order of courses is: hors d'oeuvre, soup, fish, poultry, roast, salad, *entremets* (literally "in-betweens," often fruit or sorbet), cheese and, finally, dessert.

This system in turn prescribed the order of wines, from the lightest to the strongest, because in theory, drinking too dark a wine with the chicken would overpower the dish and spoil the flavor of the next wine. Traditionally, therefore, champagne was served with the hors d'oeuvre, lighter whites with the soups and fish, bigger-bodied whites (or lighter reds) with the poultry, full reds with the meats, the fortified wines such as port and brandy with cheese, and finally on to the great sweet wines, the Sauternes, with dessert. This light-to-dark color-coding was supposed to be fitting to the dishes, too, and for similar reasons—so that too strong a sauce with the fish sauce didn't "kill" the chicken.

Obviously, this is more food (and alcohol) than most people want, even at formal banquets, so restaurants have made concessions. Many menus group the appetizers and soups together, and some group the meat and poultry entrees. The cheese course has almost disappeared (but any good French restaurant will have some cheese, even if it isn't on the menu, so ask).

In the United States, all but the finest French restaurants had given in to the American habit of having salad first, which was actually just a way of keeping the customer occupied while dinner was being cooked; but now that American diners have become intrigued by "authentic" dining, many restaurants have restored the old order. Some may ask which you prefer.

You may also see special three- or four-course *prix fixe* menu: That means the meal has a fixed price, but you will probably have two or perhaps three dishes in each course to choose from. *A la carte* merely means you are ordering (and paying for) each course separately.

One rule of thumb probably worth remembering: Try to avoid having more than one dish with the same sauce or in the same style, particularly if cream or cheese is involved. The richness will quickly grow cloying. If there are two similar dishes you're interested in, either ask if one can prepared more plainly, or have the sauce served on the side (if possible), or have a small salad or other palate-cleanser in between.

HOW TO ORDER AND SAMPLE WINE

The ceremony—some people would say "ordeal"—of ordering and tasting fine wines at a restaurant should be fun, not frightening.

The supposed rules of ordering wines—only red with meat, only white with fish—are oversimplified. It's true that a sweet white will not ideally suit brown meats or game, and a very big red will overwhelm shellfish. However, many people prefer lighter reds with chicken or big whites with game fowl; please yourself. And champagne lovers believe that the "bubbly" can be drunk with almost anything.

There is another thing the French take as seriously as wines and sauces: cheese. There are 400 varieties made in France alone, and although in the United States they (or more often, American imitations) are available year-round, many fine French cheese have "seasons." Some are even subspecialized: Certain Bries are eaten year-round, some only November till May. And like wines, certain cheeses may carry legal appellations—Roquefort, Parmesan—only if they are produced in particular regions. In France, cheeses are served before the sweets, often with butter, though that is not always true in the United States; they are usually served with crackers, and sometimes dark bread and vegetables, rather than fruit. (With Munster, curiously, it is traditional to serve cumin.) If the cheese is uncut, it is traditional for the host to cut into it with the knife and then pass it around.

Also, despite the accepted wisdom, many experts prefer red wines just slightly chilled, particularly with something other than red meat ("room temperature" in a medieval cellar, after all, was unlikely to have been anything near 72°); if you like yours that way, say so when you order it. Similarly, though Americans have a (deserved) reputation for liking both wine and beer overchilled, serving white wine or champagne too cold will numb the flavor. If the restaurant has overcompensated, ask them to take the bottle out of the ice bucket for a few minutes.

Of course, selecting wines is at best a passion and at worst an obsession, so we suggest you buy a wine guide if you want to know which wines really do go best with certain dishes; or ask the waiter or the sommelier for suggestions. It's their business to help you enjoy your meal.

When the bottle arrives, you (or whoever ordered the wine) will first be shown the label to make sure the correct wine has been brought out. Then the waiter will draw the cork and place it on the table beside your plate. Simply check to make sure it hasn't crumbled or dried out (it should be damp only about halfway up, or the seal is no longer tight); don't sniff it. Then a sip will be poured into your glass; you may swirl it to release the "bouquet" (the aroma) before tasting it, but again, don't go overboard. If it's good, you may either ask the waiter to pour or, if the wine is a red, let it rest—"breathe," and mellow in the air—a few minutes before pouring it. Some of this may be omitted if you've ordered an inexpensive or house wine; but in any case, if you are not happy with the wine, say so.

If you're entertaining at home, remember that the bouquet of a red wine is most accessible when served in a rounder goblet, while white wines are served in the more oval glasses. Champagne should be served in tall thin "tulips" or "flutes" rather than wide-bottomed, sherbet-style glasses so that the bubbles last longer.

COOKING AT HOME

It's probably not surprising that the French, who have made such a mystique of technique, should encourage people to think French recipes are difficult. Many certainly are; however, some of the recipes Americans typically shy away from, such as soufflés and hand-mixed hollandaise, are actually much easier and less temperamental than is rumored. The stew below is distinctively "provincial"—literally, as that's where Provence got its name—and incredibly simple. It's also perfect for entertaining, dirties only one dish from beginning to end, and can be made entirely in advance.

The Belgian gratin below is home-style comfort food; serve it with a really sit-down ale (like Corsendonk Monk's), a salad, and rice or french fries.

PROVENÇAL BEEF STEW

This tastes best (and can be made much less fattening) when made two days in advance.

2 pounds stewing beef, cut in large chunks
2 leeks, thoroughly washed and sliced or coarsely chopped
2 garlic cloves, chopped
1 large carrot, peeled and sliced into coins
2 stalks celery (strings removed), sliced
1 1/2 tablespoons extra virgin olive oil
1 bottle hearty red wine
1 bunch fresh sage or thyme or both
(or 2 tablespoons dried of each), stalks tied together
1 stick of fresh rosemary (or 1 tablespoon dried),
tied up with the thyme (optional)
2 whole bay leaves

1 2-inch strip of orange zest, minced
salt and pepper to taste

Combine all ingredients except orange zest in enameled casserole and refrigerate overnight. The next day, simmer gently 3–4 hours or until the meat is very tender. Cool, then return to the refrigerator overnight. The next day, remove all hardened oil and fat on the top and then reheat. Remove the bay leaves and the bunch of herbs, stir in the zest, and serve with noodles. (For a slightly richer flavor, cook noodles or macaroni until almost done, then toss with grated Parmesan cheese and pour a little of the stew liquid over the top to soften the cheese and meld the flavors.)

ENDIVE AND HAM GRATIN

8 medium Belgian endives, rinsed and trimmed
salt, pepper, and nutmeg
2 1/4 cups milk
3 tablespoons unsalted butter
4 tablespoons flour
8 thin slices ham
1 cup grated Swiss or Emmenthal cheese
1/2 cup fine bread crumbs

Preheat oven to 350°. Generously oil an enamel casserole with nonstick spray. Place the endives in the dish, season with salt, pepper, and nutmeg, and cover with 1 cup boiling water. Over high heat, bring the water back to a boil; cover, reduce heat to a bare simmer, and cook until tender (about 25 minutes). Remove with slotted spoon, reserving liquid, and drain.

Scald the milk. Meanwhile, melt the butter in a heavy saucepan. Stir in flour and cook just until it starts to take on color, then add hot milk and poaching liquid, whisking continually until smooth and thick. Simmer briefly, season again, and spoon a layer of sauce into the bottom of a baking dish large enough to hold all the endives side by side. Roll each endive in a slice of ham and place in the dish, cover with remaining sauce, top with cheese, and bake until top is crusty (15–20 minutes).

ITALY

It's entirely appropriate that so many people consider Italian food "Mamma's cooking": Even the French called it "the mother cuisine," and it goes back a long way.

In the first century, when the Roman author Apicus was writing about cooking, he listed poaching, braising, basting, grilling, roasting, and steaming (using the hot-water bath called *bagno maria*, known in France as the *bain-marie*) as common methods of cooking. Italian chefs were also serving egg- and roux-based sauces, cream sauces (including the one that was later dubbed "béchamel" in honor of a French marquis who adored it), fruits to offset fatty poultry (duck *a l'orange*), breads, and what sounds a lot like lasagne—and all this 1500 years before tomatoes were even "discovered" by Europeans.

Of course, many great Italian dishes have been disguised by French names: *ragus*, or stews, which became the French *ragouts; mille-foglie*, the "thousand-sheet" pastry called *mille feuille* in France. At the same time, a lot of what seems old about Italian cooking—sun-dried

BASIC CUISINE

DINNER FOR TWO:
Stuffed artichoke, carpaccio, minestrone, bass with capers, osso bucco

DINNER FOR FOUR:
Mixed antipasti, risotto, grilled chicken, rabbit cacciatore, calamari fra diavolo

STYLE:
Hearty, aromatic, smoky

KEY FLAVORS:
Olive oil, garlic, anise, rosemary, tomato

DISTINCTIVE FOODS:
Pasta, risotto, bruscetta, prosciutto

EATING UTENSILS:
Forks and knives

NUTRITIONAL INDEX:
Low sodium, medium fat

UNIFORMITY OF MENUS:
Good

COST:
Inexpensive to expensive

"THANK YOU":
"Grazie"

tomatoes, rice, polenta—is relatively new and a testament to their curiosity. Until 150 years ago, eggplant was believed to drive people insane, and only the Sicilians championed it. Sun-dried tomatoes are Native American. *Carpaccio*, the pounded raw beef that is now a standard of virtually every Italian restaurant, was invented only a generation ago, at Harry's Bar in Venice. (This bar/restaurant was made famous by Ernest Hemingway, and the peaches-and-Spumante cocktail known as the Bellini was also invented there.) Caesar salad is no older; it was invented in Acapulco by an Italian restaurateur named Caesar Cardini.

Italian cooking methods haven't changed much in the past two millenia; braising, poaching, steaming (*en papiotte*), grilling or griddling, and roasting remain the most common. There are still many villages that have one great wood-burning *forno*, or oven, in which temperatures routinely reach 1200–1500° and in which casseroles left overnight in the "cooling" section cook for the next day. We have an increasing number of such ovens in the United States, too; Mamma would be proud.

THE COUNTRY

Italy, as children are always told, looks like a boot kicking into the Mediterranean—a very ornate cavalier's boot, with ruffles over the knees in the north and a powerful heel stretching toward Albania and Greece—and the islands of Sardinia and Sicily are like stones the toe is kicking. The frill at the top of the boot is actually the snaking line of the Alps, beyond which lie France, Switzerland, Austria, and Slovenia. Another mountain line, the Apennines, runs down the middle, like a seam, and on into Sicily. Down the east coast—the boot's calf—is the Adriatic Sea, and around the sole and shin lies the Mediterranean.

All but a handful of provinces in Italy touch the sea, and even in the north, no village is more than 150 miles from the ocean. And because the country remains staunchly Roman Catholic, the fish markets are teeming on Friday mornings and almost empty on Monday. (If you're a seafood fanatic, remember that even in the United States, Italian cooks are apt to concentrate on fish dishes on Friday.) The busiest port is Genoa, on the western continental shore near the Italian Riviera.

The mountains also shape Italian cuisine, however: The plain at the foot of the Alps provides the primary pastureland, and many of Italy's cheeses and sweets come from this area. The fertile region to the east of the Apennines, Emilia-Romagna, provides fine durum wheat for pasta, rice, and maize; on the west is the great wine-growing region. Down the center of the peninsula and into Sicily, where the mountains are more amenable to olive groves than dairy cows, the use of olive oil increases.

Sardinia, over in the heart of the Mediterranean, is more than half pastureland and raises wheat, barley, grapes, and olives along with sheep and goats; it was the Romans' earliest bread factory and was seriously overcultivated for centuries. Sicily, hot but hilly, also supplies wheat, barley, and maize along with olives, almonds, wine grapes, sheep, and cattle.

THE HISTORY

Although there are plenty of archeological remnants, not very much is known about the earliest inhabitants of Italy. Egyptian records refer to Sardinia as early as the thirteenth century B.C., and the Greeks had established colonies along the southern coast by the fifth century B.C.; but the first (of many) invaders into the central peninsula were the Etruscans, who probably moved over from Asia Minor in about the eighth century B.C. They were the first to turn wheat flour into a sort of mush, called *puls*, which became the basic hardtack of the Roman legions and probably left its name behind for polenta, the cornmeal mush that made its roundabout way from the Americas nearly 2,500 years later.

The Etruscans prospered for some 400 years before the Celts (Gauls) elbowed them further south; and soon after that, the Latins and Sabines between them produced that acquisitive and martial people, the Romans. The Roman nobles were heavy meat-eaters and drinkers—the Emperor Maximus reportedly consumed 40 pounds of meat and 40 bottles of wine a day—but the great mass of citizens and slaves of the empire continued to rely on grains, chicken, and a little fish.

Thanks to the innovations and subjugations of the Roman Empire, Italy remained at the center of the universe for a thousand years, until it fell to the various eastern "barbarians" and, like France, broke into a number of competitive states. Sicily fell to the Saracens in the tenth century; the Byzantines recaptured the southern provinces, only to lose them in the eleventh century to the Normans, who in turn gave way to Spain.

Over the next several centuries, France, Spain, Germany (the Holy Roman Empire), and Austria carved off and juggled pieces of the once-great nation until, by the end of the fifteenth century, the country was loosely divided into three sections: the north, where the independent duchies of Genoa and Venice were booming; the central regions, home of the great commercial city-states, such as Florence and the Papal States; and the south, where the Spanish feudal system was taking a cruel toll.

In the north and central plateau, the thirteenth, fourteenth, and fifteenth centuries were a golden age; the Renaissance artists and writers transformed European court culture forever and, thanks particularly to the Venetian traders, transformed European cuisine as well. It was during the Italian Renaissance that most cooking techniques used today were perfected and taught to the French. (As Escoffier admitted, "If it had been an Italian who codified the world of cuisine, it would be thought of as Italian"—as if the Italians would ever think of "codifying" something so spontaneous as cooking.)

But if French chefs owe an irradicable debt to the Italians, they may have partially repaid it by preserving the techniques they had learned and returning them in the eighteenth and nineteenth centuries. And although Italy began the painful task of reunification in the late nineteenth century, its regional cuisines still show traces of the peoples who came and conquered before.

THE CUISINE

In Italy, as in France, there is some regional distinction by cooking fats: In the northern areas, near France and Germany, the cooking medium is most often butter, and tomatoes are used more sparingly. Garlic is widely used in the north (although it may sound confusing, the north of Italy is closer to the south of France, so the cooking of the northwest Italian provinces, in particular, resembles that of Provence.) In the northeast, nearest Switzerland and Austria, the fattier meats and sausages and the cheeses and floured meats are more common. In the south and in Sicily, the cooking fat is most often olive oil, as it is in Greece, southern Spain, and North Africa. And in Emilia-Romagna, the rich region that begins just beneath the "cuff" of the Italian boot and stretches across to the knee, cooks use all three fats—butter, oil, and lard.

There is also a preference in the north for egg noodles, which are softer, whereas in the south they are more apt to serve eggless pasta, which has more texture. For more on regional styles, see "Provincial Cuisines," page 39.

Italian cuisine is multicultural. The Etruscans were making wheat into flour a thousand years before Marco Polo set out for the Far East, and they certainly understood something resembling pasta. The Greeks introduced garlic, wine, and the essential oil (olive). They also introduced the concept of fish chowders—the beginning of a tradition that ultimately produced French bouillabaisse, Spanish zarzuela, and *cioppino*. Early on the Romans discovered how marinating meats tenderized and preserved as well as flavored them. Wine, vinegar, lemon and salt, bay leaves, garlic, and rosemary were the common ingredients. The Romans were also early connoisseurs of seafood, and they farm-raised oysters, caviar sturgeon, and lamprey eels.

But the Arabs and Byzantines are the unsung heros of the "mother cuisine"; they not only brought with them the Indonesian aromatics—mace, allspice, cinnamon, ginger, cayenne, clove, anise, and the peppercorns that made Venice rich—but also showed the Italians how to distill the great vinegars now known as balsamic. They succeeded in persuading the Italians to grow their own rice—which the Romans had encountered in India but never felt much need to cultivate—thereby making possible the risotto. They even whispered the secret of ice cream, something they had learned from the Chinese. Their influence is readily

Oil and Vinegar

There is a good reason that "Mediterranean" cuisine is almost synonymous with olive oil; 98 percent of the olive groves in the world are found in Italy, Spain, and Greece. Although it is no longer only epicures who specify extra-virgin olive oil, you may be surprised to find out that "virgin" is not the next level down, but the lowest of four; "extra-virgin" is followed first by "superfine," then by "fine." (The crème de la crème is just that—skimmed off the top of the first pressing—and called *afiorato*.) The grades reflect the amount of oleic acid permitted; extra-virgin has 1 percent or less (.5 percent is considered correct), virgin 4 percent. Olive oils do not withstand high heat very well and should thus be used for flavoring, not frying.

Italy is also home to the greatest of vinegars, the sweet and redolent balsamic vinegar. The real stuff—the only vinegar that can be labeled aceto balsamic tradizionale—is made from the Trebbiano wine grape and is aged for about 40 years. The batch is periodically moved from one cask to another; the casks are each made of a different wood and impart the only seasoning allowed. All the while, the vinegar is getting thicker and sweeter. Some is 100 years old and almost as costly as wine of its vintage.

Fitter Fats

In general, Italian sauces are much less fatty than French sauces, primarily because it is more common in Italian cooking to reduce the cooking liquid itself as a sauce, while the French tend to use the reduction to flavor a cream sauce or to "finish" it with butter. Nevertheless, Italian cuisine can be deceiving; many sauces and casseroles have at their base a fat called *battuto*, a mixture of minced onions and parsley browned in lard; and sometimes the "white sauce" you were expecting to be a clear broth turns out to be something far heavier.

Nobody can seriously claim they didn't know that fettucini Alfredo, whose four ingredients are pasta, butter, cream, and Parmesan, was a nutritional neutron bomb. In general, however, Americanized Italian food is more likely to be dripping oil or rendered cheese than authentic Italian cuisine is.

visible in southern specialties, such as oranges with braised artichokes, fennel salad, and baked rabbit with preserved lemons.

It was also the Byzantines, incidentally, who taught the Europeans table manners: When Teodora, daughter of the emperor Constantine, married an eleventh-century Venetian aristocrat, she was revolted by the Venetians' habits of eating with their hands and passing communal goblets. She introduced napkins, table settings (some historians refer to solid gold plates and rock crystal cups), and the fork—for which innovations she was denounced as decadent by various cardinals. It took several centuries for the fork to catch on in Italy, and 500 years later, when the de Medicis carried it along to France, they weren't wildly successful, either.

The final major ingredients came via the Spanish, who carved off pieces of southern Italy at various times; they introduced the tomatoes, corn, hot peppers, and chocolate they had found while searching for gold in the New World. (The word "salsa," used today almost exclusively for the tomato-pepper condiment in Central and South American cuisine, was picked up by the Spanish from the Italian word for sauce, which in turn had come from the Romans' lavish use of salt—*sal*.)

Italy was ravaged by wars for centuries following the Renaissance, and meat has only become affordable, and hence a major part of the diet, since World War II. Italians typically eat their pastas with much less sauce than Americans, and a good Italian restaurant will not flood your dish. And Italian pizzas are much lighter; one can only think the real *capo di tutti capi* would have paled at the sight of the kitchen-sink creations nicknamed "godfathers" in American pizza parlors.

In general, a Tuscan restaurant that specializes in grilled meats and seafood and uses the "good cholesterol" of olive oil is likely to have lower-fat fare than a northern Italian restaurant, particularly one that offers a lot of dredged and butter-sautéed dishes with prosciutto and fontina cheese. If you're worried about cholesterol, you may also want to remember that southern Italian cooking uses fewer eggs (particularly in the pastas), butter, or cream than northern styles. Even so, unless you pile on the Parmesan (which is both high-fat and high-sodium), you can eat fairly well in any Italian kitchen—including a pizzeria. Just stick to the veggie versions.

THE MAIN INGREDIENTS

SEASONINGS Thanks to the Saracens, the "brown" spices of Indonesia—mace, nutmeg, cinnamon, coriander, anise, clove, and ginger—are as much a part of the Italian kitchen as the "green" herbs: tarragon, parsley, basil, fennel, oregano, sage, chives and leeks, thyme, chervil, rosemary, mint, juniper, and marjoram. Capers, a small green bud brined in vinegar (another Arab import), and pickled gherkins are also used to provide contrast, particularly to seafood. Anchovies, balsamic vinegar, and green olives are popular in more pungent dishes; black pepper, truffles, and dried mushrooms are used in the earthier ones.

VEGETABLES AND FRUITS Anise (fennel) is one of the most characteristic flavors in Italian cooking, as a spice and as a vegetable. Bulb fennel, celery, celeriac, the chicories (escarole and radicchio) and endives, artichokes, thistles and cardoons, and jerusalem artichokes are all popular. Other large crops include cauliflower; broccoli and broccoli

---

Tavern Fare

Just as the French differentiate between bistros and brasseries, the Italians distinguish between trattorias, cantinas, and ristorantes. A trattoria is the most informal, a mom-and-pop place, often with an exposed kitchen, heavy plates, and jelly glasses for house wine. A cantina is more of a tavern. A restaurant that advertises *cucina stagionale* specializes in seasonal dishes, which is particularly authentic: In Italy, only fresh ingredients are ever used. *Cucina casalinga* or *casarecchia* is "home cooking," *cucina vecchia* is old-style cuisine, and *novella cucina* is the Italian equivalent of nouvelle cuisine—that is, lightened up (and probably hiked up pricewise as well).

rabe; brussels sprouts; eggplant; escarole; asparagus; chard; corn; sugar beets; spinach; turnip and mustard greens; zucchini; tomatoes; sweet and hot peppers; and beans, particularly peas, green beans, small black beans, and white *fagioli*, limas, and cannellini beans. Wild mushrooms are legendary, particularly the porcini and portobellas, which are flooding American menus.

A variety of citrus fruits, particularly oranges and lemons, are produced in the warmer regions, and so are tree fruits such as peas and peaches; and the great grape regions are in Tuscany and Sicily.

RICE AND GRAINS Arborio rice is a short grain and is considered the only variety suitable for making risotto, a creamy yet firm "braise" of rice, usually flavored with wild mushrooms or truffles, seafood, and Romano or Parmesan cheese. Cornmeal mush, or polenta, has been popular ever since the Arabs introduced it (trading for the Spanish, who found it in Mexico). Most polenta is a coarse yellow meal, although in the north it may be a finer white meal. Barley grains are often used in soups. Buckwheat, whole wheat, and rye flours are used not only for breads but also, particularly in the northern areas, in pastas.

DAIRY PRODUCTS Italians are among the foremost cheese producers (even the French bow to Parmeggiano Reggiano) and like both hard (Parmesan and Romano) and soft varieties (mozzarella, ricotta, fontina). These cheeses, incidentally, may be made from cow's milk, goat's milk, sheep's milk, or buffalo's milk, which is used to make the most expensive mozzarella.

FISH AND SEAFOOD As we have noted, virtually every province has access to the Mediterranean as well as to numerous rivers, and the variety is mouth-watering: salmon and salmon trout, mackerel, tuna, carp, bluefish, swordfish, pompano, sardines, herring, anchovies, smelts, butterfish, cod, flounder, sole, pike, perch, red snapper, catfish, turbot, grouper, and tilefish, plus squid, lampreys, sea urchins, oysters, clams, mussels, lobsters, shrimp, mullet roe, sturgeon caviar, and scampi, the giant Adriatic prawns. In the United States, "scampi" is frequently seen on menus but rarely in the flesh; instead, shrimp or prawns are substituted. *Baccala* is the Italian name for the Viking-dried cod now most often found in Portuguese and Brazilian food (*bacalao*). *Stoccafisso* (stockfish) is the name for the sun-dried cod that Norwegians call *stokkfisk*—the one that lasts 20 years.

POULTRY AND GAME BIRDS   Chicken is almost daily fare, and turkey, duck, and goose are fairly common, but Italians also like the spunkier flavor of game birds—squab, partridge, quail, snipe, pheasant, guinea hen, and woodcock—that stand up well to being roasted, spit-grilled, or stewed.

MEATS   Although beef doesn't appear on American menus as much as veal and lamb (*agnelli*), Italian beef cattle are highly prized, particularly the Razza Chianina, a buffalo-like animal raised in Tuscany and Umbria. Veal, or *vitellone*, can only be marketed as that if the calf is 3 or younger; at 3 1/2, it becomes *manzo*. Liver and onions is a Venetian invention, not a school principal's, although it's more likely to be veal liver than calf's.

Pork and suckling pigs are popular as roasts and chops; but most often they are cured or salted: The word "prosciutto" usually refers to a raw, air-cured ham (although *prosciutto cotto* is cooked ham), and *pancetta* is a fine bacon from the belly. Pork and veal are ground into sausages or meatballs. The hams and sausages of the north are particularly good. Italians pay close attention to organ meats and offal, from jowls and pigs' feet to tripe and testicles; but only the "tamest" of these—brains, kidneys, livers, and sweetbreads—are apt to appear on American menus. Gamier meats are also popular, particularly wild boar and venison. Intriguingly, Italian cookbooks tend to group rabbit recipes under "poultry." (We *told* you it tasted like chicken.)

THE MAIN DISHES

Like French provincial cooking, Italian regional specialties may be made in any part of the country, but unlike the French, the Italians prefer to improvise a bit. They also insist on seasonal ingredients; you won't see asparagus risotto in the fall—not in Italy, at least. These are some of the more common dishes; for regional specialties, see "Provincial Cuisines," page 39.

ANTIPASTI   These are appetizers, some of which are served hot (*caldi*) and some cold (*freddi*). *Bruschetta* are toasted bread crusts rubbed with garlic, olive oil, or butter; *crostini* are similar but are topped with garbanzo spreads, anchovies, or chicken livers. Mixed antipasti plates generally include olives, marinated mushrooms, hard-cooked eggs, and roasted vegetables, particularly sweet peppers mated with anchovies, carpaccio (pounded-thin, raw beef drizzled with oil and dusted with black pepper and shavings of Parmesan cheese), prosciutto, or even salami. Other likely choices include stuffed artichokes, clams or mussels, grilled or fried calamari, and garlic-sautéed scampi. *Fritto misto* just means a mixed fry and can include anything from sweetbreads and livers to mushrooms and cheese. See also "How to Order," page 43.

SOUPS   The vegetable soup Americans know as "minestrone" is a Genovese dish and combines vegetables with string beans and cannellini, pancetta, prosciutto, tomatoes, and wine. Small stuffed pasta such as tortellini are frequently served *en brodo*, floating in broth. Seafood soups called *burridas* or *cacciucco* (from a Turkish word for fish) are extremely fine. Lentil soups, chicken soups with meatballs, and green vegetable soups—broccoli, escarole, spinach—are also common.

SALADS   The mixed greens used in Italy (radicchio, escarole, arugula, romaine) tend to have body and a touch of bitterness that is tempered by simple dressings of olive oil and lemon juice or vinegar. Fresh mozzarella cheese paired with tomatoes is usually served only with oil. The Tuscans in particular are fond of *panzanella*, a bread, tomato, and olive oil salad that is a Mediterranean universal; this is sometimes called *caponata*, but in the United States, that word is usually short for *caponata di melanzane* (see the section on Sicilian regional cuisine, page 41).

VEGETABLES   The Italians generally prefer their vegetables, like their seafood, fairly simple, partly because the vegetables are so fresh. Most often they are steamed or briefly boiled, then dressed with oil; they may also be blanched and then sautéed. Artichokes, carrots, and the bitter greens such as endive and escarole are often mellowed through braising or fricasseeing; cabbage, radicchio may be cooked this way, too, or fried, or wilted under hot dressings, as spinach is. In the northern regions, vegetables such as spinach and escarole are often steamed and creamed. Onions and cabbages are stuffed with pork or veal and sautéed. Carrots and green beans are usually lightly cooked in butter, though white beans and lentils are boiled and usually mixed with either bitter greens or a little meat. Eggplant used to be found only in the south, but nowadays *melanzane alla parmigiana* is available almost everywhere. Potatoes are less frequently "done" in Italy than in France, but they do show up pan-fried, or as croquettes, or mashed for gnocchi.

MEAT   Meat in Italy was traditionally long-cooked, and much of it still is over there, although in the United States, chops and roasts are more easily ordered rare. A classic Tuscan dish, *involtini*, features beefsteak strips pounded, then layered with salami, raisins, pine nuts, orange zest, and cheese, then rolled up and sauced with a thick, sweet wine sauce; there is also a veal involtini, flavored with cinnamon and cloves and stuffed with sausage. *Bistecca alla Fiorentina* is a giant porterhouse steak that would make a Chicago cattleman proud. Beef kebabs, marinated in olive oil, lemon, red wine, and garlic, recall their Persian heritage, as does the immensely popular *osso bucco*, veal shanks stewed with tomatoes until the meat falls off the bone, served over saffron rice. *Stinco* is veal shank braised with anchovies. Veal cutlets or scallopini are commonly dredged in flour and sautéed, after which they may be flavored with lemon, marsala wine, or cream, depending on the region. *Saltimbocca* is a sort of open-faced "sandwich" of veal, prosciutto, and mozzarella, strongly flavored with fresh sage and so delicious it jumps—*saltare*—from the pan to the mouth, or *bocca*.

Lamb is roasted, served upright in racks, and stewed, particularly with artichokes or fennel. Organ meats are usually sautéed or braised. Pork may be roasted, served as chops with German-style, sweet-and-sour cabbage, or Sicilian-style with mint and oranges. But almost any other sort of dish—beef, veal, pasta, even seafood—may well include prosciutto or mortadella ham as a flavoring.

FISH AND SEAFOOD   *Fra Diavolo*, or "brother of the devil," is a peppery tomato-and-wine sauce often used with lobster, clams, squid, or mixed seafood; marinara, the milder version, is also commonly used with shellfish. (When restaurants list "clams with red or white sauce," marinara is the red sauce they mean.) Seafood stews are made with pesto or saffron, depending on the region; whole fish are most often either grilled simply with lemon and capers or garlic, glazed with wine, or dredged and fried; but particularly in the central plains, hollandaise sauce, or *salsa olandese*, is popular with steamed and poached fillets. The Byzantine flavor shows up when fish are sauced with ground almonds and grapes or raisins.

CHICKEN AND GAME BIRDS   Poultry may be common, but it gets lavish treatment: grilled with rosemary, stewed with green or black olives, prosciutto, and chicken livers, or stewed with peas and pancetta.

The gamier birds are tenderized either by hanging—the traditional treatment for pheasant—or by larding the breast, which is standard for pigeon and guinea hen. Duck and goose, on the other hand, are roasted to render the excess fat, then braised or stewed. Chicken *alla campagnola*, or country-style, has been skillet-fried with potatoes, sausages, and green peppers; *cacciatore* means hunter-style and is similar but uses tomatoes instead of potatoes and red wine instead of white.

RICE AND GRAINS   As mentioned, risotto is the most popular way to serve rice; it requires slow cooking and regular coaxing with broth. Among the most popular risottos are those flavored with wild mushrooms, eels, peas and pancetta, asparagus, and squid and scallops. Rice is also habitually paired with peas and nicknamed *risi e bisi*. Sicilians roll rice into balls with various fillings (prosciutto and mozzarella, chicken livers, ground veal) and then fry them into what are called *arancini*, oranges. The phrase *riso nero*, black rice, usually means a dish flavored with squid ink, but if it's listed under the desserts, it means a chocolate-flavored rice pudding. (Incidentally, while pasta is always served as a separate course, rice can be served alongside an entree, unless the rice has meat or seafood of its own.)

Polenta is a cornmeal mush that is cooked, left to cool, cut in slices, and then baked or fried; it can then be topped with almost any sort of meat, vegetable sauce, or poultry. Polenta slices are also used like fat pasta noodles in fancy "lasagna."

SWEETS   Like everything else in Italian cooking, desserts echo the topography. Not surprisingly, it was the Venetians, with their Byzantine connections, who first grasped the extravagant potential of sugar, so Venetian desserts are particularly ornate, involving spun sugar, custards, and so forth. Chocolate ricotta cheesecakes, ricotta-stuffed canoli, and *tiramisu* (espresso- and liquor-soaked ladyfingers or spongecake) originated in the regions closest to Germany, where pastries and creams are common; in the Piedmont, where honeybees and nut trees are farmed, there are some almost Greek-style sweets. In Sicily, near North Africa, rice is flavored with orange and cinnamon, rolled in flour, fried, and finished with powdered sugar. Nevertheless, such rich desserts are eaten far more rarely in Italy than in the United States, and at home Italians generally finish meals with fruit or cheese.

BEVERAGES Italy is the second-largest wine-producing country in Europe, and its most important centers are in Tuscany, which produces the Chiantis and Brunellos; neighboring Umbria, which produces Amarone and Orvieto; Veneto, home of Valpolicella, Amarone, Soave, and Bardolino; and the Piedmont, home of the sparkling Asti Spumantes, Barolos, and Barbarescos. Sicily is a major wine-producing region, although underrated; Marsala is among its best. Grappa, a powerful (90 proof) distilled spirit made from the lightly pressed skins of wine grapes, has become increasingly popular in the United States, and many better restaurants now offer a dozen or so choices, flavored with various herbs, after dinner. Italians are also fond of beer and coffee; the Capuchin monks are credited with inventing cappuccino.

PASTA

There are entire volumes on pasta, and there could be encyclopedias. Some of those volumes have whole chapters devoted to the question of whether the Italians invented pasta or whether Marco Polo brought it back from China. There is, in fact, a pasta museum—in Bologna, where the Italians believe pasta originated. We're not taking sides, just being grateful. As Sophia Loren once put it, "Everything you see I owe to spaghetti."

However, there are a few simple things to remember about pasta. First, the shape is intended to complement the sauce. Thin or slippery sauces—tomato sauces, thinner cream sauces—are better matched to the busier shapes that will hold the sauce; and sturdy meat sauces go with thicker, flat noodles, such as linguini or fettucini.

Among the straight pastas are *capellini d'angelo*, or angelhair, the thinnest round noodles; spaghetti and *bucatini*, which is like a hollow spaghetti; and the flat pastas—linguini, fettucini, *pappardelle*, and of course the broad lasagne sheet. Probably the most common in Italy itself is *tagliatelli*, a medium-width pasta.

Most pastas are named for their shapes. Among the spiral pastas are *fusilli* and *rotelli*. Tubular noodles can be smooth but cut with angled ends (*penne*, meaning "pen" and referring to a nib) or grooved (*rigatoni*). *Conchiglie* are little clam-shell shapes ("conchs"); *orecchiette* are "little ears"; *farfalle* are "bowties," pinched in the middle; *lombrichelle* are

Waiters in American restaurants are usually instructed to offer you both ground Parmesan and ground pepper for your food (and now that "fresh-ground" refers to cheese as well, watching young waiters juggling pepper grinders and cheese graters simultaneously can be pretty entertaining). However, many Italians consider cheese a flavoring for plainly dressed pastas or those with vegetable or seafood sauces; meat sauces, according to this school, do not take cheese.

Waiters also offer you large spoons, but these should only be used to serve from the platter, along with a serving fork. To eat pasta noodles, turn the tines of the fork downward and cage a few strands, then twirl the stem of the fork with your hand until the noodles wrap around the fork. Do not use the bowl of a spoon as a twirling aid or cut the noodles with a knife or with the side of your fork. If you can't manage long noodles, order the smaller, individual pastas, such as penne or agnolotti.

"worms," hand-made and irregular (and also called *stringozzi*, or "shoelaces"). *Semini* are seed-shaped (like the orzo of Greek kitchens), and *radiatorre* are waffled—almost tripe-like, but rounded into little radiators.

There are a number of stuffed pastas, too: *Cappellacci* are round dumplings ("little hats") made by placing the meat or cheese filling onto one sheet of pasta, covering it with another, and then cutting out rounds; *ravioli* is similar but squarish; and *agnolotti* are sort of a "half-portion"—pasta first cut into disks, then filled, folded into half-moons, and pinched around the edges. Tortellini are "little rings," and tortelloni not-so-little rings. Manicotti, which is a square of pasta rolled around a filling of ricotta and prosciutto, literally means "hand-roll" and is named after a woman's muff. Add chicken, and it becomes *cannelloni*—"cannons."

Pasta, particularly linguini and fettucini, are often made with vegetables to add flavor and color to the dish: Spinach, artichokes, tomatoes, beets, pesto, red pepper, garlic, and mushroom are the most familiar additions, but black pasta, colored with squid's ink, can be very spectacular.

Strictly speaking, gnocchi is not pasta but dumplings, made of mashed potatoes rather than flour; it's more common in the north, near Germany.

PIZZA

We're not going to get into the question of who first invented pizza, either: We're just going to pass along that the Greeks settled in the south of Italy 2,500 years ago, and the Romans who followed them certainly ate something like white pizza. Tomatoes, of course, only arrived in the early seventeenth century. The first pizzeria on record opened in 1830, in Naples.

Italians make bread out of an astonishing array of flours: hard wheat, semolina, whole wheat, soy flour, barley, bran, cornmeal, walnut or almond flour, rice (which also shows up in some fritto mistos, rendering them something like transplanted tempura), and rye. The same dough can be used for bread, rolls, breadsticks, bruschetta, focaccia, calzone, or pizza. The only real difference between pizza and focaccia is the thickness of the crust: Traditional pizza crust is thin, and something an inch or two thick (or, as it's called in the United States, deep-dish, Sicilian, or Chicago-style pizza) is focaccia. Fold the dough in half over the fillings and seal it up and you have a calzone.

Unlike Americans, the Italians consider the crust the pizza, and the topping just that—a light layer. The most famous types are *pizza margherita*, with tomatoes and mozzarella; *napoletana*, a margherita with a dash of capers and anchovy; *frutti di mare*, margherita plus clams, mussels, squid, and/or shrimp; *al quattro formaggi*, with four cheeses (chef's choice); and *pizza al formaggio*, the traditional white pizza (except that sometimes pizza al formaggio turns out to be cheese bread).

Most bread is leavened, but *torta*, a flat griddle bread, is something like a cross between pita bread and a pizza crust. *Panettone* is a puffy sweet bread, studded with raisins, candied fruit, and citrus zest, traditionally served at Christmas; *colomba* is a similar loaf bread served at Easter.

PROVINCIAL CUISINES

As Italian food becomes more popular in the United States, chefs are less satisfied with calling their food "northern Italian" or "home-style." Increasingly, at least in the menus' small print and in restaurant reviews, you'll see Italian cuisine described with reference to the province, and these cuisines are some of the more distinctive styles.

EMILIA-ROMAGNA   Among the region's major cities are Parma, Ravenna, and Bologna, and to a great extent, a restaurant in the United States that advertises "northern Italian" cuisine is talking about Bolognese or Parmesan food. Spinach lasagna includes veal and beef and prosciutto; Romagna-style macaroni has sweetbreads, prosciutto, and truffles; and a Bolognese macaroni is topped with a pancetta, veal, chicken liver, and heavy cream ragout. Pastas with "four cheeses" were invented here. Earthy flavors—eels, kidneys, rabbit, salt cod—are common. The classic meat sauce, a poor imitation of which was many Americans' earliest experience with Italian food, is actually made of a combination of ground meats: pork, veal, and beef, with pancetta, red wine, and milk as well as tomatoes. But that is only one of the region's claims to fame: Tortellini originated here, and there are scores of stuffings, ranging from cheese to chicken to veal to walnuts and cream.

GENOA   Genoa is the centerpoint of a long, skinny seafront region on the western coast of Italy; it adjoins France and bears some family resemblance to Provençal cuisine. The dishes there are apt to be baked and solid—lasagna, pastas with meat sauces, ravioli with walnuts, cauliflower with anchovies. A dish prepared *alla Genovese* is likely to have both basil and garlic as primary flavorings; soups are served with pesto, as is rice. In fact, nearby Portofino—a postcard-pretty resort of multicolored villas that has catered to the likes of the Duke and Duchess of Windsor and Bogart and Bacall—claims to be the home of pesto. Genoa is Italy's finest port, so seafood stews, seafood risottos, and seafood-sauced pastas are fine here. However, the residents also make fine game in season, characteristically with walnut or chestnut sauces.

LOMBARDY AND THE PIEDMONT   The Piedmont region, in the northwest "frill" of the boot, adjoins France and Germany, so you are apt to find cheese fondue here and heartier farm dishes such as pork sweetbreads; offal stews; garlic and anchovy sauces; potato gnocchi; stuffed peppers; and veal chops stuffed with prosciutto and cheese, dredged, breaded, and cooked in butter. Both regions are landlocked. The Lombards use vegetables more freely than many other provincials, often stuffing pasta with pumpkin or spinach; they also frequently stew tripe. Ossu bucco and veal piccata are classic Milanese dishes. Eggs and cheese are important here, and the rich mascarpone cheese, a sweet creamy cheese used primarily in desserts, is very common. Frying is more common here than in the south, and among the characteristic dishes are fried sweetbreads and brains. You are also apt to find sauerkraut, sausages, juniper berries, bay leaves, and even strudels in this region.

NAPLES   Naples is on the lower western coast, in an area known for hearty simplicity; *neapolitano* is almost a synonym for "family-style." Typical dishes include herb-stuffed squid and octopus; brains with capers and olives; spaghetti with clams, mussels, and/or plain tomato sauce (the origin of that classic menu item, "clams with red or white sauce"); pastas with tuna or anchovies; and a lighter version of *fettucini carbonata*, a pancetta and mozzarella fusilli with tomatoes and dry white wine. Steak neapolitano is an underrated dish of filet mignon broiled on a bed of chopped mushrooms, parsley, and prosciutto. Here, as in most of the south, grated cheese as a pasta topping is optional rather than habitual. Naples is also one of the centers of hard-sugar or "boiled" frosting and doughnuts.

SARDINIA   Sardinia is more than half pastureland, used primarily for the wheat the Romans exploited, olives, grapes, sheep, pork, and goats; it has an abundance of tuna, squid, mullet, eel, lobster, crabs, and, obviously, sardines (though they export most of them—maybe they're sick of the taste). One of its famous dishes is roast suckling pig, traditionally split in half and roasted head down beside the fire rather than whole and horizontal.

SICILY   This island, which was occupied by the Saracens, likes a strong dose of Middle Eastern flavorings, particularly pine nuts, raisins, fennel, and fresh sardines. It was also the bastion of eggplant when, elsewhere, that vegetable was believed to be dangerous; and the home of *caponata*, which originally included tomatoes, celery, capers, olives, roe, and lobster but nowadays is usually something like a sweetish, olive-flavored ratatouille. Pastas are usually paired with a minimum of ingredients at a time: for example, onions in wine, anchovies, garlic, tomato and basil, eggplant and tomato, broccoli and pine nuts, fried bread crumbs and raisins, zucchini, tuna, dried cod. Steak Sicilian-style is sauced with black olives, chili peppers, garlic, and capers, as well as tomatoes. Sicily is also only about 80 miles from the coast of Tunisia, and Sicilians make a great seafood version of couscous.

TUSCANY   In the past decade, Tuscany has become as hallowed a spot in the culinary hagiography as Paris used to be, with the cosmopolitan Florence at its heart and the Chianti vineyards in its backyard. Tuscan cooking is famous for its wood-burning stoves, used for roasting meats, fish, poultry, and even breads; for rabbit and wild duck cacciatore; for brown rather than tomato sauces on pasta (red-wine hare sauce, for example); and for massive open-faced sandwiches that may be the ancestors of American heros and subs. A traditional Christmas dish seems straight off the boat from Mexico: wild boar with sweet-and-sour chocolate sauce and dried fruits. Fish stews are substantial, bouillabaisse-style entrees here, not appetizers; whole fish are also grilled in crusts of either pastry or, sometimes, coarse salt. Rosemary is a classic Tuscan herb, particularly in grilled and roasted dishes, since it holds up well; rosemary, basil, tomatoes, tarragon, and olive oil are all most Tuscan chefs need. It is not true, incidentally, that *alla Fiorentina* means a dish has spinach in it; rather, it refers to the simplicity and freshness of the ingredients. Umbria adjoins Tuscany and has a similar cuisine but is particularly noted for its risottos and Amarone wines.

VENETO   Both Venice and Verona are in this province, so dishes described as Veronese or Venetian are apt to be rich and redolent of Persian spices. The classic local pasta is *bignoli*, a round and somewhat thick noodle not rolled but pressed through a special sieve that looks something like a sausage grinder. Bignoli are served with anchovies and sardines, duck and chicken livers, and hearty sauces that match the heftier noodles. Gnocchi is also popular in this region and is expected to carry its weight under veal, livers, and even snails. The famous *pasta e fagioli*, noodles with white beans, is typical. Sauce *puttanesca*, or "made in the whore's style" (not exactly *bonne femme*), is generally said to have originated in the Venetian red-light district; it's a bawdy mix of anchovies, hot peppers, garlic, capers, and olives. This has become a major center for the sparkling wine industry and is sometimes called "Little Champagne" (though not by the French). There is also a major lake district, which supplies lake shrimp, salmon trout, perch, tench, and eels.

HOW TO ORDER AND EAT LIKE A NATIVE

Italians eat in courses and, perhaps in deference to the Dogess Teodora, on clean plates for each course. The first is the *antipasti*, or hors d'oeuvre, followed by the *minestra*, or soup. Then comes the first course, called either *primi piatti* or just *i primi*, generally a pasta or rice dish, though in the south the soup may also be included here. Often "the first" is also the major dish, and the *secondi piatti*, the meat course and any vegetable side dishes, are smaller. This is the healthier way to go about it, since you fill up on the carbohydrate first—unless the first dish is fettucini Alfredo and the second a grilled flounder.

After the meat comes the salad (*insalata*); cheese (*formaggio*) or sweets (*dolci*)—usually one or the other, rarely both; and, finally, fruit (*frutta*).

If the meal is particularly leisurely or fancy, there may be a sorbet or other palate-cleanser between the main courses. In some areas, too, *piatti di mezzo*—in-between dishes—come after the primi and are usually some variation on quiches or pies: meat or vegetable tortas, frittatas, soufflés, and so forth. A *sformato* is a molded egg-custard dish that can be filled with vegetables (artichokes, fennels, spinach, zucchini), game, or sweetbreads.

Two people can easily split a stuffed artichoke and a plate of cold meat, either carpaccio or prosciutto. Follow with minestrone or an escarole soup, then order one fish (sea bass with capers and lemon) and a meat (ossu bucco or veal piccata). Alternatively, skip the appetizers and share a simple pasta after the soup. Finish with a green salad and fruit.

For four people, the restaurant may prepare a mixed antipasti platter; if not, order mussels or fritto misto, then, as your primi piatti, a risotto or vegetable ravioli dish to share. Split a grilled chicken, rabbit cacciatore, calamari fra diavolo, or other seafood dish.

COOKING AT HOME

In the old days, entertaining Italian-style (as nearly every budget-conscious student and young married couple did) meant a red-and-white checked tablecloth, empty Chianti bottles as candlesticks, and over-sweet Americanized lasagna. Nowadays, it's much more fashionable to do it up Tuscan-style, dining al fresco if possible and using an assortment of brightly colored and painted ceramic dishes. And since this style is so chic, all sorts of franchise home-supply boutiques carry these dishes. Of course, you probably don't have a wood-burning oven, but you can always rub a fish with olive oil and rosemary and pop it on the grill.

Dress the table with fresh flowers, a variety of breads, and cheese. If you have a few days' notice, infuse some extra-virgin olive oil with rosemary, basil, and a clove of garlic by dropping them all directly into the bottle; then serve the oil instead of butter for dipping the bread.

Making fresh pasta is not difficult and requires only cutting tools and maybe a drying rack. There are even fairly inexpensive machines that do it for you—add flour, egg, and water, and it churns out noodles. However, there is so much good dry pasta available now, both flavored and plain, that there is no reason to feel obligated to make your own. Just be careful not to overcook pasta; it should be *al dente*, which means "to the teeth"—that is, it should still have a little body but no raw flavor.

The seafood dish is Genovese; the white bean salad is typically Tuscan, as is the penne with Swiss chard. All are quite simple and quick.

SEAFOOD WITH POTATOES

1 lb. potatoes
1/2 cup olive oil
1 tablespoon garlic, minced
1/4 cup parsley, chopped
salt and pepper
2 pounds firm-fleshed fish (mackerel, anchovy, bluefish, cod),
calamari, or combination

Preheat oven to 450°. Peel and thinly slice potatoes, rinse in cold water, and pat dry. Toss with half the oil, garlic, and seasonings, mixing thoroughly, and place in an enameled casserole. Bake 15 minutes. Add fish or seafood, top with remaining seasonings, and bake 15 minutes more,

basting fish with juices once or twice and gently stirring potatoes if needed. Serve in large bowls with fresh bread or over rice.

WHITE BEAN SALAD

1 lb. dried white navy beans or cannellini
1 small onion, cut into chunks
1 carrot, cut into chunks
1 stalk celery with leaves, cut in large pieces
1 whole bay leaf
2 cloves garlic, crushed but left whole
1 branch or large twig each of fresh rosemary, sage, and thyme
3–4 tablespoons extra-virgin olive oil
salt and pepper
2 tablespoons each of fresh thyme, sage, and rosemary leaves

Rinse and soak beans overnight. Drain, pour into large saucepan, and
cover with fresh water; add onion, carrot, celery, bay, garlic, herb sprigs,
and 1 tablespoon olive oil. Bring to simmer and cook 45 minutes, season
lightly with salt and pepper, add more water or a splash of wine or broth
if necessary, and cook until just tender, 15–20 minutes more. Drain,
remove vegetables and herbs. Toss with fresh herbs, salt and pepper, and
remaining oil to taste.

PASTA WITH CHARD

4–6 canned anchovy fillets in oil
1 pound Swiss chard (kale can be substituted)
1 pound firm, largish pasta such as penne or rigatoni
salt and pepper
3–4 cloves garlic, minced
1 tablespoon dried red chili peppers
2/3 cup extra-virgin olive oil
1/2 cup parsley, chopped
bread crumbs and grated cheese for garnish

Drain and lightly mash anchovies with a fork. Rinse the chard and chop,
including stalks. Bring a large pot of salted water to a boil, add pasta and
chard, and cook them until the pasta is al dente. Meanwhile, sauté garlic,

anchovies, and pepper flakes in oil until garlic is soft and golden but not brown. Drain pasta and chard, add parsley, and then toss with hot garlic/anchovy mixture. Top with bread crumbs and just a bit of cheese if desired.

THE IBERIAN PENINSULA: SPAIN, PORTUGAL, AND THE BASQUE

Iberia may never have produced a "great" cuisine, but it did forge revolutionary alliances. Whether conquered or conquering, the Spanish and Portuguese were always willing to come to the enemy's table.

Spain and Portugal fell to the Phoenicians, the Greeks, the Romans, and the Moors—and ate heartily on the offerings of all four—until they too became seagoing conquerors and began dining out on their colonies. The Portuguese all but monopolized the Indian and Asian trade routes, while Spain frog-jumped from the Americas into the Philippines. In 1494 the Iberian rivals even persuaded the Pope to divide the "non-Christian world"—a sweeping assumption that covered Asia, Africa, India, and the Americas—by drawing a line that fell through the bulge of South America (which is why Brazilians speak Portuguese and most South Americans speak Spanish).

Along the way, they became the great culinary go-betweens, first between Europe and Asia, then between Europe and America. They absorbed Roman olives and Middle Eastern rice, hauled cattle into Mexico, appropriated Aztec tomatoes and Indonesian garlic, and monopolized olive oil in the New World and chocolate in the Old. They were given much, and returned (or sold) even more. Like the alchemists of legend, they transformed the ingredients of disparate continents into "Mediterranean" gold; see also the chapters on North Africa and on Mexico and Central America.

THE HISTORY

Although the peninsula is named for the Iberians, who emigrated from Africa 7,000 years ago, they were not the original inhabitants of the region; the often-overlooked but extraordinarily resilient Basques, who still live in a sort of hybridized French-Spanish region around the Pyrenees, have probably been there since Paleolithic times (they are almost certainly the people who created the cave paintings at Altamira). They are the oldest distinct ethnic group in Europe, they speak a language unrelated to any other, and they disdained the Iberians and every other ethnic wave that has swept over the region. Even Christianity took only a slow hold among the Basques, who were not converted for several hundred years after the rest of Europe. (Once converted, though, they showed their mettle by producing St. Francis Xavier and St. Ignatius of Loyola, among others.)

The Spanish and Portuguese, on the other hand, are closely related, became implacably Catholic, and were for most of their history a single nation. Though they had already been conquered several times, the Iberians became perhaps the most Romanized of all imperial subjects, vigorously taking to the innovations of language (Latin, from which both Spanish and Portuguese derive), agriculture (particularly olives and wine grapes), and politics (they produced two Caesars, Hadrian and Trajan).

They took to "multiculturalism" even more readily. The next invaders, the Visigoths, were Arianists (and heavy meat eaters), but they allowed the Iberians to remain Catholic; many of the coastal dwellers had Byzantine ties and were already experimenting with exotic spices, and most cities had vigorous Jewish communities. When the Moors swept in from North Africa in 711, they showed the Iberians how to expand the arable territory beyond the river valleys, thus permitting the cultivation of rice and groves of flowering almond and citrus trees and date palms. Their influence was industrial and aesthetic as well; the crafts and industries they fostered—Toledo steel, Cordoban leather, "Damascene" silver, Seville oranges, and Granadan silk—remain legendary.

However, it was the long battle to expel the Moors that inspired the Spanish and Portuguese to build empires of their own. Here in the United States, the Spanish conquistadors' victories in the Caribbean, Mexico, and South America are familiar stories, but the Portuguese were just as bold: Within a single 25-year span, from 1495 to 1520, Portuguese navigators rounded the Cape of Good Hope and established strongholds in India and Goa, Malaysia, Hormuz (on the Persian Gulf), the Caribbean, and Brazil. They began a highly profitable trade in spices and slaves—so profitable that in 1580, the covetous Philip II of Spain added Portugal to a list of possessions that included Sicily, Naples, Sardinia, the Netherlands, and virtually all of North and South America (he had valid claims to England and France, as well).

THE CUISINE

During Philip's reign, Spain was so dominant a world power that other European courts paid tribute to him by hiring Spanish chefs. Philip was overly fond of rich German sauces and suffered from gout as a result, but he also revolutionized Spanish culture and cuisine in a completely serendipitous fashion: He moved the capital to Madrid, which was known as "the city of 300 taverns" and one of the first societies so devoted to the art of dining out. It was in this milieu, and the culinary revolution wrought by the tomatoes, peppers, and beans brought back from the Americas, that the Spanish practice of late dinners began. So much time was devoted to gossip and afternoon snacks that supper had to be put off until 10 P.M., and entertainments, as they came into vogue, were scheduled for midnight or later. It was also in Madrid that the tapas bar first appeared (see "Tapas," page 55).

The great irony of Spain's role in culinary history is that except for chocolate, which they managed for a time to monopolize, the Spanish vastly undervalued the agricultural riches of the New World. They were more concerned with the influx of New World silver and gold, the precious metals that not only took such a high toll on the natives but also set off a chain of inflation so great that it ultimately bankrupted the empire. And by handcuffing Portugal, the Spanish exposed the East Indies to Dutch predation and thus lost the great fortune of the Spice Islands as well.

THE COUNTRIES

Today, Spain and Portugal remain primarily agricultural countries and travel resorts. Portugal's summers are hot throughout the country; winters are fairly mild on the coasts and more severe inland. It has little fertile territory—another reason for its relentlessly outward-looking explorers—and most of that land is used to cultivate wheat, grapes, sugar beets, barley, olives, and citrus fruit. Most of the poorer land is used to graze sheep. Fishing is a major industry, and sardines, anchovies, and cod are major exports as well as food sources.

Spain is divided from France by the Pyrenees, which run from the Mediterranean to the Atlantic, and has a climate (and crops) similar to Portugal's. The center of Spain is a great plateau with limited arable land; and the whole country is striated east to west by mountain chains and rivers. Because of its topographical segmentation, many of the regions have distinct dialects and cultural traditions: The Galicians, in the southern part of Spain, speak a Portuguese-influenced dialect; and Catalan, the language of Barcelona, is similar to Provençal French. Basque, as noted above, is related to no other language; however, most of the (very few) Basque restaurants in the United States either call themselves Spanish or Portuguese or translate their menus into English.

THE MAIN INGREDIENTS

SEAFOOD   The great gift of Rome was olive oil; the great concept of the Moors was irrigation; the great prize of the Americas was vegetables. But in the beginning was the sea. Monkfish, cuttle fish, sole, hake, mullet, cod, sardines, skate, mackerel, sea bass, swordfish, tuna, squid, octopus, crabs, spiny lobsters, scallops, clams, crayfish, and eels are all harvested here. *Paella,* Spain's most famous dish, is a showcase for shrimp, mussels, and clams (and there, but rarely here, freshwater snails as well); *zarzuela,* the soup version, is similarly embellished.

The sea fever the Portuguese seemed to inherit genetically also accustomed them to foods that could be preserved and stored for months at a time: They learned to pickle, salt-cure, smoke, and dry meats and fish early on. *Bacalhau,* dried and salted cod, is one of the most famous ingredients in Portuguese cooking (from the Greek *bakaliaros*), and though it may sound plain, the legend is that there are 365 recipes for it, one for every day—enough to keep a Portuguese Popeye happy.

STARCHES   Bread is part of every meal; baked daily, it is grilled, dunked and, if it gets a day old, fried. In the rural areas, it may be the only "meat" of the meal: Samuel Pepys, who visited Spain in 1683, wrote that "the greater part of Spain eat nothing but what they make of water, oil, salt, vinegar, garlic and bread, which last is the foundation of all." Rice is most often served spiced or flavored in the fashion of the Moors and is usually served with, not instead of, bread.

MEATS   From the mountainous north come the hearty goats, sheep, and hogs that made Spanish hams and sausages famous. Spicy *chorizo* and blood sausage are popular; so are the delicate organ meats such as brains, sweetbreads (particularly lamb), tripe, and tongue. Ham is so highly prized that, as in Italy, different regions have perfected subtle flavorings; in one area of Andalusia, black pigs are raised only on acorns to produce a nutty-flavored meat.

POULTRY   Chicken is a staple, and so are eggs, particularly hard-cooked or deviled; the turkey, another American transplant, is highly admired, and darker wildfowl, such as pheasant and quail, are popular, too. However, one bit of nonauthenticity in Spanish restaurants in this country is probably welcome: The Spanish traditionally like both their pork and their poultry extremely well aged. Pheasants were usually hung to the rotting point, and prime hogs still swing in butcher windows for years. Fortunately for the American palate, such practices are prohibited here.

VEGETABLES   The vast number of what are now the staple vegetables were brought back from the Americas: potatoes (white and sweet), onions, tomatoes, corn, sweet peppers, pumpkin, peas, and beans (garbanzo, white, black, red, fava, and lima). Artichokes, lentils, eggplant, beets, zucchini, and greens such as cabbage, chard, and kale were brought in from the Middle East.

SEASONINGS   The combination of Old and New World flavors is extremely characteristic of Spanish food, and many names evoke this. *Ramillete albaicinero* is an herb bouquet, usually combining mint, parsley, oregano, savory, and bay, that is named for the last section of Granada that the Moors held. A dish called *a la chilindron* has a sauce that combines garlic, onion, tomato, sweet peppers, and ham. *Veracruzano* refers to the Mexican port where the Spanish learned to cook fish with tomatoes and onions.

Among the most characteristic flavorings are almonds, anise, cloves, coriander, garlic, pine nuts, peppercorns (white and green as well as black), bay, chilies, cinnamon, cilantro, cumin, rosemary, thyme, fennel, olives, oregano, paprika, and the sovereign powder saffron—the golden-red stamen of the saffron crocus and the most expensive spice in the world. Pimenton is a pungent paprika that can be either sweet or hot. Up the Mediterranean coast toward Provence, the proportion of garlic increases; so does the use of fine vinegars, a natural in a region that so prides itself on wines and sherries.

THE MAIN DISHES

SOUPS One of the most famous Spanish dishes is gazpacho, the raw vegetable soup that depending on region and home recipe may be coarse or chunky, sweet, tangy, or peppery. The simplest versions are just bread, tomatoes, olive oil, and flavorings, but regional (and Americanized) recipes may include red onion, cucumber, sweet bell peppers, and even an heretical avocado. As we noted above, bread is almost a meat, used in soups and stews and for *migas*, little fried bread salads. Bread soups go back to early Roman times, and gazpacho and miga are both examples of Spain's role as intermediary—both are derived from Middle Eastern dishes, and both were carried from Spain to Mexico.

Thick bean-and-greens soups, given the generic name *caldo verde*, usually combine white beans and kale or chard. *Berza*, an Andalusian specialty, could be considered a Spanish cassoulet, combining ham hocks and necks, chickpeas, white beans, blood sausage and chorizo, pumpkin, chard, and the tangy brown spices of the clove family. Garlic soup by itself is extremely popular, too, as is the garlicky vegetable *pisto*. *Sopa de pescado* is a fish broth-based soup served as a first course.

SHELLFISH *Ceviche* (or seviche) is raw fish and scallops "cooked" by a marinade of lime juice, onions, and chilies. The famous fried shellfish mentioned includes squid, sardines, anchovies, and even white-fleshed fish in chunks, all lightly dusted with fine-ground flour and fried in the purest, freshest olive oil; these are staples of tapas bars, but very few representatives in the United States escape greasiness.

The dishes of the Basque region reflect a heavy Provençal influence; here the flavors are dark, almost exotic: baby "spaghetti" eels sautéed in chili-flavored oil, squid braised in its own ink, onions roasted in olive oil.

FISH Even in these calorie-conscious days, fish is rarely served just grilled or braised in a Spanish restaurant; it's usually baked whole with potatoes, onions, peppers, tomatoes, and sherry; with rich wine-flavored cream sauces; and, particularly on holidays, wrapped in puff pastry and baked. And when it is "grilled," it often shows up on a bed of coarse salt. In Spain, fish is fried to a pure crispiness that is rarely re-created in the United States. Salt cod is sometimes shredded and tossed with oranges and olives in a dish that hearkens straight back to the Moorish occupation.

CASSEROLES AND STEWS Since

Shell Game

Coquille St. Jacques, curiously, though a French invention, was created because so many French Catholics were joining the Spanish in pilgrimages to the tomb of the miraculously restored body of the patron saint of Spain, the martyred disciple James —Jacques in French, and Iago, hence Santiago, in Spanish. One of the miracles associated with the saint's body, which according to legend was discovered just in time to help rout the Moors, had to do with restoring a drowned bridegroom, who reappeared covered with cockleshells. Hence the pilgrims wore cockleshell badges, and chefs served scallops in wine sauce on cockleshells.

Spain's cuisine blends so many influences, it seems perfectly appropriate that its "national dish" combines European foods with Middle Eastern rice and Asian and American spices. Paella is a richly flavored but not heavy stew of shellfish, chicken, sausage, ham, shrimp, peas, artichoke hearts, sautéed onions, and tomatoes all bedded down in a round flat pan of saffron-tinted rice. It is traditionally prepared for a group, but it has become so popular that in the United States it is fairly common for a restaurant to offer paella for two. (Once the Spanish had perfected paella, they found it hard to live without; it is also a standard dish in Mexico, Cuba, and the Philippines.)

Zarzuelas are both filling and fascinating, all made slightly differently; some are almost platters of mixed shellfish, such as crabs, clams, scallops, shrimp, and even lobster; but most have a fragrant broth and some tender vegetables; one school "finishes" the soup with swirls of sherry. (Some menus describe zarzuela as a Spanish bouillabaisse, but it is much less oily or garlicky.)

MEATS Main courses also display a variety of influences, from peasant heartiness (stuffed oxtails, braised pig's feet) to Moroccan richness (lamb stewed in honey and nuts) and pure Mediterranean earthiness (roast pork ribs with cabbage). Both lamb chops and kid are popular, and roasted legs as well. The Spanish also enjoy sauced veal and pork, and they often play off sweet-and-sour or spicy ingredients, such as sherry, olives, and crushed peppercorns, with oranges and sweet peppers. The meat-eaters' answer to paella is *cochida Madrileno*, a weighty stew of white bean or chickpeas with flank steak, ham, sausage, onions, potatoes, kohlrabi, and usually a generous portion of garlic.

POULTRY Chickens are baked plain with lemon and garlic or in rice casseroles with saffron; roasted with almond sauce or garlic; and stuffed with sausage and vegetables. Quail are frequently grilled and eaten whole, or stuffed with raisins and rice (the Moorish influence again) and braised. A tavern-style recipe obviously based on a New World dish calls for baking quail in lima beans.

DESSERTS Iberians enjoy fruit, often mixing it with cheese in a dessert or

In recent years, Iberian restaurants in the United States have lightened up a little on the olive oil that, combined with the cuisine's rich meats, often made dishes seem greasy. However, the fat level is still fairly high; zarzuelas or roasted meats are fairly light choices.

Portuguese dishes are generally similar to the Spanish versions, particularly in the United States, but may come as a shock to those who have lost the taste for heavy salt. Both the bacalhau and many pork dishes, even those cooked with potatoes or rice, remain very salty. Other seafoods and shellfish may be wine-pickled, if not brined, before cooking; and *mariscada*, the Portuguese zarzuela or bouillabaisse, tends to be saltier than either the Spanish or French versions. However, there are also paella-like dishes—sometimes called, with deceptive simplicity, "Portuguese rice"— in which the rice tends to absorb the seasonings.

predessert course. Oranges—both thick-skinned varieties and the famous Seville oranges, bitter and thin-peeled—are foremost among a crowd of citrus fruits. *Cherimoyas* (also known as custard apples), dates, pomegranates, raisins and grapes, peaches, and bananas are also popular;

these are often served with cream or thin vanilla-flavored custards. *Membillo*, a sort of quince gelatin or aspic, is traditionally served with the salty, coarse manchenga cheese.

However, the entire region is passionate for sweets, the best-known of which is flan, a burned-sugar custard twin to the French crème caramel. Chocolate is a specialty, particularly bittersweet (as it was known in the very beginning), but there are also a number of what might be called junk-food indulgences, such as the sugar-powdered fried dough twists called *churros*.

TAPAS

Toward the end of the nineteenth century, when the light opera called zarzuela (just like the dish) was in its heyday, Madrilenos became fond of bars where they could come and go and eat small meals with drinks. These tapas—four- or five-bite dishes intended to while away hours of drink and conversation—are becoming the rage all over the United States.

There are scores of tapas possibilities, and a single restaurant, particularly in Madrid, may offer as many as 40 or 50 choices, both hot and cold. Even here, a restaurant may offer 25 or 30. Among the more common tapas are sausages, olives, grilled squid, white beans or bean salads, eggplant, tortillas (which, in the Spanish style, are potato omelets, not corn or flour pancakes), stuffed squid or baby octopus, tripe, *sobrasada* (a sort of spreadable chorizo), fried smelts or squid, various types of empanadas, almonds, deviled eggs, artichoke hearts stuffed with serrano ham, roasted sweet pepper salads, cheeses, carpaccio (usually beef, but occasionally the trendier tuna), grilled quail, clams, anchovies, and sometimes miniature paellas.

Tapas bars in Spain almost routinely offer pork ribs with cabbage, slices of roast suckling pig, and sautéed *criadillas*, or pig testicle; but these items are less common here. Instead, trendy American restaurateurs are racing to invent novel tapas, such as vegetarian pâtés and stacked tamale "napoleons," designed to bring in younger crowds.

Tapas are traditionally served before lunch and again before (or what Americans would consider right through) the dinner hour, which in Spain is no earlier than about 10. Tapas are usually either served in a separate room, like a country bar or tavern, or displayed along the bar for you to admire and point to; however, in the United States, many restaurants allow you to eat tapas in the dining room as appetizers. The most enjoyable tapas bars may offer flamenco music or even dancing in the evenings, and wine-drinking contests from those bellowslike squeeze bags.

HOW TO ORDER AND EAT LIKE A NATIVE

Dining in Spain is a full-time occupation, beginning with the two breakfasts (about 7 and 11), tapas about 1 as a warm-up to lunch at about 2:30, tea and cakes at 6, more tapas at 8, and dinner—the real stuff—about 10 or even later. Fortunately, dishes are generally more flavorful than rich and are not generally creamy, though they may be oil-dense to American tastes. The Portuguese have more European habits, dining at 8 or 9; and Spanish and Portuguese restaurants in the United States tend to accommodate both styles.

Menus in the United States are divided up by courses, and some of the hors d'oeuvre may replicate tapas dishes or even be called tapas. A selection of them may also be listed as *entremeses variados*—mixed appetizers.

Two diners here can easily share an order of gazpacho and a tortilla and entrees of either baked fish or shrimp and roast quail. A party of four might share two soups (sopa de pescado and miga) and ceviche, plus roast pork, baked chicken, and paella.

If you are planning to order paella, a dish that requires a fair amount of preparation, you may have to call the day before or specify paella when you make your reservations. Unfortunately, since it can be a lengthy process and Americans are notoriously impatient, partially precooked paellas are becoming more common here; make sure to ask that it be made up fresh. A larger group should check out a tapas bar (where, depending on the kitchen, you may be able to sample paella as well).

With tapas it is traditional to drink sherry, though there are many fine Spanish wines, particularly red wines; and more and more diners are ordering beer. (The Portuguese, incidentally, are among the world's most prolific producers of rosé wines.) Although most Americans are only familiar with sweet sherries, there are a wide range of styles, from the dry *finos* and *manzanillas*, which make fine aperitifs (there are also good Spanish vermouths), to the nutty, midrange *palo cortadas* and *amantillados* and *olorosos* and cream sherries. With dessert, you may drink a wide variety of sweetened fortified wines, not only sherry but also Madeira, malmsey, or ports.

Spanish and Portuguese restaurants are usually only moderately expensive, although there are more white-linen restaurants opening up these days. Tapas bars are like dim sum or sushi bars, because you pay by the plate, so you can spend a little or quite a lot.

COOKING AT HOME

The most important utensils in a Spanish or Portuguese kitchen are the flat, supple steel pans used for paella and the similar but smaller skillets used for tortillas and for frying (the wide rather than deep layer of oil allows for quick and even heating). Nonstick skillets and those of high-quality aluminum will do fine. Most dishes are cooked on top of the stove, in the skillets or soup pots, or grilled over open fires, with the exception of bread, which is made fresh constantly; however, some roasted entrees require baking dishes.

TORTILLA (POTATO OMELET)

1 1/2 tablespoons olive oil
1 large onion, sliced
1 sweet or mildly hot pepper, seeded and sliced
3 large potatoes, peeled, thinly sliced, and patted dry
6 large eggs
salt and pepper to taste

Heat 1/2 tablespoon oil in a nonstick skillet; sauté onion and pepper until soft and remove to a plate. Add another 1/2 tablespoon oil and sauté potatoes briefly, turning to coat, then return onions and peppers to skillet. Season, cover, and cook 15 minutes over medium-low heat, turning occasionally, until potatoes are lightly browned and tender. Set aside to cool slightly.

Meanwhile, lightly beat eggs with a pinch more salt and pepper; add potatoes to egg mixture bowl and wipe skillet clean, then add remaining oil and heat. Pour egg mixture into skillet, spreading vegetables evenly, and cook about 5 minutes or until bottom is brown but eggs are still slightly soft in the middle; put a plate over the top of the skillet, invert it, and then slide the tortilla back into the skillet just until the underside is brown and tortilla is firm but not dry. Slice into wedges and serve (with roasted red peppers if desired).

PAELLA

4 tablespoons olive oil
1/2 pound chorizo or other spicy sausage, sliced 1/2-inch thick
4 chicken breasts, legs, or thighs
1 large onion, chopped
4 cloves garlic, minced
1 sweet red pepper, seeded and diced
1 small hot pepper, seeded and diced
1/2 pound small or medium shrimp, shelled
1/4 pound squid, cleaned and cut into rings
4 small rock lobster tails or langoustines
1 1/2 cups short-grain rice
1 bay leaf
1/4 teaspoon saffron threads, crushed
1/4 cup fresh parsley, chopped
3 cups defatted chicken broth, clam juice,
or dry white wine, or a combination
1/4 pound ham, preferably Jubago or Parma
8 mussels, scrubbed and bearded
8 clams, scrubbed (optional)
4 ounces fresh small peas, cooked, or frozen and thawed
4 artichoke hearts, halved
salt and pepper to taste

In a paella pan or large skillet, heat 1 tablespoon oil; cook sausage until brown and remove with slotted spoon, leaving grease behind. Lightly season chicken and brown; set aside. Add a little more oil if necessary and sauté onion, garlic, and peppers until softened; add shrimp, squid, and lobster, cook them just until opaque, and remove to plate. Add 1 tablespoon oil and rice, stirring to coat rice grains; stir in bay leaf, saffron threads, and parsley and add broth. Cover pan lightly and cook about 10 minutes, stirring occasionally. Add peas and artichokes; arrange chicken, ham, seafood, and shellfish around pan and cover tightly; cook until all liquid is absorbed, rice is tender (add more liquid if needed), and shellfish have opened. Discard any shells that do not open, then serve.

GERMANY AND AUSTRIA

German food is a lot more familiar than many Americans expect; in fact, you might not even recognize it as "ethnic," because so many family-style American meals, from family diner blue-plate specials right down to the quintessential Fourth of July picnic, have German roots. Potato salad, deviled eggs, pickled beets, dill pickles, sugar cookies, meatloaf, mashed potatoes, pot roast, beef stew, chicken and dumplings, and chocolate cakes and cookies are all typical German fare. A popular PBS series on Amish and Pennsylvania Dutch cuisine is called "Heartland Cooking." The whole meat-and-potatoes concept is primarily a German import, not to mention beer: Every year, 35 gallons per person of this quintessentially German brew is consumed in the United States. Hamburgers and frankfurters even get their names from German cities, and what could be more American than they?

A huge percentage of Western European strains within the American melting pot—not just Germans and Austrians but also Angles, Saxons, Franks, Burgundians, Lombards,

BASIC CUISINE

DINNER FOR TWO:
Vegetable soup, schlachtplatte, schnitzel, roast duck

DINNER FOR FOUR:
Schmeerkase, sausages, potato salad, duck, sauerbraten, pike in cream sauce, schnitzel

STYLE:
Sweet-sour, doughy, smoky, gamey

KEY FLAVORS:
Vinegar, bay, sour cream

DISTINCTIVE FOODS:
Sauerkraut, sausages, sauerbraten, game, beer

EATING UTENSILS:
Forks and knives

NUTRITIONAL INDEX:
High fat, medium sodium, high cholesterol, high carbohydrate

UNIFORMITY OF MENUS:
Good

COST:
Inexpensive to moderate

"THANK YOU":
"Danke schön"

Bavarians, Icelanders, and Teutons—all lead back to the Germanic tribes who stood Rome off and finally broke down her door. Germans spawned the "greats" of various countries: Charlemagne, who invented France; Otto I, who cobbled together a Holy Roman Empire; Frederick of Prussia, whose prescient appreciation of the potato prevented a pan-European famine in the eighteenth century; and Victoria, that sable symbol of British imperial propriety. And though German immigrants were not the first to settle the New World, their Reformation, which sowed similar Protestant and political upheavals across Europe, made its settlement inevitable.

In this century, and particularly since World War II, German food, which had a long and hearty frontier tradition in the United States, has become politically unpopular; more subtly, it has acquired an unsophisticated, out-of-step image as well, thanks to the increasing social prejudice against meaty, starchy "comfort foods." However, Germany's rich sauces, its delicate asparagus, fragrant hams, earthy, musty breads, and eye-watering mustards, and its almost legendary balance of assertive, gamey meats with green herbs and rich compotes make it one of the great cold-weather cuisines.

In the United States, German and Austrian restaurants, along with Swiss and even sometimes Alsatian ones, are indistinguishable. However, those particularly interested in Swiss and Alsatian foods should also see the sections on Italian and French regional cuisines, and the discussion of Eastern European foods, particularly Hungarian, may interest Austrian devotees.

THE COUNTRY

One of the reasons "German food" can be somewhat tricky to define is that Germany not only borders Poland, France, Belgium, the Netherlands, Switzerland, Denmark, Russia, and Austria; at various times it has also *been* Poland, France, Belgium, and so forth, or at least controlled portions of them.

Germany is physically at the center of Europe, with equally close ties to the Slavic east, the Mediterranean south, and the Scandinavian north. A natural watershed, it slopes from the Alps across forestland and pastureland to the sandy lowlands of the Baltic, watered by rivers so powerful—the Danube, the Elbe, the Rhine—that for centuries they served as boundaries between ethnic rivals.

The mountainous south is turned over primarily to cattle and dairy farms, wheat and barley pastures, and vineyards: The wines of the Rhineland and the beers of Bavaria, Munich, and Würzburg are all famous. The Black Forest is to the east, and its wild game, game birds, river trout, and tart fruits are among Europe's finest. The central plateau, a long narrowish belt that includes Dortmund, Dresden, Weimar, and Frankfurt, is hilly and wooded; the famous spas are here, among orchards and herds of sheep. And the north coast is sandy and low, similar to its neighbors the Netherlands and Poland; grains are the most common crops here, particularly the potato. In 1774 Frederick the Great of Prussia commanded that the potato be planted all over his empire, and now it has become an integral part of the northern European and Scandinavian diet.

Germany has been divided innumerable times, by dynasty, by alliance, and by religion. The current boundaries of East and West Germany (now unified), Poland, Austria, and the Czech/Slovak countries date only to this century. Ethnically, however, Germany and Austria are fairly homogeneous, with significant Slavic, Turkish, and Italian minorities. Austria, which has spent much of its history as a battleground between the Celts and Romans, Slavs and Germans, spent more time occupied by the Moravians, Magyars, and Turks; its cuisine is richer, more aromatic, and more sweet-spicy than sweet-sour.

THE HISTORY

Not a lot is known about the indigenous tribes of the region. Although the Greeks mentioned meeting them trading in Norway in the fourth century B.C., there is little other record of them for another couple of millenia, when they began to stretch their legs and territories. They were halted on the west by the Celts and on the east by the Romans, who basically drew lines at the Danube and Rhine rivers. Tacitus, writing in the first century, described a taciturn people who lived on black bread, gruels (millet, oats, and barley), wild berries, game, and milk.

In the fourth and fifth centuries, the "Germanic tribes," who were closely related to the Slavs, began to break the Roman stranglehold, gradually making their way into England (as the Angles and Saxons), France and Belgium (Franks and Burgundians), and Lombardy and Germany (Goths and Visigoths); as the Roman Empire disintegrated, Europe came under invasion from the Norsemen, the Turkic Magyars, and the Slavs, who carved off chunks of France, Hungary, Poland, and Romania. Europe's national borders shrank and shifted until 962, when Otto I declared a Holy Roman Empire that at various times covered Germany, Austria, Moravia, Burgundy, the Netherlands, the papal states, and Sicily. Though the empire existed at least nominally into the early nineteenth century, its influence was diminished by a series of sundering blows—Martin Luther and the expanding waves of Reformation, the Thirty Years' War, and finally Napoleon, who, however briefly, reconfigured the whole of Europe. The empire rose again to prominence in the late nineteenth century, thanks to Bismarck and alliances with Russia and Austria-Hungary; but its colonial ambitions in Africa and its ties to the Ottoman Turks gradually estranged it from the rest of Europe, and internal upheaval culminated in the outbreak of the First World War and, in a sense, the Second World War as well.

THE CUISINE

German food may remind one of that existential joke that goes, "If we had ham, we could have ham and eggs, if we had eggs." The Germans had a meat-and-potatoes kind of philosophy even before potatoes were discovered in South America and long before they made their meandering way to central Europe. Like its neighbors, pre-Renaissance Germany was somewhat hobbled by poor agricultural methods and the need to preserve food rather than present it. (See the chapter on France for a digression on the evolution of European cuisine.)

Nevertheless, German cuisine is not nearly so straightforward as it is stereotypically portrayed. Its influences range from the Dutch and Danish, with whom it was closely allied beginning in the thirteenth century; to the Italians, whose cookbooks were standard in the sixteenth and seventeenth centuries; to the Turks, who dominated Romania, Bulgaria, Hungary, and Yugoslavia; to the Spanish, whose monopoly on chocolate made them wealthy beyond imagination; to the French, who elevated cooking to "cuisine" in the nineteenth century. Using other European traders as middlemen, Germans picked up Peruvian potatoes (via English privateer Sir Francis Drake, who picked up provisions in Cartagena), Malaysian mustards (via the Poles, who got it from the Caucasians), and Persian almonds and saffron (via the Baltic markets). Going even farther back, it was the Chinese who taught the Romans how to make sauerkraut, and the Romans who taught the Germans—and the Tatars who reminded them how, more than a thousand years later.

Because of the shifting political influences, and the topographical differences as well, Germany's cuisine shows some regional tendencies, though they are not extreme. For example, flour doughs are more common in the south, and the starches —particularly *Spaetzle*, tiny egg and wheat-flour dumplings—are grain-based. Butter is

Buds 'n' Spuds

There is a kernel of truth in the German stereotype of sauerkraut, sausage, bread, and beer. But to give them credit, Germans make dozens of kinds of sauerkraut, scores of sausages, and hundreds of kinds of breads. And there are probably even more beers than that.

Sauerkraut does have a basic recipe—cabbage is shredded, salted, and allowed to ferment—but beyond that, it can be steamed, fried, or mixed with apples, pineapple, or potatoes. (And it is classically soaked and drained before cooking, a step that is often overlooked but that makes quite a difference in the flavor.) Sausages can be made of pork, beef, lamb, rabbit, veal, venison, boar, blood, liver, brains, and tongue—but you can't always tell by the name: *Leberkaas* means liver cheese, but it contains no liver and may not have cheese, either. Bread might be white, wheat, whole wheat, rye, cracked wheat, caraway, pumpernickle, poppy seed, graham, black, egg, potato, sour, sweet, or sprouted. And beer might be dark, light, *bock* (dark and

Buds 'n' Spuds
Continued

aged), pilsner (like most American beers), lager (left to age), *Weissbier* (weak wheat beer), *Malzbier* (low-alcohol malt brew), or *Marzenbier* (the Oktoberfest type). And that doesn't include the raspberry, cherry, double-bock, Maybock, and so forth.

Potatoes may be historically the newest addition to the menu, but their use has been thoroughly explored, too: They are boiled, mashed, or turned into soufflés, salads, stews, soups, dumplings, pancakes, fried patties, and even bread doughs.

commonly used for sautéing. In the middle and north, potato flour is the dumpling base, and bacon drippings are the cooking grease.

In the south, fresh game and birds are common and are often stewed with dried fruit, showing a Turkish influence; in Austria, which was often bound up with Hungary, goulash stews, with their Turkish paprika, are very popular. French and Italian dishes—pâté, trout meunière, frogs' legs, and veal shanks, and asparagus with hollandaise sauce—are also more common in the south.

In the central forestlands, meats are smoked (raw Westphalia hams, short ribs), sauces are green with wild herbs (sorrel, chervil, borage, chives, tarragon, and dill), and stews and game are flavored with apples and pears and bread crumbs.

In the north—near the Netherlands and Scandinavia, where warmer-weather food had to be stored for bad weather—dried fish, dried and pickled meats, dried fruits, pickled eggs and vegetables, smoked eels, and fatty pork sausages are mainstays. Cream and sour cream sauces are most common here, along with those other Norse staples, herring and salt cod.

THE MAIN INGREDIENTS

FLAVORINGS Vinegar, sour cream, caraway, bay, juniper, black pepper, red wine, allspice, sour cream, and honey are the most famous seasonings in German cooking, but paprika, cinnamon, cloves, poppyseed, dill, almond, ginger, fennel, horseradish, and honey are also essential.

VEGETABLES AND FRUITS Green cabbage is king and potato its consort, but onions, carrots, turnips, asparagus, kale, spinach, white beans, red cabbage, sweet peppers, cauliflower, peas, and a wide variety of mushrooms are also important. Tomatoes, which were introduced belatedly, have less of a role here than in most of Europe; and although the Germans took to Middle Eastern–style, stuffed cabbage and green peppers, eggplant is rarely served.

FISH AND SEAFOOD Herring, cod, mackerel, pike, salmon, trout, tench, and carp are plentiful, along with lobsters, oysters, prawns, and eels. Occasionally frogs' legs and mussels are harvested, too.

MEATS Traditionally, the German cuisine is rich with game—venison, roebuck, boar, bear, and hare—as well as the beef, veal, lamb, and pork more common today. They also prize offal and organ meats, from sweetbreads, kidneys, liver, tripe, tongue, and brains to trotters, snouts, knuckles, hocks, and so on. Anything that's left on slaughter day is usually turned into sausage on the spot.

POULTRY Goose and duck are the favorites, followed by game birds (partridge, pheasant, squab, woodcock, marsh hen, and quail) and chicken. Rabbit (as opposed to wild hare) is generally treated as chicken would be.

EGGS AND DAIRY Butter, cream, sour cream, eggs, curds, cream cheese, and cheese are major ingredients, but cheese and eggs (most often shirred or boiled, and frequently pickled) are often eaten as main dishes as well. Among the best-known cheeses are Tilsit and the Bavarian blue cheeses Muenster and Limburger; Leiderkranz is actually an American invention. Germans both drink milk and buttermilk and use them in recipes. *Schmeerkase* is a sort of sour cottage cheese with dill that is spread on bread.

Our Daily Bread

Although nowadays the Germans tend to eat three meals a day, with a lighter lunch and heavier dinner, they traditionally ate five meals a day, with a second breakfast of coffee and pastry (called *Brotzeit*, or "bread time") and a late-afternoon meal of sausages and cheese. The midday meal was a hearty one, a practice passed on to millions of American laborers. The evening meal, called *Abendbrot*—literally, "evening bread"—bore a very strong resemblance to the Scandinavian smorgasbord: It was a meal of buttered breads and assorted cold cuts, cheeses, and condiments, which were assembled into open-faced sandwiches and eaten with knives and forks.

Even the big midday meal tended to be fairly plain, usually featuring an *Eintopf*—literally, a "one-pot" stew—which could be prepared and left to cook itself. Most of the dishes served in German restaurants are, in fact, just that: restaurant fare, derived from court and city cuisine rather than home cooking.

THE MAIN DISHES

APPETIZERS Both hot and cold appetizers are popular, including the "continental" classics—foie gras, oysters, smoked salmon, caviar, sautéed mushrooms in split puff pastries, etc. Cold sausages and hams, cheeses and breads, pickled fish and eggs, and vegetable salads—particularly potato and cole slaws and pickled beets—are common; in the central lowlands, French-style mixed green salads are popular.

SOUPS The word to use about all but the clear soups is "hearty." The clear soups are not only French in style, they are often called consommés; they may include spaetzle or even liver spaetzle. Pureed soups—pea, cauliflower, bean, beet, lentil, or potato—may have garnishes of ham, bacon, sausage, or smoked fish. The cream soups are similar but are thickened with cream or sour cream and often egg yolks; there are also bisques with eel and crayfish and oxtail soup. Cabbage and bacon soup is particularly popular in the north. There is even a beer soup, which includes sugar and eggs. Both soups and stews may be thickened with bread crumbs.

Dumplings, incidentally, need not be plain dough; they can be made with spinach or liver, stuffed with meat like ravioli, and flavored with anchovies or sauerkraut.

VEGETABLES Potatoes, as we mentioned above, are prepared in a number of ways, as is sauerkraut; these two are almost condiments. Red cabbage and apples (used in so many dressings and stuffings that they're almost more vegetable than fruit), spinach, green beans, asparagus, carrots, and peas are other vegetables served more or less plain. Cabbage and green peppers are stuffed, mushrooms and onions sautéed. Any of them may be creamed.

FRUITS Unlike diets that use most fruits raw, the German tendency is to either dry them and cook them into compotes to offset meat and poultry dishes (in which case they may have some vinegar) or simmer them in syrup for preserves or desserts. There are some almost habitual pairings: ham with cabbage, pork with apples, goose with cherries, duck with prunes.

MEATS Beef is used as broadly, nose to tail, as it is in Vietnam: boiled, ground into meatloaf (*Hackbraten*), smoked and served cold, dried and then smoked, rolled around pickles and mustard, and braised (*Sauerbraten*) with vinegar, wine, or even buttermilk. *Braten* is simply roast of whatever kind. *Pfefferpotthast* is the original "pepperpot" or New England boiled dinner: short ribs or brisket given a little punch with bay leaves, capers, cloves, and black peppercorns.

Pork too is consumed entirely, with chops, the loin, and the hams the most popular cuts for smoking or grilling; it is also smoked or pickled and used to flavor primarily vegetable casseroles—kale, turnips, and so on. Its affinity for mustard is well-known, and chops are sometimes coated with mustard before being rolled in bread crumbs. *Bierschinken* is a smoked ham snack made a little saltier than normal, to be eaten with beer. Whole suckling pig (and boar piglet) are festival staples.

Veal is often turned into cutlets (schnitzel) and either breaded or sauced; the most elaborate version, Holstein schnitzel, named for the baron whose favorite it became, combines the cutlet, smoked salmon, caviar, a poached egg, and capers. (A simpler recipe—just a one-knight stand, so to speak—replaces the smoked salmon and caviar with sardines.) *Weisswurst* is a very light veal sausage with eggwhites. *Hasenpfeffer* is hare stewed with wine and peppercorns; venison is usually roasted or served as cutlets or fancy sausages, as is boar. Organ meats, particularly sweetbreads, are referred to in the French manner as ragouts and involve eggs and wine. A *Schlachtplatte* is a mixed plate of sausages and cold cuts, potatoes, and sauerkraut—the ploughman's lunch.

POULTRY   Goose is roasted and smoked; goose liver pâté is considered a luxury. Duck is marinated in beer or wine or stuffed with apples and prunes and perhaps sour bread crumbs; game birds are usually marinated before being roasted or grilled. Chicken is most often stuffed and baked or braised in wine French-style; both chickens and ducks are caponized (that is, castrated to increase body fat).

SEAFOOD   Herring is fried, marinated, smoked, and turned into a sour cream salad with potatoes. Eel is smoked and made into sausage (it is also made into a stew). Fish are braised in wine and served with cream sausages and occasionally sweet-and-sour dressings; trout is served in several classic French styles, including steamed in foil or parchment.

DESSERTS   Between the French and their layered pastry doughs and the Viennese and their ornate fillings, German and Austrian pastries became extremely elaborate. Under the French influence, honey, which had been the favorite sweetener, was replaced by sugar; under the

Ottoman influence, the Austrians used jams as well as nuts in their sweets. Strüdel is a yeast dough filled with jam; rice pudding, gingerbreads, raisin breads, almond cookies, and hazelnut cakes all show their Middle Eastern ancestry. An even more obvious example is marzipan, the ground almond-sugar paste that is made into elaborate fruits, vegetables, and decorations and tinted to perfection.

Although the region offers hundreds of famous sweets, among the most common on American menus are Black Forest cake (a layered chocolate cake with cherries) and Sacher Torte, which is actually a sort of trade name, not a generic recipe. Developed by Metternich's chef, Franz Sacher, it is a chocolate cake with a stiff chocolate shell that conceals apricot puree—and technically, the only "authentic" rendition is that served at the Sacher Hotel in Vienna.

HOW TO ORDER AND EAT LIKE A NATIVE

There are only a few tricks to eating as the Germans do. The first is that open-faced sandwiches are eaten with a fork and knife, as they are in Scandinavia; the second is that smoked eel is eaten with the fingers. In fact, it's eaten by itself, accompanied only by plain bread; and at the end of the meal, the waiter traditionally pours not water but schnapps over your hands to remove the odor. Otherwise, eat as you would at home.

German food is not only rich in texture; it's rich in flavor as well and ought to be dealt out slowly on both accounts. Two people might order a vegetable soup and a mixed platter of sausages with bread to start, then a schnitzel dish and duck or goose. If it's spring, large platters of plain asparagus may be offered. Four people should try schmeerkase, mixed hot sausages, hot potato salad, roast duck, sauerbraten or hasenpfeffer, fish in cream sauce, and schnitzel.

With dinner you may drink either beer or wine, although most German wine tends to be fruity and/or sweet. Remember, dessert will be waiting.

COOKING AT HOME

Your mother cooked this stuff. If she didn't, your school cafeteria cook did. You probably have everything you need to cook anything in this chapter.

SAUERBRATEN

1 cup dry red wine
1/2 cup red wine vinegar
1 cup beef broth, stock, or water
1 onion, sliced
6 black peppercorns, crushed
8 juniper berries, crushed, or 1/4 cup gin
2 bay leaves
1 3-pound beef rump roast or top round
2 tablespoons oil
1 carrot, finely chopped
1 stalk celery, finely chopped
1 leek, finely chopped
2 tablespoons flour
2 tablespoons powdered ginger (optional)

In a nonreactive saucepan, combine wine, vinegar, broth, onion, peppercorns, juniper berries or gin, and bay leaves and bring to boil; let cool. Meanwhile, place roast in an enameled casserole or Dutch oven just large enough to hold it, and pour the marinade over it; cover and refrigerate, turning occasionally, for at least 48 hours, preferably several days.

On the day of cooking, remove meat from marinade and pat dry; strain and reserve marinade. In a deep casserole, heat oil and brown on all sides, adding more oil if necessary. Remove meat to a platter; add chopped vegetables to oil and cook until soft; sprinkle with flour and ginger until colored and smooth. Pour in marinade and bring to boil; return meat to casserole. Cover, lower heat, and simmer until tender, about 2 hours. Remove meat to platter; strain the liquid, skim off as much fat as possible, and boil down slightly to thicken. Slice meat and pour sauce over it. Serve with potatoes, potato pancakes, and red cabbage.

POTATO PANCAKES

3 pounds potatoes, peeled and grated
3 eggs, beaten
2 small onions, grated
1 1/2 teaspoons salt
1 teaspoon pepper
4 tablespoons flour
oil for frying

Press potatoes between paper towels or dishtowels to remove moisture; turn into bowl. Combine potatoes with eggs, onions, seasonings, and flour. Pour oil about 1 inch deep in skillet and heat; drop in spoonfuls of potato batter; brown, turn, and drain on paper towels.

ROAST DUCK WITH APPLE STUFFING

1 5-pound duck
salt and pepper to taste
1/2 pound veal, ground
1/2 pound sirloin or round, ground
1/2 pound lean pork, ground
2 tablespoons raisins
1 egg, beaten
3/4 cup dry bread crumbs
1/2 teaspoon dried sage
pinch nutmeg
pinch allspice
2 tart cooking apples, peeled, seeded, and diced

Preheat oven to 450°. Meanwhile, rinse duck inside and out and pat dry. Season cavity with salt and pepper; with meat fork, prick skin all over.

In a large bowl, combine all remaining ingredients except apples with a little more salt and pepper; then add apples and stuff duck, leaving space for expansion. Skewer or sew cavity shut and truss bird. Place breast up on rack in shallow pan and roast 15 minutes or until lightly browned, then remove from oven; reduce heat to 350°, pour off accumulated fat, and return to oven for 1 hour or until juices from thigh joint run clear (start testing after 45 minutes). Remove and let rest before serving.

SCANDINAVIA

Mention Scandinavian food, and most people think "smorgasbord"—and while it may be oversimplifying things to suggest that all Norden food is one big buffet, that word is a fair reminder of the cuisine's homey abundance and straightforward simplicity.

Scandinavian cuisine may not offer great variety or elaboration; but it seems to come almost directly from the land itself, with its tra-ditions nearly intact. The salmon and herring, goose and wildfowl, reindeer and mutton, root vegetables, mushrooms, and berries that charac-terize Scandinavian cuisine are the constant gift of its long coastlines, snow-melt rivers, thick timber plateaus, lakes, and marshes. The food does not come easily, but its fats and proteins offer strength; and it is best enjoyed in compa-ny—another hedge against the long winters.

Perhaps because food doesn't come easily here, good (and tireless) cooks are highly prized. In Denmark, the farmwoman in charge of the kitchen is addressed as *madmor*—"food mother." And that food involves hard work makes even more admirable the Norwegian farmwives' tradition of hanging baskets filled with fresh flatbread, butter, sausage, and a clean cloth under the storehouse eaves for any hungry person that happens by.

THE HISTORY

Denmark's "dual citizenship"—culturally associated with Scandinavia and geophysically joined to northern Europe—has made it a natural crossroads between the regions. In fact, in prehistoric times, a broad land bridge existed across what is now the strait between Copenhagen and the southern tip of Sweden. The Danes had probably settled there by 2,000 B.C., but they left few records before the ninth century, when the Vikings launched the first great raids on northern Europe. In their heyday, the Danish and Norwegian Vikings—or "Norsemen," which was eventually corrupted to "Norman" (hence the "Norman Conquest" of England)—ranged as far as Spain, France, the Low Countries, Germany, and Great Britain. Their influence waxed and waned, but never collapsed, for several hundred years. (Denmark's periodic "enlightenments" produced at least one fine irony: Danish nobles, who had once forced a king on the English, eventually hobbled their own king by forcing him to sign a declaration closely copied from the Magna Carta.)

Finland, which shares a long border and strong ethnic connections with Russia to the east, has also been a sort of bridge and not infrequently an actual battleground between Sweden and Russia. It was probably first inhabited about 7000 B.C. by nomads who followed the retreating ice north in search of game and fish; in the early centuries A.D., their descendants, the Samis (formerly known as Lapps or Laplanders), were gradually forced to the extreme north by the Finns. Sami cuisine and culture is still as thoroughly centered on the reindeer as the American Prairie tribes' were on the bison.

Sweden, the more hospitable country, was inhabited first; traces of settlement go back nearly 12,000 years and evidence of trade with Europe around 4,000 years. Not close to their Scandinavian neighbors—the "Vikings" with whom they are often confused—the Swedes actually spent most of their early history battling Norway and Denmark and expanding east across Russia to the Black Sea. Throughout the Middle Ages, Sweden was a potent military and political presence in Europe, but it emerged after the Napoleonic Wars as an early and visionary liberal society (one of Napoleon's idealistic and eventually estranged generals became the King of Sweden). It is the most eclectic culture in the region and the only one to have established a serious court cuisine. Veal Oscar, in fact, is named for King Oscar II, who preferred his veal cutlets topped with asparagus, bearnaise sauce, and lobster meat.

THE COUNTRIES

Scandinavia looks something like a drooping lily with three long, irregular petals—Norway on the west, Sweden in the center, and Finland on the east, bordering Russia, which actually forms a fourth petal—and, to the south, several dropped "seeds" that comprise Denmark. Although the northernmost part of the Scandinavian peninsula is subarctic tundra (a third of Norway lies above the Arctic Circle), the central regions are humid, fertile, and rich in both wildlife and fresh- and saltwater fish.

Because of its somewhat warmer climate—the edge of the Gulf Stream keeps it between about 30° and 60°—Denmark is much more widely cultivated than its neighbors; three-quarters of its land is devoted to pasture and agriculture. Not only is Denmark richer in grains than most of its Norden neighbors (which may be one reason they drink more beer than the others), the Danes are also much more reliant on pork as a source of protein. This is not coincidental: In the latter half of the nineteenth century, the Danish government actively encouraged its farmers to shift their emphasis from grain production (they tended to "buy American," as we say) to dairy and pork, and as a result, Denmark became the most prosperous small-farming economy in Europe. Even today, although it has greatly expanded its industrial base as well, pigs, cattle, and poultry remain as important as cereals and root vegetables.

Heavily forested and, like Norway, with a third of its territory lying above the Arctic Circle, Finland is dotted with some 55,000 lakes and vast marshlands. Only about 9 percent of the land is arable, and the primary commodities are grains (hay, oats, barley, wheat, and rye), sugar beets, potatoes, poultry, cattle, hogs, reindeer, and sheep.

Norway, a 1,100-mile-long and often narrow strip of coast, is 60 percent mountain and has even more lakes than Finland—nearly three times as many, in fact. It remains a heavily fishing-dependent society; only about 3 percent of its land is devoted to farming. The mountain pastures are given over to cattle and sheep and reindeer in the north. The northern region of Norway, like that of Finland, is dominated by Finns and Lapps or Samis.

Sweden's climate ranges widely from the mountainous northern region, which comprises nearly two-thirds of the country, to the densely populated south. Like its neighbors, Sweden is more than half forest. Only 8 percent of its land is arable, and most of that land is devoted to sugar beets, potatoes, grains, and fodder for the poultry, hogs, and cattle.

THE CUISINE

The Vikings knew early on how limited the food supply was—it was one of the primary reasons behind their aggressive quest for new territories—and they also knew how to make the most of it. Their methods of preserving foods, salting, smoking, and drying, are still in use today; in particular, their reliance on dried cod during long sea voyages inspired many Portuguese dishes and allowed the Europeans to make their own long treks to distant nations. The Finns even cure lamb in their saunas!

Although few so-called Scandinavian restaurants in the United States are particularly authentic, and most tend to mix Danish pastries with Norwegian lamb, there are substantial differences in each country's cuisine, primarily having to do with topography. Denmark, the farthest south (and a near neighbor to Germany), is a green and dairy-rich nation whose food is thick with creams and butter. Danes prefer sweet cream, the others primarily sour cream. Norway, long and exposed, has a spare, sturdy style strong on mutton and cheese. Sweden, down the center, is the wealthiest and most eclectic, with elements of French, German, Polish, and Russian styles; and Finland, the most heavily forested, delights in earthy flavors—wild game, lake fish, wild mushrooms, and black sour breads. (Whether or not it has any basis in fact, an old saying has it that "The Danes live to eat, the Norwegians eat to live, and the Swedes eat to drink.")

One of the great ironies of Scandinavian history is that despite the apparent ubiquitousness of salt, there isn't enough hard sun, and the Baltic isn't sufficiently saline, for the Scandinavians to rely on the evaporation method of producing salt for preserving foods. So German and Low Country merchants managed to take over the salt trade, particularly in connection with herring and made immense profits.

THE MAIN INGREDIENTS

FISH AND SEAFOOD This is so much the major class of food in the region that many restaurants list the lunch special as *dagensratt*—"fish of the day." Cod, salmon, Arctic char, trout, pike, and mackerel are eaten with dedication, but the greatest regional fish is herring, the alpha and often the omega of Scandinavian meals. Shrimp is also popular, particularly the small, delicately flavored baby shrimp; and the warmer regions offer eels, oysters, mussels, langoustines, crayfish, and *muikku*, a tiny type of salmon with a delicate roe.

POULTRY AND GAME BIRDS Chicken is widely raised, though more for eggs, it seems, than fricassees. Game and "free-range" birds, with their more assertive flavor, are more popular: snow grouse, goose, pheasant, duck, woodcock, and the dark-breasted ptarmigan.

DAIRY PRODUCTS Cheeses may be the most obvious, but cream, sour cream, butter, and an extraordinary number of soured or fermented dairy foods (curds, buttermilk, and particularly one called *skyr*, which is something like yogurt) are also popular. Nothing goes to waste: In some regions, fermented milk and whey are used to make cheese.

MEATS In the northernmost regions in particular, reindeer is a whole grocery store, providing tongue, sausage, meatballs, marrow, saddle, cutlets, milk and cheese, liver, stew, steaks, sandwiches, and pâté. (Actually, to the Sami, it's a whole general store, providing skins for boots and clothing, horns for utensils and souvenirs, and transportation and portage as well.)

Pick and Choose

It is possible, though difficult, to avoid a lot of salt and fat when eating at a Scandinavian restaurant. First of all, you're expected to butter the bread at the smorgasbord, and if you don't, the toppings will drip on you. Second, a great number of dishes (on either the smorgasbord or the regular menu) have cream sauces or mayonnaise; many pastry-wrapped dishes do, too. Even a lot of meat stews have heavy or sour cream mixed in. Your best bets are roasts, ham, dry-cured lamb or mutton, wild game, poached fish, and shrimp. Fermented dairy products, such as buttermilk and yogurt, tend to separate out the fat and are thus better than whole cream or butter. Vinegar is better than salt, so pickled fish is better than salt; smoking is better than either. But all things considered, sodium is a passing problem, while fat hangs around a long time, so choose salty dishes over creamy ones.

Pork is more popular farther south, particularly smoked and salted; and since reindeer is quite lean, pork provides much of the fat of non-Sami diets. (One of the features of Valhalla, the Viking heaven, was that it served a perfectly roasted wild boar that could be consumed every night but reappeared whole the next morning.) Beef is most common in Denmark—partly because the reputation of Danish ham is so high that much of it is exported. Goat, lamb, and mutton are common, but the Scandinavians, particularly the Finns, also prize game meats: elk, venison, bear, hare, even whale and horse (although the last two are unlikely to appear on any menu in the United States). Here, too, everything is used: tongue, tripe, jowls, and even calf's head, which is the "mock turtle" of the soup.

VEGETABLES AND GRAINS Since winters are long and sunlight short, roots and winter vegetables that can be cold-stored are the most important: potatoes, onions, celery root, parsnips, carrots, leeks, kale, cabbage, rutabaga, and some greens. Wild mushrooms are especially plentiful in Finland, where some 50 varieties are eaten (including some shunned elsewhere as poisonous). Barley and rye are raised in the south, wheat and oats further north.

FRUITS AND NUTS From the forests come a variety of berries, sweet and tart, including lingonberries, strawberries, cloudberries (golden raspberries), cranberries, blueberries, honeyberries, and rowanberries; they are used not only as fruit but as seasoning elements, especially to offset rich game. Nuts are also harvested but are primarily served in desserts.

SEASONINGS Dark green, "fruity" spices are prominent, including green and black pepper, juniper berries, pine needles, allspice, anise, dried citrus peel, caraway seeds, bay leaves, and coarse salt. Vinegar, lemon, honey, and sugar are the other main flavorings.

THE MAIN DISHES

SOUPS Scandinavian meals contain both hearty stews and chowders and more delicate vegetable bisques. The lighter ones are generally Danish cream of shrimp soups or light mushroom-barley soups, but the more traditional include fish chowders; beer and bread soups; thick pea soups; the Viking-era "black soup" (*svart soppa*), made with pig and goose blood (but nowadays tamed with wine, port, cinnamon, and ginger); hotpots of mixed veal, pork, and beef; and "slaughter soup," which uses all the offal. The sometimes-Russian Finns make borscht.

FISH AND SHELLFISH Herring, cod, and salmon are served nearly every way possible: boiled, baked, smoked, pickled, poached, dried, grilled, salt-cured, poached, "moussed," or boiled in soup. On special occasions, fish is baked *en croute*—wrapped in pastry—or roasted whole. Salt- and sugar-cured salmon is called *gravlax*. *Lutefisk* is a very common dried and lye-cured codfish that is soaked and then turned into soup; plain dried cod is *stokkfisk* (which lasts up to 20 years), and salted cod is *klippfisk*. There is even a fermented and potentially explosive herring called *surstroemming* that only a madmor could love. (For more on herring, see "The Smorgasbord," page 82.)

POULTRY AND GAME BIRDS Pickled goose (called "burst goose") is boiled with vegetables or served hot with a chilled horseradish cream; fresh goose is stuffed with apples and prunes. One of the preferred sauces for game birds, and game meat as well, is a combination of goat cheese and cream.

VEGETABLES Most vegetables, as we noted above, are rooty and tough; they are most often used in soups or stews, braised or boiled, or chopped and then creamed; this method is used for spinach, cauliflower, cabbage, carrots, and so on. Potatoes are eaten relatively plainly—baked, skillet-fried, julienned for fritters, or mashed into dumplings—but they are eaten a lot. Swedes venerate the potato as much as the Irish do, and for similar reasons; it saved them from famine in 1771. Some Swedes eat as many as four or five potatoes a day.

MEAT Danish hams and bacon are famous but are expensive, because so many are exported, and thus are eaten sparingly; thin-sliced mutton and smoked lamb are often substituted. Pork loin is frequently stuffed with prunes and apples and accompanied by red cabbage, particularly in the regions near Germany; it is also sometimes ground and stuffed in or even around cabbages. Pork is often stretched by being combined with veal, especially when it's ground; it may be turned into meatballs or a sort of meatloaf or even into fried croquettes.

Lamb is stewed, roasted, dried, salt-cured (both legs and whole chops), and sometimes smoked—or, in the case of the Norwegian *fenalar*, dried, salted, *and* smoked. The Swedes have a dish called *lokdolmar* that is surely related to the Middle Eastern dolmas (lamb-stuffed grape leaves), only since grape leaves are not available, the Swedes use blanched, softened, and separated onion layers. Beef is roasted, pot-roasted with anchovies, stewed with beer ("seaman's stew"), or hash-browned and chopped with diced beets and onions into a sort of ham-burger with internal relish. A really macho dish is the Finnish *vorshmack*, a mixture of ground mutton, beef, salt herring, garlic, and onions.

BEVERAGES Meals are accompanied by beer and distilled liquor, specifically the fiery caraway-flavored clear grain alcohol called, with for-givable enthusiasm, *aquavit*—the "water of life." Also popular are berry-flavored teas that are nearly juices. Finns prefer vodka.

BREADS All shapes, types, and flavors are made in the region, from the huge flatbread to the sweet *pulla,* a yeast bread or roll usually served with coffee (which perhaps explains the use of the word "Danish" to mean a sweet roll) to crisp (hardtack) to rye to the "black" bread used for the smorgasbord. *Limpa* is a sweet Finnish rye popular at Christmas.

DOUGHS AND PANCAKES Scandinavians make plenty of sweet and nonsweet doughs, particularly waffles and pancakes (usually served as desserts, not breakfast) and crepes. The Danish are fond of crisp-edged crepes filled with baby shrimp in dill and cream. There are dumplings stuffed with pork and dipped in butter, and there is also some pasta. The Finns make Russian blini and a version of piroghi. Pastries are occasionally made to be stuffed, like the sour-cream dough stuffed with meatloaf called *lihamurekepiiras;* if you see it on the menu, just point.

DESSERTS Denmark, partly because of its proximity to Germany, is particularly rich in pastries, huge cream-and-cake tartes, whipped cream–berry mousses, and fruit-flavored liqueurs. The *romfromage* is a soft whipped-cream meringe suffused with dark rum. Berries are also popular in crepes; and the Finns, who are particularly fond of ice cream, sometimes make dessert blintzes. In the north, however, plain fruit and cheese are more frequently the finale.

THE SMORGASBORD

A smorgasbord meal is a series of courses always beginning with her-ring—lots of herring—and eaten over dark multigrain "black" bread. The bread is sliced thin and placed on round flat disks to the left of the dinner plate, called *smorrebraet* (literally, "buttering boards"). The bread is always buttered, which serves as a sort of seal for the toppings. After the bread is buttered, it is moved to the large plate, where it becomes the base of the open-faced sandwiches (*smorrebord*) that make up the smorgasbord (the whole "bread-and-butter table"). Everything that is not bread or butter, incidentally, is *paalaeg*—"laid on."

Herring is the whole first course, but there may be a dozen dishes of it, pickled, salted, peppered, sugared, smoked, fried, marinated, and poached in aspic. You may even see the daunting surstroemming. The pickled herring (which is slightly sweet, as opposed to the marinated herring, which is vinegary) generally appears first with onion and then perhaps with dill sour cream, curry sauce, mustard sauce, sweet-and-sour sauce, Madeira, and so on; first you taste the herring, then you toast with the aquavit.

After the herring comes the second course, and a clean plate; now you get the other fish (smoked salmon, gravlax, eel, poached salmon with mayonnaise, and lobster or crab salad), hard-cooked eggs, apples, and some sort of salad or pickle to offset it. The third plate consists of meats and salads: roast beef, ham, salami, liver pâté, sausage, pasta salad, hard cheese, pickled tongue. Then come the hot dishes: meatballs, herring croquettes, egg and bacon tartes, omelets, potatoes. Finally, the cheese board arrives (and then dessert, although that may be delayed while you recover).

All these courses are prepared, served, and eaten with the familiar utensils, *exclusively*—that is, even things you might expect to pick up with your fingers, such as the tiny sandwiches of the smorgasbord, are cut up in the European manner (fork, tines down, in the left hand, knife in the right) and eaten off the fork. This may take some getting used to, especially for curry-sauced, hard-boiled eggs, but that's how they do it. (It's actually a good idea, since most of the sauces are creamy and the thin bread crumbles easily.)

Incidentally, about those Swedish meatballs: As an appetizer or part of the smorgasbord, meatballs are served without gravy. As a main course, over rice or pasta, they are served with sauce.

HOW TO ORDER AND EAT LIKE A NATIVE

As the old saying goes, the Danes live to eat, and traditionally they eat a half-dozen meals a day. Here, however, Scandinavian restaurants have adopted the American hours and the common menu organization. Nomenclature and menus are fairly standard, and you should have no difficulty ordering.

Meals generally begin with multiple appetizers—pickled or salted fish, open-faced cucumber and onion sandwiches, some cheese—followed by soup (most often a dill-flavored fish and potato chowder) and then the main courses of fish and meat.

A good meal for two might include some pickled fish or a plate of fine smoked or dried meats, followed by potato and fish chowder or creamed vegetable soup and, if possible, a main course of either reindeer or venison along with poached salmon; pastry-wrapped fish or lamb would be a good alternative. Ask for cheese (sliced Finnish *lappi* or the Swiss-like *vasterbotten*), fruit salad, or berry pie for dessert. A party of four would add a stuffed pork roast or goose, stuffed veal rolls, and perhaps a couple more Danish pastries—unless of course you go to an all-you-can-eat smorgasbord place. Then you're on your own. Just remember: Herring always comes first, and cheese is always last.

Be sure to ask for special imported beers or aquavit.

COOKING AT HOME

It is probably easier to make lowfat Norden food at home than in a restaurant. Now that more and more specialty markets import game, reindeer is not hard to find and is certainly the most flamboyant dish to offer guests. (Elk, venison, or even buffalo are acceptable substitutes) Start by laying out pickled herring and rye or cracked wheat bread, some cheese, and strong drink—aquavit and beer, for example. The pork roast can be accompanied by red cabbage and apples. Serve the reindeer stew over mashed potatoes with a side dish of parsnips and carrots, and pass lingonberries or cranberry relish.

STUFFED PORK ROAST

8 pitted prunes, soaked in hot water or apple cider
1 tart apple, peeled, cored, and cubed

1 teaspoon lemon juice

3 1/2–4 pounds boned center-cut loin of pork

salt and pepper

2 teaspoons thyme

2 tablespoons butter

2 tablespoons oil

3/4 cup white wine or vermouth

1/2 heavy cream (or substitute half-and-half or sour cream)

1 tablespoon currant jelly

Preheat oven to 350°. Drain prunes and pat dry; sprinkle apple with lemon juice and add to prunes. With a sharp knife, cut a slit down the length of the loin to make a pocket reaching almost end to end; season with salt, pepper, and thyme, stuff with fruit, and sew up the pocket with kitchen thread. (If you prefer to buy the roast already rolled, cut a tunnel all the way through with a skewer, widen it with a wooden spoon handle or knife sharpener, and force the fruit down either end of the tunnel, alternating prunes and apples.)

In a casserole just big enough to hold the loin, over medium heat, melt 1 tablespoon butter and 1 tablespoon oil; brown the roast on all sides, adding more oil if needed. When it's brown all around, pour off fat and add wine. Whisk in cream, bring to simmer, and cover; then move it into the oven and bake until tender (75–90 minutes). Remove to platter and let rest. Meanwhile, on top of the stove, skim the fat from the cooking liquid and bring to a boil; reduce to about a cup, add jelly, and simmer until dissolved and smooth. Slice roast and pass with sauce.

SAMI REINDEER STEW

3 tablespoons butter

3 pounds boneless reindeer meat, shoulder or roast, frozen

2 cups coarsely chopped onions

1 cup sliced mushrooms

1 cup sour cream (optional)

2 tablespoons crushed juniper berries or gin (optional)

salt and white pepper to taste

Melt the butter in an iron pot. Slice the frozen meat into slivers and add to pot; cover and simmer until all the water from the frozen meat has evaporated and the oil is clear. Add a little water and onions and continue simmering until tender (about 30 minutes). Add mushrooms, sour cream, and juniper berries or gin if desired, simmer 5–10 minutes more, then serve.

CELERY ROOT PANCAKES

1 large celery root, peeled and coarsely grated
1 onion, coarsely grated
1 sweet bell pepper, cut into matchsticks
1/2 cup cooked, canned, or frozen corn, drained
4 eggs, lightly beaten
3 tablespoons fresh dill
2 teaspoons chopped hot pepper or 1/2 teaspoon hot pepper sauce
3 tablespoons flour
1/2 teaspoon baking soda
4 tablespoons butter or margarine
3–4 tablespoons oil
salt and pepper to taste
optional garnishes: sour cream, crème fraîche, caviar, sliced red onion

Wrap grated celery root in a dishtowel and squeeze moisture out; turn into a bowl, repeat with grated onion, and add to bowl. Add peppers, corn, eggs, flour, baking soda, and seasonings and toss until well mixed.

In a skillet, melt half the butter and half the oil and heat to medium. Drop spoonfuls of vegetable batter into hot oil and flatten slightly; fry about 2 minutes on each side, drain on paper towels, and continue, adding butter and oil as needed, until the batter is used up. Garnish as desired.

RUSSIA, POLAND, AND EASTERN EUROPE

BASIC CUISINE

DINNER FOR TWO:
Blini, kulebiaka, roast lamb

DINNER FOR FOUR:
Pelmeni, borscht, roast duck, veal paprikash

GROUP DISH:
Zakouskis

STYLE:
Doughy, smoky, gamey

KEY FLAVORS:
Sour cream, smoked and salted fish, paprika

DISTINCTIVE DISHES:
Piroshki, kulebiaka, kasha

UNIFORMITY OF MENUS:
Fair; spellings in particular vary by region

EATING UTENSILS:
Forks and knives

COST:
Moderate to expensive

NUTRITIONAL INDEX:
High cholesterol, high sodium, high fat

"THANK YOU":
"Spacebo" (Russian); "Dziękuję" (Polish); "Koszonom" (Magyar)

From the culinary standpoint, as from many others, the Cold War was a terrible waste. Russian food, once one of Europe's most admired cuisines, is known to most Americans only at its extremes—the corruptly opulent Kremlin caviar fare on the one hand and the borscht and boiled potatoes of quota lines and black markets on the other. And too many of the Russian restaurants in the United States seem to cling to their own form of continental nostalgia, focusing more on "name" dishes (chicken Kiev, beef Stroganov, steak tartare, charlotte Russe, veal Orlov) than authentic ones. Polish cuisine, once similarly imitated, has been similarly slighted, reduced to ball-park sausages and beer gardens.

But with the advent of glasnost and the economic reconstruction of Eastern Europe, we can hope for a revival of not merely classic Russian and Polish dishes but Hungarian, Romanian, Czech, Azerbaijan, or even Ukrainian ones as well. These are substantial cuisines, meaty, rooty, smoky—part comfort food, part extravagance. Over a vivid, passionate crazy-quilt of

Greek, Byzantine, Asiatic, Scandinavian, Turkish, and Germanic influences was installed a layer of eighteenth-century European custom and economy; and despite decades of reckless and ruthless agricultural "redevelopment," many parts of the former Soviet sphere remain fertile and potentially prosperous.

THE COUNTRIES

Even in the post-Soviet era, Russia (or the Russian Federation, which comprises 20 republics and several territories) remains physically the largest nation in the world, covering some 6,600,000 square miles, stretching 5,000 miles from the Baltic Sea to the Pacific, and crossed by geographical belts that run virtually the entire climactic range.

The Ural Mountains are generally used to divide the northwest, "European" region of Russia, including Moscow and St. Petersburg, from the Asiatic subcontinent of Siberia, which bred four great ruthless and incredibly adaptable tribes—the Scythians, the Mongols, the Manchus, and the Huns. In the northern tundra, fur-trapping, fishing, reindeer herding, and sealing remain major occupations. The central steppes are among the great grain pastures of the world, producing wheat, oats, and rye (and supporting the dairy herds that graze on them) as well as sunflower seeds and sugar beets. Siberia is 40 percent forest, and many of the game foods that became famous in Russian cooking originated there.

The southern belt is subtropical, and Georgia's produce and cuisine resemble that of Turkey and Georgia's other Middle Eastern neighbors: citrus fruits, some wine grapes, tobacco, tea, poultry, pigs, and cattle. (It was to Georgia, intriguingly, that Jason led his Argonauts; along with the Golden Fleece, they discovered the pleasures of pheasant.) Ukraine, the region that adjoins Romania and Poland, is the breadbasket of the old empire; it produced 25 percent of the staples consumed in the old Soviet Union, primarily wheat but also corn, rice, barley, potatoes, beets, and vegetables.

The Danube River creates fertile plains down through the central plateau of Hungary, through the northern plains of Bulgaria, and into Romania. Much of the region has cold winters and hot summers, with only short intermediate seasons; farmers here primarily produce grains (wheat, barley, rue and corn) but also grow potatoes, beets, and grapes (wine-making is widespread) and raise pigs, sheep, and some cattle.

Ethnically speaking, the Slavs are a nonhomogeneous blend of Turko-Tatars, Mongols, Greeks, and Finnish and Germanic tribes; more than 60 ethnic groups are represented. The greatest single bond among them is their speech—more than 300 million people speak a Slavic language. However, the cultural rift emerges even here: The Russians, Bulgarians and Macedonians use the Cyrillic alphabet because of their affiliation with the Russian Orthodox Church, while the western Slavics write in the Roman alphabet, reflecting their Roman Catholic background. (Even more pointedly, the single language spoken by the Croats and Serbs is written in Roman by the Croats and in Cyrillic by the Serbs.)

The two non-Slavic languages in the region are Romanian, which, like French and Italian, is a Latin derivative; and Magyar, or Hungarian, a language that also came out of the Siberian Urals but is part of the Finnish/Turkish family.

THE HISTORY

The Scythians left Siberia about 3,000 years ago and worked their way west until they were halted by Alexander the Great. A series of Asiatic armies—Goths, Huns, Avars, Magyars—pushed into Germany and the Balkans, bringing Chinese noodles, red meat, soured dough, and the indispensable *kasha* (a buckwheat grain) into the fruit-heavy Persian and Byzantine diet. Meanwhile, the Norsemen who lent their name to the region—Varangians, sometimes called "Rus" or "Rhos"—instilled the practices of salting and smoking fish.

Kiev, on the trade route between Scandinavia and Constantinople, was a major commercial center and spice market by the fifth century; this is one reason why cardamom, cinnamon, and ginger were known in the north. Poland, which was part of a Lithuanian/Hungarian empire that stretched from the Baltic Sea to the Black, served as a link between Scandinavia and Italy, importing some potatoes and oils to its eastern neighbors.

But just after the turn of the thirteenth century, Genghis Khan stormed through China, Persia, Eastern Europe, and the Balkans; within decades the Mongols had left their culinary marks all across Russia, particularly the use of yogurt, sweet fermented alcoholic drinks, boiled meats, and a variety of bread and pasta products from the steppes. To the south, the Byzantine Empire (including Bulgaria and central Hungary) fell to the Ottoman Turks, who preferred spitted meats and pilafs to fruit-sweetened stews. And at the beginning of the eighteenth century, when Peter the Great became determined to bring Russia into full commerce with the rest of the European world, Russia was suddenly launched on an almost unprecedented culinary binge.

Peter imported European-trained chefs, a practice that became routine among Russian aristocracy. (Alexander I's personal chef was the celebrated French gastronome Careme, the father of "grande cuisine," who had already worked for Talleyrand and turned the future King George IV down to cook for Baron Rothschild.) Over the next decades, the influx of Dutch, French, and German dishes; the introduction of vegetables such as potatoes, asparagus, and lettuce; and the techniques of making sauces, mincing meats, and blending pastry transformed Russian cuisine forever.

Devouring the Black Sea territories of the faltering Ottoman Empire, Russia also grabbed up fields of bell peppers, tomatoes, and eggplants. So successful was the synthesis that under Catherine the Great, Russia was the chief power and social presence of continental Europe, and Russian-style banquets—particularly the ornate appetizer courses called *zakouskis*—were all the rage.

Poland had an early advantage in the culinary competition. Like France, it had the benefit of a food-savvy Italian queen—Bona Sforza of Milan, who in the sixteenth century married the Polish heir Sigismund and brought along pasta and ice cream with her dowry. But in the eighteenth and nineteenth centuries, Poland was annexed right off the map, gradually devoured by Russia on the east and Austria and Prussia to the west. As a result of these enforced alliances, Polish cuisine adopted German-style smoked meats and pastries and learned to produce desserts that rivaled those of the Viennese. Even today, Polish, Lithuanian, and Hungarian dishes betray the influences of their Central European neighbors, such as Italy, Germany, and Austria.

Romania, Yugoslavia, and particularly Bulgaria, whose culture was nearly eradicated by the Ottomans, retain much stronger ties to their

Turkish and Middle Eastern alliances and even incorporate a few Mediterranean flourishes. Though Russia is still dominated by Christians, who fast but are permitted all foods at other times, in the south and central regions there are many Muslims, whose dietary taboos, primarily pork, are consistent. There are also still strong traces of Jewish kosher-inspired cuisine in the Eastern European areas.

THE CUISINES

To a great extent, the evolution of the region's cuisines parallels those protracted and uneasy meetings of East and West—Europe vs. Asia, Roman vs. Byzantine, Turkic vs. Germanic. Here the medieval European fascination with sauce and display meets the crude vitality (and protein) of those meat-and-bread-wolfing Tatars who conquered the known world.

There are two great paradoxes in traditional Russian cuisine: The first is the almost unequaled abundance of wild game and fowl; conflicting with the huge number of fast days—250 of them—mandated by the Russian Orthodox Church, which banned not only meat but also milk or eggs. Fortunately, the region's seas and rivers produce great numbers of fish, particularly sturgeon (source of the almost mystically prized caviar), salmon, sable, mackerel, shad, whitefish, carp, pike—including Hungary's famous fogas, and trout, along with crawfish, eels, frogs, and oysters.

The other is the cheerful eclecticism of its starches—the Middle Eastern grains, the European potato, and the quintessentially Oriental dumplings, noodles, and *kasha*.

In medieval times, Russian foods—not just the large cuts of meats, such as legs or roasts, but vegetables, poultry, and fish as well—were

---

Hard-Hearted Fare

One of the regional distinctions involves the cooking fats. In Georgia, for example, housewives use a clarified butter called *erbo* that seems to bridge the gap from India's ghee to Morocco's smee. Around the Baltic, butter and cream are extremely common. Traditional Czech and Slavic recipes called for bacon grease; in Hungary, with its strong Turkish influence, olive oil dominates. Hungarians, displaying the Viennese influence, are fond of richer flavors in general: They specialize in gamey wild boar and venison and the fattier pork; they prefer to cook with lard or goose fat rather than oil; and they thicken virtually all stews with either a flour-lard roux or sour cream. Almost all East European food, in fact, is a cardiologist's nightmare.

cooked whole, not chopped or sliced. And since the Russian wood-burning "stove" was usually only an oven built into the wall of one room and extended as a bed platform and heater into the next, there was no direct-heat cooking, either; meals were braised or boiled or baked. Hence the preference for stuffed and poached or boiled noodles and dumplings over the long, fast-boiled noodles adopted elsewhere. Fish could be smoked in separate smokehouses, or they were even more commonly salted and brined—again, caviar.

Not until Peter the Great's forcible Europeanization of Russia did stove-top cooking become known (or even possible). Then the grinding and chopping of meats became almost a national pastime. And the methods of making egg-dough pastry that Russians learned from their European tutors transformed their braised and baked meat dishes into the glorious variety of *piroghis*, *kulebiakas*, and *piroshkis* that became signature dishes. Most Russian/Polish sauces are French transplants, particularly the white béchamels, salad dressings, and cheese sauces; sour cream and yogurt are used primarily as toppings, not as ingredients.

Among other regional distinctions: The Turkish strain, and the fondness for grilling meats, remains more important in the southern regions. While Hungarians cook sour cream into a recipe, Polish cooks generally stir sour cream into a dish after it has been removed from the heat and just before serving.

THE MAIN INGREDIENTS

SEASONINGS   The most important herbs and spices in the northern regions are parsley, dill, horseradish, bay leaves, cloves, pepper, and mustard. Onions and mushrooms are used widely for flavor, but garlic is used very sparingly, particularly in Poland (maybe Dracula should have relocated). In Georgia, which served as a stopping-off point for caravans trading between Venice and Baghdad, such eastern herbs as basil, cardamom, barberry, coriander, marigold, cinnamon, allspice, and ginger are popular; even peanuts, which came in from Indonesia, crop up occasionally.

Paprika, Hungary's most famous spice and its greatest contribution to regional cuisine, is also Turkish (and much more aromatic and pungent than the adulterated powder that used to pass for it in the United States). So is the poppy seed, quite common in Eastern European cooking but almost unused in Western Europe.

EGGS AND DAIRY PRODUCTS   Yogurt, sour cream, *smetana* (whey, thinner than American sour cream), and cottage cheese are among the staples in these cuisines. Eggs are used most frequently as an ingredient in doughs and pastries; when they are cooked separately, even as a layer in kulebiaka, they are usually hard-cooked.

GRAINS AND BREADS   The nutty kasha groats, which serve as stuffing, side dish, and entree, remain Russia's characteristic grain; rice comes in a distant second. (Since kasha entered Middle Eastern markets the long way around, it is also called "wheat bulgar," or Bulgarian wheat.) Many bread grains are cultivated, including rye, barley and semolina, but wheat—essential for the pastry in dumplings, blini, and pies—is the greatest of these. Cornmeal is common in Romania, where it is served as a mush or polenta called *mamaliga*.

Russian breads are generally leavened, but the Hungarians are addicted to a deep-fried and garlic-topped bread called *langos* that is purely Mongolian.

VEGETABLES AND FRUITS   Produce that can be preserved for year-round consumption, either in cold storage or by pickling, are the most common. Beets (essential for borscht), cabbage (sauerkraut), eggplant, mushrooms, potatoes and tomatoes (which were both introduced in the late sixteenth century), onions, peas, lentils, kohlrabi, turnips, brussels sprouts, savoy cabbage, and cauliflower are plentiful; the more westerly regions also grow spinach, sorrel, and vegetable marrow (what we call zucchini). In the south, Turkish eggplant, squashes, pomegranates, dates, and figs are plentiful. Preserved lemons, pickled watermelon rind, and pear and plum preserves remain popular. Sour cherries, raspberries, and gooseberries in particular are used for desserts and for a variety of strong, sweet liqueurs.

GAME BIRDS AND OTHER POULTRY Wildfowl are particularly popular in classic Russian and Eastern European cuisine, among them pheasant, partridge, duck, quail, grouse, goose, turkey, chicken, guinea fowl, and even (for really elaborate banquets) crane, swans, and peacocks.

MEATS Thanks to the breadth and variety of topography, meat dishes cover the spectrum, from game (including rabbit and hare, reindeer, elk, venison, and bear) to the lighter meats, such as veal and suckling pig, and the heavier ones, such as beef, smoked pork, and mutton. Organ meats are relatively popular, particularly in Hungary, where brains and kidneys are not only used in stews but also ground and stuffed inside dumplings.

THE MAIN DISHES

SOUPS The most famous recipes in the region are borscht, called *barshch* in Polish; and the Hungarian *Szegedi halaszhe*, a fish chowder named for the city that reputedly perfected it. Other common soups include *kharcho*, the Armenian meat and vegetable stew related to Hungary's heavier *harcho* (see below); bouillons with or without dumplings; and cream soups of potato, cauliflower, sorrel, and dried beans or peas. Cold fruit soups are also popular, particularly in Hungary and Poland.

DUMPLINGS, PIES, AND OTHER DOUGHY DELIGHTS
The doughs—pies, pastries, crepes, dumplings, and ravioli—of Russian and Eastern European cooking are ubiquitous; they can also be hard to differentiate. Some are divided by size: Piroghis are large pies, big enough to cut, while pirorzhkis are little pies that can be held in the hand. Some are classified by dough type and some by stuffing. *Kreplach* and Yugoslavian *bourek* are ground meat dumplings, but they usually show up poached or in soup. Some are nicknamed by shape: *Rastegai*, the nick-

name for canoe-shaped pastries pinched together at the ends but with the stuffing exposed in the middle, means "unbuttoned." Some are boiled, some are fried, and some might be served either way.

There are other dough substitutes as well. Polish and Lithuanian chefs are famous for their *latkes* (potato pancakes) and *knishes* (potato turnovers). The Hungarian *tarhonya* is a granulated pastry, something like the Greek orzo, made by forcing noodle dough through a sieve; it is then cooked like rice. The dumpling doughs themselves can become stuffings, rolled in bread crumbs and deep-fried into croquettes (or *kromeskis*), although the croquettes more often contain a nugget of chicken, fish, ham, or pâté. Almost anything stuffed can be fried in this culture: Polish *golomaki* are stuffed cabbage rolls that are breaded and fried. The utmost in cholesterol indulgence might be *bourreki*, dumplings of thickened béchamel sauce mixed with cheese, rolled into balls, encased in noodle dough, rolled in eggwash and breadcrumbs, and then fried.

MEATS Hungarians still like to roast on spits, using whole joints or fowl and carving them rather than cutting them up for the skewer. Hungarians also have one speciality with a characteristically Persian flavoring—the mutton stew called *harcho*, which is flavored with pickled plums.

Kebabs, called *raznijici*, are popular in Romania; the ground-meat type is called *lule* (*cebapcici* in Yugoslavia). Romanians also

---

Name That Noodle

When it comes to dumplings and such, near-identical names can breed confusion. Russian *pelmeni* are small, noodle-dough ravioli stuffed with potatoes, cheese, ground beef, cabbage, or mushrooms; they can be served either boiled in soup or fried with sour cream (the Siberians prefer to use a mustard or vinegar dressing). The Russian *piroghis* are large, rectangular, brioche-style pastry doughs stuffed with meat, fish, or kasha and mushrooms. The Polish *perogies* aren't piroghis, however—they're what Rus-sians call pelmeni. So are the Ukranian *varenikis*, although they are more likely to be cheese-stuffed noodles, like Afghani aushak—but *valenikis* are cheese-stuffed blini (buckwheat pancakes or crepes) rolled up and deep-fried. Kulebiaka (or coulebiac in the French style) is another large pie, a double-crust layering of salmon, rice, and either hard-boiled eggs or filet of salmon or sturgeon. Polish *kulebiac* may be fish, but it may also be cabbage. *Kurnik* is another piroghi, this time with a chicken and hard-boiled egg stuffing. The Russian pirozhki and the Hungarian piroshki are, fortunately, the same—a pastry-dough turnover filled with ground meat or perhaps shredded cabbage and rice and deep-fried.

like mixed grills called *mititei*, which combine cigar-shaped lule with smoked beef and bacon. *Shashliks* are thinly pounded, marinated then skewered and fried; relatives of the donner kebabs, they are often served with purely Persian pilafs.

Polish cuisine, not surprisingly, is primarily Russian but with a strong German/Austrian streak in its sausages, particularly the garlicky kielbasa (or *kolbasz*), and its smoked meats.

STEWS Another widely served and multiply named family of dishes is the paprikash or goulash. Generally speaking, goulash (or gulyas or gylas or goulasch) involves larger pieces of meat, usually veal or beef, braised and flavored with paprika and tomatoes and sometimes sour cream; it commonly includes potatoes and, in some areas, cabbage. Paprikash (or paprikache or paprykarz) is similar but generally involves a white meat or fish in sour cream with paprika. *Tokany* is a variation on paprikash with thinly sliced meat (and perhaps more than one type of meat). *Szekel gylas* is a pork and sauerkraut version. *Porkoit* is another stew, but one in which the onions are more prominent than the meat.

The Polish national dish is "hunter's stew," a glorified leftover of mixed meats or sausages, sauerkraut, mushrooms, apples, and tomatoes; "Warsaw-style" stew ups the ante with red wine and potatoes.

POULTRY AND FOWL Chicken can be given a paprikash sauce, too, but it is more frequently served as *koltetki*, ground and seasoned then breaded and fried; or *tabaka*, whole marinated game hens pressed and grilled. Wildfowl may be dressed with berries, preserved citrus, or even Persian-style walnut sauce.

BEVERAGES Even the popular drinks reveal the region's multiplicity of influences: tea from China via Siberia and Central Asia; *kefir*, a fermented milk of Mongol ancestry; coffee from Peter's European wanderings; and wine and grapes from the Middle East and France. Vodka, of course, is the national drink, distilled from potatoes, wheat and occasionally rye. (The Russian fondness for strong drink is nothing new: A sixteenth-century book describes the frequent banquets as involving

> ### Salt of the Earth
>
> The Russian word for "hospitality" is *khlebosol'stro*, from *khleb*, meaning "bread," and *sol* for "salt." *Khlebdasol* means, in effect, "bon appetit." Hence one should always place a saucer of salt on the table so that bread can be spread with butter and then dipped into salt.

Greek and Italian wines, both cold and hot; beer and the sweet beerlike *kvass;* brandy; and a variety of fruit liqueurs.) Hungary in particular produces many fine wines, the best-known being white Tokay, and an apricot spirit called *barack*. Bulgarian and Romanian red table wines are increasingly popular as inexpensive table wines here.

ZAKOUSKI

The zakouski are the smorgasbord of Russia and Poland (where the word is *zakaski*) and for centuries were served to announce a host's prosperity as well as his generosity. They were also polite excuses for extending the cocktail hour. The zakouski course became the rage in the rest of Europe as well, and they may represent the beginning of the great caviar craze.

Like a smorgasbord, the zakouski were more than hors d'oeuvre, although they were sometimes preliminary to a full dinner; the table itself comprised a banquet, and there were unspoken (and sometimes spoken) rules of etiquette that dictated its laying out and provisioning. Among typical zakouski were cold meats, ranging from cold cuts to cold roast fowl to steak tartare; chicken, pigs' feet, fish, eggs, ham, and even asparagus and brains in aspic; jellied pork and veal and pâtés of both; pickled beets, mushrooms, or gherkins; boiled salmon with mayonnaise, horseradish, or "Greek" (tomato-vegetable) sauce; hard-cooked eggs; sautéed mushrooms; and greens, kidneys, tripe dumplings, herrings, sardines, anchovies, meatballs, and multiple kinds of caviar and breads, laid out with dozens of garnishes, mustard, horseradish, and chopped onion.

Blinis are a descendent of zakouski, and one that is particularly popular here. Buckwheat crepes are brushed with melted butter and topped with caviar or sour cream—but not both in combination, an American corruption—and then rolled and served with more melted butter; other fillings include hard-cooked eggs, smoked salmon, salted herring, or other fish.

HOW TO ORDER AND EAT LIKE A NATIVE

Traditionally, Russians ate four meals a day: breakfast at about 8, consisting of buns, open-faced sandwiches, and cold cuts; a substantial lunch of fish, meat or vegetable casseroles, crepes and perhaps dumplings, at 1; the multicourse dinner (and primary social meal) at 6, which would involve at least three or four courses, beginning with the zakouski, even without company; and, at 9, an almost immediate last supper of piroshkis and desserts.

Here most restaurants limit themselves to a half-dozen zakouski, and you may be able to order a pre-assembled platter with several types.

Caviar at a restaurant is apt to be fairly expensive, but if you order blini you'll get a good sampling automatically and a more filling dish for the money. Blini, as mentioned, are dressed with melted butter and either sour cream or caviar, but not both. In the old days, plain blini (or bliny) might be rolled up, dipped in butter, and popped straight into the mouth (although that was considered macho or unpolished); but nowadays they are rolled up (preferably with two spoons, in the French fashion) and eaten with knife and fork. An order of blini is probably enough for two people to share; four diners should also order pelmeni or perogies and borscht. For main courses, look for kulebiaka, roasted game, or wildfowl; and beef lovers should take the chance to order stroganov or steak tartare—nobody does it better.

Polish restaurants will also have a variety of stuffed dumplings to start, and they may have smaller kulebiakis to be shared. Duck with apples is a classic dish, and there are many fine rabbit stews and ragouts as well; but the Polish are also masters of frequently overlooked organ dishes, such as brains and livers. In a Hungarian restaurant you will probably find a soup with dumplings and some type of perogi; for a main course, look for a veal goulash or paprikash, wild game (particularly boar), and goose or duck.

These meaty cuisines are suited to the hearty red wines of the region (the Hungarian wines aren't called "bull's blood" for nothing). Russians like the stronger and sweeter fortified sherries and ports and brandies. They drink a great deal of tea, thanks once again to the Mongols, who picked up the habit in China; it is brewed strong and diluted to taste with hot water.

COOKING AT HOME

A zakouski party is a great idea and can be the entire buffet if you like. Marinated mushrooms, pickled eggs, herring, cold ham or smoked turkey, and fish mousse or aspic is typical. And no party would be complete without at least some caviar.

Caviar should be kept cold until a few minutes before serving, and the entire container or bowl should be set in ice. You could even lay out a color wheel of caviars without going into bankruptcy if you are willing to pass on the very finest grades: Lumpfish roe is actually beigey-gray but is usually dyed either black or red. Cod roe is pink; salmon roe is orangey-red; whitefish is often golden (though not to be confused with the Iranian gold); flying fish roe is a deeper scarlet; and many new varieties from China and even the United States are pearly gray. (Unopened caviar will last several months; but once opened, caviar should be contact-covered and eaten within three or four days.)

Use small bone, lacquer, tortoise, shell, ivory, glass, or even wooden utensils to serve caviar, as silver gives it a metallic tang. Serve with toast triangles or fancy but not strongly flavored crackers and set out wedges of lemon, chopped hard-boiled egg, and sour cream. Other hors d'oeuvre that could be topped with caviar include small new potatoes cooled and cut in half or stuffed with sour cream; potato pancakes; beef or tuna carpaccio; or artichoke bottoms. The traditional beverages would be champagne, vodka, and aquavit.

Vodka is served ice-cold (it will not freeze, so the bottle can be left in the freezer compartment or even frozen inside blocks of ice in clean milk cartons), but not over ice, as the texture would be affected. You can buy vodkas flavored with hot pepper, caraway, saffron, anise, garlic, dill, lemon, cherry, even buffalo grass, but it's just as simple to pepper your own by dropping a jalapeño or even white or black pepper into the bottle and letting it steep anywhere from four days to two weeks, depending on your daring.

The Polish traditionally drink vodka with hors d'oeuvre but wine or beer with dinner. Beer, incidentally, is served in small tumblers, not huge mugs. Coffee is served after dinner, never with.

Incidentally, although most restaurants in the United States serve beef Stroganov over rice or buttered noodles, it was traditionally presented over very thick, fried potato wedges.

BEEF STROGANOV

1 1/2 pounds sirloin tip or filet
salt and pepper to taste
1 1/2 tablespoons flour
oil for cooking
butter (optional)
1 medium onion, chopped
1 cup bouillon or beef stock
1 teaspoon Dijon or Pommery mustard
1 1/2 tablespoons tomato paste
1/2 cup sour cream
minced parsley for garnish

Cut the beef into longish strips about 1/4-inch thick, season with salt and pepper, and sprinkle with flour. In a heavy-bottomed skillet, heat 1 tablespoon oil and 1 tablespoon butter (if you are using it) and begin browning beef in batches—only one layer at a time in the skillet—and remove browned meat to a plate. Repeat, adding a little oil and butter as needed, until all the beef has been sautéed; then add a little more oil and sauté onions until golden. Add stock, stir in mustard and tomato paste, and simmer until thickened; return beef to skillet and simmer for only 3 to 5 minutes. Remove from heat, stir in sour cream, adjust seasoning, and sprinkle with parsley.

Variations: Less expensive and/or leaner cuts of beef, such as rump roast or round steak can be used, but for these cuts you should increase the simmering time about 15 minutes or until the meat is tender. The oldest Russian recipes use less sour cream; Polish versions use more. Many people also like sliced mushrooms in their stroganov; if so, sauté them with the onions to reduce liquid. Other optional seasonings include a splash of red wine or brandy and a dash of worcestershire sauce.

BEEF SHASHLIK

1/2 cup dry red wine
juice of 1/2 lemon or 1 small lime
8 cloves garlic, minced
1 small onion, minced
1 tablespoon peppercorns, crushed
3 pounds boneless lamb or beef sirloin, cut in 1 1/2-inch cubes
3 small onions, cut into wedges
3 sweet peppers, seeded and cut into wedges
12–15 large mushrooms (optional)
12–15 cherry tomatoes or 3 tomatoes, cut into wedges (optional)
olive oil or vegetable oil spray
salt to taste

Combine wine, lemon or lime juice, minced garlic and onion, and peppercorns, and marinate meat, refrigerated, for 8 hours or overnight. Return to room temperature before cooking. Toss onions, bell pepper wedges, mushrooms, and cherry tomatoes (if you are using them) with olive oil or spray to coat; pat meat cubes slightly and alternate meat and vegetables on metal skewers. Grill or broil skewers, basting with marinade; serve with rice.

PART II

AFRICA

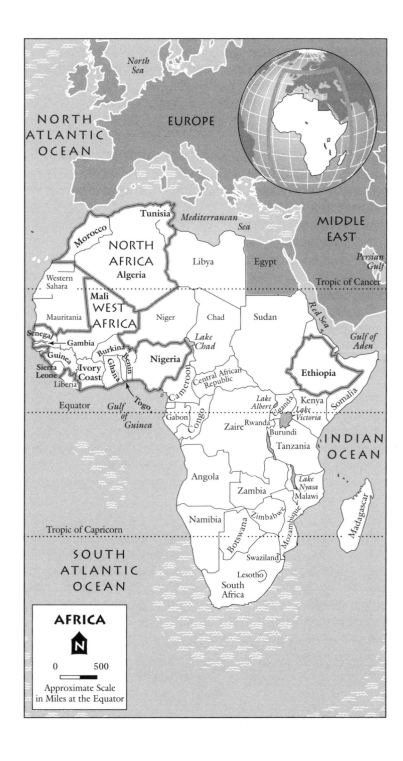

NORTH AFRICA

The most misleading thing about North African restaurants may be the name; for while Morocco, Algeria, and Tunisia are physically locked to the rest of Africa, they are culturally continents apart, their roots one-third in Europe and two-thirds in the Middle East.

These are Mediterranean countries, full partners in the creation of that cuisine, and their inhabitants speak French and Spanish as well as Arabic and Berber. Their rich food, served abundantly and enjoyed communally, conveys a panoply of civilizations. The Phoenicians brought in Lebanese wheat and Syrian olives and lentils and carried back Tunisian dates; they were also probably the first to sample nutmeg and cinnamon from Malaysia. The Carthagenians adopted West African okra and peanuts; the Persians tasted Afghani yogurt and mixed it with African honey and Asian almonds. The Greeks discovered Egyptian rice and traded it for lemons; the Romans transplanted Indian eggplants and dosed themselves with Indonesian garlic; the Moors planted orange trees in Spain. The Arabs imitated Mongol kebabs with Spanish mutton and Basque wildfowl and gave up Chinese tea in favor of Ethiopian coffee.

In Tunis and Algiers, the North Africans exchanged Lebanese chickpeas and Armenian melons for Italian sardines and French carrots. Once the Spanish returned from the New World with tomatoes, potatoes, and chilies, Mediterranean cuisine was all but complete.

THE COUNTRIES

North Africa is topographically as well as historically a part of Europe: The Atlas Mountains, which occupy most of the region, are part of the Alpine chain. Most of the arable areas are near the coast; the mountains and dune areas gradually give way, in the south, to the Sahara.

Morocco remains the most ethnically mixed area; the official language there is Arabic (the Alamite dynasty, established in 1660, remains on the throne), but many residents also speak Spanish, French, or Berber. The main crops are olives, fruit, grapes, and grain, and there is some industrial fishing as well.

Algeria is larger than its two neighbors, but much of the arid Saharan south is suitable only for livestock grazing. Algeria's principal crops are wheat and barley, potatoes, citrus fruits, tomatoes, tobacco, figs, and dates, as well as olives and grapes. In Tunisia, the most easterly of the three, sugar beets are also profitable. Livestock—sheep, poultry, goats, and cattle—are all commonplace.

THE HISTORY

Beginning halfway across the north coast of Africa and stretching just around the curve of its left hip, Tunisia, Algeria, and Morocco were settled by Berbers. These are a mysterious but ancient people, variously said to be related to the Phoenicians, the Celts, the Basques, and the Canaanites, and referred to in Egyptian wall paintings dating to about 2400 B.C. There are still several million Berber-speaking inhabitants of the North African region, and it is they who lent their name to the Barbary Coast, not the "barbarian" mercenaries of medieval pirate fleets.

The Berbers remained more or less unaffected by a millenium of Phoenician rule and rather prospered under their Roman successors. Rome invested heavily in roads and aqueducts in the region and planted groves of olives and dates and citrus fruits. The Roman occupation was

so successful that the Berbers were widely converted to Christianity—
St. Augustine was Algerian—and remained Christian for several hundred years.

However, the great Muslim Arab invasions of the seventh and eighth centuries marked a sea change in the Berber culture. The majority of the Berbers converted to Sunni Islam, and they became so prominent a part of the great westward Islamic expansion that the Spanish term for their Islamic conquerers, "Moors," actually derives from "Moroccan." (And despite Hollywood, very few Moors were either literally Arab or particularly dark-skinned.) During their centuries in Spain, the Moors transmitted so much of their agricultural and culinary knowledge to the Iberians that the ethnocentric French developed the saying, "Africa begins just south of the Pyrenees."

The Moors were finally driven back into North Africa, and after generations of invasions and counter-invasions, the empires settled into a somewhat uneasy coexistence. By the nineteenth century, however, the tactical importance of North Africa became more and more obvious to the European powers, and first British, then French, Spanish, Italian, and Maltese colonizers moved in. France and Spain ultimately agreed upon a division of power, and despite the German occupation of the region during World War II, French and Spanish people are still the primary European minorities.

THE CUISINE

The formal cuisine of North Africa is almost an oxymoron, as it is primarily a matter of family recipe, handed down orally from mother to daughter (cooks are almost uniformly female) and still susceptible to melting-pot influences. The staple carbohydrate of North African food is *couscous*, a semolina or millet meal that is not only nutritious but also cooks quickly and is increasingly popular as a rice alternative in the United States. In fact, couscous (the word can refer either to the pasta alone or to a prepared dish involving chicken, lamb, and vegetables) is far and away the best-known regional dish, eaten at least twice a week in the average North African home and popular not only in nearby Greece and Turkey but even as far away as Brazil.

Dishes are eaten by hand, using bread as a scoop and sauce mop, which explains why no place settings are needed (although restaurants in the United States frequently, and resignedly, supply them upon request). The one exception is couscous, which is eaten with a spoon. Since recipes are generally family variations passed down by word of mouth, there are almost no measuring cups or spoons, either: Large ladles, either worked metal or wood, are used for stirring the pot and turning the dish out on the table. Otherwise, North Africans basically get by with butcher and utility knives, a mortar and pestle for spices, perhaps a spatula or perforated spoon, and a charcoal brazier or plain open fire.

THE MAIN INGREDIENTS

MEATS AND FISH After couscous, lamb and poultry are the most commonly offered entrees, with goat a distant fourth; pork is almost unknown because of the heavy Muslim presence. Game meats may be offered on special occasions. (The dominant role of meat is by itself a clue to the heavy Middle Eastern influence on this coastal diet.) All North African meats are cooked until the meat falls off the bone, and they can—must—be eaten with the fingers (see "How to Order and Eat Like a Native," page 111). Lamb is typically spit-roasted (called *mechoui*). Grilling is a popular style of cooking and is used for chicken or game hens and sometimes skewers of beef or shrimp. Organ meats, particularly lamb brains, kidneys, and livers, are popular in Africa but more hesitantly offered by restaurants here, although they occasionally appear as sausage. Seafood may be fish or shrimp, with shellfish offered less frequently.

SIDE DISHES Vegetables are most frequently prepared as salads or marinated and served as appetizers or sometimes condiments: They include carrots, tomatoes, chickpeas, lentils, and eggplant. (Mediterranean lentils, incidentally, are smaller and darker than Indian lentils and do not soften as much in cooking.) Fruits include pomegranates, dates, and figs.

SEASONINGS The most characteristic condiments are a pair of chili pastes: a wetter one called *harisa* (or harissa), which combines garlic, chilies, and olive oil; and a dry paste, more popular in Tunisia, called *ras el hanut*, which uses roasted red chilies, black pepper, cinnamon, and cloves. Its Indonesian origins are striking, so on American menus it is often confusingly identified as curry—particularly in the case of "shrimp curry"—although some North African restaurants do make Indian-style cumin and lemon dishes.

The other most popular flavorings are honey, coriander, cumin, cinnamon, chestnuts, preserved limes and lemons, olives (green and black), gray verbena, mint, and *za'atar*, an intensely aromatic hybrid of thyme, marjoram, and oregano. Scented water, redolent of rose petals or verbena, is one of the most evocative remnants of Persian culture imaginable.

COUSCOUS

As we noted above, there are very few cooking utensils in North African cuisine, but the exception is for couscous. The traditional preparation of couscous requires its own dedicated steamer called, not surprisingly, a *couscousière*. It resembles a double boiler, with the stock (or in the more traditional manner, the main-course stew itself) in the lower pot and the grains in the upper bowl; perforations in the upper tray allow the steam to circulate and the couscous grains to absorb it. (One explanation for the name couscous is that it imitates the sound of steam escaping through the holes.)

Couscousières can be simple ceramic or iron pots or even elaborate copper; some cooks collect them in various sizes, as American cooks might acquire casseroles or saucepans. Interestingly, although Tunisians tend to cover the couscousière, Moroccans and Algerians leave it uncovered; hence, Tunisian couscous tends to be a little softer and moister and the others fluffier. Similarly, Tunisians more frequently mix the couscous directly into the stew before serving, while Moroccan and Algerian cooks tend to make a "bowl" of the cooked couscous on the plate and put the stew in the center.

The stew usually mixes lamb, chicken, and such vegetables as potatoes, carrots, onions, and greens; but there are as many variations as there are home cooks. Some are smoky-savory, such as the Djerba-style mixture with a jerky-like preserved lamb, dried sardines, and *tewebil*, a Tunisian-mixed spice paste of fennel and anise seeds, coriander seeds, caraway, red pepper, and so forth; some couscous versions are vegetarian, using fava beans instead of meat; and some are quite sweet, involving dates, raisins, and nuts.

The traditional drink with couscous is buttermilk; but more often nowadays you will be invited to select a North African wine or beer.

THE MAIN DISHES

SOUPS Dinner often begins with a soup—a substantial one, not a consommé—and the most popular is *harira*, a lentil soup made of lamb stock and flavored with lemon, onion, parsley, coriander, cinnamon, and perhaps tomatoes. Sometimes it appears with noodles, and it is occasionally thickened with eggs. The other most popular soup is a spicy thick chickpea soup with potatoes, ginger, and lamb or chicken stock.

The Arabic word for "soaked bread" is "gazpacho," and the Spanish learned it from the Moors, who used it for a version of the Persian *fettoush* of bread soaked in olive oil, lemon, and garlic. The Moors were expelled from Granada just as Columbus was running into North America, so they missed his triumphant return from the New World bearing tomatoes and peppers, which became the heart of Spanish gazpachos. Eventually, of course, the Spanish brought these vegetables to North Africa, where they became popular in salad form.

SIDE DISHES Salads are beautifully assembled and usually offered in combination—a fascinating display of texture, flavor, and color. Carrots might be shredded and dosed with cinnamon, lemon, and honey; green peppers and tomatoes are roughly chopped, dressed with olive oil and lemon, and sometimes studded with chilies. Eggplant is usually grilled or baked and then stirred with coriander, lemon, garlic, cumin, and oil—a lumpier adaptation of the Middle Eastern baba ganouj. Beets are also cooked before being dressed with oil and sometimes sugar. The fruit and nut mixes, usually orange with walnuts and lemon, sound familiar but get a distinctively Mediterranean twist with the addition of olives and even rosewater.

STUFFED PASTRIES AND PIES One of the most popular dishes besides couscous is called *bastilla* (which is one of the few dishes to receive varied spellings in America, showing up as bisteeya or bestila): It is a cross between pastry and chicken pot pie, a flaky filo-dough loaf stuffed with squab, game birds, or chicken, and flavored with ground almonds and powdered sugar.

A sort of family dish, popular among Tunisians in particular, is *brik*, a griddle-fried semolina pancake or tortilla that is filled with potatoes and onions and a raw egg before being folded up and fried; the egg cooks inside, and the brik winds up being a cross between a quesadilla and a frittata.

STEWS The most popular type of main-dish stews are *tajines*, or *tagines*, which are fruit-sweetened meat stews—again, usually chicken, flavored with preserved lemon and olive oil, but occasionally lamb stewed with prunes or dates—slow-cooked in earthenware pots with characteristic conical lids. Other lamb stews feature chickpeas and carrots, or honey and almonds.

Moroccans in particular are fond of meat salads, really organ-meat appetizers of brains or liver, but these are seldom offered in American restaurants, which depend heavily on set multicourse dinners. Some chefs will, if asked, rustle up kidneys. Similarly, vegetable tajines are quite common there, particularly on fast days, but such long-cooked dishes are not often seen on restaurant menus

SWEETS AND BEVERAGES Dessert may be elaborate sweet pastries with almonds or dates or fried couscous drizzled with honey; more frequently, it is "home-style," meaning just a bowl of fruit and nuts. North Africans most frequently drink tea or mint tea with their meals, and observant Muslim restaurant owners may not even apply for an alcohol license; but wine is more and more popular in the United States, and many owners seem to be importing North African cabernets in bulk.

HOW TO ORDER AND EAT LIKE A NATIVE

North African dining resembles Ethiopian in that bread is the sole utensil and the entire meal is served on a low, hourglass-shaped table. Rather than woven baskets, however, these tables may be elaborately carved and filigreed wood inlaid with mother of pearl and, especially at restaurants, may be surrounded by pillow-laden sofas, loveseats, and overstuffed ottoman stools rather than chairs. Typically, North African restaurants use fabrics in dark reds—burgundy, claret, maroon, brick, and rust—to evoke the traditional rugs and tent hangings.

As at Ethiopian restaurants, too, the use of the fingers for eating leads to an elaborate welcoming ceremony: At a Moroccan dinner, a servant or junior family member will pour water over each guest's hands into a basin and then offer the guest a towel; here, of course, the person performing these services is usually a waiter. In some cases, or in more casually Americanized restaurants, you may be offered a wet washcloth

Tread Lightly
Like formal Japanese restaurants, a few old-style Moroccan restaurants may require the removal of your shoes at the door (to preserve the rugs), but that is very rare in the United States. Still, remember the carpets, and wipe your feet.

instead of the water cascade; frequently the towel or cloth will be left behind, so that you may use it (subtly) to dab at spills. Another variation on this theme is the individual water bowl, into which you may dip your fingers between bites; but the natives lick their fingers rather than waste flavor.

Meals are served communally; all dishes are placed in the middle of the table, and diners help themselves from the platters. The bread served with the meal may be pita, either anise- or onion-flavored or plain, and either in roll form or flattish. Take a whole piece from the basket and put it on your plate; you may scoop with it, use it as a palate cleanser, or just squeeze it with your fingers to wipe them clean. If you want to spice things up, reach for the ever-present bowl of harisa and mix it into your stew.

The great majority of North African restaurants here offer only a few a la carte dishes; most have set multicourse menus, perhaps a large and a deluxe. Such package meals generally begin with soup and various vegetable salads, followed by bastilla, then a choice of the first main dish (usually chicken or perhaps seafood), then a choice of the second, meatier entree (lamb stew, long-roasted meat, kebab, etc.) and couscous. Remember, there is nothing under "well done," and the chili adjustments are made individually.

If you can order specific dishes, get one grilled meat, perhaps a kebab platter, and one tajine seasoned with olives or preserved lemons, and split a bastilla; for four, order a dip such as hummus, a vegetable salad, bastilla, one sweet stew, and one hot stew. For larger groups, definitely order a family-style couscous with sausages or lamb and chicken, raisins, chickpeas, parsley, and carrots.

The set-price dinners range depending on the number of courses and choices, but dinner will probably cost between $18 and $28 per person.

COOKING AT HOME

Because Moroccan food is generally cooked over braziers or grills—many North African cooks don't even own ovens—it is fairly simple to reproduce at home. Although you probably don't own a couscousière, you can use a colander over a pot; but if you prefer to buy quick-cooking couscous, you can make it in a regular saucepan.

The eggplant salad that follows, for example, would be grilled over a brazier, but the oven will do just fine. Get out those hot washcloths and a tablecloth that doesn't require dry-cleaning and throw around all the large pillows you own.

EGGPLANT SALAD, RABAT-STYLE

1 eggplant (about 1 pound)
1 clove garlic, peeled and slivered
2 tablespoons chopped parsley
2 sprigs chopped coriander (optional)
1/2 teaspoon paprika
1/2 teaspoon ground cumin
2 tablespoons olive oil
1–2 tablespoons lemon juice
salt to taste

Use the point of a knife to make slits in the whole eggplant, then stud it with garlic slivers. Bake in 400° oven until blackened, even blistered, and softened or "collapsed." Remove and let cool before rubbing off skin and squeezing pulp to release bitter juices (alternatively, scoop out pulp and drain in sieve). Discard liquid and mash or force pulp and garlic slivers through a food mill (do not blend or process—it would get too homogeneous). Add chopped herbs and spices and mix well; fry in oil over moderate heat, turning often with a spatula or perforated spoon, until all the liquid has evaporated and the eggplant is reduced to a thick dark jam (15–20 minutes). Sprinkle with lemon juice and adjust seasonings to taste. Serve warm or slightly chilled.

VEGETARIAN COUSCOUS

2 1/2 cups tightly packed fennel greens (or fresh dill, or a mixture)

1 cup tightly packed parsley leaves

1/4 cup tightly packed celery leaves

1/4 pound leeks, white and pale green parts (or scallions or a mixture)

1/2 cup chopped onions

1 cup chopped bulb fennel

1/4 cup olive oil

2 tablespoons tomato paste

2 teaspoons paprika

salt to taste

1/2 teaspoon ground coriander seed

1/2 teaspoon ground caraway seed

2 teaspoons dried red chili flakes or pepper sauce

1 cup defatted chicken broth or vegetable stock

1 1/2 cups uncooked couscous (not instant)

1 16-ounce can garbanzo beans, rinsed and drained

1 fresh green chili, minced

1 sweet bell pepper, cut in quarters

3 cloves garlic, peeled

1 small whole onion, studded with cloves

Wash, drain, and chop all greens; wash and chop leeks. Fill the bottom of a couscousière or double boiler with water and bring to boil; place perforated top, colander, or steamer dish over it and steam greens and leeks, covered, for 30 minutes. Drain, cool, and squeeze out excess moisture; set aside. Refill the bottom of the couscousière and bring back to boil.

Meanwhile, sauté chopped onions and fennel bulb until softened in olive oil; stir in tomato paste, paprika, salt, coriander, caraway, and chili and simmer until blended. Add stock and simmer 15 minutes more. Remove from heat and add uncooked couscous, stirring well; repeat with greens and leeks; finally, add the green chili, bell pepper chunks, garlic cloves, and whole onion. Place top back over boiling water, add cooked vegetables and garbanzos, and steam, covered, for another 30 minutes. Pour the cooked couscous mixture onto a tray, pick out the garlic cloves, bell pepper, and studded onion, and use serving fork to break up any lumps. Stir 1/2 cup water into couscous, cover with aluminum foil, and let rest in warm place for 10 minutes before serving.

Serve with harisa (available at Middle Eastern markets) or liquid pepper sauce.

Nonvegetarian variations: Add cubes of lean lamb to the skillet when adding the stock and before adding dry couscous, then add raisins before steaming and add cinnamon stick with clove-studded onion and garlic cloves (but remove it before serving). Add pan-browned chicken pieces to cooked vegetable mixture when it is placed in the top of the cous-cousière and before steaming, or pan-cook chicken separately and serve on the side.

QUICK COUSCOUS WITH CHICKEN

1 3-pound chicken, cut into serving pieces
salt and pepper to taste
2 tablespoons cooking oil
1 onion, sliced
1 large carrot, diced
3 garlic cloves, minced
1 28-ounce can peeled whole plum tomatoes, drained and chopped
(about 1 pound fresh tomatoes)
1 teaspoon ground cumin
1 teaspoon ground allspice
1/2 cup defatted chicken broth or vegetable stock
1/4 cup dry white wine
1/2 teaspoon dried red chili flakes, harisa, or other hot pepper sauce
2 small zucchini, diced
3 tablespoons tomato paste
1 15-ounce can cooked chickpeas, rinsed and drained
4 tablespoons chopped fresh cilantro or 3 tablespoons chopped fresh parsley
1 1/2 cups defatted chicken broth or vegetable stock
1 1/2 cups quick-cooking (sometimes called "instant") couscous
1 tablespoons butter or margarine (optional)

Rinse chicken, pat dry, and season with salt and pepper. Heat oil in large casserole or Dutch oven, brown chicken, and remove; add onion and carrots and sauté until softened; add garlic and cook until softened. Add tomatoes, cumin, and allspice and cook for 5 minutes, stirring; stir in stock, wine, red chili flakes and return chicken to casserole. Cover and simmer 15 minutes; add zucchini and simmer until chicken is tender (20–30 minutes more). Stir in tomato paste, add chickpeas and half the chopped cilantro or parsley, heat through, and serve.

While chicken is simmering, bring chicken broth (and butter if you are using it) to a boil and add quick-cooking couscous; stir well, cover, and turn off heat. Let couscous stand 5 minutes, fluff with fork, and spoon onto serving platter. Arrange chicken and vegetables around it, pour some sauce over the top, and garnish with remaining cilantro. Serve with harisa or other liquid pepper sauce.

ORANGE AND OLIVE SALAD

4 navel oranges
2 tablespoons black olives, slivered
1 tablespoons pine nuts, toasted
1/2 cup chopped fresh mint
1 tablespoon olive oil
1 clove garlic, minced
pinch sugar
pinch salt
1/2 teaspoon dried red chilies (more to taste)
1 teaspoon lemon juice (if needed)

Peel oranges, removing all pith, and remove skin from segments, working over a bowl to retain juice. Cut segments into bite-size pieces and mix with olives and pine nuts. Whisk together mint, olive oil, garlic, sugar, salt, chilies, and reserved orange juice, plus lemon juice if needed to thin. Adjust seasoning, toss gently, and refrigerate until serving.

ETHIOPIA

It's surprising that so many American diners let themselves be unnerved by the apparent difficulty of eating Ethiopian food. After all, in a country whose Big Three foods are hamburgers, pizza, and PB&J, eating with the hands is more familiar than using a fork. And unlike chopsticks, fingers require little practice.

Still, there is no denying that many first-timers feel extremely awkward faced with *kitfo* or *doro watt*. But any uncertainty can be erased in a matter of moments. Ethiopian food is deceptively simple—a breeze to order—delicious, nutritious, a rich choice for vegetarian diners, and a bargain as well. And the communal-platter style of service makes it a truly sociable experience. We only have one suggestion: Wear comfortable clothes, since you'll be leaning over the platter. And don't wear white the first time.

THE COUNTRY

Ethiopia is a roughly bell-shaped nation nearly twice the size of Texas, primarily made up of high plateaus—one reason it has been historically distinct from most of the rest of Africa—

BASIC CUISINE

DINNER FOR TWO:
Doro watt, beef alecha

DINNER FOR FOUR:
Doro watt, lamb with chili, kitfo, potato and carrot alecha

GROUP DISH:
Mesob

STYLE:
Spicy, soft, slightly sour

KEY FLAVORS:
Red chili, sourdough

DISTINCTIVE DISHES:
Watts, alechas, injera

EATING UTENSILS:
Fingers

UNIFORMITY OF MENUS:
Good

COST:
Inexpensive

"THANK YOU":
"Ama sekanada"

but divided diagonally down the middle by the Great Rift Valley. It's bounded by the Sudan to the northwest and west, Kenya to the south, and Somalia to the east. The northeast border, which meets the Red Sea, is the territory of Eritrea, which has struggled for independence against Italian, Egyptian, and Ethiopian forces all jealous of its coastal access: In fact, the name "Eritrea" comes from the Roman name for the Red Sea, *Mare Erythraeum*, and its ports were the region's earliest power centers.

(Although most restaurants in the United States refer to Eritrean and Ethiopian cuisine interchangeably, some are quite sensitive about the distinction. You can sometimes get a hint from the name of the establishment, since they are frequently refer to the owner's original home: Axum, Asmara, and Massawa are all in Eritrea; Addis Ababa, Diredawa, the Blue Nile—or the Abbai, as it's known there—and Harar are in Ethiopia proper. In addition, Italy's long domination of Eritrea has left behind the odd culinary clue, usually lasagna and seafood pasta.)

Ethnically, Ethiopia is fairly diverse, predominantly Christian but with large Muslim and other recognized minorities and with identifiable Greek, Armenian, Italian, Saudi, and Indian/Pakistani populations.

THE HISTORY

Though it is a troubled and undeveloped nation today, Ethiopia—the Abyssinia of mysterious allure—has many great civilizations in its past. According to legend, it was founded 3,000 years ago by Menelik I, offspring of the famous liaison between King Solomon and the Queen of Sheba (whose progenitor, the original Sheba himself, according to the Bible, was a direct descendent of Abraham). Ancient Egyptian records suggest that trade with Abyssinians stretched back a thousand years before that. And Ethiopia's great Lake Tana in the north is the fabled source of the Blue Nile, which drew so many oddly obsessive Europeans.

By the fifth century B.C., Ethiopia was a regular stop for Arab traders; 300 years later, the capital of Axum dominated Red Sea coastal trade and served as a juncture for the emerging Mediterranean civilizations, one source of the myriad ethnic minorities among its populace.

The country was officially converted to Christianity (Egyptian Coptic) in the fourth century. The first Jewish settlers probably arrived about 200 years after that, establishing a line of Beta Israel (children of

Israel) or "Falashas" that to this day have remained rigorously observant; some 25,000 of them were airlifted to Israel during the mid- and late 1980s. However, with the increasing power of the Islamic nations, Axum's role declined, and its ties to the Byzantine Empire were effectively severed. Isolated from the vital trade routes, the country gradually turned feudal and fractious.

Europeans—the Portuguese, as usual—began trading in the early sixteenth century, but Ethiopia had limited interest for the colonial powers until the opening of the Suez Canal in 1869, when it suddenly acquired strategic value. Italy bungled one invasion attempt at the end of the century, but in 1935 Mussolini succeeded in driving Emperor Haile Selassie (whose real name, Ras Tafari, became the password of his messianic cult) into exile. He was restored by British and South African forces in 1941 and brought the country into the United Nations; but it remained poor and oligarchical, with power in the hands of the few landowners. Selassie was deposed briefly in 1960 and permanently in 1974, launching a period of civil strife that, coupled with repeated drought and famine, has devastated this once-prosperous nation.

THE CUISINE

Though the main ingredients of Ethiopian cuisine are fairly straightforward and have remained almost unchanged at least since the importation of New World chilies, they are enhanced by intense and addictive seasonings that recall its years at the crossroads of the spice routes.

Introductory Ethiopian cuisine is as simple as one, two, three—one utensil, two stews, and three sauces. *Injera* is a spongy, slightly sour bread, made from fermented *tef*, that is napkin, plate, spoon, and staple all in one. *Watts* and *alechas* are the major types of stews, the first always spicy and the second either mild or hot. The three sauces—*berbere*, *awaz*, and *mitmitta*—are all hot; but the greatest of these is berbere.

THE MAIN INGREDIENTS

GRAINS AND STARCHES The Ethiopian economy is predominantly agricultural and rural; the vast majority of Ethiopians are subsistence farmers. The country's cultivation of barley, millet, and sorghum stretches back long before recorded history (they are still among its primary crops), and the millet-like tef (or teff) remains the staple starch.

Tef, the grain used in the making of authentic injera, is grown only in the Choke Mountains and is difficult and expensive to get over here, so those restaurants that offer the real thing may have slightly higher prices than the others (though no Ethiopian restaurant is ever very expensive). However, transplanted chefs have become quite adept at substituting other grains, and many of the buckwheat and soured wheat versions are very tasty. Along with grains, Ethiopian farmers rely on potatoes, peas, and plantains for starch.

MEAT AND PROTEINS Ethiopian farmers raise a variety of livestock: sheep, goats, cattle, and poultry. Not surprisingly, they consume beef, lamb (though not mutton), some goat, and a great deal of chicken. They raise animals not just for meat but also for eggs, milk, and a sort of clabbered cheese like sour cottage cheese. They are fond of certain types of organ meats, particularly tripe, though kidneys and livers do not interest them as much. (Many restaurants in the United States leave organ meats off their menus, as they are not popular here, but if you do like them, ask—they may be available anyway.) Those who either can't afford to or don't wish to eat meat get protein from peas, lentils, and peanuts.

Sometimes fish, and more frequently shrimp, are available, particularly in Eritrean restaurants. (Since Ethiopia proper is landlocked, a long list of seafood dishes is another clue to a kitchen's likely Eritrean background.)

FRUITS AND VEGETABLES   Greens, particularly cabbage, collards, and kale, are common, as are chickpeas and split peas, beans, tomatoes, carrots, potatoes, and cauliflower; slightly less common are eggplant and sweet potatoes. Lentils are so popular that some version of them often appears on your table automatically, almost as a condiment. Eritrea has a slightly broader range of produce, including citrus fruits and tobacco.

HOT SAUCES   Of the three prepared condiments, berbere is the most common and the most powerful. Berbere combines red chilies, cardamom, basil, and spices; like curry powders, it has a variable recipe but may include cloves, nutmeg, garlic, cinnamon, coriander, and ginger. (Because its resemblance to the North African harisa is so strong, one has to wonder whether berbere is, literally, Berber sauce.) Endorphin freaks in search of extra thrills will be happy to know that if a watt is somehow not hot enough, more berbere can usually be had as a condiment. *Awaze* is another chili mixture but is heavily studded with garlic and onion, while the drier mitmitta combines chilies and cardamom with coarse salt.

OTHER FLAVORINGS   Among herbs and spices, the most important are salt, cardamom, turmeric, and the ubiquitous red and sometimes green chili peppers. However, varieties of basil and garlic are frequently used, and nutmeg and cloves are added not only to stews but also to the rich, powerful Ethiopian coffee. Honey is both used as a seasoning and eaten straight from the comb.

Ethiopians tend vast hives of wild and domesticated bees, and guests are often served honeycomb and curds and whey—milk and honey, in other words.

THE MAIN DISHES
APPETIZERS   Since Ethiopians generally eat only (at most) two major meals a day, there are few distinct appetizers in the Western sense. Instead, fairly substantial snacks are eaten between meals, and those often appear on menus as appetizers. *Sambusas* are very similar to the Indian samosas; they come stuffed with either beef or lentils and perhaps potatoes and are usually spicy. Another popular snack is *quanta*, a salt- and berbere-cured beef jerky.

VEGETABLE DISHES   Despite the relatively heavy presence of meat on menus, Ethiopians have also developed a fondness for meatless stews—a virtue of necessity, in fact, since more than half the traditional Ethiopian calendar is given over to fast days. The Ethiopian vegetarian dishes have become the mainstay of the Jamaican Rastafarians, who have made Selassie's native cuisine into a dietary requirement.

Yemiser watt is the hot lentil stew; *yeduba watt* is pumpkin, and there is frequently a mildly spicy cabbage and carrot combination that may reconcile all those whose taste for cabbage was demolished in elementary school cafeterias. Also, a variety of greens are usually available, particularly collards, kale, and spinach; occasionally there may be zucchini as well.

MEATS   Ethiopians dearly love beef, perhaps because they were so often forbidden to eat it; and they love it not only stewed but also raw. *Kitfo* is the Ethiopian steak tartare, minced by hand and spiked with chili and kibbeh, the clarified butter. (In Ethiopia, men often devour whole slabs of raw meat around the table, biting into it and slicing off a chunk before passing it on. Americans are unlikely to witness this event; but if you do ever find yourself in such a group, dip the meat into the berbere dish first.)

Tere sega is similar, but the meat is served in cubes rather than hand-chopped (sort of like the difference between the chili in Texas and New Mexico). *Yesiga watt* is a braised beef stew. *Tibbs* is cooked meat, beef or sometimes lamb, and may be breast meat or ribs; *adulis tibbs* is usually charcoal-grilled. (In comparison to watts and alechas, which are simmered, tibbs is more apt to be dry-cooked or grilled before being sauced—something like the difference between "wet" and "dry" barbecue in the United States.)

When meat is combined with a vegetable, it is more likely the flavoring than the primary ingredient: *Zilb* is collard greens with lamb; *bozena shuro* is yellow split pea stew flavored with beef. *Dulet* is tripe, which is frequently stuffed with spiced vegetables and braised with honey and may be offered as a watt; it may also be mixed with livers.

STEWS   Again, there are two major types to choose from, the watts and the alechas (or alichas). This mnemonic may be helpful: "Watt" (also spelled "wat" or "wot") rhymes with "hot" and appropriately recalls "wattage," and it's the spicier version, thanks to the berbere mixed in. Alechas range from mild to moderately spicy. Both watts and alechas include *niter kibbeh* (or *kebbeh* or *kibe*), a seasoned clarified butter that resembles the Indian *ghee*.

Almost any ingredient—meat, seafood, poultry, or vegetable—can be prepared as either a watt or an alecha. *Yebeg watt* is lamb. During fast days, lentils and chickpeas are sometimes mashed and used as "mock chicken" in much the same way the Chinese use tofu. And a *fitfit*, or *fir-fir*, is a watt with bits of injera stewed right in.

POULTRY   Chicken dishes are extremely popular—particularly *doro watt*, which is probably as close to a national dish as there is; it's a stew of chicken pieces, hard-boiled eggs, and berbere. Chicken alecha is also very popular and is frequently sweetened lightly with honey. In some areas, other fowl such as quail may occasionally be offered.

BEVERAGES   Both of the region's fermented drinks, beer and the honey-based mead called *tej*, are extremely old—but no less powerful for age, particularly the deceptively sweet tej. Ethiopia may also be the origin of coffee, which grows wild in the mountains; and "double-boil" is a strong version drunk after meals.

HOW TO ORDER AND EAT LIKE A NATIVE

Ethiopian tables are fascinating things, large handwoven hourglass-shaped baskets with a lip around the surface and conical witches'-hat lids that make them look like the hives of huge African termites. (They might be modeled after beehives, a symbol of fertility and richness.) The table surface is a little low by American standards, and the chairs are also woven, with rounded backs for lounging, so that diners accustomed to pulling their knees up under the table—and having the tabletop safely between the mouth and the lap—may find that the distance between cup and lip leaves room for many a slip.

Most restaurants in the United States are furnished with the usual dinette table; but given a choice, you should really try the basket style; somehow, leaning forward to pick up your food and then leaning back in your chair reinforces the sociability of the occasion—it becomes part of the rhythm of conversation.

Traditionally, since diners will be eating with their hands, restaurants provide a pitcher of water and a basin with a sort of colander in the

Made up in pizza-sized rounds and served (usually folded in fourths) in a basket, injera should be torn into small pieces and used to soak up sauce or pinch up bite-sized morsels of the other dishes; then you pop the whole tidbit into your mouth. As in most cultures, you must use only your right hand. If you are making a fuss over someone, or honoring a guest, you may prepare such mouthfuls and hand-feed your friend, in which case these tidbits are called *gurshas*. Do not pass them hand to hand, however. Whatever main dishes you order are poured out for you on a larger and perhaps thinner sheet of injera; you may tear off pieces of the infused injera and eat that, too. You may also lightly squeeze the injera to remove excess oil or seasonings from your fingers (don't wring it out, though) and eat it plain.

middle. The waiter places the basin before you and pours the water over your hands while you rub them together and then dry them on the towel (remember, it is not a napkin) that is handed to you. Then a large round flat platter of injera, topped with mounds of the dishes you've ordered, is placed on the top of the table.

Most restaurants offer wine and beer (either Western-style or the wheat-based *talla*) along with tej, which is usually sold by the bottle or glass. However, if you order tej in a traditional-style restaurant, it may be served as it is there, in large, narrow-necked, and slightly tricky bottles called *bereles*, which are somewhere between a flask and a glass. In the traditional manner, the host may pour a little tej into his palm and taste it, just as a host or sommelier would taste wine; the custom in that case is for the taster to grimace, as if the quality is not up to the guest's due, and for the guest to exclaim over its flavor.

Ethiopian restaurants are among the best bargains in any case, but if you can't decide what you want, you might order the *mesob*, or sampler platter; most restaurants will have at least one mesob with meat and one without. The meals are surprisingly filling, so even if there are appetizers available, you may want to skip them (four people could order sambusas). Also, remember that meat dishes usually come with a vegetable on the side.

Two people should order one watt, preferably doro watt, and one alecha, beef or perhaps shrimp; if you don't like hot spices, order one alecha and one tibbs. (It may also help to know that most vegetable dishes are fairly mild.) If you have a group of four diners, one person should certainly order kitfo and another doro watt; with all the injera, a third dish may be all you need, but good additional choices would be chili-dressed lamb or shrimp and the potato-carrot stew.

COOKING AT HOME

To be honest, making injera at home is not hard—it's like making large crepes, using the bottom of a nonstick or well-seasoned cast-iron skillet—but unless you can find tef, it's not really the same. There are also imitation recipes involving pancake mixes (see below), but you should try to buy some real injera. Alternatively, serve doro watt with pita or Indian flat bread or even rice. Similarly, first- or even second-time Ethiopian chefs may wish to substitute harisa, available at many Middle Eastern markets, for homemade berbere, although the recipe below uses mostly familiar ingredients.

QUICK INJERA

3 tablespoons all-purpose flour
1 1/2 cups sourdough or buckwheat pancake mix
1/4 teaspoon baking soda
1 12-oz. bottle club soda
1 1/2 cups water

Combine flour, pancake mix, and baking soda in a large bowl. Whisking or stirring constantly, slowly but continuously pour in club soda and then water until the batter is smooth and fairly thin.

Meanwhile, heat a nonstick or seasoned 9-inch skillet over moderate heat. (Test the heat by dropping a spoonful of batter into the pan—it should solidify instantly but not brown). Lift the skillet off the heat, pour in 1/4 cup of batter, and tilt the pan to spread evenly. Cover partly and cook just a minute, or until tiny air holes turn the top spongy while the bottom is dry (but not crisp or brown). Remove this piece to a plate and pour in more batter; you should end up with about 8 or 9 pieces altogether.

To serve, place 4 or 5 pieces around the inside of a basket, overlapping them like petals; fold the others into quarters and arrange them in the middle.

BERBERE PASTE

1/4 teaspoon ground allspice
1/4 teaspoon ground cardamom
1 teaspoon ground ginger
1/2 teaspoon ground coriander
pinch ground cloves
pinch ground cinnamon
1/2 ground nutmeg
1/4 cup minced onions
1 tablespoon minced garlic
2 tablespoons salt
1/4 cup dry red wine (not cooking wine)
1 1/2 cups paprika
2 tablespoons cayenne
1/4 teaspoon black pepper
1 cup water
dash vegetable oil

In a nonstick or enameled heavy saucepan, toast first 7 ingredients, shaking the pan to keep them from scorching, until hot and fragrant. Cool, then combine with onion, garlic, half the salt, and wine into a blender and process at high speed into a smooth paste. Return saucepan to heat and briefly toast paprika, cayenne, pepper, and remaining salt, again shaking the pan to prevent sticking. (Don't lean over the skillet, because the aroma may burn your eyes or throat.) Lower heat, whisk in water in a slow stream, then add paste. Stirring constantly, cook on very low heat for 15 minutes. Scrape into jar, and tap the jar on the counter to remove air pockets. Let cool, then top with a thin film of oil. Cover with plastic wrap and refrigerate. Always replace the oil film after use; this way the paste will keep for several months.

DORO WATT

1 3-pound chicken, cut into serving pieces
1/4 cup lemon juice
1 tablespoon salt
1 tablespoon black pepper

2 cups chopped onion
4 tablespoons (1/2 stick) unsalted butter
1 tablespoon minced ginger
1/2 teaspoon ground fenugreek or anise
1/2 cup berbere paste
1/2 cup dry wine, preferably white
1 cup water or broth
4 eggs, hard-cooked and peeled

Rinse chicken and pat dry; rub with lemon juice, salt, and pepper and let it marinate. Meanwhile, melt butter in a skillet and bring it to a boil; as soon as it is covered with white foam, reduce heat to the lowest setting and let it cook undisturbed until the milk solids separate at the bottom. Pour off clarified oil and reserve.

Spray heavy enameled or nonstick casserole very lightly with cooking spray; cook onions over moderate heat for about five minutes, until soft and dry. Then add clarified butter and berbere and heat to simmer; add wine and water or broth, bring mixture to a light boil, and let it bubble until thickened. Dry chicken again and add to casserole, turning to coat with sauce; reduce and simmer, covered, about 15 minutes.

With a fork, puncture the whites of the eggs in several places and add them to the saucepan; cover again and cook until chicken is tender (about 15–20 minutes). Turn out into platter and serve.

WEST AFRICA

BASIC CUISINE

DINNER FOR TWO:
Akras or fried yucca, grilled fish, chicken in peanut or coconut sauce

DINNER FOR FOUR:
Grilled shrimp, yam croquettes, chicken yassa, bluefish chebjen

GROUP DISH:
Calaloo

STYLE:
Nutty, creamy, smoky

KEY FLAVORS:
Palm oil, hot chilies, peanuts, okra, yam

EATING UTENSILS:
Fingers, spoons

DISTINCTIVE FOODS:
Gumbos, peanut stews, spicy fish

UNIFORMITY OF MENUS:
Limited

NUTRITIONAL INDEX:
High starch, high cholesterol

COST:
Inexpensive

"THANK YOU":
"Dieuredieuf" (Senegalese); "Odima," "Adupe," or "Avo" (Nigerian); "Merci" (French Mali, etc.)

The emergence of West African restaurants in the United States is a recent phenomenon—and oddly appropriate. For though West Africa was exhaustively exploited by supposedly benign European colonizers, West African cuisine absorbed virtually nothing from European food; the cultures remained intractably segregated. On the other hand, though they were not so benignly imported, West Africans had an indelible influence on American food; and now the United States is returning the favor by providing a wealth of ingredients and a hospitable market.

It was primarily transported Gambian slaves, long accustomed to cultivating rice in their swampy river valleys, who brought prosperity to the South Carolina and Georgia rice plantations and a whole new cuisine to the Caribbean, by transporting and transplanting rice, yams, peanuts, black-eyed peas; they sent home corn, okra, coconuts, hot peppers, plantains, and string beans which had been gathered between South and Central America and home. In some areas, West African cooking and words can be found almost unchanged after 300 years:

The word *gumbo*, used for one of the most famous Southern dishes, comes from *gombo*, a West African term for okra. Africans were literally sold for peanuts in South America; they returned good for evil by transplanting them in North America.

But Americans owe much more than peanuts to the West Africans. Homesick slaves not only preserved traditional "soul food" but also helped stew up the trendy Creole cuisine and a fair portion of Cajun as well. And just recently, with the development of an educated, entrepreneurial black middle class whose members are inclined to take advantage of modern techniques and trends, West African cuisine has begun to evolve in a calculated manner. Like West African textiles and music, the food speaks of home to thousands of black Americans who have never laid eyes upon Africa itself. To American Southerners both black and white, the obvious resemblance between West African cuisine and soul food—"gitchee cooking," as it is called in the Carolina and Georgia island patois—can be eye-opening.

THE COUNTRIES

The West Coast of Africa—the area around and under the dip of ice cream on the cone of the African continent—is widely, if not densely, populated; more than 200 languages are spoken within Cameroon alone. The countries of the region include Ghana, Nigeria, Togo, Mali, Benin, Senegal, the Ivory Coast, Sierra Leone, Guinea, and Gambia.

The topography of the region swings from sandy beach to savannah, from plateau to forest, from swamp to desert. There are great networks of rivers whose names ring in history—the Niger, the Volta, the Gambia—and cities built entirely on stilts and traversed by canals rather than roads. The coastal areas, particularly Gambia, have become busy tourist attractions in the post-*Roots* era. But the region is still predominantly agricultural and thus susceptible to widespread famines, such as the ones that began in the 1970s.

In terms of religion, West Africa is a mix of indigenous cults—the Yoruban tradition in particular remains influential, having taken root in Haiti (and hence Louisiana) as voudon and in Brazil as Candomble—and Catholicism and Islam, in various proportions. Consequently, a substantial number of vegetarian dishes are prepared, particularly during the Lentan and Ramadan fasting seasons. There are also identifiable Indian,

Lebanese, and Arab minorities, whose members have added to the mix their own bits of culinary variety (curries in particular, and the occasional fried samosa).

THE HISTORY

West Africa was the site of several great empires, beginning with the Nok in Nigeria; by 2000 B.C., they had mastered iron- and tinworking, and their terracotta work was highly sophisticated. In Ghana, a great trading power dominated the trans-Saharan caravan routes for some 800 years before declining in the thirteenth century; and in the fourteenth century, Timbuktu was a byword of Islamic scholarship.

The primary European colonial influences were the Portuguese, who were the first traders to heavily exploit the West African market, beginning in the mid-fifteenth century; the British, who established their influence particularly in Ghana, Nigeria, and Gambia; and the French, who maintained at least some control over "French West Africa"— 2,000,000 square miles of it—into the 1960s. The region also endured colonial incursions by the Dutch, the Belgians, the Germans, and even the Danish, but it has one irrevocable historical tie to America: the slave trade, which the Portuguese initiated even before the New World was discovered.

The slave trade had a triangular pattern: From Europe, ships filled with rum, textiles, jewelry, some money, and guns would sail south to Africa and buy slaves; then the slavers headed west to the Caribbean and American coasts to exchange the slaves for cotton, tobacco, molasses, and coffee, which were destined for Europe. At the trade's height in the seventeenth century, Europeans were buying an estimated 20,000 slaves a year, and the general assumption that Africa existed entirely for commercial exploitation is reflected in the fact that contemporary maps read like commodity exchange reports: the Slave Coast, the Ivory Coast, the Gold Coast. (It also says much about why hotels and "establishment" restaurants in West Africa still have French or Portuguese menus.)

THE CUISINE

Traditional West African food, although hearty and comforting, can seem heavy, starchy, and overcooked to American palates—as veterans

Although it is evolving toward a lighter style, traditional West African cuisine can be both starchy and fatty, particularly the stews. The primary oils are palm and palm kernel oil, which are extremely high in cholesterol. Although nutritional concerns have persuaded some restaurants in the United States to experiment with other cooking oils, few have actually switched, because the flavor of palm oil is quite characteristic and difficult to reproduce. Also, many stews are given extra flavor and "body" by the addition of organ meats or offal, which are high in cholesterol and fat. And although okra is quite low in fat, the other common thickeners—manioc, coconut milk, and peanuts—are anything but.

of southern U.S. soul food can testify. This is partly because the diet was heavily dependent on starch to begin with and was often stewed with a small bit of salted pork or fish for flavor.

In the poorer areas, cattle and goats had to be butchered conservatively, as milk was a much more reliable source of protein than meat. Black-eyed peas, peanuts, and soybeans provided additional protein but not much flavor; hard-cooked eggs were often substituted as well.

It was also true that what meat there was, primarily mutton and beef, tended to be lean and somewhat stringy. Even in the more prosperous regions, where goats, lambs, and even oxen were also raised for meat (depending upon the dietary restrictions of various religions), meat had to be tenderized, by either pounding, marinating, long cooking, or all three. Meat was also typically "stretched"—thickened with okra, manioc flour, or peanut butter.

In the coastal and river delta regions, of course, there was protein aplenty from the fish and shellfish. (And one of the characteristics of coastal West African cuisine is that meat and fish are frequently stewed together.) Yams and rice were always available, however, and revered for their reliability and versatility. In Ghana, the Ashanti use yams in the rituals that celebrate birth, death, marriage, and sometimes the survival of a serious illness or accident.

THE MAIN INGREDIENTS

GRAINS Rice is the major starch here, but maize and the cornlike millet are also heavily planted, and a manioc flour is pounded from the cassava root. All of these starches can be left to sour, thus providing greater variety of flavors.

MEATS AND SEAFOOD West Africans raise chickens, pork, goats, sheep, and some beef. A fair variety of fish—primarily red snapper, croaker, and bluefish—are available; but shellfish, particularly shrimp, is far more common there than one would realize from reading American African menus. (Cameroon, after all, was named by the Portuguese for its abundance of fine prawns, or *camarones*.) Giant freshwater snails are considered a delicacy there, and some restaurants here compromise by offering French-style escargots.

POULTRY Along with the chickens, which are prized for their eggs, West African farmers raise turkeys, ducks, and guinea hens. In some areas, small wildfowl and even songbirds are consumed (although you're not likely to see that on a menu).

VEGETABLES AND PRODUCE Tomatoes and onions are extremely popular and are used in the most popular sauces, either as a stew or sweetened and thickened into a sort of barbecue sauce. Okra's prominence is obvious, and other common vegetables include eggplant, greens (usually spinach or cassava), string beans, carrots, cabbage, potatoes, sweet potatoes, and sweet peppers.

> ### Dine 'n' Debate
>
> Many West African cafes in the United States do quadruple duty as market stall, open-air dining room, political debating stage, and lively late-night hangout. That's because restaurants aren't just commercial establishments in West Africa, but cultural and political centers as well. In the major cities, the town square serves as marketplace by day, open-air restaurant bazaar at dusk, and political rally center by night. This central role of the market is one reflection of a strong matriarchal tradition; in Africa, the women who manage the markets have the greatest grassroots influence. In Togo, such women are addressed as "Nana Benz," because so many drive Mercedes-Benzes.

FRUITS Though most Americans would be surprised to be reminded of it, many areas of coastal Africa are tropical in the truest sense, and there are plentiful fruits, including bananas and plantains, pineapples, oranges, papayas, and mangoes. The palm nuts and coconuts provide essential cooking oils and fats; we may have to limit those fats today, but they were essential to many West Africans, whose meat consumption was limited.

SEASONINGS Among the most common herbs and spices are fiery habanero peppers (although many West African restaurants in the

United States pull their punches on peppers), ginger, mint, and scallions, plus a black pepperlike seed called "grains of paradise" that predates the pepper trade and remains a characteristic flavoring in West Africa; here, pepper usually substitutes. Sorghum is widely raised, and its molasses, along with some wild honey, provides the major sweetener.

THE MAIN DISHES

FIRST COURSES   Full-service restaurants are rare in West Africa. Outdoor vendors hawk barbecued turkey legs, beef brochette, grilled fish, or fried yam balls to be eaten while talking or shopping. Consequently, West Africans here enjoy lingering over appetizers, particularly fried sweet potatoes (one term for this is *patate sauté*) or fried plantains; peppery goat soup; or tomatoes dressed in a tangy turmeric-flavored "vinaigrette"—really, an emulsion thick as hollandaise or mayonnaise and served with almost everything.

Akras are salt cod fritters, the precursors of those popular in the Caribbean, served with a spanky green chili dip. Smoked fish sometimes appears as a spread, and occasionally seafood is offered fried. Hard-cooked eggs and, among the more acclimated cafes, grilled shrimp and chicken tidbits are popular. *Kose* is a stew of black-eyed peas flavored with chicken gizzards; it appears either as a first course, like a heavy salad, or as a main dish.

BREADS AND STARCHES   Rice still dominates in West African cuisines, although a few restaurants offer millet grains instead. There is almost no baked bread, but there are cornbreads, flatbreads, and the slightly sour fermented dough called *akassa* (corn) or *gari* (manioc). *Kpekple* is a cornmeal mush or farina frequently served with stewed fish.

POULTRY   Chicken and eggs are both extremely popular, and scrambled or hard-cooked and chopped eggs are often paired with beans and rice in place of meat. Poultry may be smoked, grilled, barbecued, or stewed. Among the most common dishes are chicken stewed with cassava and palm oil; chicken stewed with vegetables and ground peanuts or peanut butter (in Togo called *azidessi* and in Senegal called chicken *maffee*); and *moyo de poulet fumé*—smoked chicken braised with peppers, tomatoes, and onions. Grilled chicken may come sauced either with the barbecue sauce or a strong, lemony marinade often called *yassa*.

SEAFOOD   Fish may also be smoked or dried as well as fresh-caught and grilled, fried, or braised. Very fresh raw fish is sometimes filleted, salted, and then "cooked" ceviche-style in a mixture of coconut milk, lime juice, grated vegetables, and peanut oil, but it is rarely vinegar-cured as it is in the Caribbean. *Shika shika* is a lemon-flavored braised fish, often red snapper; croaker and other small fish are often fried and served with a hot sauce for dipping. *Cheb jen*, a spicy tomato-sauced bluefish, is a particular Senegalese favorite, served with rice. Some restaurants offer a sort of Americanized Africanized crab imperial—crab meat mixed with green onions, celery, garlic, and (here, at least) bread crumbs, but with the telltale addition of habanero peppers.

MEATS AND STEWS   Although the average quantity of meat in West Africa has improved, spit-roasting or grilling goat and lamb is still a mark of abundance or hospitality. Whole roast suckling pig and whole roast lamb are available at many restaurants with advance notice. Pork is often smoked and served with greens in a manner soul-food aficionados will find extremely familiar. Organ meats and offal (the original chitterlings and ham hocks) are frequently included in stews.

Kpete (or *kepete*) is a stew originally prepared primarily for banquets and festivals (for which there are frequent excuses); traditionally it features lamb, but sometimes cooks substitute goat or even occasionally duck. The lamb is butchered and the blood mixed with salt to prevent its coagulating; the meat is rubbed with garlic, bay, and pepper or grains of paradise and allowed to marinate before being stewed with the almost ritually scrubbed intestines (forerunner of the American chitterlings), the blood, the chilies, and the onions.

As we mentioned above, many stews combine beef, smoked fish, and okras, flavored with palm nuts or ground melon seeds. A particularly festive dish called *calaloo* combines spinach, lamb, shrimp, fish, and crabs and is served with cornmeal cakes; it sounds more like a translation of "paella" than Caribbean calaloo and may be the ancestor of jambalaya.

BEVERAGES   Traditionally, meals were eaten with water or palm wine, but West Africans under European influence—particularly those in the United States—have shifted to cocktails and beer. (Among the most popular brands is the super-economy-sized Maruka.)

Although many West Africans enjoy tossing huge all-day, all-village feasts or noshing their way through the market, commercial dining establishments were traditionally reserved for the European colonials and tourists. Consequently, West African restaurants in the United States are struggling with the formalities—trying to organize their menus in a recognizable (that is, "foreign") form and yet offer traditional cuisine. Portion size varies widely; you may want to ask just how large some appetizers actually are. Recipes are a matter of family tradition: Spicing runs the gamut, and even two versions of chicken with peanut butter may taste quite different. Nor is there much standardization of names; menus list a confusing mishmash of French, African, and English dishes. However, most thoughtfully provide "translations" or descriptions.

Gnamacoudji, an Ivory Coast specialty, is a sort of mint-ginger ale mixed with pineapple juice and sugar.

HOW TO ORDER AND EAT LIKE A NATIVE

In West Africa, many dishes—grilled fish, for one—are eaten by hand to prevent extraneous flavors from interfering. Consequently, it is traditional in West African, as in Ethiopian, restaurants to bring guests a basin of water to rinse their hands; as a matter of fact, guests are greeted this way even in private homes. However, many restaurants in the United States do not expect American patrons to eat with their fingers and will automatically set the tables with foks and spoons.

Two people will eat handsomely on an order of akras or fried yucca, a grilled fish dish, and chicken in peanut or coconut stew; four can probably consume some grilled shrimp, yam croquettes, a chicken yassa, and Senegalese-style bluefish chebjen. If kpete or calaloo is available, by all means order one or both.

COOKING AT HOME

No particular equipment is needed to prepare these dishes; in fact, African kitchens are quite spare, and dishes indoors are usually stewed, while larger roast animals or grilled fish or chicken are prepared outdoors. If you wish to try food finger-style, consider beginning with brochettes of beef or shrimp and warming your guests up to the idea of the chicken.

SMOKED CHICKEN STEW

1 medium smoked chicken, skinned and quartered
1 28-ounce can peeled tomatoes chopped, with juice
2 onions, thinly sliced
1/4 cup chicken stock, broth or water
1 tablespoon oil
1/2 tablespoon dark worchestershire-style sauce or soy sauce
2 habanero chilies, pierced two or three times with the tip of a knife

Place all ingredients in a dutch oven. Bring to a boil, reduce heat, and simmer uncovered for about 30 minutes. Serve hot over rice.

Variations: Add 2 tablespoons peanut butter; add 1/2 cup tightly packed fresh greens.

VEGETARIAN GUMBO

1 cup fresh black-eyed peas
1 cup loosely packed dark greens (spinach, kale, collards, etc.)
1 pound small fresh okra, stems trimmed
2 ripe tomatoes, peeled, seeded and chopped
(or 1 28-ounce can plum tomatoes)
1 habanero pepper or 2 jalapeños or bird chilies, halved and seeded
pinch ground coriander
salt and pepper to taste

Boil peas until almost done (time will depend on size, but test after about 10 minutes); drain. Rinse greens, leaving water on leaves. In heavy saucepan combine peas, okra, greens, tomatoes, and pepper; simmer 15 minutes or until okra is tender. Season to taste and serve over rice.

Variation: This can be used as a sauce for fish, chicken, or crab, or a little smoked pork or smoked fish can be stirred in.

PART III

THE MIDDLE EAST, PERSIA, AND INDIA

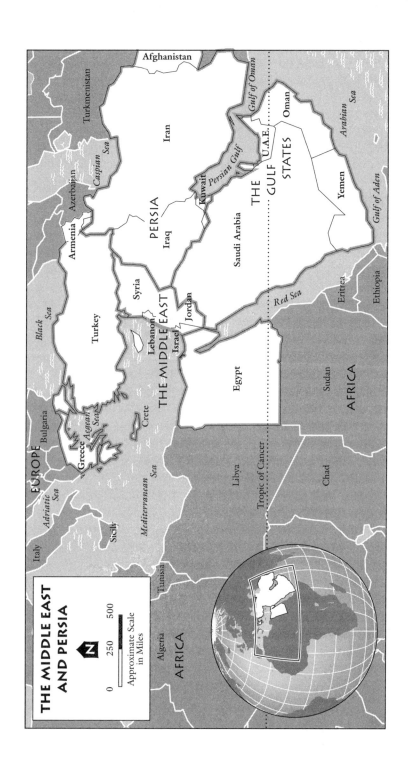

THE MIDDLE EAST AND PERSIA

Approximate Scale in Miles

0   250   500

GREECE AND TURKEY

On those old literary gazetteers of Western civilization, a great "X" must have marked this spot—the Aegean Sea between Greece and Turkey, where a pinwheel of road signs pointed toward Byzantium, Tyre, Mesopotamia, Macedonia, Persia, Egypt, Rome, Jerusalem. Troy lay here, and Crete, with its bulldancers. Odysseus roamed this region, and Xerxes and Alexander the Great and Suleiman the Magnificent and Barbarossa and Lord Byron, who swam across the Dardanelles and died fighting for Greek independence.

This area, which has always had such an immense hold over our imaginations, has had only a secondary place in our culinary affections, probably because up until relatively recently, the importation of many ingredients essential to Greek cooking—the grape leaves and goat cheeses and in particular the olive oils—was slow and unregulated and the quality questionable. Greeks restaurateurs only rarely prospered beyond the family-kitchen level, and Greek tavernas, with their hearty, village-tradition manners, were generally considered glorified greasy spoons.

Fortunately, both the cultural and commercial gaps have narrowed dramatically. Extra-virgin olive oil is a staple even in chain supermarkets, and fine calamata olives and grape leaves, *kasseri* and *kefalotiri* cheeses, and even the unmistakably resin-flavored retsina wine are readily available at specialty markets and food boutiques. Improved refrigeration and storage has allowed for a lighter touch in the grilling of fish and meat, thus bringing Greek food more into line with the American palate. Greek chefs in the United States have also modified the amount of oils cooked into dishes and left more to diners' discretion, broadening its appeal even further.

(In this chapter, Turkish cuisine refers primarily to the cooking of that portion of Turkey that lies in Europe and of the westernmost portion of Asian Turkey. Central and western Turkish cuisine more nearly resembles other Middle Eastern styles, shading toward the Persian influence; see the chapter on the Middle East for more information.)

THE COUNTRIES

Separated by a strait of water as thin as one mile in some places, Greece and Turkey together stretch from the Ionian Sea on the west to Iran and the Black Sea to the east. They literally "bridge" Asia and Europe: A small portion of Turkish territory lies north of the Dardanelles (the classical Hellespont) and the Bosporus in continental Europe. Though both have fairly large land masses, neither has much arable territory: Greece is three-quarters mountains, and the great central plateau of Asian Turkey called Anatolia lies above 3,000 feet, with only strips of coastal lowland. Greece has no navigable rivers (a situation that contributed to the early and jealous statism of its people); Turkey, which is fed by the Tigris and Euphrates, among other rivers, is able to cultivate more grains and fruit.

Both countries produce corn, wheat, citrus fruits, olives, tomatoes, grapes and currants, beets, and potatoes; Turkey also produces a fair crop of rye, oats, and rice. Sheep and goats are plentiful in the entire region, but cattle, which require more grazing territory, are more common in Turkey. Pigs are popular in certain areas of the Greek islands. Chickens, of course, are ubiquitous; lemon-rubbed and rotisserie-grilled chicken was a Greek staple long before U.S. fast-food restaurants picked it up.

This is one of the oldest wine-making regions of the world, although not one of the most famous; some wines are quite sweet (such as *mbro-daphne*) or literally turpentine-scented (like retsina, which contains pine resin and is definitely an acquired taste). However, there are many fine wines produced in Greece, and imports are expanding. *Ouzo* is the Greek equivalent of Pernod, a strong and potent licorice-flavored liquor that is clear in the bottle but turns cloudy over ice. Turkey is 99 percent Muslim, and many observant Turks do not consume alcohol; instead, their favorite stimulant and social medium is coffee, and the Turkish-style coffee made all over the region is extremely rich and strong.

THE HISTORY

Although so nearly related in geography and experience, the Greeks and Turks are ethnically distinct. The indigenous Greeks were manufacturing and trading as early as 4000 B.C., and by 600 B.C. they had colonies stretching from the Black Sea to North Africa, and from Sicily to Mediterranean France and even Spain.

The first known civilization in Turkey was Hittite, dating from about 1800 B.C. Troy may have been one of its first great centers, and if so, the Trojan War set a pattern: It was from Turkey that the Persian armies repeatedly invaded Greece.

With the victories of Alexander the Great, however, the histories of Greece and Turkey began to intertwine. Although Alexander's empire dissolved soon after his untimely death, the rise of Rome had begun, and by the middle of the second century B.C., both Turkey and Greece were under Roman control. The eastern (Byzantine) half of the Roman Empire endured into the eleventh century, but repeated attacks by Turks and Mongols from the east and European Crusaders from the west splintered it; Constantinople finally fell to the Ottomans in 1453, and despite Greece's crucial role in the rise of "Western" civilization, it became politically estranged from Europe—more an object of archeological veneration than of cultural exchange.

THE CUISINE

Nomadic, itinerant, warlike, and seagoing, the various ancestors of the Greeks and Turks didn't take the time for elaborate cooking or eating.

Oil, Olé

Unless you pay close attention to what you order, it is difficult to have anything resembling a low-fat Greek meal. Olive oil is considered essential for flavor as well as lubrication, so there tends to be plenty in any baked dish (although, as we noted above, chefs in the United States have begun to lighten the dosage). Also, Greek cheeses tend to be fatty and salty and may "weep" more oil into a dish. Even grilled fish may have been coated with oil beforehand. The best bets are roasts—lamb or chicken—or kebabs, even those that have been marinated beforehand.

The most prevalent form of cooking is grilling—a souvlas is a spit, hence souvlaki, the marinated kebabs that are Greek lunch shops' most famous offering—or the casserole-baking of one-pot dishes. Grilling over open coals is one heat-reducing maneuver, and in many Turkish homes, the coal fire is still preferred to the stove.

The other "air-conditioning" method is communal baking. In Greece it is still commonplace for women to carry a casserole to the village bakery for cooking. This association of village market and family dinner is one reason that so many Greek restaurants in the United States are built around courtyards or employ flagstone flooring evocative of the old tavernas. Food is a social event, and you should be prepared to enjoy it.

Greeks are predominantly Eastern Orthodox and pay allegiance to the Patriarch at Istanbul. Both their religious beliefs and their convoluted shoreline have made them masters of seafood—an obvious fact, perhaps, but one that might surprise Americans accustomed to thinking of Greek food only as moussaka, souvlaki, and stuffed grape leaves. The Muslim Turks, too, observe many fast days, but they rely less on seafood for alternatives than the Greeks do.

The main meal is the midday dinner, and feasts in particular are all-afternoon affairs. Portions are bountiful, particularly of the savory pies and roasted (frequently whole) lamb or kid. Eating utensils are basically the same as in the United States, at home and in restaurants. Unlike the Europeans, Greeks never considered the elaboration of cutlery a badge of civilization; hence, a salad fork is an entree fork is a dessert fork.

Incidentally, if you hear the cheer "Opa!," duck—a flaming platter is passing by.

There is little variety or fussiness in the food; it depends more on freshness. Menus are similar year-round, except that the emphasis shifts with the seasons; lamb is most popular in spring, as is suckling pig, hence their association with Easter feasts. Although special breads are baked for holidays, particularly sweet or fruit breads, both leavened doughs and flatbreads are daily fare.

THE MAIN INGREDIENTS

SEASONINGS   The most characteristic flavors in Greek cooking are lemon, olives, and olive oil, which are used not only as ingredients but also as table condiments. Turkish dishes lean a bit more to the Persian influence, with more yogurt and eggplant, wheat and grains. Both emphasize fresh herbs—parsley, mint, bay, rosemary, dill, marjoram, and the Greek oregano called rigani. Pine nuts and raisins, poppy seed, sesame seed, walnuts, and honey suggest the Persian influence.

VEGETABLES   Greeks place slightly more emphasis on greens than the Turks do, particularly spinach and wild leaf greens, which frequently appear in soup or combined with white beans or cheeses. Leeks, onions, garlic, and artichokes are particularly popular here.

MEAT AND SEAFOOD   Lamb is the most popular meat, particularly when it comes to the organ meats, such as sweetbreads or liver; farmers' treats such as pig's trotters and jellied pig's head are banquet food in Greece but not often seen in restaurants in the United States. Goat and lamb are both roasted; seafood is usually grilled or fried but is sometimes stuffed, especially whole fish and octopus. And almost anything—meat, vegetables, cheese, or sweet—is apt to show up packed into the flaky buttery dough called *filo* (or *phyllo*).

STARCHES   Rice is a regional staple, of course, but so are egg noodles and bulgar, and Greeks are particularly fond of a rice-shaped durum wheat pasta called *orzo*. Turks make a sort of ravioli called *manti*, related to the Persian aushak.

DAIRY PRODUCTS   Cheeses are usually fresh in the summer, salted or preserved in winter. The most famous Greek cheese is feta, a sharp, salty, semisoft cheese used in salads and filo pastries. *Kasseri* is a mild, provolone-like cheese that is sometimes fried and served flambé; this dish is called *sagnaki*, but the word is now sometimes used as an adjective meaning flaming, as in "shrimp sagnaki." *Mizithra* is a cheese that is soft when fresh but hardens as its ages; *kefalotiri* is another hard cheese. Yogurt is used as both ingredient and condiment.

THE MAIN DISHES

APPETIZERS Some of the most famous dips in the world are Greek and Turkish: *taramosalata*, the whipped carp roe/lemon juice/olive oil mixture; *baba ganouj*, the roasted eggplant spread; and hummus, the pureed chickpea spread. The Greek version of mashed potatoes—called *skordalia*, it's pureed with olive oil and a great deal of garlic—is a dip rather than a side dish, as we would use it. *Tzatziki* is a dip or salad of shredded, drained cucumbers in garlic-flavored yogurt.

Other appetizers include *keftedes*, small spicy meatballs; *dolmas*, those lemon-flavored grape leaves cigar-rolled around rice and ground meat (and, in Turkey, sometimes served with raisins and pine nuts as well); and *tiropites*, cheese-filled filo puffs. *Spanakopita*, filo pie stuffed with spinach and feta cheese, may be offered as either an appetizer or a main course. *Lakerdes* and *bakaliaros* are salted and dried fish served as hors d'oeuvre. Squid is also likely to be offered fried as an appetizer, as are smelts. Grilled sausages, such as the fennel-flavored lamb version called *loukanika*, may be served in appetizer portions.

SALADS Although the Greeks have adapted to American tastes, lettuce is not really in their repertoire. Instead, they make *melitzanosalata*, an eggplant salad; *patzari* is sliced or cubed beets in yogurt. Beets are also often mixed with oranges. Marinated baby octopus or squid are often served as salads. The typical "Greek salad" made in America combines greens, tomatoes, onions, olives, feta, lemon juice, and olive oil.

SOUPS *Avgolemono* is the Greek version of chicken soup, an egg-rich broth flavored with lemon and often thickened with rice; *kakavia* is a seafood soup with vegetables. The traditional Easter soup, called *mageritsa*, is a fringe benefit of all the lamb roasting going on that time of year: It includes rice, lamb organs and intestines, and lots of herbs, and you'll probably never see it on an American menu, even if it's lurking in the kitchen.

ONE-POT MEALS The most common main-course casseroles include moussaka, an eggplant dish layered with ground meat and noodles and set in béchamel custard; *pastitsio*, a Greek lasagna that may or may not have tomatoes; eggplant stuffed with rice, pine nuts, and tomatoes or with ground meat and mint; stuffed cabbage leaves; and various *kapama* dishes—shrimp, lamb, shanks, or chicken—cooked with wine, tomatoes, and onions.

Spinach/feta/onion stuffing is almost a seasoning in itself and may be used to pad whole fish, chicken breasts, breast of veal, or leg of lamb. Artichokes are a fancier alternative: *Exobikon* is a lamb stew with artichokes, calamata olives, and cheese wrapped in filo. Vegetable stews—artichokes with potatoes, carrots, and leeks, for instance, or the leek pie called *prasopita*—are often baked in or covered with filo.

MAIN DISHES   Most meats are marinated before being grilled: *Kelftiko* is the marinated roast lamb that is the mainstay of every Greek church picnic. Chicken is generally rubbed and stuffed with lemon before grilling. Kid and pork are also grill fodder, and livers and kidneys are increasingly visible on American menus. Occasionally, sweetbreads or brains will be stewed in wine or as part of a mixed grill. Pork is also stewed with celery or onions; in some regions, the first two weeks of Carnival are an almost exclusively porcine feast.

A particularly beloved and characteristically Turkish dish is *donner kebab*, in which layers of lamb, veal, and beef are marinated, layered, rolled and tied, grilled, and then sliced pinwheel-style and served with a tomato and yogurt sauce; because of the amount of work involved, many Turkish restaurants only offer this on weekends or by advance reservation.

SWEETS   Greek and Turkish pastries are obvious carryovers from Persia, extremely sweet and rich. The most famous is *baklava*, a filo pastry drenched in honey and nuts. (Unless you have a serious sweet tooth, one will generally be enough for two people.) Rice pudding is a lighter alternative and generally has a dusting of cinnamon or nutmeg.

HOW TO ORDER AND EAT LIKE A NATIVE

Most Greek menus are divided in the European fashion into hot and cold appetizers, soups, salads, and main courses. Two people should ideally test one dip—taramosalata or baba ganouj—and a finger dish, such as stuffed grape leaves; for four, add a platter of olives and red peppers, a large salad, or fried squid sprayed with lemon juice.

For the main courses, two people might consider one grilled and one roasted dish, perhaps fish and lamb; four people could have a lamb dish, roasted chicken, a fish or seafood dish, and either moussaka or pastitsio. Remember, the desserts are strong; ditto for the retsina and ouzo, both legendarily deceptive. Pace yourself.

Coffee is prepared in traditional Middle Eastern fashion and served with the pow-der-fine grounds mixed in. Be sure to give it time to settle: It may be served in a small cup or in a miniature pot, but in either case the bottom third will be sludge, and you only want to sip off the top half, at least until you get the feel of it. It's very rich (and speaking of decep-tive, two cups could wake a genie).

Greek food is generally inexpensive (particularly in the souvlaki shops) to moderate (for roasted entrees and seafood). Rarely will an entree top $15 or $16.

COOKING AT HOME

You won't need any special equipment to prepare these dishes at home, although if you happen to have invested in one of those chicken-roasting racks that stands it on end, you'll come closer to replicating rotisserie chicken. And if you want to roast a whole lamb, you'll have to dig a pit and install a spit; we'll leave that up to your imagination. Otherwise, your usual pots and pans will do. For company, set out a lot of flowers and some brightly painted stoneware or pottery platters and put lively music on the stereo.

"MOUSSAKA" WITH EGGPLANT

2 onions, finely chopped
2/3 cup olive oil
18 ounces minced (or coarsely ground) meat
2–3 tomatoes
1 bay leaf

1 garlic clove
salt and pepper to taste
4 or 5 eggplants
flour for dredging
oil for frying
2 cups béchamel sauce (see recipe below)
1/3 cup grated Parmesan cheese

Soften onions in 2/3 cup oil; add meat and sauté 10 minutes, then add tomatoes, bay leaf, garlic, and salt and pepper to taste and simmer one hour.

Meanwhile, wash eggplant, trim stems, and slice into rounds. Soak in salted water for an hour, drain, and pat dry. Dredge in flour and fry in very hot oil; drain on paper towels. Then layer a pan with half the eggplant slices, top with half the meat mixture, and repeat. Top with béchamel sauce, sprinkle with grated cheese, and bake at 375° for approximately 25 minutes. Cut into squares and serve hot.

BÉCHAMEL SAUCE

2/3 cup flour
2/3 cup extra virgin olive oil
1 1/2 cups milk
2 eggs, beaten
salt and pepper
grated nutmeg
2/3 cup kefalotiri or Parmesan cheese, grated

Pour oil into pot, stir in flour, and cook over medium heat, stirring constantly, for about 5 minutes; meanwhile, warm milk in separate pan. Whisk warmed milk into flour mixture, then eggs and seasonings, and simmer, still stirring, for 5 minutes more. Add cheese; if the mixture becomes too thick, thin with a little more milk.

TZATZIKI (CUCUMBER DIP)

1 cucumber, grated and drained
1 pint plain yogurt, drained
4–5 cloves garlic, finely grated

2 tablespoons olive oil
2 tablespoons vinegar
salt and pepper to taste

Combine cucumber and yogurt; add garlic. In alternating portions, add oil and vinegar, mixing constantly (preferably with a hand mixer). Season to taste. Serve with pita bread.

FETA SPREAD

1 clove garlic, minced
1 small red chili, seeded and minced
1 tablespoon extra-virgin olive oil (more if needed)
2 sweet peppers, roasted, peeled, and seeded
1 1/2 cups fresh feta cheese
1 teaspoon lemon juice (optional)

Combine garlic, chili, and oil in food processor; puree, scraping down sides as needed. Add roasted peppers and repeat; add feta and puree. Taste, add lemon if desired, blend, then serve.

This spread can be used as a pita or vegetable dip; spread over cauliflower and baked; or stirred into chickpea or other vegetables as seasoning.

THE MIDDLE EAST

BASIC CUISINE

DINNER FOR TWO:
Fettoosh, baba ganouj, kebabs

DINNER FOR FOUR:
Dolmas, aushak, hummus, fessanjan, grilled chicken

GROUP DISH:
Mezze

STYLE:
Tangy, sweet-and-sour, nutty

KEY FLAVORS:
Sesame, lemon, yogurt, olives, honey

EATING UTENSILS:
Pita and other breads, skewers, spoons, and forks

DISTINCTIVE DISHES:
Kebabs, basmati rice, dolmas

UNIFORMITY OF MENUS:
Good

NUTRITIONAL INDEX:
High carbohydrate, medium fat, medium sodium

COST:
Inexpensive

"THANK YOU":
"Shukaran" (Arabic); "Tasha kur" (Afghani)

It is as much a metaphor as a geographical definition: the Middle East, midpoint of two worlds, cradle of civilization, source of mystery and religion.

Seeing photographs today of the region—the great deserts, vast steppes and mountain ranges, and caravans of camels and horses as well as more modern trucks—it's hard to imagine that this was once literally the garden spot of the world. The Garden of Eden or its historical counterpoint must have lain somewhere in or near Mesopotamia, the fertile delta region between the Tigris and Euphrates rivers, in what is now southern Iraq. Many of the culinary basics were discovered here, none more important than wheat, but none more popular than fermentation, which made possible not only leavened bread but also beer, the earliest archeological evidence of which dates to about 3,500 B.C. (or even earlier, if you believe some Mesopotamian scholars).

Nowadays, it is a region of problematical agriculture, and consequently depends either on laborious irrigation or periodic flooding—or, as in the case of the aggressively modern Israeli kibbutzes, hydroponic techniques. Even Egypt, with its long Nile River valley, is only 5 percent cultivated.

THE HISTORY

The Middle East, lying at what was for millenia the center of the commercial world, has given birth to more civilizations (and been invaded by more upstarts) than any other region. Consequently, although Americans tend to view Middle Easterners as a homogeneous group, they are quite heterogeneous, even within particular countries. For example, although Iran is 95 percent Shiite Muslim, it also has Eastern Christian, Jewish, Roman Catholic, Protestant, Sunni, Zoroastrian, and Bahaian minorities, speaking Farsi, Turkish, Kurdish, Armenian, Arabic, English, and French.

Lebanon, which now looks back on its cosmopolitan past as a sort of golden age, was invaded by the Egyptians, Babylonians, Jews (fleeing Egypt under Moses), Philistines, Assyrians, Babylonians again, Persians, Greeks (under Alexander), Jews again (under the Maccabees), Romans, Persians again, Romans again, Arabs, North Africans, Western European Crusaders, Marmeluk Turks and, finally, the Ottoman Turks—and all that by the sixteenth century.

The earliest civilizations in the region date to about 5000 B.C., which is when there is evidence of wheat cultivation in the Nile River valley. The Sumerians, who moved out of India into Mesopotamia about 4000 B.C., developed not only one of the earliest writing systems and fine art but, more practically, the barter system: They traded crops for metal, stone, and wood. The first inhabitants of the Caspian Sea and Palestine (the so-called Holy Land, generally comprising Israel, Jordan, and Egypt) were herders and farmers, but by 3000 B.C. there were commercial markets all the way from Babylonia to Egypt; from the Lebanese coast, the Phoenicians traded all around the Mediterranean, on both the European and African coasts.

Despite the fairly lengthy rule of the Greeks and Romans, it was the long domination of the Arabs and later the Turks that defined the region's character. Not until the turn of this century did the European nations make even a slight mark on the Middle East.

THE CUISINES

Middle Eastern cuisine has been far more influential than is generally understood; the very word "gourmet" comes from the Farsi "ghormeh" (stew) and probably was picked up by unsophisticated French Crusaders stunned by the lavish consumption of their Muslim enemies in the Holy Land.

The phrase "Middle East" is generally taken to encompass Syria, Jordan, Israel, Kuwait, Asian Turkey, Egypt, Iraq, Iran, Afghanistan, the Gulf States, Yemen, and Armenia, and all have distinct preparations and specialties; but in the United States, Middle Eastern cooks tend to favor one of two broadly defined styles. Lebanese, Israeli, Turkish, and Egyptian restaurants have a somewhat more "western" or Mediterranean flavor, while Iranian (or, as they are more frequently referred to, Persian), Armenian, and Afghani restaurants have a much more exotic, "eastern" cast.

This generally reflects the rival historical influences of the region: Israeli and Lebanese food displays closer ties to the Turkish and Greek cuisines (thanks to the domination of the Ottoman Empire), while the eastern cultures show the heavier stamp of the Persian cuisine, which the Muslim revolution carried east to India and China and west to Spain. The rule of thumb in distinguishing the Persian influence from the Ottoman is that while the Persians enjoyed combining fruits and meats in the same dish and spicing the mix richly, even sweetly, the Ottomans tended to cook their meat separately and more simply.

But people after people and army after army marched through the Fertile Crescent, and there are scores of other ethnic signatures scrawled across this vast region. Afghani cuisine is among the simplest of cuisines, but even it is almost hieroglyphic in its ingredients: yogurt, borrowed from the Russians, and ravioli-like dumplings, a Chinese hand-me-down from the Mongols, who swept as far west as Iran and Syria. Many Middle Eastern flavors—cloves, allspice, and green and black peppercorns—originated in the Spice Islands, while cumin, turmeric, and garlic were transmitted via India, which in its turn adopted the *tanur* (in India, *tandoor*) oven and the Persian *samosas* and *kofta*. West African traders brought in okra and took back spinach, which is native to Iran. Tomatoes were introduced by the Moors, who got them from the

Spanish, who brought them back from the Americas. Even the Portuguese, who briefly established settlements on the Persian Gulf in the sixteenth century, contributed the chilies they had discovered in the Caribbean.

THE MAIN INGREDIENTS

Broadly speaking, the regional staples include wheat and rice, most famously the basmati rice of Iran, along with other grains; legumes, particularly chickpeas and lentils (which have been cultivated in this region, according to some sources, for 8000 years); purslane greens and spinach; poultry, beef, and lamb; fish; vegetables; and citrus fruits. But from the Mediterranean coast to the Afghani hills, the soil and climate ranges widely.

THE "WESTERN" COUNTRIES The Mediterranean coast, with its long, hot, dry summers and cool, rainy winters, remains one of the more fertile portions of the Middle East, and these nations have a wide variety of fruits and vegetables in their diets.

Syria's primary crops are wheat, potatoes, sugar beets, barley, cotton, chickpeas (garbanzos), fruits, and dairy products such as cheese. Turkey's fruits and vegetables—particularly eggplant, peppers, zucchini, onions, tomatoes, cherries, apricots, plums, and loquats (so-called japanese plums)—are highly prized. Israel has to import additional wheat and barley, as well as beef, but it has abundant fruits, including avocados, melons, bananas, peaches, eggplant, and tomatoes, plus olives, peanuts, grapes and cotton.

Egypt's primary crop is not edible but exportable: cotton. Its subsistence crops include rice, corn, wheat, millet, onions, beans, barley, tomatoes, sugarcane, citrus fruits, and dates. Poultry, cattle, sheep, goats, donkeys, and even buffalo are also common.

THE "EASTERN" COUNTRIES As you move east, there are fewer fruits, more grains, and more meat in the diet. Iraq's plateau regions and sandy soil make it ideal for growing dates, grains, and vegetables; Iran, most of whose cultivated territory is in the region of the Caspian Sea, produces primarily wheat but also rice, barley, and corn, as well as fruits, nuts, and dates. Iran also benefits from Caspian seafood, particularly salmon, carp, trout, pike, and the sturgeon that produces the world-famous Iranian and Russian caviar. And mountainous Afghanistan, with its Tatar and Mongol legacies, is much more heavily dependent on the grazing herds of fat-tail sheep, which provide not only food and fats but also wool for clothing and rugs and skins for huts.

SEASONINGS The most common flavorings include limes and lemons; turmeric; *zatar* (a kind of thyme); dill; mint and parsley (both dried and fresh); garlic; tahini (a sesame-seed butter); cumin; cinnamon; poppy seeds; pomegranate; saffron and sumac (not the poisonous American variety); eggplant; okra; zucchini; dried fruits, particularly cranberries, cherries, and citrus fruits; and yogurt. Hot and sweet peppers, fresh and dried, are extremely important, and most cooks make their own chili pastes from family recipes. In the more eastern regions, swirls of flavored oils are used to "finish" soups and stews.

MEZZE

One way to get to taste a lot of Middle Eastern dishes, particularly at a Lebanese or Persian restaurant, is to order *mezze*—which, depending on the region your menu-writer is from, may be spelled mezza, meza, mazzah, or some other variation. Mezze, a tableful of mini-servings or appetizers designed for sharing and conversation, is the Turkish tapas (or, more likely, tapas are the Spanish mezze). It is the most sociable of meals, and some restaurants boast of offering scores of options, although Americans, to be frank, will be lucky to experience one score. Unlike tapas, however, mezze platters (that is, preset combinations) are often served all at once, and some hot things may get cold, so consult your menu. Among typical mezze dishes are baba ganouj, hummus, stuffed grape leaves, cheese- or spinach-stuffed filo pastries called *borek*, fava beans or string beans with tomatoes, grilled sausages, fried smelts, stuffed eggplant, shredded zucchini pancakes, brains in vinaigrette, hot peppers, olives, and *lamajun*, the pizza-style topped bread that is traditionally folded in half before being eaten.

Somewhat similar to the mezze is the *mokhalafat*, which also contains a number of small dishes, but these are served as condiments rather than appetizers: pickled garlic, stewed beets, and *boryani*, or yogurt with spinach. Such condiments can also be ordered as appetizers, in which case they are usually called *sabzee*.

THE MAIN DISHES

APPETIZERS The tidbits usually gathered up in mezze are often offered singly as hors d'oeuvre. The stuffed grape leaves called *dolmas* are found throughout the region. Pita is particularly well known in this area as the accompaniment to hummus, the sesame-flavored chickpea dip, and baba ganouj, the eggplant version of hummus, called *mutabbal* in some places. Wood-grilled lamajun, or "Lebanese pizza," is increasingly popular. And stuffed pastries, filled with ground lamb, spinach, and pine nuts, or even zucchini and cheese, are common.

SALADS The Lebanese salad called *fettoosh* (also spelled fattoush or fettoush) combines day-old bread, parsley, lemon, tomatoes, cucumber, and mint. Another version combines tomatoes, cheese, chili peppers, bread, and onions. *Tabbouleh*, the lemon-flavored salad of bulgar and parsley, has been popular in the United States for a long time, as have *felafel* (garbanzo croquettes) and *pilafs* (rice dishes studded with almonds or raisins). *Kofta* is ground beef, while *kibbeh* is ground meat and chickpeas fried together; both are often grilled on kebabs.

SOUPS Although there are some broths, Middle Eastern soups tend to be thick, filling, and nutritious. Turkish favorites include lentil with purslane soup, chicken and tomato soup with plain dumplings, peppery broths with spiced meat and grain dumplings, and hearty lentil, white bean, and garbanzo soup with lamb broth. A common Persian soup combines bread and white beans—a dish transmitted to Tuscany and still popular there. *Ful* or foole is an Egyptian specialty, a thick bean stew of fava or white beans or chickpeas topped off with olive oil, tahini, and sometimes chopped fresh tomatoes. Israelis mix meat, vegetables, eggs, and rice into a stew called *cholent*, usually served on the Sabbath.

FISH AND SEAFOOD Unlike the more western Mediterranean countries, Middle Eastern cultures are generally cool toward seafood. Shellfish is forbidden to kosher-keeping Jews, although they can eat fish—including, of course, the famous smoked and salted lox and nova salmon (see "A Note on Kosher Food," page 160). The Egyptians are also fond of mild fish like the carp and mullet that populate the Nile; they are often baked with tomato sauce or occasionally with curry spices.

MEATS *Kebabs* (or kebobs or kababs), grilled skewers of marinated chicken or lamb, have been common in the United States for a long time but nowadays may also include veal, lamb chops, filet mignon, quail, goat, and shrimp. (The Persian kebabs are the originals of the Greek *souvlaki* and the Indonesian *satays*.) A number of Iranian- and Afghani-run restaurants in America serve almost nothing but kebabs and the rice pilaf that accompanies them. *Donner kebab* is a fancier, Sunday-dinner version in which various meats are sliced, marinated, layered, rolled, rotisserie-grilled, and then sliced pinwheel-fashion and topped with yogurt sauce. (In the United States, however, it is often just one meat, usually lamb.) *Chowpan zheek* is a sort of Mongol answer to kebab-to-go: grilled rack of lamb and drippings served over thin bread.

Meats are also turned into various kinds of sausages, smoked or dry-cured hams, and pastramis. (But if you hear something referred to as an "Israeli hot dog," it's actually felafel.) *Saniyeh* is a brisket or pot roast flavored with tahini.

POULTRY   Grilled or roasted chicken is a Middle Eastern classic, and Greek and Lebanese immigrants were among the first to jump on (actually, they probably built) the rotisserie-chicken bandwagon. *Fessanjan* (or fessanjen) is a classic Persian dish (usually made of chicken but sometimes duck or even lamb) stewed with walnuts and pomegranate.

STEWS AND CASSEROLES   The eastern cuisines are more fond of mixed meat and vegetables stews, or the classic meat and fruit combinations. *Koresh* (or koresht or khoresh) is the general word for "stew." *Ghormeh sabzee* are lamb shanks braised with chickpeas, scallions, onion, garlic, sumac, and dried lemon or lime. *Koresh bademjan* is lamb braised with eggplant. *Mizrah gasemi* is a variation of baba ganouj that includes tomatoes. Stuffed cabbage often has a lamb and wheat bulgar filling and a pomegranate sauce. The more upscale kitchens may offer stewed or grilled brains or other organs as well.

Among characteristic Afghan dishes are *korma-e-seib*, apples baked with tomato sauce, prunes, walnuts, split peas, and lamb; and *shalgram*, a stew of turnips baked in brown sugar and ginger and generally served alongside lamb. *Zardack palow*—sliced carrots and chickpeas stewed with walnuts and prunes and served over rice—is made with or without lamb (or beef). In fact, many Afghan dishes can be converted to vegetarian entrees, and eggplant, pumpkin, and spinach often appear as stews.

DUMPLINGS AND TURNOVERS   *Aushuk* (or *aushak*) is the best-known Afghani dish, a sort of inside-out ravioli or boiled dumplings stuffed with leeks or scallions and topped with a yogurt and mint sauce. The Turkish version is called manti and is stuffed or sometimes topped with ground lamb. *Boulani* is a vegetarian version, stuffed with leeks and potatoes and topped with yogurt. Afghan *sambosas* are usually stuffed with chickpeas and meat, rather than the Indian-style potato stuffing. A *knish* is a savory meat or potato-stuffed pastry brought to Israel by Russian immigrants along with *latkes*, pancakes of shredded potato and onion.

SIDE DISHES Vegetable dishes are generally rather simple, using familiar presentations but relying on freshness and visual appeal: grilled or sautéed eggplant, zucchini, and tomatoes in a sort of ratatouille but topped with yogurt; marinated green beans; and spinach with yogurt. Middle Easterners stuff a variety of vegetables—zucchini, sweet peppers, artichokes, and pumpkins, as well as grape leaves—both with meat and raisin stuffings or rice and pine nuts. *Shakshuka* is a dish borrowed from North Africa, but it sounds almost Central American; it's a hash of sautéed onions, tomatoes, and peppers, with a fried egg on top.

RICE The Iranian variety, called *basmati*, is considered by many—and not only Iranians—to be the best in the world. A firm, slightly nutty- or smoky-flavored long-grain species, basmati is grown only in the Middle East and in portions of India ("Texmati" rice is an American imitation). After it is cooked, it is called *chelo* or chellow. The characteristic flavor is produced by three days of smoking in a closed earthen chamber; the Iranians merely season it with saffron and a bit of oil or butter, or stir in a raw egg and powdered sumac. This egg-thickened version is also sometimes crisped in a skillet and broken into pieces to be eaten with stew; then it is called *chelo ta dag*. When rice is mixed with other ingredients it is called *polo*, or pilaf.

BREADS AND DOUGHS Throughout the region, breads—particularly flatbreads—are essential parts of any meal. The flatbreads are both leavened and unleavened, including the zatar-flavored breakfast breads, griddle cakes, and versions of pita or whole wheat "pocket bread"; but lighter breads and pastries such as filo are common, and in fact some scholars believe that filo is another Persian invention. In a style that is as familiar in Turkish kitchens as in Tandoori ones, flat disks of bread are often slapped against the hot wall of the bread oven to puff up before being hauled out. *Challah*, the most famous Jewish bread after the unleavened matzoh, is the original egg bread.

BEVERAGES   *Dooghs* are yogurt-based drinks flavored with mint. Coffee is still the stimulant of choice, particularly since alcohol is forbidden to observant Muslims; so a few Middle Eastern restaurants may not offer even beer or wine, although most have made that concession to American habits. Lebanese and Israeli beers are pretty good. *Arak* is an anise-flavored aperitif related to the Greek ouzo or Italian sambucca; ayran is a watered yogurt beverage.

SWEETS   Middle Easterners have a very sweet tooth, particularly for honeyed filo pastries, candied fruit, and fruit sherbets and ice creams served with almond cookies. The honey and nut-filled filo *baklava* is the most familiar to Americans, but *kataif*, a wheat pastry dough, makes pastries that are less overwhelmingly rich. One kataif dessert is something like funnel cake, in which the batter is poured into a colander-like container and "strung" onto a hot griddle; the strings of dough are then bundled up and topped with heavy flavored cream.

HOW TO ORDER AND EAT LIKE A NATIVE

Most Armenian, Egyptian, Iraqi, and Israeli meals are still served all at once, at a Western-style table. Jordanian, Syrian, Turkish, and Lebanese restaurants generally serve meals in courses. Iranians and Afghanis traditionally serve dinner on the carpeted floor—one reason they take such care in making rugs—and with plenty of cushions. Dishes are served in large bowls and eaten communally—even the soups (first a dumpling, then soup)—but nowadays diners are given individual bowls as well. Restaurants with a mixed clientele may even offer both Western-style seating and carpeting. In general, however, restaurants in the States have switched to table seating.

(Ethnic Yemenis are the most traditional: They segregate the diners by sex, and the men frequently eat first. Conversation is also segregated: There is little talk over the meal but much over coffee and dessert, which is served in another room. Many Yemenis also retain the one-pot, communal dining tradition.)

In America, most menus are divided into soups, salads, and main courses. Mezze may be a category, listing either a number of dishes or a preset tray of dishes. If mezze is not offered, two diners should order fettoosh and baba ganouj (and more dips if you think you can manage) and some kebabs. For four, order dolmas, aushak, a stew (preferably fessanjan), and a grilled marinated chicken.

Most Middle Eastern restaurants are inexpensive, or moderately expensive, and fairly authentic.

A NOTE ON KOSHER FOOD

There was a time when only observant Jews even knew where kosher restaurants were. Nowadays there are not only a growing number of kosher (meaning "proper") Middle Eastern establishments but also a rather astonishing supply of kosher Chinese restaurants, with rabbi-certified kitchens.

According to dietary laws laid down in the Old Testament, observant Jews may not eat shellfish; fish are allowed so long as they have scales and fins (no eels or sturgeon). Pork and carrion are both banned, as are birds of prey and animals that crawl on their bellies—such as snakes, which have had a bad reputation since Genesis. Only those animals that both chew their cud and have cloven hooves (i.e., sheep and cattle) are acceptable; and both meat and poultry must be purged of blood (or pickled) before cooking. In addition, meat and dairy dishes and utensils must be kept separate, and kosher cooks not only keep two sets of dishes but also, ideally, two kitchens. Milk or dairy products should be eaten first; in fact, if a meat dish is consumed first, the dairy foods should wait several hours.

There are requirements for kosher butchering as well. If you are concerned with keeping kosher, make sure the restaurant is *kashrut*—observant in every way, and so certified by a rabbinical board—and not just "kosher-style."

COOKING AT HOME

Most Middle Eastern kitchens are quite limited, perhaps with a small stovetop but most often with open fires or the large pit ovens that are built alongside the homes but kept separate, to limit the heat. Once these fire pits are lit, most of the dishes are cooked in quick succession so as not to waste heat or have to extend the fire.

LENTIL AND LAMB STEW

1/2 cup green lentils
3–4 cups Swiss chard, rinsed and drained
1/2 pound lean lamb, minced or processed with steel blade
1 tablespoon olive oil
1 medium onion, chopped
1 teaspoon hot pepper sauce or dried chili flakes (or more to taste)
1/2 tablespoon tomato paste
1 cup beef broth or water
1/2 cup canned or cooked dried garbanzos
1/4 cup bulgar wheat or kasha
1/2 tablespoons finely minced or mashed garlic
3 tablespoons lemon juice
dried mint leaves, salt, and pepper to taste, plain yogurt

Rinse lentils, cover with 2 inches fresh water, and bring to a boil; cover, lower heat, and simmer until done (about 30 minutes). Drain, reserving cooking liquid. Blanch chard in boiling water, drain under cold water, and roll in clean dishtowel; squeeze dry and chop.

Heat 1 tablespoon oil in Dutch oven and sauté minced lamb until it looses its red color; lower heat, add onion, and cook just until they start to soften. Add pepper sauce, tomato paste, and broth or water. Bring to a simmer, cover, and cook 15–20 minutes. Increase heat and add bulgar, if using, lentils, and 2 cups of their cooking liquid (add water if necessary), and garbanzos. Bring to boil, then lower to simmer again and cook, covered, another 15–20 minutes. Add greens or kasha, if using, garlic, lemon juice, salt, and pepper. Simmer 15 minutes again and serve; top with mint and yogurt.

TABBOULEH

1 cup wheat bulgar
3 cups cold water
1/2 cup chopped green onion
1/2 cup chopped mint
3 cups chopped fresh parsley leaves
1/4 cup extra-virgin olive oil
3 tablespoons lemon juice
1 1/2 teaspoons salt
1 teaspoon ground white (or black) pepper
3–4 ripe but firm tomatoes, peeled, seeded, and diced
lemon wedges for garnish

Soak bulgar in water 30 minutes; drain well, pressing out excess moisture, then spread on clean tea towel to dry another 30 minutes. Pour into bowl, add onions, parsley, and mint, and mix well. (It's easier to mix with the hands.) Whisk together olive oil, lemon juice, salt, and pepper; add to bulgar and mix well. Gently stir in tomatoes; cover and chill before serving; serve with extra lemon wedges for seasoning.

EGGPLANT "CAVIAR"

1 large eggplant or 4 small Italian eggplants
2 large ripe but firm tomatoes, peeled, seeded, and finely chopped
2 scallions, trimmed and chopped
2 tablespoons chopped fresh cilantro or mint leaves
2 cloves garlic or 1 clove mild elephant garlic, minced
salt and hot chili pepper to taste

Roast whole eggplant, skin generously pricked, on a cookie sheet in a 425° oven until blackened and slightly collapsed or soft (usually 20 to 30 minutes, depending on size). Cool, remove skin, and puree meat in food processor. Stir in tomatoes, scallions, cilantro, garlic, salt, and chilies to taste; serve with pita bread.

HUMMUS (GARBANZO DIP)

2 cans cooked garbanzos (chickpeas), rinsed and drained
1/3 cup tahini (sesame paste)
1/2 cup lemon juice (or more to taste)
2 cloves garlic
1/2 teaspoon salt (or more to taste)
liquid pepper sauce to taste
chopped parsley or mint for garnish
1 tablespoon extra-virgin olive oil

Combine garbanzos, tahini, and lemon juice in food processor and puree. "Cream" garlic and 1/2 teaspoon salt into a smooth paste, add to processor bowl, and blend. Add pepper sauce, and additional lemon and salt if desired, and blend again. Turn dip into serving bowl and make a small depression in the center; pour oil into hollow, sprinkle with parsley or mint, and serve with pita bread.

INDIA

Almost everyone knows something about Indian food—curry with chutney—and almost everything they know is wrong.

"Curry," the word the British casually applied to the spicy golden lamb and chicken stews they so enjoyed in Calcutta and Bombay, is probably a mistranslation of the word *kari*, the generic term for sauce. The "curry powder" marketed in the United States, usually a rather flat blend of turmeric, cumin, and rice-powder filler, is something of a joke in India, where spices are not only roasted and ground fresh for each meal but are nearly always used in combinations of at least a half-dozen flavors. Curries aren't always spicy-hot and aren't always stewed—they might be fried, roasted, or grilled—and many curries aren't even yellow: They can also be green, red, and even white. And the chutneys most familiar to Americans, like "Major Grey's," are cooked; but authentic chutneys, like real salsas, are raw and fresh.

What we think of as "curry spices" are those same Spice Island treasures that inspired virtually all the European colonial expeditions;

but they had been passed along to the Persians and Arabs so far back in time, and so thoroughly assimilated into Moghul cuisine, that the British—who, after all, have never been famous for their sophisticated use of spices or sauces—felt as though they were just discovering them. And though they were intrigued with "going native," like most European colonials in Asia, they only wanted to go so far.

This reduction of Indian cuisine to a single recipe robs it not only of its complexity but of much of its opulent history. In fact, Indian cuisine is almost a perfect melding of Middle Eastern, Mongolian, and Malaysian cooking, and for the most part it uses the healthier parts of each. Persian pilafs, Turkish flatbreads, Moghul kebabs, and Indonesian flavors are the mainstays of Indian foods; and the high proportion of vegetarian and even vegan dishes makes it hospitable to every diner.

Although this chapter refers almost exclusively to Indian food, it can be used as a guide to several related cuisines—Bangladeshi, Nepalese, Ceylonese, and western-central Burmese, particular the Mandalay region. Most Pakistani restaurants are also similar, although a few with chefs from the west, toward Afghanistan and Iran, may offer menus more reminiscent of Middle Eastern kitchens.

THE COUNTRY

A slightly cockeyed diamond-shaped or toothy mass that juts into the Indian Ocean, India is the second most populous nation on earth, with an estimated 850 million inhabitants; two dozen cities hold more than a million people apiece. It is an extremely heterogeneous population, however, with anthropological roots in four races (Caucasoid, Mongoloid, Australoid, and Negroid) and 1,500 languages and dialects.

Four-fifths of the population is Hindu, 12 percent is Muslim, and the rest is a mixture of Christian, Buddhist, and Sikh (itself a monotheistic mix of Sufi Islam and Bhakti Hinduism). Most of them are employed in agriculture, either in subsistence farming or on the large tea, tobacco, and coffee plantations. Although the caste system, which placed the Brahmins at the top and the "untouchables" irreversibly at the social bottom, has been officially outlawed, it continues to exercise considerable influence.

Physically, India is walled off along the northeast diagonal by the Himalayan crest and along the northwest by desert; almost parallel to

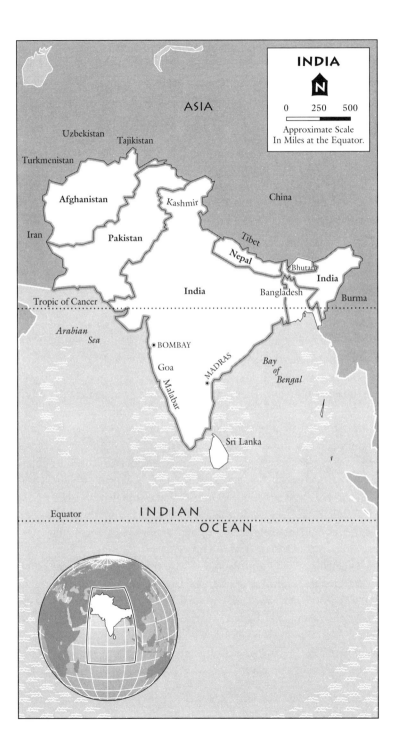

ASIA

Uzbekistan

Tajikistan

Turkmenistan

Afghanistan

Kashmir

China

Iran

Pakistan

Tibet

Nepal

Bhutan

India

India

Bangladesh

Burma

Tropic of Cancer

Arabian
Sea

BOMBAY

Goa

Malabar

MADRAS

Bay
of
Bengal

Sri Lanka

Equator

INDIAN

OCEAN

these lines, however, run two of the great river systems: the Indus River, in what is now Pakistan, and the Ganges, below Nepal. The alluvial plain of the Ganges is the most arable territory in the country, along with the tropical east coast; the west is semiarid and best suited to raising grains and livestock, but the entire country suffers from periodic drought, famine, monsoon, and flood.

THE HISTORY

Although much Indian archeology is relatively recent, it is known that a flourishing and sophisticated civilization in the Indus Valley rose to its peak between 2500 B.C. and 1500 B.C. This civilization was heavily involved in trade with the Mesopotamian societies and early on served as the exchange point for the two great staples of Asia, taking Middle Eastern wheat east to China, and bringing Chinese rice back. This set the pattern for centuries of intracontinental recipe-swapping: The Syrians and Persians swapped garlic, nuts, and oils for squashes and eggplant, which grew in India in dozens of delicious varieties, and then traders in the West Indies doused all these new foods with mustard, cinnamon, ginger, mace, coconut milk, and peppercorns.

Large portions of India were at times part of Persia, and in conquering the Persian Empire, Alexander the Great also conquered the western regions of India. The dynasty that wrested India free established a Buddhist society, but as the Indi and Persian civilizations declined, two distinct regional influences emerged that would be echoed in the development of regional cuisines: Aryans, early Asiatic and Turkish Hindus, moved across the north as far as the Bay of Bengal, and the Greeks who had followed Alexander into Afghanistan and Turkey established a related, Indo-Hellenic culture in the northwest. In the south, on the other hand, active trade was maintained with the evolving Roman empire and the merchants of Malaysia and Indonesia.

The Islamic influence crept in slowly with the Arab sea traders, but as the Muslim revolution spread, overland raids became more virulent, and in 1192 the Muslim army captured Dehli and established a vast sultanate that eventually ruled everything but Kashmir and the remote south. (Shahriar, husband of that Scheherazade who passed a "thousand and one nights" telling stories, was emperor of both Persia and India.) Tamerlane, the legendary Turk who claimed descent from Genghis

Khan, marched in at the end of the fourteenth century; another Turk, Babur, who claimed descent from Tamerlane, established the great Moghul (i.e., "Mongol") empire, which witnessed the evolution of the ornate Indo-Islamic art and architecture epitomized by the Taj Mahal. Nevertheless, Islam never won over the hearts of the Indian majority.

The Portuguese established their sphere of influence about the same time: Vasco de Gama landed at Calcutta in 1498, closely followed by Cabral. The British, French, and Dutch were close on their heels, as the route around Africa made importing West Indian spices much more profitable than it had been via the overland route, and the British eventually dominated; but it was not until the mid-eighteenth century, when repeated Persian and Afghani insurrections weakened the Moghul rulers, that the British Empire actually claimed the entire territory. Britain's withdrawal reignited the historical Muslim-Hindu struggle, and an estimated 50,000 people died in the riots that accompanied the partitioning of Pakistan.

> ## Milk of Kindness
>
> Intriguingly, the Aryans brought cattle with them, and beef was originally a common food in India. They quickly discovered that the indigenous breed was better adapted to the climate and began raising it instead, but that breed gave less milk, so it had to be protected from slaughter, because the amount of milk a cow produces daily far outweighs in nutritional value its one-time use for meat. Eventually, as prolife religions such as Jainism and Buddhism spread, even barren cows became sacrosanct. And when the Moghul conquerors began eating meat, it only made the subject touchier.

THE CUISINE

As we mentioned above, the two great influences on Indian cuisine are Turkish and Indonesian; and though there are scores of regional cuisines in India, in the United States Indian restaurants generally only describe themselves as northern or southern in style. Loosely speaking, that suggests an emphasis on meat (in the north) or vegetables (in the south), drier dishes and breads (in the north) or wetter stews and rice (in the south).

The one very general rule of thumb is that the farther south you go, the hotter the food tends to be, partly because the chilies were introduced by the seagoing Portuguese rather than the overland traders and

For all their casual attitude toward the fleshly pleasures, it was the early Indians whose cosmic vision most concerned food. They saw the earth as an island surrounded by seven concentric seas. The first was composed of salt; the second of jaggery, or raw palm sugar; the third of wine; the fourth of ghee; the fifth of milk; the sixth of curds; and the seventh—only then—of water.

thus "landed" on the coasts, working their way into the interior more gradually. The difference is not only in the amount of chilies used but also in the handling of them: In the north, the garlic, onions, and spices are usually slow-fried together before other ingredients are added, while in the south, the uncooked and unmellowed spices are added at the end of the cooking process.

The Moghul influence explains the heavier use of meat in the north; tandoori cooking, though now fairly widespread, was until the last generation known primarily in the northwest quadrant. (Not only is the tandoor oven Middle Eastern, but the traditional tandoori marinade—yogurt, lemon, ginger, and turmeric—is classically Turkish as well.)

Since the influence of the old Persian Empire is strongest in the northwest, the rich Moghul cuisine features cream, sweets, and almonds; and the chutneys involve more fruit, while southern chutneys are often based on mint or fresh fruit. There are other geographic distinctions as well: In the cooler, drier north, wheat grows more plentifully and is the primary starch for bread. However, the Persian love of rice, particularly basmati rice, makes Moghul biryanis famous.

In cities with larger Indian populations, some restaurants may define their cuisine more specifically: Punjabi, Kashmiri, Goan, Gujurati, Bengali, and so forth. Kashmir is in the far northern point, where Pakistan, Afghanistan, and western China come together; Kashmiri Bhahmins do not eat beef, garlic, or onions, so most Kashmiri dishes are lamb.

The Punjab is one of the major states in the northern neck, so "Punjabi" is often used as a synonym for tandoori cooking. However, the Punjab is also the stronghold of the Sikhs, whose vegetarian cooking is fairly well known in the United States, thanks to a "chain" of Golden Temple restaurants and cookbooks. The Punjab is one of the richest grain-growing regions; it produces primarily wheat but also corn, millet, and barley, and Punjabi chefs are, not surprisingly, famous for their breads.

Goa, an Arabian Sea port with a long history of Middle Eastern trade, was a Portuguese colony for nearly 400 years, and Goan cooking uses a bit more vinegar, tomato, and garlic; and any pork dish is almost certainly Goan. The hot-and-sour vindaloo style of curry, which uses a vinegar marinade to tenderize the meat, is Goan. (The word itself comes from the Portuguese word for vinegar.) Cashews and coconuts are also popular in this cuisine.

Bombay is part of Maharashtra, and "Maharashtran" cuisine employs both rice and millet. Because it lies on the west coast and had the closest ties to Arab and African traders, Maharashtrans are fonder of peanuts, okra, and bananas than other Indians are. "Malabar" also refers to the west coast.

The west point of the Indian diamond, between Bombay and the Pakistani border, is the state of Gujurat, which produces primarily vegetarian curries with tangy green chutneys. It is home to the Jainists, who reject slaughter of any life and thus are entirely vegetarian; many even avoid root plants, such as onions, because insects may be displaced or killed in the harvesting. Though there is little meat, Gujurat's Persian heritage shows in the popularity of such flavors as cardamom, almond, saffron, and pistachio.

In the south, where the Hindu tradition is strongest, little meat is served (and little is available, anyway), but an abundance of tropical vegetables provide an almost endless supply of dishes. In the east, along the Bay of Bengal, fish is a major part of the diet. Bengali cooking (and the neighboring Bangladeshi cuisine) tends to be fairly spicy and more heavily mustard-flavored. Coromandel, a term familiar mostly from old novels, was on the east coast. Madras is also on the east coast, and "Madras-style" is usually a version of "hot!"

Off the southern tip of India lies Sri Lanka, formerly Ceylon; though its cuisine is similar to southern Indian food, it is even more "tropical," with a much wider variety of seafoods, including squid and crab. It also shows a strong European influence; for 150 years it was under Portuguese control, and the Portuguese were followed by the Dutch, who introduced butter and eggs and baking doughs. One of the most popular Sri Lankan dishes is a yeast-dough bun stuffed with curried beef

The various cooking oils used lend particular flavors to Indian dishes—now all the more so, because the relatively neutral ghee, the clarified butter that was the common cooking fat in the north, has become much more expensive and is thus used less. Unfortunately, the replacements, while more aromatic, are not much less cholesterolic: The alternatives include sesame oil, peanut oil, coconut oil, almond oil, and mustard oil. The best of them is peanut oil, but you may not always get a straight answer from the waiter about which is being used.

However, aside from the oils and the foods that are fried in them, Indian cuisine has much to recommend it as a healthful choice: Many dishes are steamed, roasted, grilled, or baked; there is little meat and a high proportion of grains and legumes; and in many regions there is almost no dairy except for the lower-fat yogurt. However, any thickened or "wet" curry is apt to hide secret butterfat from condensed milk, skimmed-off cream, or coconut. It is also a low-alcohol diet; most of the spirits served in Indian restaurants—gin, Pimm's cups, or beer—are remnants of the Raj.

and potatoes—a perfect hybrid of all three ethnic cuisines. Sri Lankans like their curries extremely hot.

THE MAIN INGREDIENTS

SEASONINGS The wealth of spices and flavorings in India, which has been at the crossroads of East-West trade since the beginning of history, is overwhelming. *Garam masala*, which is closest to the spice combination Americans know as curry powder, actually just means "mixed spices," and every cook makes his or her own. The most common ingredients are fresh ginger, cumin, turmeric, coriander, cardamom, mace, nutmeg, cloves, and fennel. Other frequently used spices include bay, dill, mint, poppy seeds, sesame seeds, sorrel, asafoetida (a garlicky-flavored but less aromatic herb common in American health-food stores), rose hips, and oregano. Jaggery, a raw palm sugar, is similar to unsulfured molasses. Madras cooks are particularly fond of fenugeek, Bengalis of brown mustard seeds and mustard oil. Garlic is fairly common in the north, but it is not as widely used as in most Asian cuisines; many Indians believe it inflames the passions.

VEGETABLES In India, lentils and beans are such a large part of the diet that they are often a menu category in themselves. The generic word *dal* may refer to any of a half-dozen kinds of lentils (black, red, yellow, orange, white, green), chickpeas, pigeon peas, green peas, red kidney beans, mung beans, split peas, and sometimes tiny black beans. Lentils are used not only as protein but also as starch; lentil flour and fermented lentil doughs are frequently used for breads and crepes and as a thickener for curries.

Among the other vegetables, the most important are the greens (categorically, *palak*)—especially mustard, spinach, and kale—and eggplant, potatoes, cauliflower, broccoli, carrots, gourds, squashes, pumpkins, and tomatoes.

FRUITS   Indian mangoes are as diverse as Indonesian bananas—there are dozens of varieties—and Indians think the mangoes available in the United States a rather poor alternative. They also grow oranges, lemons, limes, pineapples, pomegranates, tamarinds, plums, peaches, guavas, and bananas. Papayas are used both as a fruit (and medicine) and as a tenderizer for meat or fowl.

MEATS   There is less to say on this subject in Indian cuisine than almost anywhere else. Between the Muslims (and west Indian Jews), who eat no pork, and the Hindus, Buddhists, and Jains, who eat (or are supposed to eat) no meat at all, pigs are unknown in India. Beef is limited, but goat and lamb, the Persian and Moghul favorites, are plentiful and the most popular here as well.

POULTRY AND SEAFOOD   Chicken is surprisingly expensive in most parts of the country, though in the north and central game birds are fairly common; and duck is a west coast and Bombay specialty. (Chicken, of course, is extremely popular in Indian restaurants in the United States, where it is not expensive.) Fish—salmon, especially—and shrimp are popular in the coastal regions.

EGGS AND DAIRY   The most important dairy products are cheese and yogurt, which is quite thick, almost curdlike (goat's-milk and sheep's-milk yogurts are said to have more authentic flavor). Yogurt is stirred into many curries as an alternative to coconut milk or cream, but it is more frequently seasoned—either with hot spices or chilies or simply mint or spinach—and served as a condiment, called a *raita*. Some menus refer to "yogurt curries," but those are generally raitas rather than entrees. Cheese is frequently used in curries, usually in combination with a vegetable, such as peas or spinach. However, Indian cooks also boil milk and condense it, or allow it to separate and then skim off the thick cream, called koa; both condensed milk and *koa* are also used to thicken sauces.

Eggs are used as a main course but very rarely as a sauce ingredient or binder. The most common way to serve eggs is to hard-boiled and halve them, then top them with a curry sauce; in the south it's usually a coconut curry. Eggs are also scrambled, frequently with fish, a memento of the British breakfast habit.

GRAINS AND STARCHES The breads of India are made from a variety of flours—white, whole wheat, lentil and occasionally rice—although potatoes are not commonly used for doughs. Rice, both the fine Middle Eastern basmati grain used in biryanis and the shorter, stickier Asian grain common in the south, makes up a substantial portion of the diet.

CURRIES

Like other inhabitants of hot climates, Indians adhere to the theory that spicy food makes you sweat and thus cools you off; it also excites the appetite and aids in digestion. Perhaps that's why there are such an abundance of "exciting" dishes.

Curries come in a variety of colors: red, which includes tomatoes; yellow, which has the heaviest concentration of the turmeric and cumin flavors Americans traditionally associate with "curry powder"; green, which can either mean spinach, mint or cilantro, or green chilies; and almost black, from the Sri Lankan habit of roasting the spices until they are the color and richness of coffee. Coconut-based stews, which are particularly common in south India and Sri Lanka, are referred to as "white curries," and the addition of coconut milk turns a curry from "dry" to "wet." Tomatoes are also more common in the south and along the coast, where they were introduced by the Europeans.

Since the word "curry" has little meaning in India, many restaurant menus use it erratically, and there are several types of dishes that

Americans would tend to include in that category. Most of the terms have to do with the manner in which the main ingredients is prepared: A *korma* is a meat curry, a *keema* a minced-meat curry, and a vindaloo a stew of vinegar-marinated meat. These all have sauces and are closest to what we think of as curries.

However, many dry dishes also involve curry spices: *koftas*, the Middle Eastern–style minced meats (or lentils) formed into meatballs or sausages; *raan*, which means a roast that was probably spice-rubbed; and tandoori dishes, which have been marinated in lemon, yogurt, and (usually mild) spices. *Josh* refers to a curried meat in a yogurt or cream-thickened sauce. The term *bhuna* refers to a stir-frying technique in which all the liquid is cooked out and the spices left behind. Kebabs can be curried as well, especially those with the word *tikka* (pieces), which means the meat or poultry has been cut up and marinated.

Curries involving vegetables are generally called *bhaji* and are relatively dry; curries in which the vegetables are mashed or cooked into a pureelike consistency are *bhartas*. The words *takari* and *sabzi* just mean vegetables, either raw or cooked; these dishes may include curry spices, too. And some things you just have to take for granted, like samosas, the stuffings of which are almost always spiced.

THE MAIN DISHES

APPETIZERS The word for snacks in Indian is, pleasantly, "chat," and most of the dumplings and fritters listed on American menus under "appetizers" are really snacks. ("*Mathai* shops," which may be found in cities with established Indian communities, are combination convenience stores and bakeries and sell dozens of varieties of chat and sweets.) Among the most popular are *samosas*, triangular fried pastries stuffed with either curried potatoes and peas or minced lamb or beef; *kachori*, lentil-stuffed samosas; *pappadam*, the crispy lentil-flour cracker bread; *vadas*, chickpea or lentil dumplings served with raita; *pakoras* (sometimes called *bhajias*), batter-fried vegetables, meat, or sometimes fish; *dosai*, fried patties of fermented rice and lentil flour; and *bondas*, fried mashed potato balls, the Indian knish. *Pani puri* are deep-fried puffs filled with chutneys or split peas or spiced potatoes. *Chakli* (or chakri) are fried spirals or "rounds" of lentil or rice-flour dough, pressed out through a special tool into hot oil—something like a cross between a bagel and a funnel cake. Rice pancakes and potato straws or even baked potato slices, cooked and seasoned, are also popular.

Occasionally restaurants may offer miniature versions of main courses, such as single skewers of chicken tikka. *El maru* is a sort of north Indian trail mix, combining rice, nuts, and crispy noodles. *Oothapam* is a south Indian crepe stuffed with sautéed onions, tomatoes, and peppers.

SALADS   There is no separate course or real menu category here. What raw vegetable mixtures there are resemble Middle Eastern or North African salads and condiments: cucumbers with lemon and mint; eggplant with tomato, shredded carrots, and raisins; even a sort of gazpacho of raw onions, tomato, chilies, coriander, and a touch of sugar. Cold spiced potatoes, cucumber in yogurt, and occasionally cold spiced eggplant may be used as a combination condiment and appetizer.

SOUPS   "Mulligatawny soup" is probably the best-known Indian soup, but like curry, the Anglicized version is the one most familiar to us. The original *mulegoothani*, or "pepper water," has been thickened with beef and soup bones, coconut milk, onion, and curry spices. The other most popular soups feature lentils, split peas, lentils with mixed vegetables, and occasionally pumpkin or squash. *Sambor* is a curry-seasoned soup thickened with pureed lentils.

VEGETABLES   Again, there are dozens of lentils and beans, and any of them may be offered as a stew or puree, spiced or mild; so may squash, potatoes, beans, cabbage, pumpkin, mushrooms, okra, or any of the greens. Potatoes were only introduced toward the end of the eighteenth century but quickly became extremely popular; potato and pea is a very common combination (called *alu mattar*), as are spinach and cheese (*sag paneer*), cauliflower and potato (*alu gobi*), and pea with cheese (*mattar paneer*). Thickly stewed eggplant (*banghun bharta*), mixed baked vegetables (*tandoori sabzi*), stuffed cabbages or green peppers, and fried eggplant slices are popular from India to the Mediterranean.

RICE AND GRAINS   Biryanis and pilaus are central to the Indian diet; the first is only a richer (more Persian-influenced) version of the (more southerly) second. Both are cooked very slowly so that the flavors blend, and both are considered main dishes. Pilaus may be mixed with vegetables (peas, chickpeas, lentils) or spices (saffron, cinnamon, almonds or pistachios, lemon, dill), minced meat, yogurt, and even a little shrimp or coconut. Biryanis are highly aromatic, flavored with mutton, lamb, chicken, nuts, cinnamon, cardamom, chilies, or even rosewater. *Kitchri* is a dish that features rice and lentils cooked together.

SEAFOOD Prawns (*jingha*) are quite popular, either in coconut-flavored curries or skewered satay-style. Tandoori-marinated fish, though a slight of oxymoron (it's hard to find salmon in the north of India), has become extremely popular in the United States. More authentically, fish (*machi* or *machli*) is curried, stuffed with seasoned rice, and broiled or baked, deep-fried, minced and fried, steamed in banana leaves Malay-style, curried with tomato (both fish and tomato are southern specialties), or grilled. Where shellfish is available, it is usually steamed.

POULTRY Chicken (*murgh*) may be marinated and tandoori-roasted; prepared in dry or wet curries, in a vindaloo sauce, or with coconut milk but without hot spices; chopped and fried; or mixed with vegetables. *Tikka* are small skewered morsels like satays. Chicken (or shrimp) *kadai* is stir-fried, usually with tomatoes, onions, and green peppers. Chicken Mahkanwala is a twice-cooked dish—tandoori-roasted meat sautéed in butter and tomatoes. Chicken is also used to flavor biryanis, curried with cashews, stewed with lentils and vegetables, and occasionally deep-fried. Although organ meats are not generally considered edible in India, chicken livers (probably thanks to the British) are sometimes served grilled or even curried.

Small game birds are cooked the same ways as chicken. Duck, which is fattier, does not respond as well to tandoori preparations (the marinade cannot penetrate the fatty layer), so it is more frequently prepared with a vindaloo sauce or in some other offsetting, tangy manner (with tamarind, ginger, papaya, etc.). "Bombay duck," incidentally, is not poultry at all but a dried fish that is fried and served as a salty seasoning, the way Americans used bacon bits.

MEATS Lamb is far and away the most popular meat, followed closely by goat and distantly by beef; mutton, the stronger flavor of which is often mellowed by marination, is also popular. Lamb is rubbed with spices and roasted; rubbed with spices and skewered; or soaked in vinegar and stewed with tomato and yogurt (*rogan josh*, which might be the national dish if more Indians ate meat). *Badami gosht* is pure Persian: lamb flavored with saffron, cinnamon, ginger, almonds, and yogurt, but no hot spices. Lamb is made into meatballs, kebabs, coconut curries, and biryanis; in a few extravagant Goanese dishes, it may even be combined with pork. Most other lean meats can be cooked in the same ways; however, since meat fat (and fat meat) are not common in India, meat is not made into sausages or cured (except perhaps by the European trade). Organ meats and offal are discarded. Buffalo and horse are common meats in India, though camels and dogs are "unclean"; none of these four are apt to appear on an American menu in any case.

CONDIMENTS Chutneys, like salsas, are mixed fruit and vegetable or spice mixes eaten alongside and sometimes with main dishes; *sambals*, another feature of Indonesian cooking, are flavorings—onions sautéed with lemon and chilies, for example, or perhaps highly seasoned vegetables. Raitas are yogurt-based condiments and can include simply cucumber mint (the version most familiar in the United States) or bananas, tomatoes, spinach, and so forth. Chutneys may feature coconut, mango, papaya, chilies, eggplant, mint, coriander, lemon, or pineapple.

There are also a variety of sweet-and-sour pickles: lemon pickle (which is widely known here), mango, green coconut, tomato or green tomato, and so on. The table may be set with small dishes of dried coconut, nuts, banana chips, tiny dried fish, and so on, for customizing your meal.

BEVERAGES The spiciness of most curries has made beer the most common American accompaniment, though some people believe the carbonation makes the spices burn hotter. There are both sweet and savory yogurt drinks (called *lassis*), along with mint drinks and spiced teas. *Faludas* are jellylike sweetish drinks flavored with rose syrup and milk; fruit and milk drinks are sometimes called *fools* (another European appellation). Rice beers and a sugarcane and melon alcohol are popular among the rural people, but if they are available here, it's only under the counter.

DESSERTS Like their Persian forefathers, the Indians like sweets and generally serve a couple at the end of a meal. (In some areas, dinner begins with a sweet dish, and in the west, one of the main dishes may be sweet.) Rice puddings, banana puddings, bread, vermicelli, nut and raisin puddings, fried sweetened nut doughs or cookies, honey- or syrup-covered sweetmeats (*laddu*), and fruits or cheese balls are common. *Halva*, a honey-flavored semolina confection, comes in a variety of flavors.

Ice cream and frozen fruit sherbets are also popular, particularly in the United States.

HOW TO ORDER AND EAT LIKE A NATIVE

A typical Indian meal consists of five or six dishes, and traditionally meals are served family-style, all at once, on a platter called a *thali*, which somewhat resembles those deviled-egg plates picnickers used to use: It's a circular tray with a number of small bowls or cups nestled around the outside and a pile of rice or chapati in the middle. It is customary to eat with the hands, using the fingers for the meat or vegetable and the chapati or rice to absorb sauce. However, as in other countries, only the fingers of the right hand are used. Most restaurants that serve in the traditional manner will bring a pitcher of water and basin to the table, or at least supply fingerbowls; a few use wet cloths.

In most cities in India, Western-style service—that is, plates and forks—is now common. However, the physical arrangement is similar: Rice should be put in the center of the plate, with various curries and condiments around it, and only one dish at a time should be tasted. The rice should also be the predominant part of the meal.

Two people might split an order of samosas and some paratha or a crepe; tandoori chicken; and rogan josh. Four people should share samosas, pakoras, and lentil soup; benghan bharta; chicken Makhanwala; lamb vindaloo; and a pilau or biryani. A group might ask about a thali: Although such "sampler" platters are now often served for one or two people, a real family-style dinner may be forthcoming.

COOKING AT HOME

Except for a tandoori oven, for which a broiler or grill will have to substitute, most Indian utensils and techniques can be reproduced fairly easily in an American kitchen. The most important pan in Indian cooking is called a *karhai*, a slightly deeper version of a Chinese wok, used for stir-frying (hence the descriptive phrase "karhai" on menus). But if you don't have a wok, any deep frying pan will do. Although roasted spices are traditionally ground in a mortar, a small nut grinder or mini–food processor works fine.

There is no standard recipe for garam masala, and even those available in Indian groceries vary from brand to brand; but it's simple to make your own, and the flavor (and the house aroma) will be better. You can make up your own version; and in a pinch, ground allspice plus a little chili powder will get you by.

GARAM MASALA

1 tablespoon black peppercorns
1 1/2 tablespoons cumin seeds
1 tablespoon golden or black mustard seed
1 tablespoon cardamom seed
2 tablespoons coriander seed
2 teaspoons whole cloves
2 teaspoons whole allspice berries
2 sticks cinnamon, broken in smaller pieces
2 teaspoons ground nutmeg

Using a small skillet or Japanese sesame seed pan, toast all the spices except the nutmeg one type at a time; as the seeds become fragrant, turn them into a bowl to cool. When they have all cooled, grind them together. Keep in an airtight jar.

CHICKEN MOGHULI

1 3-pound roasting chicken, cut into serving pieces
2 tablespoons canola or peanut oil
1 large onion, thinly sliced
2 cloves garlic, minced
2 teaspoons fresh ginger root, minced
1 tablespoon ground turmeric
1 teaspoon salt
2 tablespoons garam masala
1 cup thick yogurt

1/4 cup chicken broth or hot water
1/4 cup cream (optional)
1/4 cup cashews or slivered almonds
chopped coriander for garnish

Remove skin and fat from chicken pieces, rinse, and pat dry. In a large heavy pan, heat oil and sauté onions until soft, then add garlic, ginger, turmeric, salt, and garam masala and fry gently until spices are softened (10 to 15 minutes). Add chicken pieces and cook, turning, until lightly browned on all sides. Stir in half the yogurt, the chicken stock, and the cream (if you are using it); cook gently until chicken is tender.

Meanwhile, grind about two-thirds of the nuts. Remove chicken pieces to warm platter; add remaining yogurt and nuts to skillet, adding a splash more water if necessary, and heat through. Return chicken to sauce, then serve, sprinkling remaining nuts and coriander on top. Serve with rice and chapatis (or whole wheat pita bread).

Note: To thicken commercial yogurt, drain in yogurt strainer or strainer lined with cheesecloth so that the whey separates out.

TANDOORI-STYLE LAMB

1 half leg of lamb, sirloin section, trimmed of fat
2 cloves garlic, minced
2 teaspoons fresh ginger, minced
1 teaspoon salt
1 tablespoon garam masala
pinch chili powder
pinch turmeric
1 tablespoon lemon juice
1/2 cup thick yogurt
2 tablespoons cashews or pistachios, ground, or 1 tablespoon nut butter

With the point of a sharp knife, make 1-inch slits all over the lamb. Combine the next 7 ingredients into a paste (use more lemon juice if needed) and rub it over the meat, pushing spice mixture into slits. Combine yogurt and cashews and coat lamb; let it marinate, covered, in the refrigerator for at least 8 hours, though 24 or even 36 would be better.

Preheat over to 450°; place lamb, still covered, in oven and cook 30 minutes; reduce heat to 350° and cook another 40 to 45 minutes or until cooked through but not dry. Serve with rice and tomato-cucumber salsa or chutney.

BENGHAN BHARTA

2 large eggplants, or about 2 pounds of the smaller variety
2 tablespoons mustard or peanut oil
1 onion, chopped
1 small chili, chopped
1 teaspoon fresh ginger, chopped
1 tablespoon garam masala
2 tomatoes, chopped (peeling is optional)
1 teaspoon lemon juice
salt (optional)

Cut eggplants in half and cut slits in meat; place on foil in oven and bake at 350° until skin mottles and partially collapses; remove, cool, peel, and discard any liquid. Coarsely chop or mash meat.

Meanwhile, heat oil and sauté onion until soft; add chili, ginger, and spices and cook 5 minutes; add tomatoes and cook 5 minutes more. Add eggplant, stir, and simmer until the dish resembles a puree. Season with lemon juice and salt if desired.

PART IV

SOUTHEAST ASIA, INDONESIA, AND THE PHILIPPINES

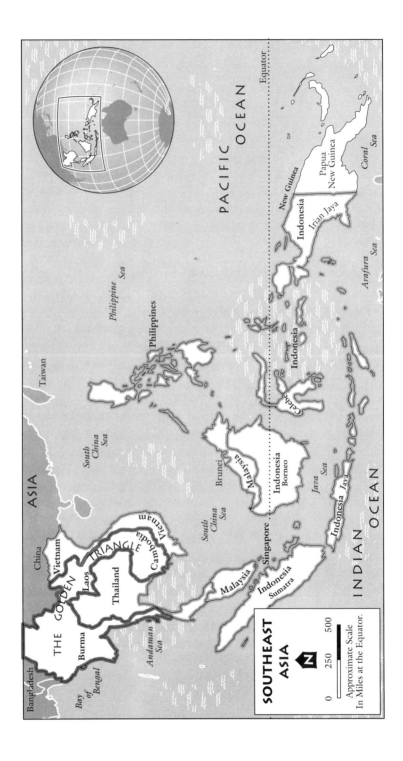

SOUTHEAST ASIA

0 250 500

Approximate Scale
In Miles at the Equator.

THAILAND

BASIC CUISINE

DINNER FOR TWO:
Lemongrass soup, larb,
beef curry

DINNER FOR FOUR:
Hot-and-sour soup, beef
or squid salad, pad thai,
chicken curry, soft-shell
crabs

STYLE:
Very spicy, fishy,
crunchy, low-fat

KEY FLAVORS:
Nuoc mam, chilies,
vinegar, coconut, lemon-
grass

EATING UTENSILS:
Fingers, spoons, chop-
sticks

DISTINCTIVE DISHES:
Pad thai, pra goong,
larb, curries

UNIFORMITY OF MENUS:
Good

NUTRITIONAL INDEX:
High fiber, high sodium,
low fat

COST:
Inexpensive to moderate

"THANK YOU":
"Kap kuhn"

Thai food has become tremendously popular in the United States, and for several reasons: Like many Asian cuisines, it is relatively simple, low in fat, and high in flavor. On the other hand, it is quite distinctive, reflecting far less Western influence than most of its neighbors. Among Southeast Asian countries, Thailand alone has never been colonized; in fact, the Thais' own name for their nation, Prathat Thai, means "Land of the Free." And although not all Thai dishes are as hot as rumored, many are, so Thai restaurants have also been picked up by the hot-chili and Cajun-spice bandwagons.

Unlike some of their neighbors, the Thai people "do" restaurants, and they do them up in style. Eating out is a national pastime, and there are garden restaurants in Bangkok that will seat a thousand people at a time. The names and styles of Thai dishes are relatively standardized, so ordering in a Thai restaurant is easily mastered; and since the Thai people use chopsticks only when eating noodles (which, like the chopsticks themselves, are Chinese imports), the fork-dependent—or rather, the spoon-dependent—can feel perfectly at home. (See "How to Eat Like a Native," page 193.)

THE COUNTRY

Thailand, known for centuries (and in American theatrical history) as Siam, is at the heart of the Southeast Asian peninsula. It forms the base of the region's "flower" part and stretches partway down the stem, toward Malaysia to the south. Myanmar (Burma) borders it on the west, Laos lies to the north and east, and below Laos, Cambodia curves around the east and southeast.

Thailand is permeated with water, both fresh and salt. It is criss-crossed by streams and canals; the Mekong River provides much of the Cambodian-Thai border, and the southern peninsular region is squeezed between the Andaman Sea (part of the Indian Ocean) on the west and the Gulf of Siam (the South China Sea) on the east. Not surprisingly, the great central plateau of the country is all but turned over to rice paddies; rice is not only the staple food but also the largest export commodity. Thailand is in fact the world's leading exporter of rice, shipping out 4.5 metric tons a year, which is even more amazing when you consider that the average Thai eats the cooked product of three-fourths of a pound of dry rice a day.

The northern region, however, is hilly and difficult to farm, and in many areas has been denuded by the harvesting of teak, another primary export. The southern peninsula is mountainous, too, but thickly jungled. It served the United States as a major staging area during the Korean and Vietnam wars; consequently, Thai immigrants have had a relatively easy time relocating (and establishing restaurants) here.

THE HISTORY

The Thai have always had a fiesty, independent streak. Their own historical "exodus" out of south-central China occurred near the end of the thirteenth century, when they migrated to the hill country rather than live under Kublai Khan's Mongols; and although Thai speech is related to Chinese and other Southeast Asian languages, its alphabet was borrowed from the Cambodian Khmer and is written "backward"—that is, left to right, rather than right to left as Chinese is.

Ever since its establishment as a nation, Thailand has knocked elbows and frequently worse with Burma, Cambodia, Laos, France, England, and Japan. It was first exposed to Western culture in 1511, when the ever-adventuresome Portuguese traders and missionaries first explored what were long called the East Indies; the Dutch and English were shut out for nearly 200 years, and after the French financed an abortive coup in 1688, Europeans were locked out again for another century, which they whiled away by colonizing and influencing Malaysia, Burma, and Indochina. In the decades just after the American Civil War, Thailand was gradually reopened and then determinedly "Westernized" by King Mongkut, or Rama IV (the "King" of Siam memorialized in "The King and I"), and his son, Chulalongkorn, also known as Rama V. Except for the period between 1930 and 1950, when the newly named Thailand—then renamed Siam, then renamed Thailand—was pulled in and out of the Communist Chinese orbit, Thailand has remained Western-oriented.

Although the greatest religious influence is Buddhist—members of the royal family also serve as religious figureheads, which partially explains the almost shrine-like portraits of Thai rulers seen in many restaurants here—there are Hindu and Muslim minorities, and a wide variety of religious holidays are observed in the country.

THE CUISINE

Thai food has only one rule: balance. Thai meals, and even single dishes, are supposed to combine the four essences: hot, sour, salty, and sweet, or *prik*, *preeo*, *khem*, and *wan*. Thai food has room for creativity and adaptation—another reason Thai restaurants have flourished in the West—so long as the essential quality and balance are preserved.

On Thai menus, curry dishes are often listed in a sort of color chart: red, green, yellow, and "country style," usually referring to the northern-style dishes without coconut milk. Curry paste is usually indicated by the word *panaeng*, also spelled pakaeng or even kaengpaa. *Kaeng* by itself means both curry and the sauce itself, so it can also be used for any soupy or heavily sauced dish.

Cooking styles are also simple; indeed, in most traditional Thai houses, the kitchen is a separate shack out back, with woks, steamers, strainers, and assorted utensils hanging around a gas or wood stove. Even in the United States, many restaurant kitchens are surprisingly basic, depending on cleavers and mortars and pestles in place of grinders or food processors, and centering on the gas flame. Curries are usually simmered, meats and fish grilled over charcoal, and whole fish sometimes fried or wrapped in banana leaves and grill-steamed. Vegetables are generally julienned or chopped (or even grated) and served raw or lightly stir-fried.

THE MAIN INGREDIENTS

SEASONINGS The most characteristic flavors in Thai food are *nam pla* (the nuoc mam of Vietnam), an anchovy-based fish sauce that is to the Thai what soy sauce is to the Chinese; chilies, ranging from fairly mild (the yellow *prik num* or banana chilies) to very hot (dried red *prik haeng* and fiery multicolored *prik kee noo* or bird chilies); coconut milk; and curry pastes, also ranging in heat from mild to incendiary and either prepared at home or available in markets.

Common herbs and spices include lemongrass, only the lower stalks of which is used (bruised or flattened to break the woody fibers and then sliced or minced); kaffir lime leaves; the Thai basil known as *gaprow* (also called "holy basil"); cilantro (also called coriander or Chinese parsley); and mint. The most prevalent flavors are basil, black pepper, galangal and its near cousin ginger, and garlic. Next to the Koreans, in fact,

Thais have the greatest per capita consumption of garlic in the world—about a pound per person per year.

The major condiments are chili-vinegar dipping sauce, a sort of Thai vinaigrette, and the peanut sauce used for satays. Bottles of nam pla and rice vinegar are usually set on the tables with the salt and pepper. Dried minced shrimp is often used to punch up salads and noodle dishes; so is roasted ground rice.

PASTAS AND STARCH Rice is the basis of all meals: In welcome, the Thai say "*Kin khao!*"—"Eat rice!" In comparison to the Thais' consumption of three-fourths of a pound every day, Americans average less than a half-pound a month, and even that average has gone up in the years since Asians began immigrating in such numbers. The preference in the north is for "sticky rice," called *kao nio* and related to the sweet rice of Japan; in the south, the longer-grained and intensely fragrant jasmine rice is standard.

Like other Asian cuisines, Thai cooking features a range of noodles—thick and thin, flat and round noodles, made of rice, wheat, and buckwheat, and those so-called cellophane or glass noodles made from bean starch—but even many noodle dishes are served with rice alongside.

MEAT AND POULTRY Pork and beef are the most common livestock, providing steaks and roast sections for grilling along with variety of organ meats and offal; but the Thai rarely eat lamb, which is considered an Asian—that is, Mongol—

Hot, Hot, Hot

In some cases, ordering is as simple as picking beef, chicken or shrimp and then "color-coding" the sauce. Green chilies are the hottest and tend to announce themselves immediately; red chilies move to the back of your tongue and then gradually take hold. Yellow chili pastes usually get their color from the addition of turmeric, suggesting more Burmese or Malay influence. "Dry curries," which sound to American ears as if they ought to be spice rubs but look much like yellow curries, omit the coconut milk in favor of a tamarind paste.

This is probably the time to point out that while northern or Isaan (sometimes transliterated as "Eesan") cooking, with its green and red curries, is notoriously hot, many Bangkok-style dishes are just as powerfully and persistently incendiary. If you see a listing for something like "tiger steak," remember that the dipping sauce or marinade served with grilled steak is called *seua rong hai*—literally, hot enough "to make a tiger cry." However, not all Thai dishes are hot; and most menus have stars or asterisks (or even little chili pods) to indicate the degree of spiciness. To be sure, ask your server.

import and too strong-smelling. Chicken is popular, and to a lesser degree, so are duck and quail.

SEAFOOD Though most Thai restaurants in the United States tend to offer only a couple of types of fish, particularly flounder and red snapper, at home they prepare a wide variety of salt- and freshwater fish, such as catfish and bass. Squid and shrimp are the most common shellfish, followed by mussels. Soft-shell crabs are becoming a staple in Thai restaurants, at least on the East Coast.

VEGETABLES Thai markets are frenetic places, and they stock many kinds of produce rarely seen (or prepared) here. There's a catalogue's worth of eggplants, for instance, from pea-sized bitter plants often found in curries, to white or pale green golf ball–sized "Thai eggplant" used in stir-fry, to the so-called Japanese eggplant, which are small, nearly seedless, and so sweet they do not require the pretreatment big European eggplants do. Other stable vegetables include bok choy and related cabbages, "yard-long" green beans, fresh bamboo shoots, onions, carrots, broccoli, sweet potatoes, and both fresh and dried mushrooms.

FRUITS Although they are infrequently included on menus, except perhaps as desserts, more than 30 varieties of bananas alone are available in Thailand, along with lychees, mango, pineapples, papayas, and jackfruit, which is the Limburger cheese of the fruit stand—delicious, but so odiferous that many hotels won't allow it in. It almost never appears on an American menu, but some Thai kitchens that cater to other Thai diners—and know you well—may admit to having some in the back.

THE MAIN DISHES

NOODLES AND RICE Probably the most famous Thai dish is the straightforwardly named *pad thai*—Thai noodles—which is served by street vendors in Thailand the way hot dogs are in New York. Pad thai combines rice noodles stir-fried with bean sprouts, chicken, pork, shrimp or tofu, dried shrimp, egg, green onions, and chopped peanuts, along with whatever else takes the chef's fancy (or happens to be at hand).

Among other major noodles dishes are *meekrop*, flash-fried and puffed noodles tossed with a sweetish-sour dressing and chicken or seafood; and *rad nar* or *guay tio rad nar*, fat rice noodles stir-fried with broccoli and chicken, pork, or beef and dressed with oyster sauce or fish sauce and a pinch of sugar. *Joke*, or jooke, is a thick rice porridge related to Chinese congee.

Among the most popular curries are *nam prik num*, a thick green vegetarian stew, and *nam prik oong*, made from ground meat and probably as close to American chili as Asian cooking gets. Both are northern in origin and should be eaten with sticky rice, using your fingers.

SOUPS Although Thais traditionally eat all their "courses" together, restaurants in the United States generally serve soups first. The most common are lemongrass-flavored broths with chilies, mushrooms, green onions, cilantro leaves, and either chicken (*tom yum gai*) or shrimp (*tom yum goong*). (Don't try to eat either the woody lemongrass stalks or pieces of galangal themselves—they're strictly for flavoring.) The other most popular soup is chicken with coconut milk (*tom kah gai*), which is also sparked by chilies and galangal. *Gaeng jud taoboo* is a bean curd soup with minced chicken, shrimp, and/or pork. Other fine options include hot-and-sour soups made with either shrimp or chicken; thickish rice soups made with meat or chicken; or the hearty *guay tio rangsit*, a rice noodle-and-beef soup often enriched with organ meats.

APPETIZERS AND SALADS Like the soup course, the separate hors d'oeuvre course doesn't actually exist in Thailand; the ones listed on menus here generally started out as light meals or kanto. Among the most popular are fried chicken drumsticks or "drumettes" pulled inside out and stuffed with pork or shrimp; pork or beef or chicken satay; and crab and meat dumplings, sometimes called "puffs" or even "balls." Although it is rarely seen, butterflied raw shrimp layered with chopped chilies and garlic is a seafood revelation, even to sushi addicts.

SALADS The Thai would be baffled by the mounds of iceberg lettuce that most Americans associate with the term "salad." Theirs are light entrees. The most popular feature squid or shrimp "cooked"

Snack Attack

What are listed on Western menus as "appetizers" are generally what the Thai consider snacks. Snacking is a constant activity in Thai life, which explains why many Thai "appetizers" are almost as large as main dishes in themselves. *Kanto* is the term for street food, and the cities of Thailand are movable banquets, with hundreds of stalls handing out satays; the grilled barbecued chicken called *kai yang*; *keap moo*, puffy fried pork skins that would mesmerize George Bush; and small bowls or even banana leaves of curries and rice.

ceviche-style in lime and chilies (in America, they are sometimes blanched or poached) and tossed with onion, chilies, cilantro, and cellophane noodles: The shrimp version is called *pra goong* (sometimes pla gung) and the squid salad is *pra pla mug* (or moog). Grilled marinated beef (*yum nam tok* or *yam nua*) and roasted duck (*yum ped yang*) are also often served atop salads, seasoned with red onion, cilantro, mint, ginger, ground roasted rice, lime juice, and fish sauce.

Meang kom is a sort of finger salad that involves mixing together dried shrimp, roasted coconut, minced onion, sweet pepper, and a little sauce, all served in little dishes, on a spinach or lettuce leaf and rolling it up to nibble on.

MEATS The most common ways of cooking beef and pork are to grill them (usually thin-sliced and skewered) or to stir-fry them in one of the curry sauces. Minced raw meat salads may be available in really authentic restaurants; called *larb* (or lahb), they are a northern regional dish made of pork or beef or even water buffalo. (In the United States, however, most larb is chicken, *larb gai*, and it's cooked.) Larb is served with sticky rice, which should be formed into a patty or flatted ball and used to snag a bite of meat—something like the way Ethiopian injera is used to eat kitfo. *Nem* is a sausage made of raw meat and roasted rice and then cured—really pickled—in chili and garlic; *sai krog* is a pork sausage, usually served grilled.

SEAFOOD The Gulf of Thailand is extremely rich in shellfish and prawns as well as flesh fish, hence the high quality of seafood dishes. Shrimp, squid, and soft-shell crabs are particular favorites and are offered in a variety of sauces, usually including a curry, a ginger-and-scallion sauce, coarse black pepper and vinegar, chili paste and scallions, or black bean sauce, or in the almost universally applied gra prou style— basil and chilies. Small whole squid may be stuffed with ground pork (a dish called *pla muk sod sal*). Tiger shrimp and prawns are commonly grilled and served with sauces on the side, while mussels and seafood stews (more and more often listed on American menus as "Thai bouillabaisses") are usually prepared with coconut milk. Whole fish are often fried and offered with either black bean, ground pork, chili sauce, or sweet-and-sour sauce or steamed with ginger.

POULTRY Chicken may be grilled or skewered and served with the same choice of chili, black bean, or sweet-and-sour sauces, as well as with the curries described above. Chicken is also frequently offered in a peanut or cashew-flavored sauce; and duck may be fried or roasted. In restaurants with stronger Indonesian influences, you may see duck breast with mango and cashew or tamarind sauce. Quail, either marinated and grilled or fried, is also popular.

BEVERAGES   You will probably find that the sweet-sour vinegars and nam pla spoil the taste of wine (and those "exotic" cocktails with umbrellas are the potable equivalent of bermuda shorts and black socks). Your best bet is beer; the Thai Singha ("Tiger") brand is widely available. The primary nonalcoholic drinks are iced coffee and iced tea, both served with sweetened evaporated milk; hot tea (though not hot coffee), lemonade (rather salty to Western tastes), and perhaps soft drinks. Rice whiskey, which is rarely listed but frequently available, is highly potent.

SWEETS   Desserts may be fruits (fried bananas, plain fresh melon) or a combination of sticky rice and coconut milk with mango or banana. Coconut ice cream (particularly in the United States), lychee nuts, and sweet cakes or jellies called *kanom* are also popular.

HOW TO ORDER AND EAT LIKE A NATIVE

Thai restaurants in the United States are making fewer and fewer concessions to Western tastes, for several reasons. One is the increasing interest among American diners in real ethnic food and fresh ingredients. Another is the greater number of fresh Thai spices and vegetables available. (In the usual circular fashion, greater demand leads to more and fresher ingredients being made available, which leads to more interest, and so on.) Spicy cuisines are more than a rage; they've become standard.

The one concession Thai menus have made is in classification. Although Thai meals are served simultaneously, Thai restaurants here have adopted the Western scheme: appetizers or soups first, then salads, main dishes, and desserts. You can ask to have them all served at once, however, as the Thai do, and use a spoon to dish up the rice and top it with a little entree. You will come to appreciate the soups more if you have them alongside entrees—for one thing, you'll be able to eat a bite of rice now and then to cool off!

As with all menus transliterated from other alphabets, there are spelling differences among Thai menus (sate vs. satay, pad vs. pud, etc.). The knottiest problem for English speakers is the consonant that in most Southeast Asian languages, along with Korean and to a lesser extent Japanese, falls halfway between the English "r" and "l" and is apt to be spelled either way. (Asians tend to be soft with all consonants as a matter of style and think Western languages somewhat rude and abrupt because they have such "harsh" sounds.) There is also a rather fluid vowel that ranges between "ow" and "uh" and "ah," but most other syllables are fairly clear, and you will probably have no difficulty spotting your favorite dishes.

Generally, the menus here split up dishes into appetizers, soups, salads, meat dishes, poultry dishes, seafood dishes, and noodle and rice dishes. Two diners will probably want two dishes and a soup—say, lemongrass soup with shrimp; lahb; and beef curry. Four diners should order a soup (maybe hot and sour), squid or grilled beef salad, pad thai, chicken curry, and either soft-shell crabs or whole fish. Some rice will be served automatically, but you may find yourself ordering more.

Thai cooking, like many Asian cuisines, is relatively quick and inexpensive, putting it high on the office-lunchers' list: You can expect to have a good meal for $10 and a great one for $20.

Rice, the mainstay, is the only dish served hot rather than comfortably warm or even room temperature, often in lidded woven baskets (particularly in the case of sticky rice) or covered porcelain bowls. Each diner takes a large portion of rice and then small portions of the main dishes, supplementing them as the meal progresses. Again, there are two main types of rice, the glutinous sticky or "sweet" rice and the unmistakably fragrant jasmine rice. You may even come across a third type during your meal—uncooked rice that has been roasted and then ground into a spicing powder that tastes a little like malt or Grape-Nuts. Altogether, a Thai diner may consume three to four cups of rice at a sitting, treating what we consider the main dishes merely as gloried condiments.

In Thailand itself, especially in the country or informally at home, many people still eat with their fingers, rolling bite-size balls of rice with their fingers and then dipping them into the curry or other sauce. Otherwise, they tend to use spoons, sometimes pushing food into the flattened bowl of the spoon with forks. Noodles take chopsticks.

Traditionally, the dining table is round, with a short pedestal, and diners sit around it on the floor; but while some Japanese and Korean restaurants in the United States maintain traditional floor seating, few if any Thai establishments do. When entertaining at home, however, you could recreate the traditional atmosphere either by sitting around a coffee table or by placing a cloth on the floor itself, picnic-style. And although it is considered polite to remove your shoes before entering Thai homes, as it is with Japanese homes, that is not necessary in a restaurant.

COOKING AT HOME

Little special equipment is required to prepare Thai dishes at home; if you don't have a mortar and pestle, a spice or coffee grinder will do, or even a food processor. A wok, a skillet, and a couple of bowls will just about do it; a bamboo steamer is helpful, but a wok with a rack and steam-proof dish will do just as well.

CUCUMBER SALAD

1 cucumber, peeled, seeded, and chopped
1 tablespoon onion, minced
2 tablespoons dried shrimp, pounded into pieces
1 teaspoon granulated sugar
3 tablespoons lime juice
2 tablespoons fish sauce (nam pla)
8 lettuce leaves
2 tablespoons roasted peanuts, coarsely crushed
1 teaspoon red chili flakes

Line a bowl with paper towels. Place chopped cucumber in the bowl and gently squeeze out moisture. Remove paper and add onion, dried shrimp, and sugar. Sprinkle with lime juice and fish sauce and toss gently. Line a serving dish with lettuce leaves and mound cucumbers in the middle; top with peanuts and chili flakes. Chill and serve.

MINCED BEEF (LARB)

1 1/2 tablespoons long- or short-grain rice
4 small dried red chilies, seeded

1 pound top round steak, finely minced
juice of 2 limes
3 stalks lemongrass, finely minced
1 large red onion, finely chopped
1 large bell pepper, cored, seeded, and chopped
30 mint leaves (approximately)
2 tablespoons fish sauce (nam pla)

In a small dry frying pan over medium heat, roast rice and chilies, shaking until the grains have browned and chilies darkened. Pour this mixture into mortar and pestle or electric grinder and grind to the consistency of coarse sand.

Place minced steak in a bowl and with your hands mix in ground rice and chili mixture, lime juice, lemongrass, red onion, and green pepper. Chop half the mint leaves and stir into the meat; reserve the rest for garnish. Season with fish sauce and transfer to serving dish. Garnish with remaining mint or decorate with lime wedges, cucumber slices, etc.

Note: You may modify the recipe by lightly poaching minced meat in boiling water until it just changes color, then proceed.

CHICKEN, COCONUT, AND GALANGAL SOUP

4 cups stock or broth
4 lime leaves, chopped
4-inch piece lemongrass, chopped
2-inch piece galangal, split lengthwise into several pieces
6–8 tablespoons fish sauce (nam pla)
6 tablespoons lemon juice
8 ounces chicken breast, finely sliced
1 1/4 cups coconut milk
4 small red chilies, slightly crushed
cilantro leaves for garnish

In a saucepan, heat stock, lime leaves, lemongrass, galangal, fish sauce and lemon juice. Stirring thoroughly, bring to a boil and add chicken and coconut milk. Continue to cook over high heat, stirring constantly, until meat is cooked through (about 2 minutes). Add crushed chilies for the last few seconds, pour into small bowls, and garnish with cilantro.

SHRIMP CURRY

3 tablespoons oil
3 large garlic cloves, finely chopped
2 tablespoons red curry paste
2 cups coconut milk
4 tablespoons fish sauce (nam pla)
2 teaspoons sugar
24 large raw shrimp, deveined and peeled but with small tail shell intact
4 lime leaves, finely sliced
2 small red chilies, finely sliced lengthwise
20 leaves holy basil

In a wok or frying pan, heat oil and sauté garlic until golden brown. Add curry paste and cook briefly, then add, half the coconut milk, the fish sauce, and the sugar, stirring briskly after each addition. The mixture will thicken slightly. Add shrimp and cook until they start to become opaque, then add the remaining coconut milk, the lime leaves, and the chilies. Continue to turn shrimp in the sauce until cooked through. Using a slotted spoon, remove shrimp to serving dish, add basil leaves to sauce, stir, and pour over shrimp.

VIETNAM

BASIC CUISINE

DINNER FOR TWO:
Cha gio, grilled beef in lettuce leaves, caramel chicken, stuffed squid

DINNER FOR FOUR:
Stuffed chicken wings, beef noodle soup, banh xeo, soft-shell crabs, steamed fish, roast quail

GROUP DISH:
Bo Ban Mon

STYLE:
Light, crisp, spicy

KEY FLAVORS:
Cilantro, nuoc mam, chilies

EATING UTENSILS:
Fingers, chopsticks

DISTINCTIVE DISHES:
Pho, spring rolls, banh xeo

UNIFORMITY OF MENUS:
Good

NUTRITIONAL INDEX:
Low fat, high protein, medium sodium

COST:
Inexpensive

"THANK YOU":
"Cam ahn"

Perhaps the deceptive simplicity of Vietnamese cuisine has kept it from achieving the wide popularity one would expect of a style so clean, light, and healthful, yet so satisfying. Maybe diners lost sight of it in moving away from the more familiar, heavily sauced Chinese cooking to the spicier Thai restaurants.

However, it is an easy cuisine to like—fresh, low in fat and calories, and inexpensive, particularly in the case of the pho kitchens that specialize in one-pot soup meals. Where some cuisines emphasize variety of flavors (such as Thai) or simplicity and purity (the Japanese), Vietnamese cuisine concentrates on texture, mixing cooked ingredients with raw ones, spicy or sour ingredients with mild ones, and cold foods with hot. Cold soft noodles are topped with grilled meats and chopped fresh herbs; minced pork and shrimp are mixed with crunchy bean sprouts, chopped peanuts, and mint and wrapped in paper-thin sheets of rice flour; and marinated chicken is tossed with grapefruit sections and served over cabbage slaw.

And since nearly all foods are dipped in sauce after cooking, the contrasting flavors are exaggerated even further.

THE COUNTRY

Shaped like a gracefully extended "f" from some old love letter, never wider than about 45 miles, Vietnam stretches down the east coast of Southeast Asia along the South China Sea and up under the southern tip of Cambodia. Just larger than the state of New Mexico, it is home to 40 times as many residents—more than 65 million.

Settled more than 4,000 years ago and culturally linked to the Chinese, Vietnam was actually conquered by China about 100 B.C. and remained a subject nation for another thousand years before establishing its independence and stretching south into what had been ethnic Khmer (Cambodian) territory. Its division into north and south has long historical precedent; from the mid-sixteenth through the mid-nineteenth centuries, the country was ruled as two separate kingdoms, centered at Hanoi in the north and Hue near Da Nang in the central plateau.

The French began aggressively attempting to colonize the area about that time and gradually took control; by the end of the nineteenth century, French Indochina included not only Vietnam but also Laos and Cambodia. The region remained under French domination until World War II, when it was occupied by Japanese forces; it was "returned" to the French after the war and did not achieve independence until the mid-1950s, but French influence on the cuisine, though superficially strong (because so many restaurant menus were translated into French), is actually quite limited.

THE CUISINE

Vietnam has three geographical regions, each with its own produce and recognizable culinary styles, although in the United States the regional cuisines are less distinctive.

The cooler, mountainous north has fewer foods available—the plateaus are largely turned over to tea, coffee, and sugar plantations, with a few starches such as sweet potatoes, corn, and beans planted in between—so the cuisine depends heavily on spices for variety. Dried and preserved ingredients are common here, too, including mushrooms and fungi and dried jellyfish. Much use is made of the seafood found in colder water, such as crabs; but the plateaus are good for raising cattle, and the North Vietnamese prize beef somewhat more highly than their southern counterparts do. The North's proximity to China shows in its more frequent use of stir-frying.

The central lowlands—whose old capital, Hue, was once considered particularly sophisticated—reflect the typical courtiers' assumption that more is better: "Court cuisine" consisted of many highly and imaginatively spiced dishes served in small portions. Specially fed and fattened pork were a Hue delicacy, and pork is still highly popular here.

And the south, with its humid climate and the rich alluvial soil deposited by heavy rainfall in the Mekong Delta, produces the widest variety of vegetables and fruits, as well as the sugarcane that is used in both grilling and candying; the Indian influence is seen here in the fondness for curry spices, and the Indonesian trade is visible in the use of peanut-based dipping sauces and coconut milk and the tendency to use sweet-sour citrus fruits to refresh food, particularly seafood dishes.

Despite its strong Chinese ties, Vietnamese cooking remains remarkably distinct. The most obvious differences are a preference for cooking with water or broth rather than oil; the taste for raw rather than cooked vegetables; and the use of *nuoc mam*, also called fish sauce, instead of soy sauce except in dishes that are actually borrowed from Chinese recipes. However, the Vietnamese remain the only Southeast Asian people that commonly use chopsticks.

Delicious and Nutritious

Although some dishes, particularly those made with *nuoc mam* or *mam nem*, may seem slightly salty, Vietnamese food in general is exceptionally healthful. The Vietnamese prefer to use only a small amount of oil even when stir-frying; most dishes are either grilled (the charcoal brazier is the most important element in Vietnamese cooking), simmered, braised, or steamed. Although skewered meat and poultry are as popular here as they are in the Middle East, Vietnamese marinades are much less likely to be oil-based, and vegetables and rice far outweigh meat in the diet anyway. Soups and sauces are simmered and reduced rather than thickened with starch as in China.

The main exceptions are the whole fried fish (and unfortunately, the Vietnamese version can be extremely addictive), the fried stuffed chicken drumettes, and the Malay-influenced dipping sauces, whose fat double-whammy of coconut milk and peanut butter can turn an otherwise lean satay into a diet-buster. Also, some restaurants have a pretty heavy hand with the oil when making *banh xeo*, the giant crepes.

Vietnamese cooks in the United States have made accommodations to American tastes. At home, the Vietnamese buy all their poultry live (whatever that they don't raise themselves, that is) and have it killed, bled, and cleaned on the spot; they prefer their poultry slightly pink, which the freshness allows for. Here chicken is cooked throughout, as most Americans prefer; on the other hand, the beef and pork that we might cook less is also well done. Restaurant chefs here don't generally cook with as much garlic or chilies as they do at home. (Contrary to popular wisdom, Vietnamese like spicy food almost as much as the Thai.) Also, dishes that in Vietnam would be hand-wrapped in rice papers are frequently served either prewrapped by the kitchen or served with steamed rice instead unless you specify a preference first.

The first Europeans to trade in Vietnam were, as usual, the Portuguese, who arrived in 1535 bearing the New World's revolutionary foodstuffs: corn, tomatoes, peanuts, potatoes, watercress, peanuts, and chilies, and in return carried away peppercorns and other spices. The Dutch, French, and English arrived a few centuries later, along with a steady influx of Catholic missionaries; today Vietnam's population is divided between Buddhists and Catholics. The many fast days and the strict vegetarianism of Buddhist philosophy contributed to the number of vegetarian dishes common among Vietnamese restaurants.

The most prominent mementos of French colonization are French bread (eaten in addition to, not instead of, rice and noodles); strong French coffee (usually iced and sweetened with condensed milk, in deference to the climate); and a fondness for such vegetables as asparagus (usually canned, since cultivation is difficult) and artichokes (grown in Vietnam but most often dried and turned into tea). The French language is still spoken throughout Southeast Asia, but menus in the United States, which used to use French terms for most dishes, are increasingly in Vietnamese and English only.

MAIN INGREDIENTS

RICE AND OTHER STARCHES The two delta regions—the Red River and its extensive canals in the north and the Mekong in the south—are among the world's most productive rice fields; Vietnamese sometimes compare their bone-shaped country to a porter's pole with buckets of rice hanging from either end. The everyday rice is a fragrant jasmine or basmati, but for special occasions and as comfort food, they cook the more glutinous type, called "sweet rice" by the Japanese, "sticky rice" by the Thai, and called *gao nep* by the Vietnamese. (There is also a black glutinous rice, but it is still fairly rare in the United States.)

Some flour is made from rice, but tapioca flour and potato flour are also produced. The variety of flours results in a wide range of noodles and pastas as well as rolls and dumplings.

MEAT AND GAME   Beef (*bo*) is the favorite meat, although it is scarce and therefore expensive in some places. Organs are fairly common—particularly liver, kidneys, tripe, and brains—but are not as specifically popular as in China or Singapore. Pork (*heo*) is more expansively consumed, because it is cheaper and easier to raise, and its leftovers and fats are turned into either mild or spicy sausages. Vietnam is also surprisingly rich in game, such as buffalo, wild oxen, elk, and deer; one of the delicacies sold in markets is a sort of candied venison jerky with sesame seeds. Mutton is not eaten.

POULTRY   There is almost as much wildfowl as game meat in Vietnam, including pheasant, thrush, and waterfowl; quail is a particular favorite. Almost all families raise chicken and ducks, but the eggs are not a major dietary item.

FISH AND SEAFOOD   Restaurants here may play up the meats, because they assume Americans prefer them to seafood, but their cuisine is rich in both saltwater and freshwater fish: carp, red snapper, perch, catfish and the anchovies essential for the making of nuoc mam. In the United States they most often steam the snapper and fry flounder. Vietnam is even richer in river creatures and shellfish—shrimp, crabs, clams, oysters, langoustines, lobsters, snails, eels, jellyfish, rays, sharks, squid, and even frogs.

VEGETABLES   For any pro-fiber nutritionists looking for paradise, Vietnam might be the place. Among the common vegetables are radishes, cauliflower, artichokes, cabbages, carrots, cucumber, jicama, lettuce, spinach, watercress, eggplant, bean sprouts, bamboo shoots, leeks, scallions, snow peas, and a wide variety of mushrooms.

FRUITS   Although they appear primarily as desserts on American menus, the Vietnamese enjoy papaya, mango, coconut, bananas, jackfruit, bitter melons, pineapples, and plums. Pickled plums—actually salted, dried, and then sugared—are simmered into many meat sauces and called *xi mui*.

SEASONINGS *Nuoc mam*, which is both ingredient and condiment, is a fermented anchovy sauce. Mixed with fresh lime juice, vinegar, garlic, chilies, and a dash of sugar it becomes *nuoc cham*, the dipping sauce provided for most finger foods (which are numerous) and salads. Mixed with peanuts, a little tomato or chili paste, and soybean or hoisin sauce, it becomes *nuoc leo*. At least one of these three, if not all, will be served at some point during the meal.

The most distinctive flavorings in Vietnamese cooking, after nuoc mam, are cilantro, parsley, *ngo gai* (the "saw leaf herb" used in hot-and-sour soup), lemongrass, vinegar, ginger, garlic, garlic chives, sesame seeds and sesame oil, shallots, black and especially white pepper, tamarind, annatto (the mild orangy seed also used in Latin American cooking), five-spice powder, anise, curry spices (coriander, fennel seed, turmeric, cumin, cloves, and cardamom), coconut milk, and a variety of basils (purple Thai basil, Japanese shiso, and perilla), mints, and hot red and green chilies, particularly the tiny Thai or bird peppers.

Sweetened or sweet-and-sour tomato sauces and barbecue sauces are popular particularly on street snacks or dishes commonly cooked on the waterfront, such as whole fried fish. Peanut sauces borrowed from Indonesia are served on the satays learned from the same source. There is also an unfermented anchovy sauce, called *mam nem*; and the Chinese staples hoisin sauce and oyster sauce are also used, like soy, in those recipes that reflect the Chinese influence. Interestingly, strict Buddhists are forbidden to consume either garlic or scallions; and since they believe that all living things, including fish, have a soul, nuoc mam is also forbidden, so on Buddhist holidays it is replaced by soy.

THE MAIN DISHES

FIRST COURSES What are usually listed as appetizers in restaurants here are called *do nhau*, or "little bites," in Vietnam. They are the sort of fresh-off-the-grill finger foods that vendors hand out from food stalls in the marketplaces in Vietnam: tiny crab cakes; spring rolls; shrimp toast (minced shrimp paste spread over grilled French bread); barbecued spare ribs; chicken wings or drumettes stuffed with crabmeat and chopped rice vermicelli; minced shrimp paste wrapped around sugarcane or crab claws and then grilled; beef grilled in grape leaves; grilled meatballs; or lemon chicken. A lot of these items may be served with lettuce leaves or rice papers for wrapping up, and you could easily "graze" through a whole meal of them. (*Banh trang*, the "rice papers," are really rice-flour pancakes rolled very thin, then dried, then reconstituted by soaking in water—something like Vietnamese tortillas.)

More formal sit-down first courses might include "happy pancakes" (usually, but not always, called *banh xeo*), rice-flour omelets or heavy crepes filled with mushrooms, pork, and shrimp; artichokes stuffed with crabmeat; squid stuffed with pork; or Indonesian-style grilled beef satays with peanut sauce.

APPETIZER ROLLS *Cha gio* (pronounced "zhah zhaw"), the justly famous spring rolls, are rice-paper wrappers filled with pork, tree ear mushrooms, shrimp, herbs, and the translucent "cellophane noodles" or "glass noodles" (also called bean threads); they are fried and, like almost all these appetizers, are meant to be dipped in nuoc cham. (Adherents of cha gio shudder at the term "egg roll.") *Goi cuon*, sometimes referred to here as "imperial rolls," are unfried rolls with noodles, shrimp, scallions, and herbs dipped in plum sauce; *bi cuon* are similar but with pork fat added.

SALADS Raw vegetable dishes are part of nearly every meal, but they go far beyond what we think of as salads. They are more likely seafood (shrimp or squid) or grilled meat with raw carrot, cucumbers, lettuce, scallions, and fresh herbs all composed on a plate and presented with the rice papers for wrapping them all up and a saucer of nuoc cham for dipping. (Be sure to read the menu carefully, however: In the United States, Vietnamese restaurants frequently attempt to hand out salad bowls of iceberg lettuce and tomato, assuming that's what Americans want). Seafood and citrus combinations are also popular, such as lobster with papaya or shrimp with oranges or lemons.

SOUPS Particularly in the case of the North Vietnamese favorite called *pho* (see page 207), soups can be whole meals, but they may also be offered as appetizers, served either individually or in large family-sized tureens. Soup is frequently served as breakfast, which makes sense in a climate that may be blisteringly hot by midday. Among the popular first-course soups are crab and asparagus, chicken and rice, or chicken and noodle soups; hot-and-sour soup with shrimp or pork; crab dumpling soup; meatball soup; beef-noodle soup; and dried squid stew. Non-noodle soups are known collectively as *sup*.

PASTAS AND PORRIDGES Noodles are extremely popular, particularly rice vermicelli and cellophane noodles, and are most often served cold. The word *bun* refers to rice vermicelli. Noodles are frequently fried into crispy baskets to hold seafood or beef stews, or are stir-fried with tomato and vegetables under seafood. However, rice (*com*) is still the most popular starch and is anything but dull: The deceptively plain-looking "Perfume River rice," for instance, is flavored with lemongrass, dried shrimp, and sesame seeds. *Come tay chao* is a familiar dish to fans of Chinese mom-and-pop kitchens, a sort of congee or rice porridge topped with anything from duck to tripe. There are also a number of rice stews cooked in clay pots: *Con tay cam* is flavored with duck broth, crabmeat, shrimp, and vegetables; *come tay cam ga* is the chicken version.

MEATS Beef is relatively rare and thus more expensive—hence the tradition of presenting "Beef Seven Ways" at celebrations and banquets. Beef is often "stretched," either as part of a salad, soup, or stir-fry or as meatballs. It may also be "stuffed" or rolled around vegetables and cut in pinwheel slices; among these dishes are fragrant "cinnamon beef" with orange peel; wine-and-honey–marinated beef pinwheeled around grilled onions; and flank steak rolled around caramelized carrots. Wine-flavored bouef bourguignonne–style stews, sometimes called "Saigon beef," are often padded, with the potatoes and bread stewed right in.

Other common meat entrees include pork chops, short ribs, and venison in red wine.

POULTRY Roast duck is extremely popular over salads and rice congees, usually with the skin and fat (where the smoke or spices linger) intact. Quail is very popular, marinated and grilled and served with the coarse salt-and-pepper dip or marinated in coconut. Chicken (*ga*) is roasted, marinated, stewed in coconut milk and ginger sauce, satay-grilled, braised with a caramel sauce (sometimes made from the sweetened condensed milk the Vietnamese favor in coffee), or stir-fried with chilies and lemongrass. A chicken and rice casserole is a home-cooking favorite; although it is not often on restaurant menus, it is frequently available for the asking.

FISH AND SHELLFISH As mentioned, whole fish are extremely popular, particularly fried or steamed. Mixed seafoods are popular too, either steamed, grilled, poached, or stir-fried; and they are frequently presented in fried rice-noodle "nests." Clams and oysters are often steamed with ginger and garlic or scallions; squid often appears stuffed with pork or shrimp or even crab. Shrimp are most often grilled, but they are popular in curry and coconut milk sauces. Soft-shell crabs are a particular Vietnamese specialty, and in season many restaurants will offer them four or five ways a day.

ONE-POT MEALS   Some restaurants offer beef or even fish fondues called *lau*, which are Chinese hotpots recalling the Mongol invasions of the thirteenth century; however, the "broth" may have a very un-Mongol flavoring of coconut milk or vinegar. Similar dishes are cooked in the kitchen in clay pots. Tofu frequently is stir-fried not just instead of meats but in addition to them, flavored with roast pork or smoked duck.

BEVERAGES   With meals—particularly with "little bites" such as crabs, satays, and barbecue—the Vietnamese like beer or coffee, along with soft drinks (including a soy milk, club soda, and egg yolk "cream" called *soda sua not ga*), teas (green, black, or floral), French-style wines, or a rice wine called *ruou de* that is similar to sake.

SWEETS   The Vietnamese themselves do not serve sugary desserts—they tend to eat them in the late afternoon with hot tea or coffee, following the post-lunch siesta—and generally prefer fruit, either fresh or perhaps caramelized, after dinner. However, since most customers in restaurants here do expect dessert choices, menus are likely to include a least a simple flan, bananas flambé, or rice or taro pudding. (You may also see less likely pudding choices; some are even made with black-eyed peas.) Vietnamese iced coffee—espresso with sweetened condensed milk—is very sweet and serves as a sort of combination coffee and dessert.

PHO

Pho, the most famous Vietnamese soup, is a whole meal in a bowl and is just about the only dish *not* served communally; the word *pho* actually means "one's own bowl," because you don't share it.

Pho is a beef broth and noodle soup with raw bean sprouts, fresh green herbs, and usually a choice of up to eight or ten various cuts of beef (occasionally, but not traditionally, chicken or seafood) placed on top and served with various condiments on the side. Like most beef dishes, it was most popular in the north—some restaurants advertise it as "beef noodle soup, Hanoi-style"—but it became almost a staple in the south after the fall of Saigon and the influx of northerners. In the United States there are an increasing number of "pho houses" that offer only pho. From $4 a bowl of basics to about $10 with all the deluxe toppings, these meals are budget bonanzas.

When you order pho, the soup bowl will arrive nearly full of hot broth and noodles with whatever meat you have chosen on top; the bean sprouts, fresh green herbs, chilies, and flavoring sauces (vinegar, soy or nuoc mam, and hoisin) will be served separately. You will be given chopsticks, a soup spoon, and a small sauce dish. Stir the raw vegetables into the soup and put the dipping sauces (which are for the meats) in the small saucer. Then using the chopsticks in your stronger hand and the spoon in the other, draw up some noodles out of the broth to cool, resting the lower part of them in the bowl of the spoon. You may blow on the noodles or make a slurping noise without being impolite. In between noodles and sprouts, use the chopsticks to bring out the meats or seafood and dip them in the sauce.

HOW TO ORDER AND EAT LIKE A NATIVE

Dining is a lively social exercise in Vietnam, either out (at the food stalls that are the very heart of the markets), in restaurants, or at home, where everyone is served at once and a great hubbub arises while the dishes are passed.

In traditional Vietnamese homes, diners sit cross-legged on bamboo mats on the floor around a low table, but this practice is almost never seen in the United States. Each place is set with a bowl, a small saucer for nuoc cham or other dipping sauces, chopsticks and a flat-bottomed Chinese porcelain spoon; here a plate is almost certain. You may also be offered wet washcloths or towels for your hands. There will probably be bowls of cilantro, mint, and lettuce leaves on the table, and perhaps cold noodles on the table as well. After the salad and soup, all the dishes—generally three or four entrees—are served at once, and when the big bowl of rice appears, the noise (and pleasure) level rises appreciably.

Each diner puts rice in his or her bowl, then takes a small portion of each entree and puts it on top of the rice; it is polite to take only as much as you can manage, because the rice and dishes will go around again and again. Use the larger ends of the chopsticks to serve yourself rather than the eating ends.

Incidentally, if any of the dishes are served with sticky rice instead of banh trang, you should use the rice itself as a spoon, molding it with your fingers; see the chapter on Thailand for hints.

"Bo Bay Mon," the Beef Seven Ways banquet, is obviously a whole meal, but in the United States restaurants frequently offer customers the choice of ordering only two or three of the courses. However, if you have the full dinner, the last course will be *chao thit bo*, a beef-rice soup cooked in the broth created by previous courses of hot pots, etc. Like the pho, these dishes are served with varieties of green herbs, chilies, and lime to flavor just as you like.

Pho, is also a whole meal, but you might want to save it for a second (or solo) visit. To order from a full menu, two people should try cha gio, grilled beef in grape leaves, and, if you have fairly hearty appetites, extra appetizers such as shrimp grilled on sugarcane or the so-called shrimp beignets (minced shrimp and eggwhites quick-fired and puffed up), then caramelized or coconut milk chicken and stuffed squid. For four people, order stuffed chicken wings; either beef noodle soup or hot-and-

Merrily We Roll

The great majority of Vietnamese dishes—salads, satays, barbecues, and even the flesh of whole fish, pulled by chopsticks away from the bone—are traditionally eaten by hand. The meats, along with a few of the green herbs and noodles that will be served on the side, are wrapped in the rice-paper crepes and dipped into sauce; this rolling, dipping, and chatting rhythm makes Vietnamese dining even more sociable.

The best way to make a roll is to use the chopsticks to transfer food into the rice-paper sheet about a third of the way up, then, using your hands, turn the short flap of crepe over the filling and fold in the two remaining "long sides" butcher-paper style before tightly rolling from the filled end toward the open side. That way the food won't fall out the ends. The first few times, try putting only a morsel of two of each ingredient into the paper—they add up, and then the roll gets hard to hold together. Also, rice-paper crepes are much thinner than the Chinese pancakes you may have had Peking duck or moo shi pork in, and they tear more easily.

Menus here are logistically predictable but linguistically problematic. Although traditional Vietnamese meals do not include "appetizers" as we know them, and have "salads" we'd consider light meals, most Vietnamese restaurants have managed to arrange the menus in a way that is more familiar to American diners.

On the other hand, recognizing the names of dishes—which can be difficult in any Asian restaurant, because the words have to be spelled phonetically—seems especially tricky in this case because the phonetics themselves seem mysterious: *Pho*, for instance, is pronounced with almost any vowel you can imagine. The most undependably translated word appears to be *banh*, which literally means "cake" but which refers frequently to rice-noodle patties, sometimes to French bread, and most often to a sort of thick omelet. Fortunately, though they are unobtrusive and deferential, Vietnamese waiters are very helpful and will tell you what you want to know about your food and often show you how to eat it.

sour soup; banh xeo; fried soft-shell crabs; a whole steamed fish (remember to ask for rice papers so you can roll it); and roast quail.

A few Vietnamese restaurants serve more modern street food, some of it imported by homesick French soldiers and some probably traceable to the American servicemen stationed there: cheeses, pâtés, hero-type sandwiches on French baguettes, etc.

COOKING AT HOME

Vietnamese kitchens are among the simplest in the world. Usually they are annexes to the house, partly open to the outdoors to let the heat out, and they depend on charcoal braziers. A wok, some skillets, a mortar and pestle (or grinder), a colander, a bamboo steamer, a cleaver, chopsticks, and a couple of spoons are almost all you need either there or here; a rice cooker is helpful, but a regular saucepan will do, of course. You can either cook outdoors on a grill or use the broiler inside. (If you will be grilling on bamboo skewers, be sure to soak them in water 30 minutes beforehand.)

Pass around cold wet towels before serving. Dishes should be served at least warm or room temperature, but the rice should be hot, so make up all the dipping sauces and set out the condiments (lettuce leaves, dipping sauces, cold rice noodles, chili peppers) in advance.

NUOC CHAM

1/4 cup sugar
1/4 cup warm water
3 cloves garlic, peeled
1 Thai or bird chili
1/2 cup fish sauce (nuoc mam)
1/4 cup lime juice
1 medium carrot, finely shredded (option)

Combine sugar and warm water in blender and mix until dissolved. Add all other ingredients except carrot in blender and puree; stir carrot in last. Serve at room temperature.

GRILLED MEATBALLS (NINH HOA)

1 lb. ground pork (or mixed pork and beef)
1 teaspoon freshly ground white pepper (or more to taste)
3 cloves garlic, peeled and finely minced (or more to taste)
1 tablespoon sugar
1 scallion or green onion, finely chopped
3 leaves mint or basil, finely chopped (optional)
1 tablespoon fish sauce (nuoc mam)
3 teaspoons cornstarch or potato starch
oil for rolling meatballs
lettuce leaves for wrapping
nuoc cham (recipe above)

Combine ground meat, pepper, garlic, sugar, scallion or onion, herbs, and fish sauce; sprinkle with starch and mix again. Cover, place in refrigerator, and let flavors blend several hours.

Prepare grill or preheat broiler. Rub a little oil on your hands, then make meatballs about one inch across; place on skewers, if you are using them, and grill or broil until crispy on all sides (2–3 minutes per side). Serve with lettuce leaves for wrapping and nuoc cham dipping sauce.

RICE WITH CHICKEN IN CLAY POT CASSEROLE (COME TAY CAM)

2 tablespoons fish sauce (nuoc mam)
1 teaspoon sugar

2 teaspoons sesame oil
4 cloves garlic, peeled and finely minced
salt and white pepper to taste
6 chicken thighs, skinned, boned, and cut into bite-sized pieces
8 dried shiitake mushrooms
1 tablespoon cornstarch or potato starch
1/2 cup dry sherry or Chinese cooking wine
2 tablespoons peanut oil
4 shallots, peeled and finely minced
1 small white onion, chopped
2 cups long grain rice
2 1/2 cups chicken or vegetable broth

Mix together fish sauce, sugar, sesame oil, 1 clove garlic, and salt and pepper; add chicken and stir to cover well. Meanwhile, soak mushrooms in warm water until soft; dispose of tough stems and julienne the caps. Dissolve cornstarch in sherry.

Heat 1 teaspoon peanut oil in a skillet, sauté shallot and remaining garlic 1 minute, and add chicken mixture. Sauté, stirring, about 8 minutes or until thoroughly cooked. Add mushrooms and stir 1 minute; add cornstarch and continue to stir another 5 minutes. Set aside.

In a heavy casserole or enamel-coated pot, heat the rest of the peanut oil and sauté the onion until golden; increase heat to high, add rice, and stir-fry about 3 minutes. Add broth, stir once, and cover; reduce heat to medium, cook about 5 minutes or until liquid has evaporated, and then reduce heat to low. Continue to cook, stirring once or twice, another 10 minutes, then pour chicken over rice and cook another 10 minutes. Serve hot.

FRIED CHICKEN WITH LEMONGRASS

1 stalk fresh lemongrass (or 1 tablespoon dried)
2 tablespoons rice wine vinegar or wine
3 tablespoons fresh ginger, peeled and finely minced
2 tablespoons fish sauce (nuoc mam)
1/2 cup water
1 teaspoon cornstarch or potato starch
1 teaspoon sugar

3 chicken thighs, skinned, boned, and cut into bite-sized pieces
freshly ground white pepper
1 tablespoon peanut oil
2 cloves garlic, peeled and minced (or more to taste)
1 medium onion, cut in eighths
2 scallions, green parts only, cut in 2-inch lengths

Trim away outer leaves and upper half of lemongrass stalks; slice tender bottom as thinly as possible (soak dried lemongrass for 2 hours, drain, pat dry, and chop). Combine vinegar and ginger and set aside. Combine 1 tablespoon fish sauce, water, starch, and sugar and set aside. Season chicken with remaining fish sauce and ground pepper, add lemongrass, and mix well.

Heat oil and sauté garlic and onion; add chicken and scallions and cook, stirring constantly, about 5 minutes. Cover, lower heat to medium, and cook another 5 minutes. Add ginger-vinegar mixture and starch mixture and stir well; recover and cook 5 minutes more. Serve with rice.

The Golden Triangle: Cambodia, Laos, and Burma

BASIC CUISINE

DINNER FOR TWO:
Satay, larb, coconut
chicken, grilled fish

DINNER FOR FOUR:
Fried squash, tea-leaf
salad, whole fried fish,
eggplant stew,
"dry" shrimp curry,
"wet" beef curry

STYLE:
Tangy, earthy

KEY FLAVORS:
Curry, cilantro, fish
sauce, chili

EATING UTENSILS:
Fingers, spoons

DISTINCTIVE FOODS:
Pickled greens, sticky
rice, curries

NUTRITIONAL INDEX:
High starch, medium
sodium, medium fat

UNIFORMITY OF MENUS:
Good

COST:
Inexpensive

"THANK YOU":
"Or kuhn"
(Cambodian);
"Khop chai" (Laotian);
"Kyay zu tin par del"
(Burmese)

Even though there are growing Cambodian, Laotian, and Burmese communities in the United States, particularly on the coasts, they have established only a few restaurants here—and in fact are having to learn the business almost from scratch. Unlike Thailand and Vietnam, where dining out was an established and sociable tradition, Cambodia had no real restaurant tradition outside the royal court; most families cooked and ate at home, and the few restaurants were generally owned by expatriate or ethnic Chinese. In Laos, which is rugged, mountainous, and thickly forested, farming is mostly for subsistence, and home-style cooking is heavily borrowed from the Thai; Laotian restaurants tended to be French, or Frenchified. And although Burma has an intriguingly hybrid cuisine, influenced by India and Malaysia and Indonesia and China, there has been as yet little emigration from Burma to the United States.

Nevertheless, these countries offer intriguing side trips into Asian cuisine. Cambodia, which has a rather narrow coastal access compared to other Southeast Asian nations, has developed a cuisine that pays particular attention to meat, while the food of Laos is rather plain, emphasizing freshwater fish and some wild hogs for protein. The Burmese have developed a distinctive flavoring by cooking, eating, and fermenting green tea leaves as well as drying them.

THE COUNTRIES

Cambodia (also known as Kampuchea) is the most fertile of the three, half tropical forest and half a network of river and lake that annually floods and enriches the earth. During the rainy season, the Mekong River backs up all the way to the Tonlé Sap ("Great Lake"), turning the whole center of the country into a natural paddy. Laos, which is landlocked, is entirely dependent on the Mekong River.

Burma (known today as Myanmar) borders on Bangladesh and India as well as Laos, Thailand, China, the Bay of Bengal, and the Andaman Sea. The heavy marks of Indian and Indonesian trade show in its cooking, suggesting that at various points in its history, Burma served as a docking point between the two. Like its neighbors, Burma is a rice-growing country; the Mekong River defines most of its western border, and the Irrawaddy River runs down the spine of the country, through the legendary Mandalay to Yangon (the former Rangoon). Rice accounts for half the nation's total agricultural output, followed by corn.

THE HISTORY

Although the entire peninsula has much history in common, and much conflict, the countries are ethnically and often religiously distinct. Cambodia is 90 percent Khmer, descended from a great empire that prospered for nearly a thousand years, with its capital at Ankgor, until it fell prey first to the constant regional battles between the Thai and Vietnamese and later to the French colonials.

The Laotians are descended from the Thai tribes that in the twelfth and thirteenth centuries pushed south from China into Khmer territory; though it was also part of French Indochina, it was never really occupied, and its cuisine remains closely related to Thai food (see the chapter on Thailand). The Burmese still slightly resemble their Mongol ancestors; they are descended from tribes that roared out of Tibet in the ninth century, and they picked up a fresh infusion of blood a few centuries later, when Kublai Khan's armies swept in.

All the countries in the Golden Triangle are primarily Buddhist, but Burma (which was a British rather than French protectorate) has a large Christian population as well. The Japanese occupied the entire subcontinent during World War II but left little if any mark on the cuisine.

THE CUISINES

More than half the population of Laos lives along the banks of the Mekong River, which runs through the heart of the country; farmers depend on rice, corn, and vegetables, supplemented by river fish. Although many of the dishes are Thai in origin, and the Laotians use the Thai-style glutinous "sticky rice" rather than paddy rice, the meats are gamey, and the seasoning is much plainer and depends heavily on wild herbs and leaves, notably the mild ginger-flavored *romdeng*.

Both Cambodian and Laotian cuisines depend heavily on garden herbs and spices; since only fresh foods, including meat, are eaten (there are few refrigerators, and eating just-killed animals is a matter of safety as well as flavor), meals depend on seasonal availability, and menus can be repetitious. Eggplant has a peculiar and very distinctive role in Laotian cooking: It is highly prized as a vegetable, particularly grilled; also, it is stewed to a thick paste, then used as a thickener in stews.

Burmese cooking is veggie-heavy and uses proteins mostly for flavoring. They too like eggplant, but as an vegetable; they prefer to grind or puree chickpeas or roasted rice to thicken dishes. However, although proteins are not a large element in the dishes, they are quite varied—beef, poultry, shrimp and fish, and beans, plus peanuts, eggs, and tofu—and one of the characteristics of Burmese recipes is that they frequently

Where's the Beef?

Cambodian cuisine is meat-heavy and thus high-cholesterol. Laotians, who have limited access to meat at home, naturally value it more and so consider it an essential ingredient for restaurant customers, but the simplicity of the cuisine guarantees a certain caloric restraint. However, Burmese cooking can be deceptive, because even though it contains so many vegetables, most of the seasonings are cooked in oil before being used in sauces, and because the Burmese are accustomed to and prefer an oilier flavor than most Americans do. Also, the Indonesian gifts to Burmese cooking were delicious but even more high-fat—namely, coconut milk and peanuts.

combine several proteins in a single dish. And while Cambodians and Laotians serve vegetables raw, the Burmese generally cook theirs, even for salads, and the vegetables are often made visually more exciting by sprinklings of turmeric and fried onions.

Burmese cuisine offers more variety than the other two in style as well as substance: The Indian-style curried dishes are often served alongside and in contrast to the tart, vinegar, or fish-sauced regional dishes. (Curries actually come in two styles, "wet" and "dry." The presence or absence of coconut milk is one of the major differences, but it is not the only distinction; some curries get their liquid from the ingredients themselves.) Other common cooking techniques include braising, frying (in peanut and occasionally sesame oil), and stir-frying.

THE MAIN INGREDIENTS

SEASONINGS Where the Chinese use soy sauce and the Vietnamese use nuoc mam, the Cambodians prefer an unfermented fish sauce called *tak trey* (or tuk trey). Made of minced or ground grilled fish, it is used as either condiment or cooking ingredient. Mixed with lime juice, basil, ground peanuts, and chilies it becomes a dipping sauce called *tak kruen;* and mixed with coconut milk and ground meat, it becomes *nataing.*

Another important sauce is called *prahok katih* (*prahok* is dried anchovies and *katih* is ground pork flavored with coconut); often served with rice or raw vegetables, this sauce is essential for flavoring a popular homestyle dish of eggplant and shrimp. Other characteristic flavorings include lemongrass, galangal (a variety of ginger), peanuts, lime juice, basil, mint, black pepper, chilies and chili powder, coriander, lemongrass, garlic, spring onions, sesame seeds, dried mushrooms, cumin, coconut milk, ground fennel seed, turmeric, and the rarely imported but irreplaceable banana blossoms. Added flavor is supplied by bits of ham, powdered shrimp or fish, and, occasionally, preserved citrus.

Laotian food is, again, relatively plain: eggplant, peanuts, lime juice or pickles, malty-roasted rice, chilies, mint, and bitter greens are the most common flavoring agents.

The Burmese have been heavily influenced by Indian food and have adopted curry spices and sauces; these are typically dark red sauces, made by sautéing the onions, garlic, and ginger in oil until they brown and reseparate from the oil, then adding turmeric and chili powder and continuing to cook the raw spices before adding any other ingredients. The Burmese also prefer a little more oil in the dish than most Americans do.

The most common flavorings are the pickled tea leaves, shallots, garlic, dried fish paste, fish sauce, dried shrimp, lemongrass, cilantro, coconut milk, vinegar (pickled condiments are important for contrast), and citrus or fruit-pickle chutneys. However, there are a few more Western flavorings, including chickpea flour and roasted chickpeas and paprika. The roasted rice powder used in Thai and Lao salads is used here as well.

MEATS By Asian standards, Cambodians are extremely fond of meat; they raise cattle, buffalo, pork, and some goats and rabbits, but like most of their neighbors, the Cambodians abjure mutton. Laotians depend on the countryside to supplement their rice and somewhat limited vegetable crops: buffalo, venison, some elk, and the occasional boar replace beef and pork. Meat in Burmese cooking is most often beef.

POULTRY AND EGGS Cambodian cuisine includes quite of bit of chicken, duck, squab, guinea hen, and even tiny paddy birds or rails; in poorer areas they are generally used as flavorings rather than main ingredients, but most cooks grill or roast them. Laotians also like poultry but seldom eat eggs. The Burmese like both and frequently add eggs to dishes that already include meat, poultry, or even fish.

FISH AND SHELLFISH The Cambodians are particularly adept at the use of both fresh- and saltwater fish, shellfish, and even snails and frogs. Laotians prize freshwater eels, and the huge *pa boeuk* fish supplies a delicate roe that is often salted like caviar. The Burmese prepare quite a bit of shrimp; they also serve fish whole or minced into a paste.

VEGETABLES AND FRUITS The Cambodians are able to raise corn, peanuts, squash, pumpkins, and sugar palms. The Laotians depend heavily on eggplant, beans, mustard and other wild greens, some forest mushrooms and fungus, and some corn. The Burmese enjoy lentils, greens (mustard, chrysanthemum, and tea among them), Chinese cabbage, bamboo shoots, carrots, onions, bean sprouts, squash, eggplant, and chickpeas. Melons, bananas, papayas, lemons, limes, and oranges are the most common fruits in the region.

STARCHES   As we mentioned above, Laotians are much fonder of sticky rice than steamed rice. The Burmese prefer long-grained steamed rice, as do the Cambodians. Corn is the second most popular grain, but dough wrappers and noodles are almost solely made from rice flour. The Burmese especially love noodles, soft or fried, and serve them almost as frequently as rice.

THE MAIN DISHES

SOUPS AND CASSEROLES   Cambodians are fond of soups (*samla*), which are served at every meal. *Samla mchou banle* is a tart, tamarind-flavored fish soup, and *machu kroeng* is a hearty eggplant and beef soup. Seafood hotpots, another legacy of the Mongols, gets a twist here—the broth is flavored with coconut milk and lemongrass, and the cooked seafood is wrapped in lettuce leaves for eating in the Vietnamese style. A really hearty one-pot meal called *khao phoune* is a combination of thin rice noodles, raw salad vegetables, chili and nataing sauces, and banana blossoms, plus dried meat or meatballs.

Like Cambodians, the Laotians take soup at every meal. Most of these everyday soups are mild and vegetarian; the meats are reserved for special occasions.

At lunch and dinner the Burmese nearly always serve soup, along with little fried snacks such as chopped shrimp or meat patties, fried sprouts or calabash "fingers," and lentil cakes. However, to the Burmese soup is not just a first course but a beverage that is sipped throughout the meal; consequently, many of them, such as black-pepper soup, have palate-priming roles of their own. And some are extremely hearty: "Twelve varieties" soup combines chicken or duck with pork, liver, cabbage, cauliflower, green beans, mushrooms, onions, and so on.

The Burmese national dish is *mohinga* (sometimes moo hing nga or mohhing gha), a thick, spicy fish stew or chowder served over rice noodles and flavored with roasted rice and slices of young banana greens.

SALADS   The Cambodians often top shredded vegetables with grilled or shredded meat or chicken. Laotians also like the meat salads, eaten by hand in the Thai fashion; sticky rice is rolled into small balls or patties in the fingers and dipped in the central dish—food and utensils in one.

The Burmese make salads of raw or cooked vegetables and even fruits. *Lap pat dok* is a dish uniquely Burmese, combining green tea leaves, fried lentils, peanuts, onions, lime and chilies and often mixed at the table; the tea, which may also be added to shrimp, chicken, or pork salads as well, lends a smoky and just slightly sour taste. Frequently the onions are caramelized and the tea "pickled" for even greater contrast. Ginger salad is a hearty mix of cabbage, beans, dried shrimp, and chilies.

MEATS Indonesian-style satays are common in Cambodian and Burmese restaurants, and grilling is a popular style of cooking almost anything, from marinated pork or boneless duck to whole fish or stuffed boneless chicken. The Laotians like Thai-style ground meat mixed with spices and powdered roasted rice, but with a slight twist: The Laotians prefer to pound their meat into a paste with a mortar and pestle rather than mince it with a knife. *O lam* is eggplant with buffalo meat and fresh beans.

One unusually meat-heavy Laotian meal is a type of Sunday dinner dish called *lap* or *koy;* it is a sort of venison tartare, with the meat of the leg and liver finely sliced or chopped and seasoned with lime juice, ground roasted rice, chilies, and mints and bitter greens, all to be eaten with sticky rice. Since lap also translates as "luck," it is a common dish at weddings, housewarmings, etc.

POULTRY Fowl, especially the smaller ones, are frequently grilled. *Larb gai,* the chopped chicken dish, is extremely common. Chicken often shows an Indonesian influence, but somewhat inside-out—stuffed, rather than sauced, with a peanut-coconut mixture and then steamed.

FISH AND SEAFOOD Deep-frying is a style usually reserved for whole fish, but in general seafood is either grilled or wrapped in herbs or banana leaves and then steamed; it is often seasoned with tangy sauces featuring tamarind, pineapple, and chopped nuts or even black beans. Another hand-pureed Laotian dish is *tom pobn,* a fish and eggplant mixture spread over lettuce leaves.

RICE AND NOODLES Rice is essential for every Burmese meal, often in addition to noodles, which may be soft or fried. In fact, some dishes have both rice and noodles; a popular homestyle dish called *htamin lethoke* is a sort of mix-your-own platter of rice, fried noodles, vegetables, and flavorings. Rice is served hot, even when the other dishes are lukewarm. It is accompanied by a number of small and pungent side dishes or condiments, called *toolee moolee*, usually including coriander, chutney, fried garlic and shallots, chilies (sometimes even fried whole chilies), and fish sauce; they are primarily intended to allow every diner to, in effect, design his or her own recipe; informally, with rice, they become a meal. The most popular accompaniment is *balachaung*, a mixture of dried shrimp paste, garlic, onions, and chili powder.

Kaukswe thoke is a noodle dish tossed with dried shrimp, cilantro, chilies, and peanuts.

The Laos serve rice for all three meals. For breakfast, it is soaked overnight, steamed until soft, and eaten with mango, coconut, and perhaps pickled fish.

DESSERTS   The Cambodians and Laotians most often serve fresh fruit, though sometimes they simmer rice in coconut milk and then add the fruit. The Burmese traditionally serve fruit or digestifs (marinated fresh ginger slices) after a meal, but between meals they are fond of Indian-style desserts such as spongy cakes, flavored jellies, coconut milk sweets, and semolina, rice, or tapioca puddings.

BEVERAGES   Tea and beer are the most common beverages in Burmese restaurants. Laotians prefer tea. Cambodians also drink mild tea with meals but more often drink warm or hot water to aid digestion.

HOW TO ORDER AND EAT LIKE A NATIVE

In a Laotian restaurant, be sure to order a meat salad (a *larb*), which will come with the sticky rice to roll with your fingers. Two of you will need a soup and either a stew (eggplant-thickened if possible) or a chicken dish; four should order a fish-paste appetizer, a seafood stew (or large lobster salad), and a second stew, particularly a meat or game stew if available.

The Cambodians eat much as their neighbors do, pulling off small pieces of grilled fish or meat, wrapping it in a salad leaf with herbs and bean sprouts, and then dipping the roll in hot sauce. In a Cambodian restaurant, four people should order rice, curry, a vegetable entree, soup, and a duck or fish dish (preferably grilled). If it's offered, try a hotpot; if hotpots for two are available, this should be the first choice for a duo as well. Incidentally, Cambodians serve all dishes at once.

As we mentioned before, the Burmese prefer curries, and almost any entree—beef, poultry, pork, fish (and minced fish *kofta*), shrimp, or tofu—may be offered as a curry. A full Burmese dinner traditionally involves a half-dozen dishes, including a salad (raw vegetables or fruit); several curries of beef, fish, or pork; fresh vegetables; and perhaps lentils.

Burmese eating customs, like the foods themselves, derive from India rather than from China or Thailand; neither chopsticks, sticky rice, nor spoons are used. In Burma, diners sit at tables set with individual plates; the dishes are served communally in bowls with serving spoons, but only the fingers of the right hand are used to eat. Diners serve themselves a little of each of the six or eight dishes, beginning with the rice and using only the left hand for the serving spoons. The food is left separate on the plate, in small piles. Then little bites are taken up with the fingers—using only the right hand, remember, and only the fingers; the palm must not be used as a scoop. (In fact, *htamin lethoke*, one of the most common dishes in Burmese culture, translates simply "rice mixed with the fingers.") As in many Asian countries, it is considered rude to put more on the plate than you can eat, but second and third helpings are fine.

If you do order a dish such as lethoke (pronounced "letho"—the interior *k* is silent in Burmese), it will be preceded by a bowl of hot water and soap for washing the hands; after the meal, the hands are washed again. However, although any Burmese restaurateur will be delighted to see you eat in their traditional way, most establishments here set out forks and spoons.

Again, the Burmese meals consist of many dishes. For two diners, look for something with the green tea leaves, probably a salad; and order two curries, perhaps one wet and one dry. Four people should try one of the mix-your-own dishes, such as lethoke, or perhaps the fish-curry stew mohinga; add to that fried turnovers or fried prawns and a dry chicken curry.

COOKING AT HOME

Although many Laotian, Cambodian, or Burmese dishes are labor-intensive, few are actually difficult—primarily since kitchens in the region tend to be limited. Wood or charcoal fires are the main source of heat, and most dishes that are not simply grilled are prepared in pots (or woks). Mortars and pestles are desirable for authenticity, but grinders will do nicely.

To serve a Burmese meal, set out plates for rice, to serve as general trays, and serve the rest of the meal in bowls. Laotian and Cambodian meals are traditionally served on a large tray set down on the floor in the middle of a circle of diners; all the dishes are set on the tray, and baskets (or bowls) of rice are placed between diners. Serve weak tea or beer.

LAOTIAN PORK SOUP

1 pound lean pork chops
4 cloves garlic, minced
1 teaspoon oil
5 cups beef broth (or water)
1 tablespoon fish sauce
1 tablespoon sugar
1 tablespoon lemon juice
1 tablespoon fresh ginger, julienned
chopped fresh cilantro for garnish

Bone the chops; cut or coarsely chop pork into small pieces and enrich broth or make stock from the bones. Sauté garlic in oil until soft, but not brown, and add pork; sauté for a minute, then pour in stock and add all other ingredients except cilantro. Cover and simmer 20 to 30 minutes; top with cilantro and serve.

LAOTIAN CHICKEN

1 3-pound roasting chicken
1 teaspoon salt
2 cloves garlic, crushed
1 teaspoon oil
2 medium onions, chopped
1/2 pound lean pork, minced or ground
1 fresh red chili, finely chopped
2 tablespoons fresh cilantro, chopped
1/2 cup uncooked rice
2 1/2 cups coconut milk

1 teaspoon fish sauce (nuoc mam)
salt and pepper to taste

Wash and dry chicken, then rub inside and out with salt and one of the garlic cloves. Sauté the other garlic clove, the chopped onions, and the pork, and season with salt, pepper, and red chili. Add cilantro, uncooked rice, and 1 cup coconut milk and bring to a simmer, then cover, lower heat, and cook at bare simmer until liquid is absorbed (about 10 minutes). Use pork and rice mixture to stuff chicken. Mix remaining coconut milk, 1/2 cup water, and fish sauce. Place stuffed chicken in a deep saucepan, pour coconut milk over it, and cover and simmer until tender (about an hour).

STEAMED FISH WITH GINGER

4 6- to 8-ounce fish fillets or steaks
4 ounces fresh ginger root, preferably young
juice of 1 lemon
4 large cloves garlic
1 1/2 tablespoons cooking oil
1 tablespoon sesame oil
3 tablespoons toasted sesame seeds
2 tablespoons soy sauce
banana leaves for steaming (or foil wrap)

Wash fish, checking for any remaining scales, and pat dry. Scrape rough skin off ginger and julienne finely. Cover with lemon juice and set aside. Slice garlic thinly and sauté in the combined oils over low heat until golden; pour both garlic and oil into ginger mixture and add sesame seeds and soy sauce. Place fillets on banana leaves (or in foil packages), sprinkle with ginger mixture, and steam 15 minutes.

BURMESE "DRY" SHRIMP CURRY

1 pound large or jumbo shrimp
1 onion, chopped
3 cloves garlic
1/2 teaspoon turmeric
1 teaspoon grated ginger

1/2 teaspoon chili powder

3 tablespoons sesame oil

2 tablespoons spring onions (thin green parts only), chopped

dash of coriander

2 tablespoons cilantro, chopped

salt to taste

Shell and devein shrimp. Put onion, garlic, turmeric, and ginger in blender or food processor and puree, scraping down the sides as necessary. Add chili powder and blend again. Heat oil until smoking and add ground ingredients (it may spatter); reduce heat, stir paste into oil, and simmer; cover for 15 minutes, stirring frequently to make sure it does not stick. When the paste turns deep red and the oil begins to separate to the sides, add the shrimp and stir well. Sprinkle with coriander and cook just until opaque, then add onions and remove from heat. Serve with rice.

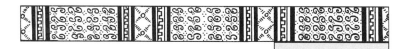

INDONESIA, MALAYSIA, AND SINGAPORE

Though there are few authentic Indonesian or Malay restaurants in the United States, they are in one sense the universal common denominator: They made virtually every other cuisine possible.

These are the legendary Spice Islands, whose riches permeated Byzantine culture; whose incalculable commercial value drove the European nations to sea and frequently to war; whose aromatics inspired the first truly worldwide trade. It was their spices—pepper, ginger, cloves, cinnamon, and allspice—that allowed cooking to become cuisine, not only serving as preservatives and masking the odors of spoiling meat but also inspiring the *creation* of actual dishes and flavorings. Like the vegetables of the Americas, which revolutionized European food, the spices of Indonesia and Malaysia made possible the curries, pilafs, stews, sautés, and salads of China, Southeast Asia, and the Middle East.

They also made possible a boom in home medication: Many of the most popular spices were used as pharmaceuticals long before they became flavoring agents, and the Europeans and

BASIC CUISINE

DINNER FOR TWO:
Satays, chicken in coconut milk, beef sambal

DINNER FOR FOUR:
Satays, soup, gado-gado, sambal, shrimp sayur or fried fish

GROUP DISH:
Rijsttafel

STYLE:
Hot, spicy, aromatic

KEY FLAVORS:
Curry, coconut, chilies, peanuts

EATING UTENSILS:
Fingers, spoons, forks

DISTINCTIVE FOODS:
Rijsttafel, gado-gado, satay

UNIFORMITY OF MENUS:
Fair

NUTRITIONAL INDEX:
High fiber and protein; medium fat, cholesterol, and sodium

COST:
Moderate

"THANK YOU":
"Terima kasih" (Indonesian)

Arabs who began trading in the powders also began boasting of their healing powers. Garlic was prescribed for migraines and menstrual cramps, lemongrass for intestinal disorders, peppers for fever and flu, cloves for toothache (clove oil is still used by many dentists to soak surgical dressings), and virtually all the hottest spices, including chilies, cinnamon, cumin, ginger, onion, and turmeric, were used for stomach disorders, dysentery, and diarrhea—all of which were endemic before refrigeration or sanitary handling.

THE COUNTRIES

Indonesia is almost like a watery galaxy—more than 13,500 islands, barely a third of them populated (though even at that there are 180 million people and hundreds of languages), flung along the equator between Southeast Asia and Australia. They form a natural barrier between the Pacific and Indian (Atlantic) oceans, so the early explorers who believed they were at the edge of the world were almost right: Indonesia is the seam of the world. Its territories are synonymous with adventure—Java, Sumatra, Borneo, Bali, the Moluccas, New Guinea, and the catastrophic Krakatoa—and tigers, elephants, crocodiles, and surreally brilliant wild birds still roam them. Earthquakes are frequent, and more than 100 active volcanoes attest to the islands' turbulent origins.

Malaysia, like Turkey, comprises two parts divided by water. Eastern Malaysia, which is mostly rainforest, forms a slightly cockeyed lid over the large island of Borneo, with the tiny but independent and extremely wealthy kingdom of Brunei as a handle. Western Malaysia is actually on the Indochinese peninsula, south of Thailand. Topographically, western Malaysia resembles a fish skeleton, with a mountain range down its spine and tiny rivers, like ribs, running east and west, and at its southern tip is the city-state of Singapore—which itself actually comprises some 60 islands.

Most of the region is quite fertile along the coasts, thanks to the volcanic soils and tropical climate. Singapore is the exception. Only about 5 percent of its land is turned over to raising fruits and vegetables; it devotes more attention to raising pork and poultry, including ducks. Fish are the major source of protein, and rice the primary crop; but several other starches—cassava, yams, and soy beans—are cultivated, along with sugarcane, coffee, tobacco, peanuts, palm oil, cinchona (the source of quinine), cacao, coconuts and, of course, spices.

THE HISTORY

Malaysia, particularly the contiguous part, was settled about 4,000 years ago by Malay tribes from southern China, who drove the aboriginals into the mountains and jungle islands where many of them still live. Throughout its history, it has been subject to invasions by and inter-marriages with Thai, Indian, and Javanese peoples; of its modern population, about 59 percent is ethnically Malay, 32 percent is Chinese, and another 10 percent is Indian or Pakistani.

Most Indonesians are either from Papuan or Malay groups, and although one of the 300 Malay dialects is the official language, English is the second. The largest ethnic minority is Chinese, and there are sizable Arab, Indian, and Pakistani communities as well. For 600 years, from the seventh to the thirteenth centuries, Sumatra was the seat of a prosperous Buddhist empire, and the kingdom of Java was Hindu; but beginning in the fourteenth century, the increasing influence of Arab traders spread Islam through the islands, and by the end of the sixteenth century, the region was overwhelmingly Muslim. Only Bali remains predominantly Hindu.

Religion is one reason that so many meals are based on fish and rice: The Malay are primarily Muslim and do not eat pork (or drink alcohol); the Indians are Hindu and do not eat beef; and the Chinese, who are primarily Buddhist, have a strong vegetarian tradition as well, though they do enjoy pork. Singapore, founded by the British in the early nineteenth century, has the heartiest and least restricted diet; meats and eggs, which are expensive and not too common elsewhere, are served relatively lavishly here.

THE CUISINE

There are two underlying principles in Indonesian/Malaysian cuisine, both related to the tropical climate. One is that the excessive heat can kill the appetite (thus ultimately weakening the body), and the other is that food spoils rapidly. So chilies and spices are essential both for preserving the food and for stimulating the palate; and meals tend to center on "market availability," so to speak, for both reasons. In general, the cuisine is not terribly fancy or varied but is fresh, bright, and colorful.

Cooking methods are fairly limited. In the old days, wood stoves were kept away from the house, in small shacks clustered together in the common back courtyard; and most dishes could either be left to themselves or cooked very quickly. Heavy woks, called *kualis*, are used for stir-frying, steaming, frying, and braising; flat iron griddles are used not only for grilling but also for baking flatbreads. The most important kitchen utensil is a heavy bowl or mortar called a *ukelan*, which is used for grinding spices into powder or paste; it is similar to the old Mexican *metate*.

The most obvious element of Indonesian cuisine is its hodgepodge of influences. The first Europeans to reach the Indian Ocean were the Portuguese, who captured Molucca in the early sixteenth century; but the Dutch, who took advantage of Portugal's internal troubles (i.e., the "Spanish captivity") to wrest away its colonies, established a hold over what came to be known as the Dutch East Indies. Their control of Indonesia lasted until the turn of this century.

There are some regional specialties and stylistic differences, notably the rich and sweetish dishes from Molucca, where the Portuguese influence was strongest; the simple but powerfully spicy curries from Sumatra; the relatively elaborate, Europeanized meals of Java; and the long, slow-simmered and more mellow, clay-pot stews from Penang. (Note, however, that Penang-style barbecue can be eye-wateringly spicy.) In addition, Malaysian cooks preserve many Indian-style recipes, particularly biryanis and kormas.

The most distinctive dishes of Singapore come from the Nonya style, a mixture of Chinese ingredients and Malay spices that evolved in the nineteenth century, when Chinese labor recruits married Malay women. (According to a more romantic explanation, the Nonya culture dates from the sixteenth century, when a Malaccan sultan married a Beijing princess, and its names derives from the Mandarin phrase *nan yang*, or "southern ocean.") Only women are called *nonyas*: The men are called *babas*, and collectively the people are known as *paranakan*. Nonya dishes are hot and spicy, most often based on a chili-onion-turmeric paste called a *rempah*. Chili crabs are so ubiquitous in Singapore that they might be called the national dish.

THE MAIN INGREDIENTS

RICE   The Balinese are among the world champions of rice consumption; they eat the cooked equivalent of a pound of raw rice every day (and also leave small rice piles on windowsills and pathways, for the spirits). The most famous meal of Indonesia, ordered up (and christened) with pleasure by the Dutch, is the *rijsttafel*, or "rice table"—a sit-down buffet, in effect, with rice in the center and 15 or 20 toppings (ceremonially, up to 50) and side dishes laid out around it. The rice is the main dish here, not the accompaniment, and although there may be meat dishes or vegetable curries as well, they are flavorings rather than entrees. A smaller version, with fewer side dishes, may be called a *nasi rames* (*nasi* is the word for rice).

Both steamed rice and the sweeter glutinous or sticky rice are common, and sticky rice is frequently used to wrap sausages, vegetables, or meats into a finger food. Rice is often fried as well. As a meal base, noodles are the only alternative to rice (and whatever their shape, they are almost always rice noodles); they are among the most obvious Chinese contributions, along with dumplings.

FISH AND SHELLFISH   Seafood—particularly crabs, cockles or clams, squid, and shrimp—and fish, both fresh- and saltwater, provide the primary proteins: *Ikan* is the generic word for fish, *cumi-cumi* is squid, *udang* is shrimp.

POULTRY AND MEATS   Beef and pork are not uncommon, particularly among Chinese families, but because of various religious prohibitions, they are served less frequently than they are here. Organ meats—brains, liver, kidneys, and so forth—are also particularly popular among Chinese families. Buddhists get most of their proteins from tofu and tempeh, the mold-fermented soy variant, which are widely used in vegetarian soups and stews; they also appear in addition to meat or seafood in "fancy" recipes.

VEGETABLES AND FRUITS   The Portuguese were responsible for bringing in the New World squashes, tomatoes, corn, chilies, and sweet potatoes; they may also have been the first to transport peanuts from Africa and eggplant from Turkey. The Dutch supplied the broccoli and cauliflower that the Chinese taught them to stir-fry with their own bok choy. Other vegetables include bean sprouts, bamboo shoots, a wide

The P-Nuttiest

There is much about Indonesian food that looks healthful—the seafoods, the satays and salads—but in fact, this is one of the world's highest fat cuisines. Palm oil, coconut oil, coconut milk are all at the top of the fat-level list, and peanuts are not far behind, so grilled and steamed dishes are better nutritional bets than sweet coconut curries and peanut-based satay dipping sauces. The Sumatran and Singapore-style dishes are often less fatty, because they depend more on chili sauces than on sweet ones; and the Indian-influenced rice biryanis are pretty good bets, too. In general, eat lots of rice, try to avoid the dishes that have oil puddling in the bottom (eat off the top if you must), and eat the satays plain.

variety of mushrooms, and okra (from Africa, courtesy of the Arab traders). Fruits include mangoes, papayas, jackfruit, and oranges (also a Middle Eastern contribution).

SEASONINGS The most important spices are ginger, pepper, cumin, curry (turmeric), cloves, lemongrass, limes, rice wine and vinegar, tamarind, cinnamon, coriander, coconut, sugar (frequently brown sugar), cilantro, basil, cardamom, sesame oil, soy sauce, garlic, nutmeg, dried fish or shrimp pastes, dried red chilies, and fresh chilies, both green and red. Ketjap, or "sweet soy"—the tomato-less ancestor of ketchup—is a blend of dark Chinese soy sauce, sugar, onions, and spices. The *kemiri* nut, also called a candle nut, is a characteristic flavoring something like macadamia.

THE MAIN DISHES

MEAT AND POULTRY Almost any meat or fowl can be curried or braised in coconut milk; chicken in coconut, called *opor ayam*, is particularly popular. Satays, which evolved from the kebabs of Persia and became more delicate, are among Indonesia's most famous foods: marinated meats (beef, lamb, pork) and chicken are skewered, broiled, or grilled, and served with dipping sauces of ground peanuts, coconut milk, and chilies. Eggs are rarely served as the main protein but often act as a medium for vegetables (in a sort of stir-fried "scramble") or seafood (like Singapore's oyster omelets).

SEAFOOD Shrimp and squid can be curried or coconut-stewed, too, but flesh fish are more frequently deep-fried whole, steamed in banana leaves, or rubbed with chili paste and grilled. In some places, shrimp is skewered and served up like a satay. Also, mixed seafood stews are fairly common.

SALADS AND VEGETARIAN DISHES *Gado-gado* is a very popular mixed-vegetable salad with peanut sauce that is often used to illustrate the region's melting-pot cuisine, since it combines European vegetables, African peanuts, and indigenous spices. *Urap* is a coconut-vegetable salad usually reserved for fancier occasions. Otherwise, vegetables (green beans, carrots, potatoes, cauliflower, etc.) tend to be served up as curries and stews and may not be any "lighter" than the meat dishes.

BEVERAGES The most popular drinks are tea and coffee, coconut milk (often served in the shell with a flavoring of lime or nutmeg and cinnamon), beer, rice wine, or fruit juices. Sweet desserts are almost a requirement here—not just fruits but thick coconut puddings, bean flour buns, sweetened rice cakes, and so forth.

> **Flavor Savor**
>
> Many Indonesian and Malaysian menus categorize dishes not by the entree—beef, chicken, shrimp, whatever—but by the style of cooking. *Sambals* are usually dishes fried with chilies but can also refer to powerful chili pastes; *sayurs* are dishes with plenty of sauce to dip rice into (see "How to Order and Eat Like a Native," below). *Kalio* sauce is heavily flavored with coriander and coconut; *bumbu* is another spice paste, usually mixed with coconut milk. Croquettes (or, from the Dutch, *krokets*) are just what they sound like—fried balls or dumplings—but may be fish, shrimp, or potato or some other vegetable.

HOW TO ORDER AND EAT LIKE A NATIVE

Indonesia and Malaysia are, like Central America, crowded with outdoor food vendors, many specializing in only one dish—even a single type of fish—and others laying out a spread of curries and sambals. In larger cities, such as Singapore and Kuala Lumpur, not only markets but also parking lots and parks at night become al fresco taverns for progressive dinners; when you sit down at a table, serving boys from nearby stalls, each representing a different chef, trot up and sing out the menus. Warm water and soap are offered as a matter of course, and larger clusters of stalls may have a sort of communal washroom. More formal restaurants differ not so much in the menu as in the presentation: They provide such items as carved vegetable garnishes and extra side dishes.

Mix and Match

Dining in Indonesian restaurants is not so much tricky as chancy. Menu spellings are not too diverse, but actual recipes, which depend so heavily on the individual chef's spice mixes, are anything but standardized, so it's possible that a dish you order in one restaurant will be quite different from the "same" dish from another chef. The Americanized versions of Indonesian and Malaysian food in smaller cities can be extremely disappointing, about as authentic as meals in "Polynesian" huts used to be; but there are good restaurants in larger cities, particularly along both coasts.

All dishes are served at the same time—even soup, which is sipped with food rather than eaten beforehand—and food is traditionally eaten with the fingers. Fingerbowls are standard tableware.

Most Indonesian restaurants here, of course, are full-service establishments; but even if they have separated their menus into what appears to be courses—soups, curries, satays, and noodle and rice dishes— remember that all dishes will be served simultaneously.

Like many other cultures, the Indonesian and Malay societies dictate that only the fingertips and the thumb of the right hand may be used for eating. (The left hand is customarily used for bathing, etc., and is thus considered unclean.) As elsewhere, the rice is formed into small balls and dipped into the sauce or curry. However, spoons are quite common, particularly for wetter dishes, and are becoming even more so, particularly among younger diners; and forks are increasingly common as well, so if you would rather not eat the traditional way, you need not. (Dishes that are eaten with a spoon and fork, modern-style, are known as *lauk pering*—"food served on a plate.") Chopsticks are generally used only for Chinese dishes.

A typical meal consists of rice; at least two curries; one fish and one meat or poultry (or all three); two or more vegetable dishes, one soupy (a sayur) and one stir-fried or in salad; and dishes of chilies, green onions, and other condiments. Many Indonesian establishments serve fixed-price rijsttafels (some with a choice of vegetarian, seafood, or meat side dishes) as well as individual curries, fish, or satays. The rice table is the most fun and allows you to taste the most dishes, but if you don't want a rijsttafel, two diners should order satays, chicken curry, and beef sambal; for four, add gado-gado and either shrimp or chicken sayur or a fish. If chili crabs are available, by all means order them, but don't wear your best clothes; you pretty much have to eat them with your fingers, and a dainty method hasn't been invented yet.

COOKING AT HOME

Many Indonesian and Malaysian dishes are easy to re-create at home with just a blender (for spices) and a deep heavy skillet, although woks are also useful. Satays can be grilled indoors or out and are particularly well adapted to small tabletop grills or hibachis. For atmosphere, drape the table with batik cloth. Set out fingerbowls with lemon slices for those who want to try eating with their fingers.

PAN-FRIED FISH IN COCONUT MILK

5 spring onions, chopped
2 cloves garlic, peeled
2 dime-sized slices of ginger root, peeled
2 small hot chilies, seeded
1 stalk lemongrass, thinly sliced
4 kemiri nuts or unsalted, unroasted macadamia nuts
1/2 teaspoon shrimp paste
2 tablespoons vegetable oil
4 fillets of mackerel or other firm fish, about 1 inch thick
1/2 to 1 teaspoon sesame oil (optional)
juice of 1 lime
1 cup condensed coconut milk or thick portion of separated canned milk
pinch salt

Combine onions, garlic, ginger, chilies, lemongrass, kemiri nuts, and shrimp paste in mortar, blender, or food processor; blend into smooth paste, adding a dash of sesame oil or coconut milk if needed. Meanwhile, heat vegetable oil in a skillet and sauté fish 2–3 minutes on each side; set aside. Add spice paste and cook until "spicy" smell fades; add lime juice and coconut milk and simmer about 10 minutes; add fish and heat through. Serve with rice.

SINGAPORE-STYLE CRABS

2 large or 4 medium live crabs
1/2 cup vegetable oil
1 tablespoons ginger, peeled and minced
2 cloves garlic, peeled and minced
4 fresh green or red chilies, seeded and minced
1/3 cup tomato-based chili sauce
1 tablespoon light soy sauce
1 tablespoon sugar (or substitute 1 1/2 tablespoons "sweet soy"
or katjap for both soy and sugar)
1/4 cup flat beer, defatted chicken broth, or water
pinch salt

Scrub crabs well; remove top shell, stomach, and lungs (or have vendor clean them); and chop into quarters. Heat oil in wok and stir-fry crabs, turning them constantly, until they turn red; remove. Add ginger, garlic, and chilies to wok and stir-fry 2 minutes; add chili sauce, soy, sugar (or katjap), and beer and bring to boil. Return crabs to sauce, lower heat and simmer 5 minutes, and serve with rice.

GADO-GADO

2 medium potatoes
1/2 cup fresh bean sprouts
3/4 cup Chinese or green cabbage, sliced
1/2 cup green beans, cut on diagonal into 2-inch pieces
1 carrot, julienned
1/2 cup small cauliflower florets
1 small cucumber, seeded and julienned
1 small bunch fresh watercress
1 hard-boiled egg, sliced
1 ripe tomato, peeled, seeded, and chopped
1/2 cake firm silken tofu, cut in 1-inch cubes
peanut sauce (see following page)

Boil potatoes, let cool, and slice. Blanch bean sprouts and drain; repeat with cabbage. Cook green beans until crisp-tender; drain. Repeat with cauliflower and carrot. Remove watercress stems and chill leaves and cucumber until crisp. Arrange vegetables either in large bowl or on platter; make sure all vegetables are visible in layers or in separate piles. Place egg slices around top and scatter tomato and tofu on top. Peanut sauce may either be poured in a circle over the salad or served on the side or in a smaller bowl in the center of the platter.

QUICK PEANUT SAUCE

1/2 cup smooth or crunchy peanut butter
1/2 cup coconut milk
1/2 cup water
1 fresh red or green chili, chopped
1 teaspoon garlic, minced
1 teaspoon dried lemon peel, 1/2 teaspoon fresh minced peel,
or 2 teaspoons lemon juice
1 teaspoon dark brown sugar
2 tablespoons dark soy
1/2 teaspoon shrimp paste or anchovy paste

Heat peanut butter, coconut milk, and water in a saucepan until blended. Meanwhile, in a mortar, blender, or processor, combine chili, garlic, lemon peel (if you are using it), and sugar into a paste; add soy and shrimp paste and blend again. Add to saucepan, along with lemon juice; add more coconut milk if mixture is too thick. This sauce can also be used for dipping satays.

SWEET-SOUR SATAY MARINADE

1 tablespoon coriander powder
1/4 teaspoon cumin
1 tablespoon garlic, minced
1 teaspoon fresh ginger, minced
1 fresh red or green chili, roughly chopped
2 green onions, chopped
1/2 teaspoon salt
2 teaspoons lemon juice
2 tablespoons dark soy sauce
2 teaspoons dark brown sugar

1 tablespoon peanut oil
(Lean pork, beef, lamb, chicken breast, or shrimp)

Combine all spices except oil in blender and process until smooth. Pour into bowl, whisk in oil, and marinate meat 3 hours or longer in refrigerator. (At the same time, if using bamboo skewers, soak them in water so they won't burn.) When ready to cook, thread meat on bamboo skewers and grill until browned.

THE PHILIPPINES

Given its geographical location—as an outrider to China between Japan and Indonesia—one would expect Philippine cuisine to be thoroughly Asian and largely dependent on seafood. Instead, thanks primarily to four centuries of Spanish occupation and 50 years as a U.S. protectorate, the food is a meat-heavy mix of indigenous spices, Spanish cooking methods, Chinese noodles, and lettuce-and-tomato salads—along with the African and Middle Eastern dishes the Arab traders left behind.

THE HISTORY

The Philippines' first residents were Negritos, a Malayo-Polynesian people, who crossed over from Sumatra and Borneo when the islands were still connected by dry land. These first Malays, who moved in 30,000 years ago, have living descendants among the most aboriginal tribes; later waves of more sophisticated Malay immigrants evolved into the people now called Filipino.

The first Javanese and Chinese ships arrived at the end of the first millenium, but it

BASIC CUISINE

DINNER FOR TWO:
Kilawin, sio mai, chicken adobo, roast pork

DINNER FOR FOUR:
Lumpia, pancit guisado, chicken guinataan, pork adobo, kare-kare

GROUP DISH:
Turo-turo

STYLE:
Meaty, tangy, rich

KEY FLAVORS:
Coconut milk, vinegar, tamarind

EATING UTENSILS:
Forks and knives

DISTINCTIVE DISHES:
Adobo, puchero, lumpia

NUTRITIONAL INDEX:
High fat, high protein, high starch

UNIFORMITY OF MENUS:
Good

COST:
Moderate

"THANK YOU":
"Salamat"

was not until the fourteenth century, with the arrival of the Arab traders and their Muslim evangelism, that much cross-cultural evolution took place. Then, in 1512, the Spanish appeared—captained by the Portuguese explorer Ferdinand Magellan, whose dream of a passage to the East had been laughed off by his own king—followed shortly by another Spanish fleet sailing west from Mexico, who claimed the islands in the name of the Infante Philip, later Philip II.

The islands were a rich find, supplying gold, silver, timber, spices, coffee, and sugar to the empire. They were also vulnerable to attacks by Chinese and English pirates, fanatically anti-Christian Moros, and the Dutch, who already controlled the rest of the East Indies. Nevertheless, the Philippines remained in Spanish hands until the Spanish-American War, when, despite their declaration of democratic independence, the Filipinos (and Puerto Ricans) found themselves in the "protective" custody of the United States.

On December 7, 1941, the same day they attacked Pearl Harbor, Japanese forces invaded the Philippines. Filipino-American forces suffered terrible losses at Bataan and Corregidor, and the Filipino government went into exile in Washington. In October 1944, the Gulf of Leyte became the site of the greatest naval engagement of all time; over the course of three days, U.S. forces destroyed the Japanese fleet. On July 5, 1945, General Douglas MacArthur was able to declare the Philippines entirely liberated; almost exactly a year later, on July 4, 1946, the independent Republic of the Philippines was finally acknowledged.

THE COUNTRY

Today, Philippine culture retains strong and somehow complementary strains from all its influences—Malaysian, Chinese, Spanish, and American. An archipelago of 7,000 islands, most of them very tiny (11 Philippine islands make up 95 percent of the land mass), it is slightly larger than Great Britain and supports about the same size population. Like Indonesia, it is a country of myriad native languages, about 70; the official language is Pilipino, and a great many people speak English (although only a small number speak Spanish). It remains overwhelmingly Christian—only about 5 percent are Muslim—and thanks to the Spanish, pork is the most popular meat in the Philippines.

Like its equatorial neighbors, the Philippines is volcanic and richly forested, subject to constant earthquakes and studded with hot springs. There are navigable rivers and large lakes, providing freshwater fish and shellfish as well as irrigation. Rice, corn, and coconut cultivation takes up four-fifths of the cropland; the rest is given over to sugarcane, yams (including a particularly sweet purple yam used in desserts), manioc, bananas, coffee, tobacco, and hemp.

THE CUISINE

Philippine cuisine is perhaps the clearest evidence of its multicultural history. The spices are indigenous, the cooking methods Spanish, the noodles Chinese, and a few of the combinations—chicken with garbanzos, pork with greens—hearken back to Africa and the Middle East. A fermented shrimp or fish sauce called *patis*, similar to but milder than the Thai nam pla, is a characteristic flavoring, along with Malay-style coconut. However, Filipino dishes are notable among southern Asian cuisines for the amount of meat consumed, the much lighter use of hot spices, and the preference for olive oil over peanut oil. And the most obvious distinction is the fact that the "national dish," called *adobo*, is purely European—it's any meat or chicken barbecued in a vinegar/ginger/soy sauce marinade, derived from the Spanish adobado.

Filipinos are also less interested in vegetables than many neighboring peoples; they prefer their tofu dried to soft; and they frequently serve meals in courses—soup, fish, meat, fruit, dessert—in a way that is obviously European. And although a few Filipinos in rural areas continue to eat with their fingers, nearly all have become accustomed to forks and knives, spoons and plates.

THE MAIN INGREDIENTS

MEAT AND POULTRY The Filipino diet is extremely meat-heavy. Livestock farmers raise hogs, water buffalo, and goats; there are

---

Fat Watch

Eating a light meal in a Philippine restaurant requires careful planning, since many of the most popular ingredients—pork, olive oil, peanuts, and coconut and coconut oil—are all high in fat. A surprisingly high percentage of dishes, including dumplings, meats, fish, even rice and tofu, are fried. If possible, stick to the grilled foods. Also be prepared to drink a lot of water; many dishes may seem very salty.

also dairy farms around the larger cities. Organ meats and some of the fattiest offal—hocks and belly—are also popular. Not surprisingly, they prefer the fattier meat of ducks to chickens and frequently raise both.

SEASONINGS Again, Filipinos prefer the flavor of the Spanish olive oil and use it fairly generously. They also like coconut milk; and the combined richness is only occasionally broken by dashes of vinegar, tamarind, ginger, or fish sauce.

SEAFOOD Among the most common fish are pompano, catfish, grouper, snapper, tilapia, and a fish greatly beloved in the Philippines but unavailable here, called *bungus* or milkfish. *Tinapa* is a smoked fish used as a topping for rice or noodle dishes. The Filipinos also enjoy shellfish, particularly the delicate Manila clams, mussels, shrimp, and squid, and several species of clawless spiny lobster, like those found in the Caribbean.

THE MAIN DISHES

Philippine foods are often referred to not by ingredients but by cooking style. By far the most popular dish in the country is adobo, which is usually pork or chicken but can be beef or goat or even shrimp or fish. It can even be stuffed into buns, like empanadas.

Another common method of cooking is *guinataan*, stewed in coconut milk. *Grisado* is just what it sounds like—"cooked in oil" (i.e., sautéed or fried). *Inihaw* refers to grilled foods, and *sinigang* is a type of stew, again either meat or fish, given a particularly sour bite by tamarind.

RICE, NOODLES, AND DUMPLINGS Rice is served at every meal, usually boiled but frequently fried. *Turo-turo*, which also refers to a kind of restaurant, is a relative of the Indonesian rijsttafel: It literally means "point, point," and what happens is that you get a bowl of rice and point to the various toppings you want. The sweet or sticky (glutinous) rice is most often reserved for desserts.

The other starch is noodles, or *pancit; pancit guisado* is fried noodles with mixed meats. *Loti* is the flat Chinese rice noodle. The Filipinos have also adopted, and adapted, the dumpling and the spring roll: *Sio mai* are open-faced dumplings with pork; *lumpia* are thin rice crepes rolled around garbanzo beans, tofu, pork, vegetables, or perhaps shrimp and dipped into a sweet-and-sour sauce; occasionally they are also served deep-fried.

FISH AND SEAFOOD   The Filipinos not only like seafood, they also like it in combination with meat; the Philippine *arroz a la paella*, with chicken, pork chops, prawns, mussels, chorizo, and lobster—and saffron—would do any Spaniard proud. Fish is most often pan-fried or braised, or even stuffed with tomatoes and onions (purely Spanish) and steamed in banana leaves (just as distinctly Asian). On the other hand, it can be "cooked" in lime or lemon juice, like ceviche, then mixed with chilies, tomatoes, and coconut (called *kilawin*).

MEATS   To say that there are numerous recipes for pork is an understatement. The Filipinos eat pork the way Koreans eat beef: nose to tail. Besides the more familiar cuts—whole roast pig, called *klechon*, and barbecued chops, butts, and satays—and the reasonably tame grilled livers and kidneys, there are offal soups (*dinuguan*), congee-style rice gruels with tripe (*goto*), fried hocks and cracklings, and recipes for jowl and snout and belly—not to mention bacon and sausage. *Menudo* is a pork stew seasoned with liver, a little milder than its Central American tripe model.

The Filipinos eat almost as much beef and water buffalo as pork, including a beef marrow soup called *bulado* and a braised roast called *mechado; almondigas* are, as they are in Spain, ground meatballs. *Porchero*, sometimes called *cuchido*, is a thick stew, often beef and chicken with lots of garlic, that is served in two parts—meat and vegetables in one bowl and broth on the side. *Kare-kare*, a popular stew, is a Mediterranean-circuit dish of oxtail, peanut, and eggplant. Goat is usually stewed or barbecued.

POULTRY   Chicken can be adobo-barbecued, deep-fried, roasted, cooked in coconut, or combined with a second meat, usually sausage or pork. Duck is popular and widely raised: *Balut* are duck eggs, allowed to fertilize and then salted.

VEGETABLES AND FRUIT   In general, vegetables are considered only mildly interesting, but eggplant, called *talong*, is the exception; it is the one constant in a sort of ratatouille stew called *pinakbet* that otherwise can include almost anything. Under the American influence, however, vegetable salads have become somewhat more commonplace and may include tomatoes and onions, potatoes, sweet potatoes, mushrooms (mostly dried), water greens and watercresses, cucumbers, and radishes. Fruits include papaya, mango, bitter melon, bananas, and the tiny finger bananas called *saba*.

SWEETS Again, thanks to the Spanish influence, the Filipinos crave desserts—sweets made of yams and rice, coconut flans, corn puddings, cookies, and sherbet-like coconut or mango ices.

BEVERAGES About a few things the Filipinos are stubbornly unpredictable. Despite the Spanish occupation, Filipinos rarely drink wine or sherry. Nor, despite the Chinese influence, do they like tea, which is drunk medicinally rather than socially. Instead, Filipinos prefer to drink water with meals and, at other times, coffee and hot chocolate and beer (San Miguel is a Philippine brand widely available here). *Halo-halo* (mix-mix) is a sort of fruit shake with sweet red beans.

HOW TO ORDER AND EAT LIKE A NATIVE

Like the Spanish, the Filipinos eat four times a day, with a late-afternoon meal between lunch and dinner (and frequently a late-morning break for coffee and sweet cheese pastries). Breakfast is either rice and fish or a spicy sausage called *longaniza*, fried in a skillet and accompanied by rice cooked in the sausage grease. The afternoon meal is called *merienda*, a cross between English high tea and dim sum: lumpia, sandwiches, sweets, and cakes are all offered together.

As we noted above, Spanish-style dinners are often served in courses, but the native dishes, such as adobo or guinataan stews, are offered all at once. Traditionally, Filipinos eat at tables with "lazy Susan" turntables in the center, and some restaurants in the United States are equipped with these. Turo-turo restaurants, the pick-your-topping rice joints, are sometimes just glorified steam tables with stools.

Adobo is "must" eating, and two diners might split chicken adobo and roast pork after appetizers of kilawin and sio mai dumplings. Four people should start with lumpia and pancit guisado before going on to try an adobo (pork) and a guinataan stew (probably chicken), with a third dish of kare-kare. A group might ask whether the restaurant has a "turo-turo" menu; if not, paella would be a good alternative.

COOKING AT HOME

Most ingredients for cooking Filipino dishes at home can be bought at the local market; the most important would be patis (the fish sauce), tamarind sauce, and coconut milk. Thai nam pla may be substituted for patis but should be slightly diluted; likewise, the vinegar generally used in making adobo is a palm vinegar much milder than the cider or wine vinegars Westerners are accustomed to, so you should either buy some or dilute rice wine vinegar with water. Rice was traditionally cooked in an earthenware pot but is now usually boiled Western-style. The Philippine version of a wok is called a *carajay* (pronounced, in the Spanish style, "cara-hai") and is good for stir-frying, though a skillet will do fine.

PORK ADOBO

1 1/4 pound pork butt or 4 meaty chops
6 cloves garlic, sliced
1 cup rice or white wine vinegar
3/4 cup water
2 bay leaves
2 tablespoons soy sauce
1 teaspoon black peppercorns, crushed
1/2 teaspoon salt
olive oil (or rendered pork fat or lard)

If using pork butt, cut into large chunks; trim fat on chops to 1/4 inch. Combine all ingredients in heavy casserole or saucepan and marinate at least 1 hour. Turn on heat, bring to a boil, and simmer until pork is tender. Remove meat and reduce marinade to thick sauce; pour through strainer into small bowl or juice separator and return fat to pan. Add oil to cover pan bottom by 1/4 inch. Return pork to pan and fry until brown all over; serve with rice and top with sauce.

Variation: Use 3/4 pound pork or small leg chops and add small chicken, cut into serving pieces. For chicken only, omit pre-cooking marinade and just cook in the adobo sauce. After cooking, remove meat and brown as above, and add 1/2 cup coconut milk to reduced sauce.

LUMPIA

2 tablespoons olive oil
1 cup chopped green onion
5 cloves garlic, peeled and minced

1 cup chopped raw shrimp
1 cup cooked diced pork
1/2 cup diced ham
1/2 cup diced chicken, cooked
1 carrot, peeled and julienned
1/2 cup bamboo shoots or water chestnuts, chopped
1/2 cup bean sprouts
2 cups shredded Chinese cabbage
salt and pepper
soy sauce (optional)
20–25 small romaine or flat lettuce leaves
spring roll or egg roll wrappers (about two dozen)

Heat oil in wok or deep skillet and cook onion and garlic over medium heat until soft; add shrimp, stir-fry until just opaque, and add pork, ham, and chicken. Stir-fry 3 minutes and add carrot, bamboo shoots or water chestnuts, and bean sprouts; stir-fry 3 minutes more and add cabbage, sprinkling with salt. Continue cooking, tossing frequently, until cabbage is tender but still crisp. Season to taste with more salt or soy and pepper, then drain off excess liquid and set aside to cool.

To serve, place one lettuce leaf on each wrapper and place a large spoonful (about 2 tablespoons) of filling in the center. Fold two edges in, then roll to enclose stuffing. Serve with dipping sauce (below).

Variation: Lumpia can also be served deep-fried, but in that case the lettuce should be omitted.

DIPPING SAUCE

1 cup chicken stock
2 tablespoons soy sauce
5 tablespoons brown sugar
2 tablespoons cornstarch or other starch
3 cloves garlic, finely minced
salt (if desired)

Place stock, soy sauce, sugar, and starch in small saucepan; simmer, stirring constantly, until thickened. Salt to taste and pour into serving bowl (or bowls) and sprinkle with garlic.

PART V

ASIA

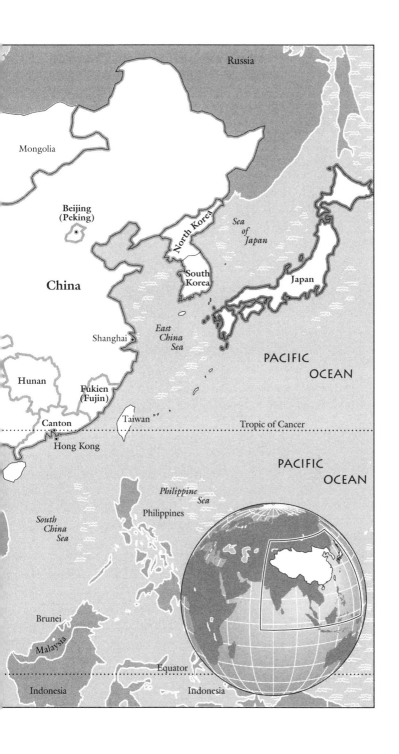

CHINA

BASIC CUISINE

DINNER FOR TWO:
Hot-and-sour soup, egg drop soup, tea-smoked duck, Hunan-style pork

DINNER FOR FOUR:
Noodle soup, steamed fish with ginger and scallions, red-cooked chicken, Szechwan-style green beans, beef in five-spice powder

GROUP DISH:
Dim sum or Chinese hotpot

STYLE:
Tangy, complex, brown-spiced

KEY FLAVORS:
Soy sauce, hoisin sauce, sesame oil, chilies

DISTINCTIVE FOODS:
Dim sum, Peking duck, stir-fried meats

NUTRITIONAL INDEX:
Low cholesterol, medium fat, high carbohydrate, high sodium

EATING UTENSILS:
Chopsticks, spoons

UNIFORMITY OF MENUS:
Fair

COST:
Inexpensive to expensive

"THANK YOU":
"Shasha nee"

The Chinese may not have established the first civilization, but theirs is the oldest existing society, and its culinary roots range far and wide. The Chinese were steaming rice perhaps as long as 8,000 years ago and millet soon thereafter. The soybean is native to the region and has served them as protein, preservative, and flavoring for at least 5,000 years; but a great many of the foods and spices we think of as Chinese were actually imports from the Middle East, Malaysia (often via the seagoing Europeans), India, and the Americas.

Like the French, the Chinese are fascinated by technique: They conceived of "recipes" 3,000 years ago and had court nutritionists even then. Some estimates put the number of Chinese dishes at 80,000. And like the French, the Chinese consider cooking a great profession; high-ranking chefs are expected not only to lord it over their subordinates but to cook only for the most important clients (who, in the United States, are more often *not* the Americans). The approved course in making Peking duck is a year long.

However, just because Chinese cuisine is so old and so accomplished does not mean that it is, or ever was, terribly rich outside of the great palaces. Only about 10 percent of the land is arable, and the tending of that fraction is so intense it requires the labor of 60 percent of the people. China is a land of limited wood and natural fuels, which is one reason that so many dishes are cooked quickly or steamed: Compare the relative "cost" of baking bread in one of those Italian ovens at 1,500° with steaming a whole dinner in stacking baskets over a single pot. Dairy products are scarce because arable land has always been too precious to serve as pasture. There were many periods of famine and warfare—several within memory—that had to be survived as well.

However, the Chinese can legitimately lay claim to two of the most important culinary inventions in history: chopsticks, the most versatile eating utensil known; and the wok, the deep, sloped-sided Chinese frying pan/stockpot/braising dish.

THE COUNTRY

China is the most populous nation in the world, with over 900 million people; it covers some 400 million square miles and, in the central and southeastern regions, has 4,000 miles of coastline and scores of rivers and lakes. The primarily dialect is Mandarin, which derives from the imperial court speech at Peking and is spoken by about 70 percent of the population—which means, strikingly, that approximately one person in every six in the world speaks Mandarin Chinese as a first language. However, there are many other dialects, 108 in the province of Fukien alone.

China is physically as well as spiritually at the heart of many cultures: At the northeast corner of the coast, Manchuria meets the peninsula of Korea; moving around counter-clockwise, China is bounded by Russia, Mongolia, several former Soviet nations (such as Kazakhstan and Tadzhikistan), Afghanistan, Pakistan, India, Nepal, Myanmar (Burma), Laos, and Vietnam.

The country itself is shaped, appropriately, like a high-rimmed wok or hotpot tilted slightly to one side, with the more populous region in the base, Tibet in the western part of the "bowl," Manchuria cocked up on the east, and the now-independent Mongolia as the lid.

The Huang He (Yellow) and Yangtze rivers cut roughly across the bottom of the bowl above the fat base; they are the cradles of Chinese culture.

Northern China is semiarid; the Gobi Desert rises into the Inner Mongolian steppes. The Tibetan plateau runs at 3,660 miles high between the Himalayas and the Kunlun Mountains, and Manchuria is mostly plains and highlands. Hence wheat is the primary grain in the north, rather than rice. Only central and southern China, from the great Huang He and Yangtze basins to the sea, are suited to broader agricultural production.

THE HISTORY

Chinese cooking could be said to go back to Peking Man, who was using fire to cook his meat nearly half a million years ago. The word "man" may be an exaggeration, and "cuisine" would be ludicrous; it is not clear that he even knew the value of salt.

A more recognizable man appeared in northern China after the last Ice Age—about 20,000 years ago—and Chinese civilization as we know it coalesced about 4,000 years ago. Its resemblances to the first Mesopotamian civilizations are strong, and some scholars have argued that Chinese civilization actually originated in the West, which would certainly upend the traditional imperial vision of China as the center of the universe.

Thanks to the preservation of so much Chinese literature and to the ongoing excavation of paleolithic and neolithic settlements, we have fleeting images of the evolution of Chinese culture and cuisine. The cultivation of first millet and then rice in the Yellow River and Yangtze River valleys allowed the early Chinese to stop living nomadically and to domesticate their first animals. In classical Chinese, the word for rice was also the word for agriculture, suggesting that rice was known back when the language was actually being formed; and in many of the Southeast Asian languages that were influenced by Chinese, "rice" is synonymous with food or meals. A 3,000-year-old book of poems speaks of the farmers raising rice and brewing wine from it, planting wheat, harvesting melons, gourds, and chives, boiling celery and soybeans, and picking dates and wild asparagus. A Chu ode written about 500 B.C. lures back the souls of the dead with promises of rice with honey, lamb roasted with sugarcane, and braised beef tendons.

The first crucial import was wheat, the cultivation of which passed from Egypt through the Middle East to India and arrived in western and northern China about 2500 B.C. The other early culinary "improvements" were also Persian, imported by an imperial spy named Zhang Xian, who marked what became the Silk Road into Central Asia in the second century B.C.; along that route came back grapes, pomegranates, squash, peas, coriander, garlic, walnuts and, most important, sesame oil, which remains essential in northern Chinese cooking. Persian-style kebabs made their way in more roundaboutly, via Indonesia, where they were lightened into satays. Meat stews became common, flavored with mustard, cinnamon, ginger, galangal, soy sauce, and fermented black beans.

About the beginning of the common era, the trick of milling flour was imported from India, and noodles were invented. Curry spices became popular. Meanwhile, in southern China, poets were speaking of oranges, coconuts, lotus seeds. The wok was in use by about the sixth century, and Turkish spirits had been discovered; a few centuries later, residents of Szechwan were distilling alcohol. The Persian trade produced eggplant and spinach, dill, nutmeg, saffron, and peppercorns. In Vietnam, a faster-growing strain of rice was discovered, and agriculture boomed.

By the end of the first millenium, regional specialties—including the pepper-rich Szechwan cuisine—were already recognized. Lamb, kid, and mutton, now almost unknown in southern China, were prominent in cookbooks of the time, but after the invasion of the Mongols, who ate so much lamb, these meats became politically incorrect.

The dynastic history of China is quite intricate, but in general, the empire had a sort of heartbeat; it would expand, often toward the west; then it would relax, become decadent, and deteriorate. Territories at the fringes would be lost, the "heart" would contract , and then a tide of new "barbarian" blood would flow in—usually from the north, as if through an artery—to conquer and eventually to assimilate. Then the empire would expand, grow fat and content, and the whole thing would happen all over again. Genghis Khan's Mongols, for example, first conquered the northern ranges and then, in 1271, put Marco Polo's idol Kublai Khan on the Imperial Throne; a century later, they were back in Mongolia.

The Mongols' rule was followed by the Ming dynasty, which was conquered by the Manchus (also from the north); it was during the Ming and Manchu reigns that the Portuguese landed (1514) and the Spanish conquered the Philippines (1565) and modern Chinese cuisine took shape. International trade brought in snow peas (called "Holland peas") from the Dutch, watercress from Portugal, and tomatoes ("foreign eggplant") and chilies from the Americas. More important for the subsistence farmers, the Spanish traders also supplied New World corn and potatoes, which flourished in areas where rice could not.

THE CUISINE

The ingredients of Chinese cuisine as we know it were acquired slowly, over a period of many centuries. Rice and wheat were among the first crops, and China remains the world's largest producer of both. They are symbolic of the country's divided economies: In the north, wheat is the primary starch, and noodles the preferred manner of consumption. If you remember that the Kublai Khan Marco Polo visited was Mongolian, you will understand how it is that the "Chinese" theory of pasta creation came about. It was the inland Chinese who first domesticated the pig, and China is also the world's largest producer of red meat. In the southern and central regions, on the other hand, rice is the staple, and fish and seafood the primary proteins.

As we have already seen, the essential seasonings came from all over—Persia, India, Malaysia, the Americas. However, the methods of cooking have remained relatively unchanged, simple and fast and fuel-efficient: boiling, braising, steaming, roasting, stir-frying, and deep-frying. There are many refinements of each: simmering, steeping, smothering, pan-sticking, and smoking, for example. Each cooking method has even further degrees of variation—there are probably a dozen ways to boil chicken, depending on exactly the texture desired for a particular dish— and the Chinese often "double-cook" dishes, boiling and then frying; but few methods require both long cooking and high heat.

Marinating, which preserves and tenderizes meat and poultry (thus shortening cooking times) as well as flavoring them, can be adjusted to permeate, crisp, or even "velvet" a dish—give it a silken, cornstarch-based coating.

Many of the aesthetic elements in Chinese cuisine were also partially inspired by the need to husband resources. Like the Japanese, the Chinese use contrast, color, texture, and cosmic "harmony" to make every dish seem more elaborate and to make eating it a more fulfilling experience. A 2,500-year-old book of etiquette speaks of seasoning with spices in autumn, salt in winter, sour flavors in spring, and bitter in summer, and offsetting them all with sweetness; it also prescribes the correct fat to be used in frying various meats. Although dishes in a meal may not be rich, they are varied—seafood, poultry, pork, tofu, vegetables—each preferably in a different sauce and, ideally, cut or sliced in different ways.

The use of ornate, metaphorical names for recipes works the same way, demanding the diner's attention to the creation of the dish and slowing its consumption. The dragon and phoenix are both considered propitious animals, so they are often invoked symbolically, the dragon usually represented by lobster and the phoenix by white chicken meat.

Authentic Chinese food is unusually healthful, and for some unusual reasons. For one thing, it is virtually free of dairy foods—milk, butter, or cheese—which not only limits the diet's cholesterol content but makes it an especially attractive choice for lactose-intolerant diners. Meat is used as a flavoring for vegetables and grains, not as a main dish, limiting the cholesterol even further. (In fact, there is no "main dish"; variety is used as another way to stretch a meal.) Grains and beans of various types are important in all regions of the country.

Because so much of the agricultural land in the central and southern regions is either regularly flooded for rice growing or naturally marshy, a surprising number of the vegetables consumed are watery and low-calorie: lotus and bamboo shoots, lily buds, water chestnuts, bean sprouts, cabbages, and so forth. For the same reasons, many are fibrous, adding another healthful element to the diet. Other "vegetables" are actually marine life, such as algae and "sea cucumbers," which supply nutrients macrobiologists venerate.

The exceptions are dishes that are fried, of course, including dumplings, buns, wontons, and fried rice as well as deep-fried fish and what are called "twice-cooked" dishes. American stir-fried dishes tend to be overly greasy and, in the cheaper establishments, may be cooked in oil that has been reused and has become rank. Corner-cutting "Szechwan" carryouts often use hot pepper oil to flavor dishes rather than taking the time to incorporate real chilies. Poached, braised, and steamed dishes, particularly those that include seafoods and mixed vegetables, are better bets, but even these dishes can be deceptive: Many meats used in soups and stews are stir-fried first, to add flavor; and noodles can also be pre-fried to extend their shelf life (again, this problem is more likely in a quick, cheap eatery). The tell-tale sign is the oil on the surface of the dish or in the bottom of the plate.

Finally, Chinese food is fairly high in sodium, most of it hidden; Chinese food is traditionally seasoned during the cooking rather than at the table.

REGIONAL CUISINES

There are regional distinctions in Chinese cooking, and luckily for Americans, more and more Chinese restaurants in the United States are specializing in regional cuisines. (Actually, it's probably more accurate to say that they are beginning to advertise their specialties in English and list them on the menus; for many years, the only way to get real Chinese food was to ask for the Chinese-language menu, wait for the host to come over and try to convince you that you *didn't* want to order the tripe in chili oil that you were pointing to, and then order precisely that.)

Intriguingly, there are Chinese writers who fear that the same instruments of "progress" that made authentic Chinese food in America possible—swifter and more reliable transport, better communication and education—may work against regional cuisines back home and that Chinese cooking may be becoming increasingly homogenized. The two greatest changes in recent decades have probably been the protection of many rare and exotic animals previously used for meat and the adoption of some international dishes—particularly around Shanghai, which was for many years an international mecca.

The five main regional styles available in the United States reflect historical as well as topographical and climactic differences. Cantonese cuisine comes from the southeast; Szechwan, from the west; Beijing, from the northeast; Hunan, from the central regions; and Fukien, from the eastern coast.

CANTONESE cuisine, generally speaking, is the most simply flavored, characterized by minimal seasonings (coriander, black beans, oyster sauce, bean cheese, and shrimp paste), the use of chicken broth as a cooking medium, and a heavy dependence on stir-frying and steaming; most dim sum, the assortment of steamed dumplings rolled around on carts, is Cantonese. It is closely related to Beijing-style cuisine, because in the mid-seventeenth century, when the Manchus swept into the Imperial City, many of the royal chefs fled south to safety. There they turned their practiced hand to new ingredients, particularly seafood.

The Cantonese generally prefer both fish and poultry slightly pink at the bone (they are bought live and cooked only at the last minute, so there is no danger), though in this country meat is usually cooked more thoroughly to satisfy the perceived American taste. Cantonese cuisine is also full of delicate fruits and vegetables, such as lychees, cashews, coconuts, pineapples, papaya, watercress, pea leaves, chrysanthemum petals, cilantro, and water chestnuts.

Because the port of Canton was the first major East-West cross-roads, and the Cantonese were the first group to travel widely to Europe and the United States, theirs was also the first style most Westerners were introduced to, and it remains the most common here. (Historians have pointed out that the Chinese laborers' healthier diet and abstinence from cheap rotgut whiskey helped them survive the crippling working conditions of the transcontinental railroads, while the Americans, downing spoiled beef and beans, suffered chronic illness.) Hong Kong is off the coast of Canton, and many Hong Kong dishes offered in Cantonese restaurants closely resemble Singaporean Nonja cuisine (see the chapter on Indonesia, Malaysia, and Singapore).

BEIJING Peking, as it was formerly spelled, was the site of the Imperial Court and thus the site of the most elaborate banquets, so Beijing cuisine is the most consciously sophisticated of the regional cuisines; it is also light and fairly delicately seasoned but uses much more garlic (as much as its neighbors in Korea) and scallions and other green onions. Rice is used less frequently in the north than elsewhere in the country; wheat, millet, and soybeans are the staples. Northerners also tend to prefer dark soy sauce almost exclusively over light soy. Wine is used as a cooking liquid, especially for meats, and so is vinegar. Soft-fried foods are a hallmark. Beijing and the closely related Shantung (or Shandong) dishes used to be called "Mandarin" as well, referring to the aristocrats of the court. (Court cuisine could be very demanding: In the sixth century B.C., the Duke of Jin is said to have executed his chef for undercooking braised bear's paw—still a northern Chinese specialty, although it is now illegal.)

Most so-called Mongolian dishes are northern Chinese in style, but because of the great grass steppes there (and the Muslim influence in the northwest), lamb and mutton are more common than pork, and some fermented dairy products such as yogurt are used. The hotpot and various casseroles that were characteristic of the

Chop Shop

Most "Chinese-American" dishes are just unfortunate adaptations of classic recipes, the best that impoverished nineteenth-century Chinese immigrants—most of whom were not professional chefs but mom-and-pop cooks—had to do with what they could get here. Because they didn't have the time or ingredients to make flavorful Supreme Stock (described on page 262), they doused fried rice with soy sauce. Since Americans were unaccustomed to delicate egg roll wrappings and disliked most seafood anyway, eggs rolls became thicker, with pork instead of shrimp. Unable to get fresh fruit, they improvised sweet-and-sour sauces out of canned pineapples and ketchup, and so on.

There is one possibly "authentic" Chinese-American dish: chop suey. According to legend, Ambassador Li Hong Zhang, who represented the Manchu court here at the end of the nineteenth century, once forgot to warn his chef that he had invited company over for supper. At the last minute, the chef combined all the leftovers and seasonings he could find into what we would call refrigerator roulette, and when his guests

Chop Shop
continued

asked him the name of the dish, the ambassador answered honestly, *"Tsap seui"*—an amalgamation of scraps. A related story has Li serving tsap seui at a diplomatic dinner at the Waldorf Astoria, of all places. A third credits the ingenuity of a San Francisco cook faced with a rowdy crowd of drunk and hungry miners. A few scholars scoff at such tales and call it an old country dish. Nevertheless, a Shanghai restaurant in the 1930s advertised "Genuine American Chop Suey."

That silliest of "Chinese" specialties, the fortune cookie, is definitely native to the United States—invented in 1916 by a California noodle maker named David Jung. Just in the last couple of years, however, a Brooklyn fortune cookie firm has been hired to build a factory in Canton. Confucius say, "There's no accounting for taste."

swift-moving Mongols are still common, though they were probably reintroduced from Inner Mongolia sometime after the Khans had been evicted. "Mongolian barbecue" restaurants are almost like Japanese teppanyaki houses, where sliced meat and vegetables are quick-grilled with a flourish of chopsticks and then stuffed into little rolls and eaten by hand. The Shantung version is a lamb stew with dunked buns. The city of Tsingtao was once leased to the Germans, which is how it came to make such good beer.

Szechwan (also spelled Szechuan or Sichuan) cuisine has become increasingly popular in the United States over the last 20 years and probably laid the groundwork for the boom in Thai restaurants here. Szechwan food is spicy and peppery and tends to be oily, as well; many ingredients are fried, wrapped in dough, and then fried again. The cooking fat may be lard or chicken fat as well as oil. Even "lighter fare" may be boiled, then stir-fried, such as Twice-Cooked Pork. China's western region has less fish than some areas, because the rivers race down from the mountains too fast for leisurely breeding, so "fish-flavored" in Szechwan cuisine refers to dishes seasoned with a rich, slightly sour barbecue sauce made from vinegar, hot bean paste, ginger, garlic, and onions. Ironically, though Chung King is one of the major names in homogenized, thoroughly un-spicy Chinese-American fare, "Chungking" cuisine is another name for Szechwan cooking.

Hunan cuisine, which in the United States is generally confused with Szechwan, is also spicy but richer; dishes are more likely to be marinated in or sauced with sweet-and-sour compotes. Meats may also be dried and preserved. Though the chili peppers used now in Szechwan and Hunan cooking originated in the New World and were not known in China until the seventeenth century, both styles were already characterized by generous doses of black and white pepper and ginger.

Fukien cuisine, which is just beginning to be available in the United States, is extremely healthful: It emphasizes "wet" dishes, particularly soups (which are filling and not fatty) and soupy dishes, stocks, wine braising, and seafood. Because Fukien (or Fujien) is on the east coast of China and has perhaps had more exchange with Japanese cuisine, Fukien cooking uses more soy sauce than some of the other regional styles and features more "fish and rice" dishes; Fukien restaurants in the United States may have sushi bars. The thin crepes called *poopia* are almost Vietnamese in style; as many as 20 julienned or shredded meats and vegetables are laid out, and diners fill and roll their own crepes. Oysterette pan-fry is a sort of omelet.

Salted and preserved duck, crabs, the original fried rice (made with Supreme Stock), and many dim sum dishes originated in the eastern regions as well. Shanghai cooking can be heavily Europeanized (cold meat aspic, for instance) but also includes such specialties as "red-cooked" pork shoulder with rock candy. Taiwan is off the shore of Fukien province, so "Taiwanese-style" cuisine is primarily Fukienese.

Most recently, Chinese foods in Hong Kong and on the West Coast of America have begun to evolve in a new direction, reflecting both the international outlook of young upwardly mobile Hong Kong professionals—called, inevitably, "chuppies"—and the increasing pride Chinese-Americans have in their dual heritage. Chop suey is back, in a snappier, fresher fashion; and some new-wave Chinese restaurants are even experimenting—as are Japanese sushi bars—with such American dairy products as mayonnaise and cheese.

THE MAIN INGREDIENTS

SEASONINGS The most prominent flavors are soy sauce, sesame oil, peanut oil, sweet wines, garlic, ginger, various onions, bean pastes, sesame paste, fermented black beans, and mustard. Salt, pepper, cinnamon, curry spices, anise, powdered ginger, chilies, brown sugar, vinegar, honey, and various dried and pickled ingredients, such as dried shrimp, dried mushrooms, and pickled cabbage, are characteristic. Dried orange peel is a particularly old and treasured flavor; the orange is native to China. A number of premixed sauces, such as hoisin sauce (a mix of soybean paste, five-spice powder, chili, and a touch of brown sugar), plum sauce (often called "duck sauce" because it was usually served with duck in American restaurants), bean sauce (fermented soybeans) and its chili-fired alternative, "oyster sauce," and chili sauce are used as condiments or season-ings. Tea is also an important ingredient: It is used as a broth, particularly for hard-boiled eggs, and tea leaves are used for smoking duck and chicken and are occa-sionally stir-fried.

One of the most important ingredients in Cantonese cooking is called Supreme Stock; each chef has his own version, but it is generally a rich broth made from a com-bination of chicken and perhaps duck or squab, ham, and pork. Like sourdough starter, this stock, once made, is then replenished, expanded, and continually re-created for years; in some epicurean circles, it is the stock that separates the cooks from the culinary stars.

Chinese soy sauce is a little less sweet and more salty than Japanese shoyu, which mixes more wheat with the soy. Dark soy has a little molasses in it and is used more with meats; light soy is more suited to seafoods, dipping sauces, and soups. "Five-spice powder" may not always have only five ingredients—the usual combination is star anise, fennel seed, cinnamon, cloves, and ginger, with anise root and Szechwan pep-percorns often added—but five is a propitious number, and since it was originally a medicinal mixture, the name emphasized and even increased its potency. Sesame oil, is a flavoring, not a cooking oil; it cannot with-stand high temperature.

VEGETABLES Thanks to millenia of trading, the Chinese eat near-ly all of the vegetables that any other culture eats, but a few—bamboo shoots, bean sprouts, water chestnuts, mung beans—are purely Chinese. Mushrooms, greens (spinach, mustard, Chinese cabbage, celery, water-cress, and many lettuces), seaweeds, cucumbers, several eggplants, peas, lima beans, string beans, radishes, squashes, winter melons, sweet pota-toes, taro root, turnips, okra, asparagus, sweet peppers, and corn are some of the most common. Soybeans provide more protein per acre and per pound than any other crop; the Chinese consume plain boiled beans, sprouts, tofu (bean curd), fermented bean paste, and soy milk.

FRUITS AND NUTS Melons, grapes, kumquats, loquats, bananas, apples, oranges, mangoes, apricots, and plums are common. So-called lychee nuts are really a fruit. Many fruits are candied or preserved to eat as snacks and occasionally as desserts, but they may also be used in sauces. Walnuts, chestnuts, lotus seeds, cashews, almonds, coconut, gingko nuts, peanuts, and sesame seeds are also prominent.

RICE AND NOODLES According to the stereotype, all Chinese food comes with rice, either steamed or fried; but that is another American (Cantonese) overstatement. In the north, as mentioned, noo-dles are the staple. Wheat is the major grain there, but barley, maize, and millet are also cultivated, and all four of these flours are used to make breads, buns, pastries, and the tortilla-like pancakes (sometimes referred to as "doilies") used in Peking duck and moo shi pork. Noodles are eaten in the south, too, but rice is the staple (the poor eat very little else), and noodles are more frequently considered light fare. The sticky or gluti-nous rice popular in Southeast Asia is used mainly for stuffings and desserts and occasionally to coat meatballs or pork. The thick "chow foon" noodles are particularly popular as a family dish; other common noodles include egg noodles, peastarch noodles, cellophane or bean thread noodles, and pale white "rice sticks."

FISH AND SEAFOOD China is rolling, or roiling, in both fresh- and saltwater proteins: bass, bluefish, bream, carp, catfish, sturgeon, trout, tuna, flounder, halibut, mackerel, mullet, perch, shad, sardines, pike, cod, herring, snapper, sole, dogfish, and shark, plus lobster, crab, abalone, scallops, oysters, clams, eels, scallops, shrimp, and squid—for starters. Nori (seaweed sheets) are used to enrich soups and sometimes to wrap fish and rice, Japanese-style; kelp is eaten as a source of iodine. "Sea cucumber," incidentally, is not a vegetable but a marine slug, also known as *bêche-de-mer*.

POULTRY AND GAME BIRDS Duck, rather than chicken, is the first choice in poultry in the Chinese diet, and a Chinese clipper ship that sailed into the United States in the 1870s brought with it the ancestors of all those Long Island and Peking ducks here now. Like the geese fattened for foie gras, ducks are force-fed for weeks before slaughter. Many Chinese restaurants smoke, dry (all poultry is well-drained of blood), and roast whole ducks and chickens and hang them in the windows as a sort of advertising, just as sushi bars display plastic fish. Chicken is a close second, followed by squab, quail, partridge, wild duck, pheasant, goose, and occasionally turkey. Duck eggs, fresh and salted, are extremely popular, again followed by hen's eggs, quail, and pigeon eggs. (Duck eggs have a slightly oilier texture than hens' eggs, and some French pastry experts claim they are essential for making *cordon bleu* pastry dough.)

MEATS Pork is the first meat in Chinese cookery, in both senses: The pink pig we know was domesticated in China thousands of years ago, and it is also the most popular meat in the diet. Pork is made into bacon, a Smithfield-like ham, and sausage—although it is hard to guess what constitutes leftover offal for sausage, given that the Chinese eat pork kidneys, livers, hearts, tripe, stomachs, brains, ears, tails, tongues, blood (in pudding), and pigs' feet, and even snouts and spleens.

Beef is only gradually becoming common (it is used far more frequently in American Chinese restaurants than anywhere in China itself), but again, little is wasted: The Chinese consume organ meats and even the shinbones. On the other hand, veal, so highly prized in European cuisines, is not considered interesting. Lamb, along with some goat, is eaten mostly in the northern regions, where the steppes are best suited to sheep grazing; in the south, a Muslim specialty is paper-thin horsemeat cooked with rice noodles, like a fondue or shabu-shabu.

THE MAIN DISHES

There isn't room to list all the 80,000 recipes, and fortunately, most menu listings are fairly self-explanatory ("shrimp and scallops in black bean sauce"). However, there are some dishes so common that they are referred to by their Chinese names, which we'll describe.

SOUPS The Chinese consider soup a part of the meal, to be drunk throughout rather than only at the beginning, and so most soups are served (to Chinese patrons, anyway) in large tureens and may be replenished during the evening. Among the standards are hot-and-sour;

egg drop; wonton; chicken with bean-thread noodles; crabmeat with asparagus; mixed seafood soups with bok choy and rice noodles; pork with winter melon, meatballs and vermicelli; and flavored broths with fish. These are relatively light soups; the simplest is merely boiled water poured over freshly minced greens. Thicker soups are generally long-simmered and are more apt to be served as lunch or light meals. Meat is usually limited to flavorings or even garnish. The "bird's nests" used in soup are not twigs but a gelatinous protein produced by a certain type of swallow; they look more like toasted coconut. Shark's fin is just what it sounds like.

There are also sweet dessert soups, usually made of fruit and seen primarily at banquets. Since the appetizers at a formal dinner often include peanuts or walnuts, a Chinese banquet can be said to go from nuts to soup.

RICE AND NOODLE DISHES   Real fried rice dishes, named for the majority ingredient (shrimp fried rice, pork fried rice, etc.) may or may not include eggs; *subgum*, which sometimes appears in the name, too, just means "many ingredients"—a sort of deluxe version. Fried rice is eaten as a meal rather than ordered as a entree among others. "Sizzling rice" dishes use the rice crusts that are left in the pan when rice is boiled; these crusts are deep-fried, and stir-fried seafood is poured over them, producing a popping or sizzling sound.

Congee or *jook* is a rice porridge that by itself is very bland but is usually just the base for a variety of toppings: wontons, sliced duck, pork kidneys, sliced fish, meatballs, and so forth. Noodle restaurants often work the same way: Only the toppings arrive on a large bowl of noodles in broth (called *yakkomein*) like the Vietnamese pho; wo mein noodles are fine egg noodles in soup. Wonton shops specialize in chewy noodles and water crescents (really soup dumplings or soft wontons).

"Soft-fried" noodles are parboiled then lightly stir-fried; "crisp-fried" noodles are used as garnish. Real chow mein calls for soft-fried, not crisp-fried noodles, boiled and then stir-fried with an assortment of meat and vegetables that were stir-fried separately; lo *mein* is similar, but the noodles are parboiled and then added directly to the meat-vegetable mixture. Dan-dan noodles are Szechwan-style, with dried shrimp, peanuts, and pickled vegetables.

APPETIZERS   Spareribs, even barbecued ones, are more authentic than you might think; but they aren't generally served as appetizers except at formal dinners or banquets. Traditionally, appetizers are cold and are more likely to include cold chicken, ham or sausage, meatballs, smoked fish, shrimp toast, pickled or parboiled vegetables, and even peanuts or preserved eggs. (Also called hundred-year-old eggs, preserved eggs are actually only about 100 days old and buried in lime.) Most of what we consider appetizers, particularly hot ones, are transplanted dim sum—teahouse meals (see page 269). Spring rolls are the original egg rolls, but smaller, more delicate than the modern version; they were originally Chinese New Year snacks. Wontons are stuffed dumplings (the things tossed on top of soup in cheap restaurants are just fried wonton skins); they can either be boiled in soup or served a dozen to a plate, deep-fried or steamed, as a light meal.

VEGETABLES   Because observant Buddhist monks didn't eat meat, the standard mixed-vegetable stir-fry is often called the Buddhist Delight. Dishes with names such as "Hard Immortal" and "Soft Immortal" or "Food of the Forest" are also vegetarian. "Mock chicken" is tofu; so are "yellow birds," "vegetarian roast duck," and so forth. Incidentally, vegetable dishes—even those served cold and resembling Southeast Asian vegetable salads—are never eaten raw; for safety, they have traditionally been boiled, salted, or pickled. Sauerkraut, intriguingly, is Chinese. Formal Chinese banquets do not include separate vegetarian dishes, only vegetables served with a meat.

FISH AND SEAFOOD   Fish is traditionally served whole, not only because it looks nicer but also because the meat of the cheeks is a delicacy and because the fish stays moister if it is cooked whole. The way a fish is cooked (steamed, simmered, fried, pan-fried, braised, etc.) is dictated by its relative thickness and oiliness. Cantonese-style steamed fish topped with julienned scallions and ginger has become so popular that it is apt to be served in almost any restaurant (try to get bass, which has a layer of fat that keeps the flesh moist but peels away). So is fried whole fish with sweet and sour or black bean sauce. In fine Chinese seafood restaurants, fresh scallops with their coral intact are also steamed with ginger. Mixed seafood is frequently served in a "basket" of quick-fried noodles. "Vinegar-slipped" fish is a northern Chinese specialty; the fish is quick-fried and then "slipped" into a sweet-and-sour vinegar sauce.

POULTRY Northern duck dishes, like Peking duck, have extra-crisp skin because the carcass is inflated before roasting to separate the layer of fat from the meat; then the meat is sliced at the table to be rolled in tortilla-like pancakes with a sliver of scallion and a dollop of hoisin sauce. Cantonese-style duck—the type that is often seen hanging around in windows—is filled with broth and seasonings and then roasted. Roast duck may be coated with honey, orange juice, or sherry; boned and braised with five-spice powder and hoisin; or chopped into two-inch pieces and simmered with fruit. "Eight-treasure duck" or chicken includes mushrooms, chestnuts, ginkgo nuts, pork, ham, shrimp, and lotus seeds. Nanking-style duck is rolled in coarse salt and crushed peppercorns, steamed, chopped into bite-size pieces, and served cold.

Chicken and other birds can be poached, steamed, deep-fried, braised, roasted, soy-marinated, and double-cooked; "white-simmered" means cooked without soy sauce, "red-simmered" with. *Kung pao* (or *gung pao*) chicken with peanuts and hot peppers is named for the "guardian of the palace" who invented it (the original version had the chilies, but used corn kernels rather than peanuts). *Moo goo gai pan* is stir-fried chicken with button mushrooms and thickened white sauce. "Beggar's chicken" is rolled in lotus leaves and baked in an earthen dish; originally the leaves were encased in mud and baked, because the beggars had presumably stolen the chicken and hidden it.

Incidentally, eggs are rarely eaten alone; instead, they are combined with meat or seafood and vegetables in omelets or soufflés. The original egg *foo yung* was an eggwhite and minced chicken breast soufflé, but in the United States it is a much heartier frittata-style pancake, either pan-fried ("home style") or deep-fried ("restaurant style").

MEAT Chinese cuisine offers more pork recipes than anything else, not surprisingly, but American diners rarely have a chance to order "five-flower pork" (belly bacon with alternating strips of fat and lean) or deep-fried roast pork squares with crabmeat. More common is "happy family" (sea cucumber, chicken, pork shoulder, ham, and vegetables in sweet and soy-sour sauce), "gold coin pork" (skewered deep-fried squares of pork, bacon, black mushrooms in sesame and anise; Chinese coins are, as this description suggests, square), "drunken pork" (boiled, then marinated in sherry for about a week) or *moo shi* pork (stir-fried pork with lily buds, cloud ear mushrooms, and scrambled eggs).

Szechwan beef is thin-cut, double-cooked, and glazed with a sweet-hot sauce, sometimes with orange; Cantonese steak is stir-fried beef with brandy and tomatoes. "Beef roll" is usually stuffed with shrimp and pine nuts and flavored with soy and brown sugar.

DESSERTS The Chinese themselves rarely eat sweets as we know them; they prefer fresh fruit or lychee nuts and sometimes preserved plums and even olives. On special occasions, apples and bananas may be battered and fried and drizzled with caramelized sugar called "silken threads," or you may be served buns filled with sweet bean paste or almonds. Restaurant desserts in China may also include almond-paste or sponge cakes. In the United States, most restaurants bring around sliced oranges after dinner, but many offer ice cream and the ubiquitous fortune cookie.

BEVERAGES The Chinese drink tea at the beginning of the meal and at the end; in the middle they prefer to stick to the soup or sip warm yellow wine (except when eating dim sum, which calls for copious consumption of tea.) In any case, they do not drink iced water, which they believe is hard on the digestion; that belief is now held by many Western doctors as well.

Shaoshing wine is a rice wine but tastes more like sherry than sake; that is the only Chinese wine most Americans will ever be offered. However, if you get friendly with the owner, you may taste *ng ga pai*, or "five companies" wine, which is almost like a whiskey; or even *pai gar*, which is closer to moonshine. *Fen*, which is 130 proof, is often used for cooking. *Kaoling* is a rice spirit that suggests vodka. These stronger spirits do not need warming. The Chinese also make a variety of liqueurs from plums, oranges, lychees, apricots, kiwi fruit, ginseng, and other fruits and herbs.

Tea is a source of great pleasure to the Chinese, and they study and evaluate tea the way the French evaluate wines. Like rice, it was first cultivated in the Yangtze River valley and is at least 2,500 years old. (The Portuguese took it back from Macao, the Portuguese princess Catharine of Braganza married Charles II of England and carried it with her, and eventually it became so profitable that the British East India Company decided to plant it all over India and Ceylon.) Green tea is unfermented; "black" tea—referred to as "red" by both Chinese and Japanese, because black has funereal associations—is fermented and roasted. Smoky teas such as *oolong* are lightly fermented or semifermented. The names are incredibly poetic, incidentally: "Pekoe" means "white hair," because young leaves have a pale fuzz and make a pale tea; "oolong" means "black dragon," and Wun Mo is "cloud mist."

Beer is increasingly popular in Chinese restaurants, particularly in the United States, where a full bar is almost standard; but happily, you see fewer and fewer of those "exotic drink" menus offering fruit-flavored grogs with tiny umbrellas.

DIM SUM

In Canton, where dim sum originated, businessmen traditionally used teahouses as their offices, often staying 12 or even 15 hours at a time. So teahouses became specialists in "snacks," particularly dumplings. Although there are literally hundreds of types of dim sum, the most traditional are *sui mei*, which when made correctly are nearly fat-free and gossamer-thin open-topped steamed dumplings filled with crab, shrimp, coriander, and freshwater chestnuts. Steamed beef meatballs are *ngau yuk mai*, pork-filled buns are *cha siu bau*. One type of steamed bun is called *manto*, or "savage's head"; "lion's head" is an extra-large meatball. Potstickers, or *guo-tieh*, are dumplings stuffed with meat and vegetables and pan-browned on the flat side. Fried rice may be wrapped in lotus leaves, and so may shrimp; bean curd can be stuffed with mushrooms and vegetables and steamed or fried. Steamed Cantonese spareribs are called *pai kwat*. Sometimes flaky buns are filled with curried chicken or minced buns or a sweet red bean paste.

Traditionally, carts of dim sum (two or three to a plate) are wheeled through the dining room, and you stop the waiter and point. At the end of the meal, your bill is calculated by how many empty plates you have accumulated. However, dim sum has become so popular in recent years that many restaurants in the United States have a special dim sum menu to order from; its increasing popularity also explains why dim sum, which for decades was available only on Sundays and usually only to Chinese-reading diners, is now frequently offered on Saturdays or even seven days a week.

"Dim sum," sweetly, means "touch the heart"—satisfy the inner man, as my father used to say.

HOTPOT MEALS

The Chinese firepot, also called the Mongolian hotpot, is a festive one-dish meal like a mixed fondue; it's similar to the Japanese shabu-shabu, among other things. The firepot is something like a wok with a chimney in the center; the "moat" is filled with a rich stock (one recipe includes a whole chicken, a ham bone, dried scallops, abalone, a pound of roast pork, pints of oysters and clams, and scallions) that is brought to a boil.

Meanwhile, each diner has custom-blended condiments—soy, sherry, hoisin sauce, sesame paste, vinegar, mustard, soybean paste, sugar, sesame oil, raw eggs—in a small bowl. Platters of paper-thin, sliced beef, pork, duck, chicken, ham, lamb, chicken livers, pork kidneys (parboiled), fish, shellfish, shrimp, lobster, squid, greens, bean curd, mushrooms, tofu, and nearly anything else are arranged on the table along with bowls of picked ginger, leeks, scallions, garlic, parsley, and so forth.

Once the stock begins to simmer, each diner picks up a single piece of food with chopsticks, dips it into the stock until it is cooked, and then returns it to his or her flavoring bowl, dips it, and eats it. (Some recipes call for setting the table with bowls of cornstarch-water mixtures as well, so that those who want to "velvet" their meats can dip them before poaching.) About halfway through the meal, noodles are added to the broth. At the end, the broth is ladled into the condiment bowl until balanced to taste; some noodles are added, and perhaps an egg is swirled into it; and the diners drink this "soup."

The Mongolian hotpot works the same way. As we noted above, the Mongolian barbecue has a similar mixture of ingredients and a bowl of seasonings, but the meats and vegetables are quick-grilled and eaten with buns or biscuits. (Rice, remember, is southern.)

HOW TO ORDER AND EAT LIKE A NATIVE

Chopsticks are about 4000 years old and, with a little practice, can be used for almost everything in the kitchen except chopping.

Chopsticks can be made of bamboo, jade, silver, ivory, fine woods, and even silver; and in the last several years, antique and artisan-crafted chopsticks have become available in the United States as well. If you have them, flaunt them; why waste trees? Besides, plastic chopsticks are slippery, and cheap wooden chopsticks have a scent that may distract from the food.

Chinese chopsticks are shaped somewhat differently from Japanese chopsticks; Chinese chopsticks are almost always square at the top, where they're held, and round in the lower half, the eating part; Japanese chopsticks tend to be either squarish all the way down or even pointed, which many people find easier to master. However, since the Chinese find it acceptable to raise the rice bowl to the lips and shovel with the sticks, it is fairly easy either way.

It is considered unlucky to cross the chopsticks or to let one fall to the floor, and a mismatched pair is said to predict difficult travel. It's considered rude to stick your elbows out, because you may inhibit a neighboring diner. Unfortunately, for the same reason, it's considered less polite to eat with your left hand.

Most Chinese dishes are eaten with chopsticks, and for some dishes, this requires a little practice. Noodles are picked up, bitten off, and allowed to gently slide back into the bowl. For poultry or beef chopped into small pieces with the bones intact, hold onto the bone with the chopsticks and then return it to the plate. Some texts say that when you eat shrimp in their shells, you should pick them up with chopsticks and pop them whole into your mouth, squeeze the meat out with your teeth, and return the shell to the plate with the chopsticks. We find it easier and as neat

Column 2

Chinese menus suffer from the same transliteration problems as other Asian cuisines, and the "official" respelling of many names during the 1980s, such as Peking (now Beijing) or Szechwan (now Sichuan), doesn't help much. Nevertheless, most dishes are themselves translated, and after a while, you will begin to recognize the various spellings.

There are several reasons to insist upon seeing the "Chinese" menu in addition to the American one. Not only will it include dozens of dishes probably not listed on the general menu (particularly the organ meats and offal), it is also more likely to put you in the hands of one of the more experienced chefs—and hopefully, one who won't dose your food with the extra sauce he assumes Americans prefer. If there is no other menu, or it's entirely in ideographs, talk to the waiter or manager about recommending dishes. If you see a party of Chinese diners eating something you don't recognize, order that. You might be surprised at how good it tastes. But whatever you get, treat it with respect. If you don't like it, don't make faces. Try a little and take the rest home—with feigned if not sincere pleasure.

According to Taoist philosophy, the entire world is divided into two elements, the feminine (yin) and the masculine (yang). These correspond to "cold" and "hot" humors—in food, in the human body, in animate and inanimate matter. "Hot-humored" food increases energy and circulation; "cold-humored" food is relaxing and cleansing. Lamb is considered hot, beef is warm, and most other meat is neutral; yellow vegetables and beans are neutral, green vegetables are cool, bean curd and mung beans are cold. Peppers are hot; garlic is warm, fruit is cool. Shrimp is hot, crab is cold.

The theory is that foods should be chosen to help balance the body in the cosmic scheme—that is, hot-humored foods should be consumed in the winter, and cool and cold foods in the summer. Consult your Chinese grocer.

to hold the shrimp near the tail, squeeze the meat out with the teeth, and replace the shell. Fingers are not allowed in either case. Similarly, bones in fish should be transferred to the plate using the chopsticks.

The Chinese believe that variety in a meal means variety in the preparation styles as well as the ingredients; so a traditional family-style meal would include appetizers; one dish per diner—fish or seafood, meat, poultry, and vegetable, stir-fried, roasted, broiled, steamed, and baked—plus continually replenished soup and rice; and, finally, fruit. Except for the appetizers and fruit, everything is served simultaneously.

When ordering, remember that pork is the favorite meat and so is apt to be offered in the most interesting ways; duck is the second choice. In the Chinese order of courses, incidentally, fish follows the meat and poultry rather than preceding it in the Western fashion. Two people might try hot-and-sour soup and egg drop soup, tea-smoked duck, and Hunan-style pork. Four people should order a family-size soup with noodles, steamed fish with ginger and scallions or kung pao shrimp, red-cooked chicken, twice-cooked pork or beef in five-spice powder, and Szechwan-style green beans or Hunan-style tofu.

Chinese restaurants in the United States are (not surprisingly) somewhat ambivalent about serving meals in the Western fashion, a course at a time, or traditionally, all at once. For the best results, ask to be served Chinese-style. All dishes are shared except rice; all diners have their own rice bowls, which they may refill whenever they wish. Food is taken from the main platter with the chopsticks and either eaten directly or placed in the rice bowl; it can be dipped into a sauce or seasoning in between. The rice bowl itself is cupped in the left hand and kept off the table top while the diner is actively eating.

COOKING AT HOME

Although a wok is the easiest way to cook almost any Chinese dish, and addictively adaptable to other cuisines as well, it is perfectly possible to recreate Chinese recipes using casseroles, skillets, saucepans, and so forth. Asian rice-cookers are a great time-saver, and the texture of their rice is more like that of authentic Chinese rice, but again, they are not essential.

If you are stir-frying a dish, it is important to remember than you cannot simply double a recipe, because the heat will be insufficient and the dish will be thin and soggy. Recipes for four or perhaps six is about the tops; for more than that, cook in batches.

When entertaining, remember that a meal should partake of at least four elements—meat, seafood, vegetable, and poultry—and varied seasonings and flavors. The table setting should include a soup bowl and/or rice bowl, a plate, flat-bottomed porcelain soup spoons, a small wine cup (like a Japanese sake tumbler), a teacup, and chopsticks.

RED-COOKED PORK

2 tablespoons peanut oil
3 scallions, cut into fourths
3 1/4-inch slices peeled fresh ginger
2 cloves garlic, crushed
3–3 1/2 pounds boneless pork loin, butt or fresh ham
4 tablespoons dark soy
1/4 cup sherry or rice wine
2 tablespoons crushed rock candy crystals (or brown sugar)
1 whole star anise or 2 teaspoons five-spice powder
pinch salt
1 pound fresh water chesnuts (or large can)

Heat oil in heavy pot or casserole dish; quickly sauté scallions, ginger, and garlic, push aside, and sear meat on all sides. Add soy, sherry or wine, sugar, anise, and salt; stir; then add 1 cup boiling water. Simmer, covered, for about 2 1/2 hours, turning meat every 30 minutes. If using fresh water chestnuts, prepare by boiling 30 minutes and peeling off shell and membrane; add after 1 1/2 hours. If using canned, rinse and drain and add for last 30 minutes.

HONEY-ROASTED DUCK

1 4–5 lb. duck, rinsed and patted dry
coarse salt
3 cloves garlic, crushed
3 scallions, minced
3 tablespoons dark soy
3 tablespoons sherry or rice wine
2 1/2 tablespoons honey

Prehaet oven to 350°. Rub duck lightly, inside and out, with salt. Combine garlic, scallions, soy, and sherry. Mix 1/4 cup of mixture (about half) with honey and rub into skin; let dry, then repeat. Pour the rest of the sauce into duck cavity and place on a rack above 3 inches water (add more as needed). Roast about 2 hours (check beginning at 1 1/2 hours), frequently basting with remaining honey mixture thinned with hot water.

JAPAN

In Japanese culture, the greatest art is that of understatement. Poetry, painting, music, manners, fashion, even food preparation, all are polished to a concentrated purity. The observer is meant to contemplate the simplicity of any object and to "see" not just the result but also the intricate process by which it has been created. It wasn't a Japanese artist who defined sculpture as cutting away all the stone that was not the statue within, but that is a philosophy any Japanese chef would understand.

Another great tenet of Japanese culture is also alluded to in the cuisine: All nature is interrelated. In the most formal traditional meals, called *kaiseki*, nature determines not only the menu but also the metaphors. Nothing should be eaten out of season, lest the harmony of the diners be disturbed; live flowers or foliage are commonly used for garnish; even kimonos and table decorations change with the seasons. And although it is a fading art, many sushi chefs (or *itamae*) trained in the old-fashioned way, with apprenticeships lasting 10 to 15 years, create landscapes and seasonal symbols

BASIC CUISINE

DINNER FOR TWO:
Sashimi, shrimp tempura, beef teriyaki

DINNER FOR FOUR:
Sushi, soft-shell crabs tempura, grilled fish, chicken teriyaki

GROUP DISH:
Shabu-shabu

STYLE:
Light, subtle, austere

KEY FLAVORS:
Soy sauce, teriyaki, ginger pickle

EATING UTENSILS:
Chopsticks, spoons, fingers

DISTINCTIVE DISHES:
Sushi, sashimi, teriyaki, tempura

UNIFORMITY OF MENUS:
Good

NUTRITIONAL INDEX:
Low fat, high protein, high carbohydrate, high sodium

COST:
Moderate

"THANK YOU":
"Arigato"

using masterfully cut fish, shellfish, and seaweed. Translucently thin sheets of *daikon* radish, themselves a marvel of knifework, are cross-hatched into "fishermen's nets" in which tiny shrimp or smelts are hopelessly tangled. Squid may be cut into matchsticks, formed into a "bird's nest," and served with a quail-egg yolk inside. More common are roses formed of sashimi "petals."

THE COUNTRY

Although it is often referred to as an island, Japan is actually four large islands and nearly 4,000 smaller ones. This island chain stretches 1,750 miles, from the snow-covered mountains of Hokkaido almost to the Tropic of Cancer—a latitude stretch roughly matching that from Montreal to the Yucatan. Much of the land is either mountainous or forested, with heavy rainfall in the summer and monsoons in spring and autumn, particularly in Hokkaido, a scenic wilderness with vast areas for hiking, skiing, and fishing.

The largest island is the intensely developed Honshu, just smaller than the state of California but with a population four times as large—124 million. Honshu includes Tokyo as well as Yokohama, Osaka, Hiroshima, and Kyoto (formerly Edo), which was the capital of Japan for most of its history. Honshu is agriculturally as well as politically the "big island," since it contains most of the productive rice fields. These fields remain a prickly issue: Because rice is a unique symbol of Japanese traditional culture, Japan is still reluctant to allow Western imports; however, growing sufficient rice for its own consumption requires the cultivation of vast parcels of land, the one resource Japan has the least of. At the same time, younger Japanese no longer consume rice as previous generations did, having absorbed the McFries habit as well as Western-style breakfast cereals and bread; and the agricultural economy is increasingly overshadowed by manufacturing and high-tech interests.

THE HISTORY

Not much is known about Japan's aboriginal inhabitants, called the Jomon after a particular style of pottery they created, but they were apparently concentrated in the area north of Toyko. Since Honshu is a long thin crescent, squeezed between the Pacific on the west and the Sea of Japan on the east, it is not surprising that the Japanese developed such a fine distinction for fresh fish. And because there was so great a variety and so constant a fresh supply, there was less reason to preserve proteins than in countries more vulnerable to seasonal shortages: There was some pickling and a bit of salt curing—sushi actually evolved around the seventh century from a method of curing meat and fish by soaking them in rice until it fermented—but little smoking or hard-curing or drying.

Rice itself took hold in the third century B.C. with the Yayoi (also named for their pottery), who migrated east from Korea, where the dredging and flooding techniques of rice growing were already firmly established. Rice provided not only food but also drink (the potent *sake*), straw for ropes and bedding, paper, fuel, fodder for animals, and oils for soap.

Sometime in the mid-sixth century, Buddhism—which, like rice, entered Japan via Korea—became the official religion of the Japanese court. Although Buddhism in Japan gradually blended with secular Confucian and pantheistic Shinto practices, it remained a pervasive influence. It is the reason that meat dishes are so few and so relatively simple, since the Japanese were at least officially forbidden to eat meat for some 1,200 years after Buddhism was adopted (see the description of sukiyaki below).

In the middle of the sixteenth century, the evangelical and commercially ambitious Portuguese fleet stumbled onto Japan and attempted to establish a monopoly on Japanese trade. The equally ambitious (but Protestant) Dutch traders soon followed, however, and fearing war, Tokugawa Ieyasu, the shogun made famous by James Clavell's novel, effectively sealed Japan off from the outside world for nearly 250 years.

Before their expulsion, however, the Europeans left their marks, and not just among the baptized. *Tempura*, or batter-fried fish and vegetables, was a Portuguese contribution to Japanese cuisine; Ieyasu became so fond of the "foreign delicacy" that he died of a surfeit of tempura, according to some historian. Sugar, corn, and potatoes, along with the tobacco that remains a Japanese staple, were all New World items then newly discovered and quickly passed along the trade routes by these avid colonizers.

When Commodore Perry forced the reopening of Japan to trade, Japanese professionals and scholars were stunned to discover how far Western medicine and science had progressed. To symbolize his desire to become part of the "civilized world," or perhaps to surrender to it, in

1872 Japan's emperor ordered a thoroughly European banquet for New Year's Day, and for the first time in more than a millenium, the Japanese began openly to eat meat.

THE CUISINE

Rice, miso soup, *sashimi* (plain raw seafood), and seaweed are all staples of the Japanese diet, but first among equals, so to speak, is rice—so much so that the common words for breakfast, lunch and dinner are *asagohan*, *hirugohan*, and *bangohan*—literally, morning rice, midday rice, and evening rice. Rice is believed to have been given to the Japanese directly by the goddess Amaterasu, and as her direct descendent, it is the emperor's duty—even today—to cultivate some small plot of rice himself.

Although vastly bastardized versions of sukiyaki and tempura have been made in the United States for 50 years, sushi has been the breakthrough for most Americans, overcoming a widespread cultural squeamishness over raw fish to become the most popular ethnic lunch since pizza. Sushi bars, or *sushi-ya*, are only one type of Japanese restaurant, however. Among the other major varieties are the *robata-ya* grills, which cook meats, fish, and vegetables over hot charcoal; noodle houses, also called *soba-ya*, which offer the hot, cold, wet, or dry noodle dishes that are the fast foods of Japan; and *teppanyaki* restaurants, those with the huge hot steel grills for tables. There are also the more traditional *shokuji dokoro* establishments, which serve a variety of traditional or semi-formal entrees; *nomi-ya*, neighborhood taverns; tempura kitchens, which like the Calabash buffets of North Carolina lay out reams of fried shrimp and vegetables; and occasionally the single-style specialty houses that quick-fix *yakitori*— skewers of grilled chicken, shrimp, and vegetables.

Sushi bars may well have robotayaki food and probably traditional one-pot meals as well. Shokuji dokoro restaurants may well have a small sushi bar, or just a "service bar" in the kitchen; the majority of teppanyaki steakhouses have no sushi bar at all.

In passing we should note that many of these "Japanese steakhouses" are only minimally authentic. The inventor of the knife-juggling routine was a publicity-savvy sportsman and adventurer named "Rocky" Aoki, who believed that Americans would be more likely to pay for prime flesh if it came with some prime-time flash. However, very few of the chain versions here employ Japanese cooks, and even fewer serve real Kobe beef.

You should also remember that at a teppanyaki house, where each grill (and cook) serves up to a dozen customers at a time, you are almost certainly going to be seated with a group of strangers, which can be fun so long as you're prepared for it. Otherwise, book a baby shower.

Two of Those . . .

How can you tell whether a restaurant serves sushi? If it's not on the sign—and frequently even if it is—there is likely to be a display of plastic but quite realistic sushi in the window, hearkening back to a time when most ordinary customers could not read. If the plastic delicacies are not visible, there will be a poster or picture menu instead. And you are entirely welcome to use the picture menu as a "cheat sheet" or even to point to what you want.

THE MAIN INGREDIENTS

The sacred three, one might say, of Japanese cuisine are rice, tea, and sake; these are the three whose names receive the honorific prefix "o-," generally reserved for social superiors. Rice is called *gohan* once it is cooked ("go-" is a Chinese remnant form of "o-"); uncooked, it is called *kome* or *okome*. Rice for sushi, tossed with seasoned vinegar, is called *shari*. Gohan is traditionally served at breakfast as well as lunch and dinner—a combination cereal, bread, and potato.

O-sake is also a rice product, and although it's primarily for drinking (see "How to Eat Like a Native," page 290), it is also used for marinating, simmering, and flavoring foods. *Mirin* is cooking wine; *kasuzake* is the mash left from the fermenting process used for marinades. *Su* is rice vinegar, essential for sushi rice. Tea is *cha* or *ocha*. You may also hear tea referred to as *agari*, but that is a slang term, to be used only when sitting at the sushi bar itself.

SOY PRODUCTS The second most important food in the Japanese diet is the soybean. Although most Americans only recognize soy in soy sauce, it it perhaps the most prolific of vegetables. Among the other most common ingredients are *miso*, the fermented soybean paste that comes in a range of qualities, from the sweeter white (used in *miso shiro* soup) to a pungent, saltier dark red; and its first cousins *tofu* (bean curd cakes, either firm, silken, or fried) and *shoyu*, or soy sauce, which also ranges from light (and now "lite") to dark. Japanese soy sauce, unlike the Chinese and American varieties, is fermented for up to two years before being bottled. Soybeans are also eaten fresh, incidentally; and boiled in their pods and lightly salted, they are called *edamame* and frequently offered as a snack food or appetizer.

SEASONINGS Monosodium glutamate (MSG), or *ajinomoto*, used to be habitually included in Japanese dishes; in fact, while the English language only defines four kinds of flavors—salty, sweet, bitter, and sour—Japanese has a fifth term just for the MSG taste, which occurs naturally in seaweed. However, in deference to the increasing dislike many Americans have for it, more and more Japanese restaurants are eliminating it from their kitchens. The tiny shaker on your table today is more likely to be *sansho* or *togarashi*, the Japanese version of ground black or chili peppers. Other familiar seasonings include garlic, ginger, and sugar.

The most distinctive herb is *shiso*, which is usually translated as "beefsteak plant" but tastes like a cross between its cousins, basil and mint. A slightly fuzzy, sawtooth-edged green (or, more rarely, purple or red) leaf, it is frequently served whole or julienned with sashimi. Occasionally, it is even served tempura-fried. Sesame seeds and sesame oil are also popular flavorings.

CONDIMENTS The *daikon* is the radish world's giant, frequently reaching three feet in length and weighing a couple of pounds. It is usually grated into sauces, or shredded and served under sashimi. Peppery-flavored radish sprouts are frequently used to garnish sashimi. Radish is almost always among the pickled vegetables, called *tsukemono*, that are served with every meal. Bean sprouts, snow peas, and carrots are often served alongside broiled dishes or sliced into long quills and pickled.

VEGETABLES What is frequently called Chinese cabbage in America (or Napa cabbage in California) is called *hakusai* in Japan and is most frequently used in soups or for pickling. There are several kinds of yams, including the so-called mountain potato, which has a sticky, tapiocalike juice and is served either boiled or raw.

Mushrooms are a treasured ingredient and range from the tiny white bulb-headed *enoki* to the familiar *shiitake* (or "forest mushrooms") to the large and seasonally available *matsutake* (usually found in autumn), which are served broiled like a steak or simmered with rice. *Nameko* are orange or yellow and have a rich, almost rot-sweet, earthy smell; "wood-ear mushrooms," or *kikurage*, are sold dried and then reconstituted; they are sometimes called "jelly mushrooms" because of their consistency.

Among the greens frequently seen are fiddlehead ferns; chrysanthemum greens; pepper-tree leaves (*kinome*), similar to cilantro or watercress; kelp; and *mitsuba*, something like celery greens. Scallions are common, particularly a large variety called negi (as in *negimayaki*, the beef dish mentioned above). White bulb onions are used in soups, casseroles, and tempura.

PASTAS Next to sushi, the Japanese are probably addicted most notoriously to noodles: fat, skinny, doughy, ethereal, white, brown, or green. (The most popular fast-food version, those skinny little ramen

---

Fat Is Beautiful

In this Buddhist society, meat-eaters (i.e., Europeans) were considered not merely unclean but completely soulless—which only goes to show that the Japanese have displayed their usual dispatch by turning Kobe beef into a byword for quality. For price, too: Real Kobe beef comes from steers that are fed and even overfed a rich diet so that they develop a high degree of fat; then they are massaged and pounded so that the fat marbles all the way through the meat, making it even richer—and more expensive. Kobe beef, in other words, are the sumo wrestlers of the meat-packing industry.

Even heavily doused with soy sauce, which has much less sodium than iodized salt does, sushi and sashimi are among the healthiest dishes available. However, the popularity of sushi has led to a surprising number of non-Japanese carryouts that dole out second-rate or possibly hours-old sushi on the assumption (unfortunately, a well-founded one) that most Americans can't taste the difference. In general, novice sushi eaters should stick to more established restaurants, or ask for recommendations, to ensure that the fish is as fresh and safe as possible.

noodles sold either dried in waves or in instant-soup cups, is another Chinese invention: *Ramen* is the Japanese transliteration of *lo mein*.) The generic term is *menrui;* among the most popular are *udon* noodles, the soft, fat, friendly ones used in *nabeyaki udon* soup; *somen*, the thin vermicelli served chilled in summer; *harusame*, called bean threads or cellophane noodles; *soba*, buckwheat noodles; and *cha-soba*, buckwheat noodles flavored (and colored) with green tea.

LIFE IN THE SUSHI LANE

Stepping into a sushi bar, especially for a novice, can be one of the most atmospherically transporting experiences in dining. As you duck through the printed-blue cloth "doors"—references to a time when each feudal lord had his own design, and such curtains declared partisanship—you hear the formal welcoming cry, "*Irasshaimase!*" A waitress in kimono bows before you, the sushi chefs nod their bandana'd heads, and you are truly in another world. Some would consider it heaven.

Sakana is the collective term for fish, shellfish, and other seafoods, including virtually all of the items available at a sushi bar. The difference between sashimi and sushi is the presence (or presentation) of rice: Sashimi is served by itself, while sushi is either draped over a bite-sized roll of seasoned rice (the style called *nigiri*), rolled with rice and nori sheets into logs and sliced (called *maki* or rolled sushi), or served as a "hand roll," an ice cream cone–shaped nori sheet half-filled with rice and then topped with fish. (*Nori* is a sheet of dark green "paper," usually referred to as seaweed but actually composed of algae.)

Some of the more fluid shellfish, such as sea urchin and scallops, are cradled in a sort of sideways nigiri: A strip of nori is wound around a small ball of rice, leaving a lip like a soufflé collar, and then the seafood is spooned in.

Osizushi—literally, "pressed sushi"—is a sort of large sandwich affair prepared in a wooden box; seasoned rice is placed in the bottom, layered with assorted fish and topped with more rice, then pressed flat and sliced into what looks like petit fours. *Chirasizushi* is an assortment of sushi left unassembled, in effect—a box of seasoned rice topped with sliced raw fish, ginger, and *wasabi*—and you can eat the items in whatever order you choose.

Not all sushi involves raw fish, incidentally; novices with qualms might prefer to start with shrimp, crab, eel, octopus, salmon, or egg-omelet sushi (*tamago*), which are all precooked, or one of the vegetable or American-style rolls. What might be called new American sushi, in fact, is a burgeoning field: Virtually every Japanese restaurant has at least one "signature" roll that incorporates American ingredients (mayonnaise or chili sauce, or even Cajun spices) or mixes and matches seafoods for a bigger-is-better effect.

Because of its vast popularity, and because of the Japanese drive to master the market, sushi is fairly easy to order. Many sushi chefs know the English words for fish even if that's all the English they do know; besides, on the table there is almost always a "cheat sheet" of pictures to go by. If you're sitting at the sushi bar, you can just point. The following is a list of the most common types of seafood you are likely to encounter.

Amaebi, small "sweet shrimp" that indeed have a sweeter taste and slightly more gelatinous texture than regular shrimp. They will probably arrive with the heads still on but the body peeled down to the last tiny tail shell. Bite right behind the heads and eat the rest whole. The heads may be brought back later, fried and crunchy and served with a tempura dipping sauce. Don't worry, they'll be so brittle and crisp—particularly the long antenna—you'll think you're eating some sort of shrimp-flavored chip.

Clams, at least a half-dozen varieties ranging in size, color, and pungency, and including the almost rubbery abalone (*awabi*), the large and small scallops (*kaibashira* and *kobashira*), the giant geoduck (*mirugai*), and the cockle (*torigai*), as well as cherrystones and other American regional varieties.

Crab, called *kani*, as well as the imitation crab stick called *surimi* that is now a common item in American grocery stores. Soft-shell crabs are increasingly popular, tempura-fried and used more and more frequently in new American sushi.

Eel, either freshwater (*unagi*) or saltwater (*anago*). They have similar tastes, resembling smoked trout—unagi is a trifle lighter in both color and flavor—and are served broiled and glazed with a sweetish sauce. Unagi is so popular that there are restaurants in Japan called unagiyas. It is also the traditional dish to serve on *Doyo-no-hi*, the hottest day of summer, because it is believed to replenish energy.

Flounder, or *hirame*, which is also used to cover a number of flatfish and whitefish such as halibut, sole, turbot, bream, and sea bass, although they are more properly referred to as *shiromi*.

Fugu, or globefish, though famous for its potentially lethal thrill (sushi chefs must be specially licensed to prepare it), is extremely rare in the United States, but it is found in the largest metropolitan cities. Even if it were worth the risk, it's probably not worth the price.

Kohada, a sort of small shad, served whole either as salad or sushi or, when full of roe, grilled.

Mackerel (*saba*), Spanish mackerel, and king and horse mackerel (*aji*) are strongly flavored, oily fish that sometimes have a grayish flesh; with their blue-striped silver skin, they resemble those leaping fish so often seen at the bottom of serving bowls.

Octopus (*tako*) is always served cooked, even when used in salads; it is either boiled and sliced—you can tell, because boiled octopus is red and white, while raw octopus is actually gray—or sometimes, in the case of tiny whole ones, glazed with a sweet sauce and eaten whole. It is somewhat chewy and surprisingly mild.

Oysters (*kaki*), most often served raw on the half-shell dashed with vinegar, grated radish, and chopped scallions (they beat Rockefeller every time). Sometimes they are served in the seaweed "cups" or fried.

Red snapper (*tai*) is often confused with, or at least replaced by, red sea bream, perch, or even porgy; it is a particularly light and sweet-fleshed fish, good for beginners.

Roe is very popular as a sushi ingredient; among the most common varieties are the large salmon roe (*ikura*), frequently served in one of those soufflé collars of nori and often topped with a (raw) quail- or chicken-egg yolk; the small, crunchy, poppy-red, flying fish roe (*tobiko*) most familiar from their use in California rolls; and smelt (*masago*) and herring roe (*kazunoko*), both of which are most often served still in the whole fish. Though salty, Japanese roes rarely are as strongly briny as traditional caviar. Recently, many sushi bars have taken to adding chili or pepper sauce to tobiko paste to make what's called "spicy tuna roll," another example of indigenous American sushi.

Salmon—called *sake*, just like the drink, but without the honorific "o-"—can also be pronounced "sha-ke," which is sort of blue-collar dialect but prevents confusion for those not yet confident around the sushi bar. It may be salted, smoked, pan-broiled, or even simmered in sake. Occasionally it is salt-marinated and then grilled (*shio-yaki*).

Sea urchin (*uni*) is actually the sea urchin roe, a mustard-gold or even orange custard whose originally delicate flavor quickly grows pungent and even bitter; in this case, quality is measured in days, if not hours. Even fresh, it has a distinctive and unique (one would almost say decadent) flavor; I usually describe it as tasting the way the sea smells.

Shrimp (*ebi*), even as sushi, is usually served boiled, but at more sophisticated sushi bars—or those with greater faith in their patrons—may be served raw. (Really favored customers may get their shrimp only moments from live, which are called *odori*, or "dancing.") The most common treatment of shrimp, of course, is tempura, even when it is served in soups. It is also grilled.

Squid (*ika*) is a sort of translucent white, not unlike onion, and is served both raw and cooked. Depending on the size of the squid, it can be chewy and occasionally has a sort of soapy texture; but the flavor is mild and picks up whatever sauce it is served with. However, it wants gentle handling or it turns tough; if it reminds you of rubber tires, as the rumor sometimes goes, that's most likely the restaurant's fault, not the squid's.

Trout (*masu*), although not indigenous to Japan, has quickly become popular, particularly for grilling and, when very fresh, for sushi. (Similarly, both orange roughy and telapia, suddenly so chic among grillers, are beginning to show up on the sushi board.)

Tuna (*maguro*) is probably the most famous sashimi and sushi fish in the world. A deep red, it tastes quite a bit like filet mignon and is surprisingly easy to swallow, even for the most dubious of first-timers. *Toro* is an extra-rich (because it's extra-fatty) portion of the tuna belly; its seasonal availability, like that of soft-shell crabs, seems to have widened considerably, thanks to the commercial smarts of seafood wholesalers. Some will find its oiliness off-putting, but it grows on you, as they say. *Chutoro*, or near-toro, is a sort of half-and-half, richer than the lean maguro but not quite as buttery as toro. *Tataki* is skipjack tuna, which is sometimes available as sashimi and is also half-rich.

Yellowtail (*hamachi*) is, like the mackerel, a branch of the tuna family, with cream-colored flesh blending to a browning red and a buttery-mushroom flavor. Because of its richness, in fact, it is often matched in rolled sushi with either scallions or the basil-like shiso.

The major condiments served with sushi or sashimi are soy sauce, pickled ginger (*gari*), and *wasabi*, the hot green spread that is sometimes called Japanese mustard but is really a type of horseradish. (See "How to Eat Like a Native," page 290.) Soy sauce is often mixed with vinegar and grated daikon radish to make either *ponzu* or tempura-dipping sauce; *nuta* sauce, usually served with spinach or octopus appetizers, is a thick miso paste. Sashimi is usually framed with edible decorations, either seaweed, radishes, or pickles.

Incidentally, if your sushi is served with scissored green plastic "doilies" underneath, you're seeing the last remnant of really traditional sushi service. In the old days, sushi was served on fresh banana leaves, cut into artistic shapes; the one seen most frequently nowadays, with two "feelers" at one end and jagged sawteeth on the sides, originally imitated a shrimp. Otherwise, if the garnishes look edible, they most likely are.

At the sushi bar, you will probably be served on wooden platters that the *itamae* (sushi chef) will place before you; then, as you order, he will reach over the glass partition and place the sushi directly onto your plate. At the bar, you may receive your sushi a few pieces at a time, particularly if you order verbally and directly from the chef; or it may be prepared all at once, especially if you mark up a sushi ticket. A few flashier restaurants have set up conveyor belts to whisk sushi orders down the length of the bar; some even have tiny rivers or canals and set the sushi on little "boats" to ride the stream to the customer. Somehow, though, these systems lack the personal touch.

THE MAIN DISHES

APPETIZERS The Japanese, with their love for artful restraint, long ago mastered what "nouvelle" masters talk of now: grazing. (*Kaiseki* is, after all, the ultimate in presentation dining, and pretty near *cuisine minceur*, at that.) *Otsumani* are the nibbling things, to be eaten either as you drink away the evening or just as a warm-up to dinner—the tapas of Japan.

Virtually all Japanese meals begin with soup, either *miso-shiru*, a cloudy soypaste broth with tofu and scallions in it, or *suimono*, a simple broth with sliced mushrooms. Pickled vegetables are ubiquitous, and bean sprout salads are becoming so. Regular customers are often served a tidbit or two as well: a tiny whole octopus grilled and glazed, a morsel of boiled taro, or grilled mushrooms. And sashimi (the filleted raw fish served without rice) is the most commonly ordered first course. Boiled spinach with sesame seeds and sliced octopus in miso dressing (*tako nuta*) are both very popular.

More Moriawase

Most restaurants list at least one sushi combination and one sashimi plate. In general, the sushi combo—often called *moriawase*, or "assorted"—will have an assortment chosen from among tuna (maguro, not toro), shrimp, yellowtail, flounder, omelet, salmon, and perhaps a couple of pieces of California roll. If there is a "deluxe" combo, it will probably add sea urchin, crab, octopus, and squid. Sashimi tends to be even simpler: tuna, flounder, mackerel, or octopus; "deluxe" gets you yellowtail and salmon. If you're unsure, it's best to ask.

However, there are many other delightful hors d'oeuvre, including *gyoza*, the Japanese version of fried dumplings; *ika soba*, squid julienned into soba noodles; and the particularly fine *ankimo*, a steamed mousse of monkfish liver so delicate that a two-star Michelin chef in Washington calls his version "foie gras of the sea." Small orders of sushi and sashimi specials are sometimes offered as appetizers, too.

CASSEROLES AND STEWS Japanese are fond of one-pot dishes, usually featuring either rice or noodles, although many noodle dishes, particularly those with broth, are served with rice on the side. *Nabeyaki udon* is a thick soup with shrimp tempura, chicken, vegetables, and thick udon noodles, often with an egg cracked over the top to poach. *Yosenabe* is a lighter seafood and vegetable version. *Kamameshi* is a rice stews, like Chinese congee. *Oden* is a sort of winter root stew, very hearty, full of potatoes, taro, fish cakes, greens, and tofu.

Donburis are rice dishes; the two best-known types are unagi donburi, which is topped with broiled glazed eel, and oyaku donburi, a combination of teriyaki chicken and egg (also known as "mother and child" donburi). And although it may surprise you, curry is one of Japan's most popular adopted foods. It's generally called kairi raisu (say it out loud and you'll understand), although it's more like the soupier American version of curry than the Indian or Thai original. It comes topped or tossed with chicken, fried pork, scallops, grilled fish, and so forth. However, it's most frequently found at specialty carryouts.

Chawan mushi is a nonsweet hot custard, usually with tidbits of chicken, shrimp, and gingko nuts baked in.

MEATS AND POULTRY Sukiyaki, as mentioned, is a sort of fondue or stew of beef, vegetables, and tofu that are sautéed, then simmered in a sweet-and-soy broth. (The Tokyo style, in which the broth is first brought to a simmer and the other ingredients are added later, is more common in restaurants where sukiyaki is offered in single portions.) Shabu-shabu is its plainer cousin, which is simmered in water and evolves, by the end of the meal into a rich broth that the diner drinks. According to one explanation, sukiyaki got its name from a time when Buddhist emperors forbade people to eat meat: Defying this rule, poor farmers in the fields surreptitiously broiled food (yaki means grilled) over campfires on the back of their farming tools (one translation of suki is "plow" or "shovel"). Shabu-shabu is said to have been named for the sibilant sound of beef being dipped into boiling water.

Among other meat dishes still commonly served are tonkatsu, a breaded pork cutlet; negimayaki, beef rolled up around sliced scallions and broiled, then pinwheel-sliced; and teriyaki, a glazed and broiled chicken or beef. And nowadays, in Japan as well as in America, one may see what is called "beef sashimi"—the Japanese version of carpaccio.

Most full-service Japanese restaurants (though perhaps not a small sushi bar) will offer beef teriyaki; but if you want *tappanyaki*—that knife-flourishing, speed-slicing, Popeil gadget of a dinner—you'll probably have to go to a so-called Japanese steakhouse. The real Japanese chef considers all that sound and fury gauche and, well, barbarian.

SEAFOODS The Japanese eat just as much cooked fish as raw. Fish, shrimp, scallops, octopus, and squid are all broiled plain, but fish is also frequently coated and briefly marinated in coarse salt (a style called *shioyaki*), then broiled very hot so that the thin layer of fat just beneath the skin melts and seasons the flesh. Seafood is also frequently steamed, braised, or simmered as well as deep-fried. The heads of whole fish, particularly yellowtail and salmon, are often broiled and served up separately (usually listed on the menu as "jaw of yellowtail," etc.). The meat of the cheeks is extremely sweet. Small octopus, large prawns, and whole fish, usually red snapper or trout or mackerel, are apt to be charbroiled on the robotai grill.

Seafood soups, called *yosenabe*, are whole meals—large pots of broth with shellfish, shrimp, and some chunks of fish, along with a gelatinous, candy-striped aspic (misnamed "fishcake") and cabbage and onions.

VEGETABLES Although the most common ways for Japanese to eat their vegetables are as pickles or tempura-fried, almost any fresh produce, from asparagus to sweet peppers to eggplant, and the large meaty mushrooms called matsutake or shiitakes, can be chargrilled. Spinach is a slight exception; it is often boiled, cooked, and then served as a palate-cleanser.

BEVERAGES Sake is the most famous; it ranges from 12 to 20 percent alcohol and is traditionally served warm, although there are sakes brewed to be served cold. Like other wines, sake ranges in quality and flavor, from dry (*karakuchi*) to sweet (*amakuchi*); you'll just have to experiment.

Sake is usually served in vaselike vessels and drunk out of small (thimble-sized, ritually) plain cups, but occasionally it's served in wider, flat-footed bowls, or even plain balsawood boxes called *hachi* (which you can sign and leave at the bar; the more you use it, the more fragrant the balsa becomes). It is most polite to lift your cup off the table when being served and, if you are pouring, to hold the bottle with both hands.

SWEETS The Japanese often end with a bowl of plain rice, but they enjoy desserts as well: green tea, red bean– or ginger-flavored ice cream, fresh fruit, or *yokan*, a red bean gelatin that tastes something like chestnut puree. On special occasions, there may be sweet doughy buns called *mochi* stuffed with nuts or sweet bean paste. Fresh fruit is common, and the mild acid of fresh pineapple or orange is considered good for the digestion.

Americans tend to drink hot green tea after the meal, like coffee, but many Japanese drink it throughout the meal along with whatever other beverage they order. Tea is made from a variety of tea leaves or flowers or even rice hulls; cold barley tea is particularly popular in summer. *Ocha* is green tea; America, Chinese and Indian teas are called *kocha*, black (literally "red") tea.

Japanese beer is also pretty good and is widely available in the United States, particularly the brands Kirin, Asahi, and Sapporo. There are Japanese whiskies as well—the most famous is Suntory—and liqueurs, such as the honeydew-flavored Midori. In particularly macho traditional sushi bars, patrons may buy a whole bottle of Suntory, label it, and leave it there from visit to visit.

HOW TO EAT LIKE A NATIVE

To begin with the utensils, the Japanese use chopsticks and a sort of flat-bottomed spoon (mostly used with the large one-pot or communal meals or to cradle the bottom of a stickful of noodles). When you sit down, you will probably see a paper-wrapped package of chopsticks, a bottle of soy sauce and, if you're at the sushi bar, a small square or round saucer to pour the soy sauce into. To prepare your chopsticks, split them carefully, then rub one against the other to remove any small splinters. If there is not a chopstick rest to lean them on, twist the paper wrapper (assuming you didn't rip it in half) around your fingers and tie a loose, flat knot; then rest the small ends of the chopsticks on that rather than the table. Or you may lean them against the soy sauce dish.

If a hot washcloth or towel (*oshibori*) is offered, it will be carefully rolled; open it and wipe your hands clean, but don't refold the cloth— just lay it neatly back in its cradle. Don't wipe your face, either.

A spoon will probably come with the soup, but the Japanese pick up the whole bowl with one hand, sip the soup directly from the lip, and use chopsticks to stir up the broth or eat the squares of tofu at the bottom. (The spoons are essential for the big soups, however.) On the other hand, while most Americans prefer to use chopsticks to eat sushi, many Japanese, particularly men, still pick it up with their fingers and pop it into their mouths.

Noodles are eaten with chopsticks, but it's not hard; if they're in a bowl, you can pick the whole thing up with one hand and bring it close to your mouth and sort of shovel the noodles in with the other hand. If the noodles are either served dry on a plate or with a dipping sauce on the side, use your rice bowl as the saucer. And don't worry about catching up the strands neatly. Noodles are fast, sloppy comfort food in Japan, and slurping is perfectly polite. In fact, it's essential, not only to keep the noodles from spilling all over the table but because sucking air in also cools the hot food.

Sushi is traditionally prepared with a dab of wasabi between the fish and rice, with more on the side; with sashimi, you add your wasabi yourself. Or you can pour a little soy sauce into the small dish provided for that purpose and use your chopsticks to stir a little wasabi into that.

When eating sushi, the correct form is to dip not the rice side but the fish itself into the soy sauce; as a handy hint, try turning the sushi on its side and picking it up with

Stick-y Situations

If you're sitting at a table, particularly at one of the older-style shokuji dokoro establishments, food is considered something of a family affair. At a sushi bar, an obvious couple may be served from one wooden tray rather than two. When sharing food at a Japanese restaurant, whether you use your own chopsticks in a communal pot has to do with the closeness of your relationships. If you're related, or at least very close, you may do so; otherwise, use the longer serving sticks provided to place food on your rice bowl or plate. If you want to exchange tidbits, use your chopsticks to put food either on your companion's plate or directly into his or her mouth, but never—this is important—never pass food from one pair of chopsticks to another. This is a method used to transport funeral remains after cremation, so it is very bad karma.

It is also extremely rude to stab your chopsticks into the rice bowl and leave them sticking out ("drumming" with chopsticks is beneath contempt but astonishingly common). Chopsticks are also used to say "when": Laying both sticks horizon-

Stick-y Situations
continued

tally across your platter means you're full. Incidentally, it is perfectly acceptable to bring your own chopsticks if you have them; the Japanese have long since run low on wood and actually import tons of cheap disposable chopstick balsam from the United States.

your chopsticks the long way, sandwiching the rice in, rather than grabbing it across the middle; it is less likely to fall apart.

Alternatively, you may eat sushi with your fingers; just make even more sure you don't over-douse the fish in soy sauce and get it on your fingers. Also, if you eat half of a piece of sushi instead of eating it all in one bite, you should hold the remaining portion in your slightly lowered hand or chopsticks; don't put it back on the plate. And if you are served an inside-out roll—that is, with the rice on the outside—finger a piece of the ginger pickle first: It will keep the rice from sticking to your fingers.

Grilled bits of chicken (*yakitori*) or fish are often served on skewers; holding the tip of the skewer with one hand, slide the food off with your chopsticks and eat it over your rice. Pick up tempura with your chopsticks and bite off what you want; you may put the rest down.

As to the seating itself, traditional Japanese dining tables are short platforms without chairs; diners are supposed to sit on the floor. However, most Japanese restaurants in America have Western-style seating; and as a concession to comfort, many of those that do have private rooms with traditional tables have a cutaway "pit" under the table for your legs to dangle.

If you are seated in a traditional Japanese dining room (called a "tatami room" after the straw matting that covers the floor), you must dine in your stocking feet, so remove your shoes and leave them on the threshold just outside the sliding door. If the entire restaurant has traditional service, you will be given slippers to wear.

HOW TO ORDER

A Japanese meal begins with soup and some sort of appetizer or salad (often served automatically), then moves through sushi and sashimi to grilled or fried seafood, then meat or poultry (or a one-pot stew). Each dish is presented and served separately (though this is not necessarily true at a Japanese home). There is one major exception—the *bento* lunch. The bento box holds four or five dishes, with rice as the mainstay—perhaps a couple of shrimp tempura, a little sushi, a little yakitori, and some pickles. Bento boxes are traditionally multi-layered nesting boxes, but some look like the old TV-dinner trays, with odd triangular dividers.

Kaiseki ryori, the most formal and elaborate cuisine, came, like the tea ceremony, from Zen tradition; and like the tea ceremony, it demonstrates the extreme sophistication and sensitivity of both chef and diner by pretending to be very simple. (The word *kaiseki* actually refers not to food at all but to the hot stones Buddhist priests used to pocket to keep warm and trick their empty stomachs into quiet.) Kaiseki is the Japanese version of a "grazing menu," multiple courses, each containing just a few bites, prepared with attention to visual presentation as well as flavor and including a variety of grilled, salted, tempura-fried, steamed, and braised or boiled dishes.

If you only want to eat sushi, it's more fun to sit at the sushi bar and watch the itamae (whose title means, literally, "behind the board") work his magic. However, you don't have to sit at the bar to order sushi—and usually you don't have to give up tempura to sit at the bar, either. Just be courteous: If your party of four is only going to have a California roll, don't take up the bar stools.

When ordering sushi, remember to keep track, as it's easy to run up quite a bill without really noticing. (This is one reason more and more restaurants are experimenting with "all you can eat" nights.) Also, when ordering sushi a la carte, check to see whether that particular sushi bar counts one order of sushi to mean one piece or two.

Although sushi meals range the most widely in price, depending on your appetite, many other Japanese dishes are fairly reasonable, particularly the one-pot meals such as nabeyaki udon.

If you are feeling adventuresome, you may ask for *omakase*—chef's choice. At some restaurants, however, an omakase meal, which depends on market ingredients, may have to be ordered 24 hours in advance.

Giant Economy-Size

While the Japanese themselves generally eat lightly and, like other Asian cultures, value the rice over the protein, Japanese restaurateurs in the United States are accustomed to the greater appetites of American diners and have increased portions to match. Remember that most restaurants serve a bowl of soup and small salad with sushi or entrees.

Omakase dinners will be more expensive, perhaps up to $50 depending on the establishment; omakase kaiseki meals can cost up to $100 a person.

COOKING AT HOME

Japanese dishes can be easily adapted to the American kitchen, often without adding new equipment. Sukiyaki and nabeyaki are prepared in cast-iron skillets or cauldrons; chicken or beef can easily be marinated in teriyaki sauce and broiled or grilled. Even chawan mushi can be prepared, with some care, in any small covered mug.

A flexible bamboo mat is needed for rolling maki sushi, but in a pinch, a stiffish grass-weave placemat would do. (And nowadays, there are good sushi carryouts all over the country.) Rice cookers, which originated in Japan, are now thoroughly Americanized and are worth owning whether you cook Japanese-style or not. Mongolian hotpots and fondue pots can be used for shabu-shabu. There are even miniature tappanyaki grills for home Benihana practice.

However, for entertaining at home, it is nice to indulge in a set of chopsticks and chopstick rests, soy sauce bowls, and covered soup bowls; at the least, a sake set and cups should be used to set the table. Don't overdress the table, either; some fresh flowers, an interesting branch or bush cutting, even just handmade pottery dishes. Remember, understatement is the key. And greet your guests as the Japanese greet you: "*Irasshaimase!*"

CUCUMBER SUNOMONO

4 tablespoons rice vinegar
3 tablespoons soy sauce
2 tablespoons sugar, mirin, or honey
1 teaspoon grated ginger with juice
1 large European cucumber or 6 scrubbed, blemish-free pickling cucumbers

In a small bowl, combine dressing ingredients. If the cucumbers are waxed or thick-skinned, you may peel them; then slice thinly and spread on papers towels to drain for 30 minutes. Then dress, toss, and divide into portions. If desired, top with crabmeat or baby shrimp.

CHICKEN YAKITORI

1/2 cup mirin
2 teaspoons grated ginger
1 teaspoon spoon
1/2 cup soy sauce
2 pounds boneless chicken breasts
4–5 green onions or scallions, cut into 1-inch pieces
2 tablespoons lemon juice

Preheat broiler or prepare grill. Combine mirin, ginger, sugar, and soy. Slice chicken into 1-inch strips and marinate 20–30 minutes. If you are using bamboo skewers, soak them in water 20 minutes.

Thread a piece of onion onto a skewer, followed by chicken (pierce in several places and slice down like ribbon); repeat. Broil or grill, turning once, about 4 minutes per side. Sprinkle with lemon juice and black pepper, if desired. Serve hot or at room temperature.

SUKIYAKI

3/4 pound fresh spinach, washed and stems removed,
2–3 green onions, cut in 2-inch pieces
or 1/2 head bok choy, sliced 1 inch wide
1 can whole bamboo shoots
1 package firm tofu, cut into cubes
1/2 pound shirataki noodles[1]
1 1/2 pounds thinly sliced beef sirloin, all fat trimmed
2 ounces beef suet or 2 tablespoons oil
1 large onion, cut into eighths
8 large dried shiitake mushrooms, soaked in hot water
cooked rice

SUKIYAKI SAUCE

1 1/2 cup beef or chicken stock
2/3 cup soy sauce

---

[1] Shirataki, white jelly noodles, are preferably bought fresh from an Asian grocery and are usually found, like the tofu, either floating in water in the refrigerator case or in sealed water packages. As a last resort, get an 8- or 9-ounce can.

2/3 cup mirin
2–3 tablespoons sugar or honey
1 tablespoon oil

Trim all vegetables: Slice spinach leaves and bamboo shoots into bite-sized pieces and refresh in cold water. Drain.

Pat excess liquid from tofu. Trim hard stems from shiitakes; cut in halves or quarters. Arrange on platter with meat.

Stir together sauce ingredients (you may substitute the shiitake soaking liquid for some of the stock). If cooking at the table, have everyone seated before beginning.

Heat oil in skillet; add half the meat and cook partially. Add half the onion and some sauce, stirring the meat so that it cooks evenly. Add half of the other vegetables, including noodles and tofu (but keep them somewhat separate). Serve and repeat with the remaining ingredients. Serve with individual bowls of rice and top with a little extra sauce. (In Japan, the bowls of rice are topped with raw eggs, which cook in the stew; but current health concerns make that practice unfashionable.)

KOREA

In many parts of the United States, Korean food is a sort of "stealth cuisine." The Korean-American community, made up largely of recent immigrants, is only beginning to move past the mom-and-pop grocery cooktop to the formal restaurant kitchen—or to put their own names on the scores of purportedly "Japanese" sushi bars opened by Korean entrepreneurs hoping to cash in on an already established market.

But Korean food, although it has old and strong ties to both Chinese and Japanese cuisines, has an earthiness, a robust kind of gustatory humor, that is very distinctive. Korean culture is at the same time Confucian and shamanistic, painstakingly ordered and richly symbolic. Early Koreans envisioned a universe of earth, fire, water, wood, and metal; and that combination of assertiveness and delicacy characterizes Korean cuisine as well—simple but not exactly subtle.

And since Koreans comprise one of the fastest-growing ethnic communities in the United States—the population increased 125 percent between 1980 and 1990—restaurants advertising Korean-style barbecue and dumplings are sprouting up all over. The main difficulty now is getting them to "go public"—that is, to supplement their frequently Korean-only signs (and menus) with English ones.

THE COUNTRY

The Korean peninsula, a powerful thumb hitchhiking from southern China toward Japan, is primarily mountainous, crisscrossed by rivers (few of them navigable), and with a penumbra of nearly 3,500 small islands, most of them uninhabitable. It divides the Sea of Japan (or, as the Koreans call it, the East Sea) from the Yellow Sea; and at its southern tip, the Straits of Japan are only 150 miles wide. Except for a very small border onto Russia, Korea has only one land neighbor—China, specifically Manchuria; and one of its most crucial roles in world history has been to serve as a cultural go-between for China and Japan. Even the language is a sort of bridge, Chinese in syntax and Japanese in morphology.

For centuries, Korean society adhered faithfully to the Chinese model—so faithfully, in fact, that in 1644, when the supposedly celestial Ming dynasty was overthrown by the Mongolian-bred Manchus, it seemed that Heaven had literally fallen to the barbarians (just what Western civilization thought when Jerusalem fell to the Muslims). Korea banned all non-Chinese influences, but Japan forced it open in the late nineteenth century and eventually annexed the whole country. Ironically, considering Korea's defiance of both the Mongol and Japanese invaders, both left indelible imprints on the cuisine. Mongols supplied the hot brazier used to grill meats (and the chopped raw steak tartare called *yookwhe*), and the Japanese made sashimi and tempura staples.

Korea's climate varies markedly, with cold, dry winters in the north and near-tropical conditions in the south. About half the farmland in Korea has been turned over to rice cultivation, with paddies not only along the coast and in river valleys but in painstakingly recovered flood plains. Livestock is raised somewhat sparingly, particularly in the north, where the uneven ground makes grazing difficult.

THE CUISINE

Because the marinated and grilled beef dishes such as *bulgoki* (rump or round strips) and *bulgalbi* (short ribs) are so well known, Korean cuisine is sometimes thought of as heavier than most other Asian styles. Like its neighboring countries, however, Korea depends most heavily on three staples—fish, rice, and noodles; the difference is in the almost forward, spotlight-grabbing seasoning.

Koreans enjoy powerfully flavored food, consuming more garlic than any other ethnic group; they also use lavish amounts of soy sauce, red chilies, black pepper, and ginger. The most famous Korean condiment, really a staple in itself, is *kimchee*, a spicy, fermented pickle or relish made from radish, red peppers, ginger, and lavish amounts of garlic. Kimchee can addict the most serious of chiliheads. At the same time, Koreans know the value of contrast; the *pajyun*, a large mung-flour pancake studded with oysters, shrimp, and scallions, could not be more delicate.

THE MAIN INGREDIENTS

GRAINS AND STARCHES Most of the Korean countryside is devoted to rice farming. However, farmers also grow several other varieties of grains (barley, wheat, corn, and sorghum) and starches (soy, azuki and mung beans, and white and sweet potatoes), which are turned into flours or pastes and from that into noodles or thickenings.

VEGETABLES Cabbage (usually either Chinese or celery cabbage), garlic, and radishes are particularly treasured for their role in kimchee, which occupies in Korean family life a near-sacred position,

Stealth Health

Korean food is fairly healthful, although somewhat sodium-heavy. Cooking methods are simple—most foods that are not served raw are either pan-fried, grilled, broiled, steamed, or braised—and what little oil is used is vegetable or sesame. Very little animal fat is used even for frying. And although meat is popular, it is eaten, as in most Asian cuisines, in combination with starch and vegetables.

At the same time, because of its long Buddhist tradition, Korea has quite a few vegetarian dishes; but for whatever reason, they are not widely offered in American restaurants. There are a few chefs, however, who prepare what is called "temple cooking"—traditional monastery fare (again, simple but not dull), including dishes such as grilled bamboo shoots and wild sesame gruel. There are also restaurants that specialize in tofu dishes, with or without additional meats. Interestingly, some Buddhists believe that although they are forbidden to eat living things (i.e., seafood), they may consume food that is washed up—presumably "offered"—on the shore; however, no chef in the United States is going to serve two-day-old oysters, so don't worry.

like that of rice in Japan. Other common vegetables include eggplant, mushrooms, leeks, limas, burdock, turnips, some squash, carrots, tomatoes; and delicate sprouts such as bamboo shoots, lotus roots, and sprouted beans are also popular.

FRUITS Although it is not generally obvious from restaurant menus, Koreans are fond of a variety of fruits, including apples, so-called Korean pears, persimmons, cherries, plums, oranges, lemons, winter melons, and grapes. These are commonly served at the end of a meal, or in the form of preserves and condiments.

FLAVORINGS Kimchee provides one of the major flavor elements of the meal, but despite its power, it is usually "doubled" by heavy doses of garlic, ginger, ginseng, perilla (the basil-mint relative called shiso in Japan), sesame seeds (which are usually crushed before being added to marinades, thus releasing a darker, richer flavor than the Middle Eastern sesame sauces offer), scallions and onions, soy sauce, red or black bean paste, a salty chili paste called *gochujang*, black pepper, dried red pepper, and citrus—particularly preserved or fermented lemons.

MEATS AND POULTRY Beef is the most popular entree, followed by chicken; rabbits are raised but rarely eaten, and pork is only slightly more common. Goat is popular in some areas, but mutton is almost never served. (In the United States, however, it sometimes appears in a version of the Mongolian hotpot).

SEAFOOD AND SHELLFISH Far and away the greatest natural food resource are the country's thousands of inlets and freshwater streams, which supply Koreans with an abundance of seafood proteins: anchovies, sardines, mackerel, tuna, cuttlefish, whitefish, pollack, flounder, fluke, whiting, cod, sandfish, herring, eel, octopus, clams, shrimp, squid, and abalone, along with algaes and seaweeds (used, as in Japan, both for wrapping sushi and for enriching stocks) and some marine vegetables.

ANJU

Like most Asians, Koreans don't think of appetizers as a first course—although they can be—but more frequently as alternative meals, food to drink and talk by, in the way the Spanish consume tapas. (Soups, in fact, are more popular as snacks or on-the-run meals.)

The Korean word for such small tapas-like dishes is *anju* and commonly includes sashimi, oysters, bits of grilled pork, hard-boiled quail eggs, a sort of thin-sliced spicy corned brisket, and lettuce or even salted cabbage leaves to roll them in (and revive your thirst). In the United States, the anju frequently appear at the beginning of the menu, like hors d'oeuvre, but are apt to be much larger than expected.

Kejaeng is a highly distinctive and addictive anju: raw crab served in the shell but chopped into two-inches pieces, cured in salt and chili paste like a fiery ceviche and served cold. Eating kejaeng requires either great skill or a certain amount of abandon; you can pick out a piece from the serving tray with chopsticks, but eventually you'll have to just grab hold with your fingers and eat it despite the chili sauce. Treat it something like an artichoke leaf, biting down on the shell to flatten it and gradually working the meat out—or just eat it anyway you can.

Gulchupan (or guljeolpan), one of the most popular sit-around dishes, is more of a group order: Small pancakes are served in the center of a compartmented tray surrounded by a variety of ingredients ("gulchupan" literally means "nine varieties"), such as dried mushrooms, stir-fried matchstick carrots, and marinated shredded beef. Gulchupan is served at room temperature and thus can be eaten at leisure, so it frequently substitutes for a more elaborate meal.

In a Pickle

Kimchee is more than a staple—it's an official, national treasure. It even has its own museum in Seoul, where the World Trade Center has a permanent exhibit of the equipment, techniques, and history of kimchee making. Kimchee (or kim chi) is at the same time one dish and hundreds, ranging from the most common variety, a fermented and garlicky relative of sauerkraut, to the hottest radish-chili pickle, called *khaktugi*. Korean markets may stock dozens of kimchees at a time, lightly spiced or incendiary, and based on cucumbers, cabbage, turnips, or even zucchini or apples; sometimes even octopus, dried shrimp, rare fruits, and small fish. A fine restaurant may serve 5 or 10 varieties. Every family has its own recipe, and every fall, in a ritual called *kimbang* that recalls the exhaustive canning and jarring that American frontier women did, the whole family gathers to salt and season a year's worth of cabbage, pack it in drums, and bury it for fermenting over the winter.

THE MAIN DISHES

HORS D'OEUVRE As we noted above, most of the items listed on American menus as "appetizers" are really light meals and can be quite filling. An order of sashimi, for instance, which might be six or eight pieces as a Japanese first course, may be literally dozens at a Korean restaurant—and that's not even the "large" size. Another dish frequently seen in the United States is *mandoo* (or mandu), Korean dumplings available steamed or fried or in soup; *cham maat* is a more general term covering dumplings and other dishes like the Chinese dim sum.

KOREAN BARBECUE In Korea, beef is prepared literally nose to (ox)tail, and there are said to be well over a hundred special soup recipes for virtually every portion, from shankbone to shoulder. However, the cuts most frequently offered in the U.S. are rump, round, short ribs, brisket, filet, tongue, liver, and tripe. Any of these are apt to be offered as "barbecue"— that is, marinated in a spicy and slightly sweet sauce and grilled over a hot brazier called a *hware*.

Bul means "beef"; *bulgoki* is usually sliced rump or round; *bulgalbi* (also known as simply galbi or sometimes kalbi) are short ribs sawed into two- or three-inch lengths. A suffix that indicates grilled food is -*gwhe: Yumtong-gwhe* is grilled heart, and *gobchang-gwhe* is tripe. *Yookwhe* (or yuk whey) is raw beef; usually made of higher-quality cuts, it is served like steak tartare, topped with pine nuts, fresh apple, and egg, but is meant to be rolled up in lettuce leaves rather than spread on bread.

Most restaurants in the United States use portable gas or propane grills instead of charcoal braziers, but some have the real thing in the

Fish Story

Korean sashimi is usually sliced more thickly than the Japanese version. Sometimes it looks almost chunky, because Koreans prefer to eat sashimi as they do meat, wrapping it in lettuce leaves with some radish or chilies for flavor and dipping it into sauces, either the traditional soy or even the hot bean paste. (This makes sashimi orders in Korean restaurants seem even larger.) Traditionally, the nori sheets used to wrap Japanese sushi are served as a side dish or condiment, brushed with sesame oil, lightly toasted, and cut up into squares to wrap around bites of rice. Korean sushi is also likely to seem more sturdy than the delicate Japanese version but is usually eaten in the traditional fashion, with chopsticks, soy sauce, and wasabi.

back, so you might want to ask. If your whole party is having barbecue, let the staff know, because many tables have built-in grill tops that allow everyone to cook at the same time and taste everything. If only one person is having grilled meat (or if the staff thinks you seem new to the cuisine), it may be grilled for you in the kitchen and brought out on a platter, which is fine but not quite as much fun.

OTHER MEATS AND POULTRY   The barbecue method is also applied to pork, poultry, and even seafood. *Dwiji-gwhe* is sliced grilled pork; *jang-gwhe* (or janguh-guyee) is grilled eel (called unagi at Japanese sushi bars); and *ojingu-gwhe* is marinated grilled squid. *Tak* is chicken, *takgoki* barbecued chicken. *Soon dae* are sausages.

OMELETS AND CREPES   *Bindaeduk* or pindaettuk are pancakes made of ground mung beans, rather than flour, and mixed with egg; they taste like a combination omelet and crepe and are stuffed with pork, vegetables, and perhaps a touch of kimchee. Pajyun or paijeon is a large version (sometimes quite large, like a pizza) often made with seafood.

NOODLES   As we noted above, the Koreans are very fond of pastas and prepare them from a variety of starches and flours. Among the most popular dishes are *naengmein*, buckwheat noodles that are usually served cold with meat, vegetables, and chili paste; *jajaengmein*, wheat noodles in brown bean sauce with meat; and *chowmamein*, a seafood version. *Mein*, the Chinese word for noodles, seen in variations all over southern Asia, is frequently spelled myon or maen as well. Interestingly, the nearest Korean version of pad thai or chowmein—stir-fried vegetables and noodles—is not called "mein" but *chap chae* (or jap chae or chap chye). *Tangmein* is usually rice noodles, the see-through kind also called cellophane noodles or bean threads; but *tang* also refers to the clear stock prepared for soups.

BIG-BOWL DISHES   While Europeans and Americans tend to segregate different dishes on the plate and eat them separately, most Korean dishes are one-pot meals; although the ingredients are served in bowls, along with the kimchee and condiments, the diner is expected to stir them all together in the largest bowl and season to taste. Among the favorites are *bibimbap*, a rice dish topped with chopped or strip-grilled beef, vegetables (usually spinach, bean sprouts, watercress or julienned zucchini, and carrots), egg, and hoisin or chili sauce, which is served layered like a composed salad and then stirred up by the diner; and *yook-whe bibimbap*, which has raw beef coated with sesame oil instead of the grilled version. Traditionally, yookwhe bibimbap is served with a raw egg, too, but like many Japanese restaurants, many Korean establishments have shifted to either serving cooked eggs or offering a choice. *Hwehdobap* (or hwaidupbap) is sort of a cross between bibimbap and Japanese chirasizushi, with thin strips of raw fish over noodles, seaweed, daikon radish, carrots, and so forth.

CASSEROLES AND ONE-POT MEALS   *Jige* is a type of soup with hot bean paste mixed into the broth: *Ke-jige* is a crab version, *dubu-jige* usually pork and bean curd, and *sook-jige* is a jumbo gumbo of cuttlefish, pork, tofu, scallions, squash, and egg. *Jungol* means "casserole" and can feature shellfish, sea cucumber, seafood, and tripe, or often, in a sort of deluxe version, all of the above; a particularly fancy variation, frequently translated as "caviar stew" or, more bluntly, "fish egg soup," features bean curd and cod or herring roe in a hot chili broth. *Haejaengook* or haejangkook is a hearty stew often prescribed as a hangover remedy, thickened with blood sausage and served with lots of scallions.

Koreans are also fond of a version of Mongolian hotpot called *sin sul lo* or shin sun ro, which uses a "steamboat" or "firepot" dish with a chimney for charcoal. (See "How to Eat Like a Native," on the following page). A similar dish involving seafood, called *maeun-tang*, can be either a light stew or a thicker gumbo.

BEVERAGES   With meals, Koreans generally drink beer or rice wines. *Makkolli*, a cloudy fermented-rice liquor particularly suited to anju, is the most popular beverage; a slightly more refined makkolli, closer to Japanese sake, is called *tongdongju* or, more slangily, *popju*; and ginseng wine is called *insamchu*. Western-style liquor is also popular.

Koreans take tea very seriously; and in the teahouses, dedicated to traditional enjoyment and contemplation of the beverage, there may be imaginative brews flavored with roasted corn or barley, wild sesame, ginseng, ginger, cinnamon, arrowroot, citron, or quince.

SWEETS   Koreans do not generally eat desserts, although they will occasionally offer children crackers or American candy; fresh fruits are more common at the end of a meal. Sweets are usually limited to holidays or special occasions.

HOW TO ORDER AND EAT LIKE
A NATIVE

Many Korean restaurants in Korea, and a growing number in the United States as well, are specialty shops, preparing only grilled dishes or sushi. A *bulgoki-jip* is a barbecue joint (literally, a "beef house"), a *saengsan-hweh-jip* the local sushi bar, a *mandoo-jip* a dumpling kitchen, and a *poon-sik-jip* a noodle counter, where you can watch the cooks hand-pull, stretch, thin, and finally cut the chewy noodles that are the third major food group. There are also what are called *suljip*—the tapas bars of Korea, serving mostly anju and cocktails and catering primarily to students and happy-hour types.

However, the vast majority of Korean restaurants in the United States are full-service establishments, where you can sample some of everything. But start slowly, because every meal comes with rice (even breakfast, when it may be a kind of gruel) or rice mixed with other grains and a number of small side orders called *panchan*—bowls of mung bean spouts, squash or spinach in sesame oil, garlic stems, raw or dried squid, dried shrimp, watercress or cilantro, grated turnip or radish, and of course kimchee. All dishes are served at once, including soup and sushi (although some restaurants here have shifted to a dual-course service). And remember that "appetizers" may be more like light entrees.

Most foods are eaten with either chopsticks and spoons, in the case of one-pot meals, or chopsticks and fingers for barbecue, sushi or sashimi, and anju. Barbecued meats are taken off the brazier with chopsticks, placed into a lettuce leaf with a bite of rice, green onion, and chili or bean paste, and then eaten with the fingers. (In the United States, especially for American customers, the waitresses may come along and take the grilled meat or chicken off the brazier for you and place it on a plate, which will allow you to eat it with chopsticks if you prefer.) *Yookwhe*, the sesame-flavored beef tartare, is eaten the same way. *Kalbi*, the short ribs, are eaten with the fingers.

The "flat dishes," such as bindaeduk, can be eaten either with your fingers or with chopsticks; the larger version, pajyun, can be torn into smaller pieces with chopsticks and then eaten either way. To eat gulchu-pan, use your chopsticks (the thicker end, not the eating end) to place the fillings into your pancake, then use your fingers to roll it up, dip it

into the sauce, and eat it; ditto for most
anju. The large-bowl dishes—the rice-
based bibimbaps and noodle dishes—are
eaten both with long-handled teaspoonlike
spoons, used primarily for stirring ingredients and seasonings together, and chopsticks. You may slurp your noodles, within
reason. For soups, use the chopsticks for
picking out the meats or seafood and the
spoon for the broth.

Sin sul lo, the hotpot meal, is eaten
communally and requires chopsticks. The
traditional firekettle looks something like a
stovepipe hat with the brim turned up and
the crown sliced off; thin slices of beef,
onions, carrots, scallions, chrysanthemum
leaves, shrimp, pork meatballs, and perhaps
walnuts or pine nuts are arranged around
the bowl. When it is brought to the table,
hot coals are transferred to the chimney, the
lid is replaced, and boiling stock is poured
into the "moat"; and as the food cooks, diners remove bits from the broth, dip them
into a sesame-flavored sauce, and eat them
over rice.

A meal for two might consist of an
order of steamed or fried mandoo dumplings,
one order of bulgoki, and perhaps a charbroiled fish or shrimp tempura. Four people
should order bindaeduk or some sashimi or,
if you don't like raw fish, perhaps soon dae sausages; two barbecues (bulgalbi and either chicken or, if available, eel) or one beef dish and a rice or
noodle dish such as bibimbap or jajaengmyon; it will be a lot of food.

If you have several people in your party, or perhaps a family group,
find out whether the restaurant offers chongsik dinners, banquet-style

meals that usually require 24 hours' advance notice; a chongsik menu is apt to run to as many as 20 dishes, including baked shellfish, meat-stuffed peppers, fried oysters, and elaborate stews as well as grilled meats. (*Hanjungsik* banquets, formal court affairs, ran to 100 dishes or more.)

Dining in Korean restaurants is typically inexpensive or moderately expensive; most dishes cost under $10. After discovering how much food it can be, you may order less and save more. The chongsik dinners may be somewhat more, perhaps $25 a person.

COOKING AT HOME

Recreating Korean food at home is fairly easy, even if you don't have a hotpot for sin sul ro; it can be made in a large wok or electric frypan, and barbecues can be made either outdoors on a grill or inside in a skillet (galbi can be broiled or oven-roasted as well). If you have a small hibachi, you can even grill tableside. Since the panchan (side dishes) can be made in advance, the meat marinated overnight, and the rice timed, you can eat whenever you decide to fire up the grill.

Traditionally, Korean men and women ate separately (aristocrats and scholars often dined in their studies) off low, wide tables like footed trays, so you could sit around the hibachi on the floor or just set the table. Use bowls only—small for the panchan (you can refill them as needed), medium for the rice, and larger for the main dishes or noodles. And offer plenty of spices: red chili paste, hoisin sauce, dried red chilies, soy sauce, and lots of kimchee. This essential relish can be obtained in any Asian market, but there are relatively quick versions, like the one offered here, that allow you to control the heat and garlic level.

Incidentally, a great many of the dishes used in Korean restaurants, particularly to serve rice, are stainless steel or perhaps brass; this is a remnant of the tradition that required all bowls, spoons, and chopsticks to be silver, because silver was believed to discolor in the presence of poison, thus conflating hospitality and honesty. Even today, bridal dowries contain some silver. However, more and more restaurant settings are simply porcelain; some of the larger one-pot dishes or casseroles are served in preheated stoneware bowls or crocks or even cast-iron skillets.

BARBECUE MARINADE
(FOR BULGOKI, BULGALBI, CHICKEN, ETC.)

6 tablespoons soy sauce
2 tablespoons mirin or dry sherry
2 tablespoons water or beef stock
2 tablespoons toasted, crushed sesame seeds or 2 tablespoons sesame oil
2 heaping tablespoons sugar
4 scallions, white and pale green, finely chopped
1 tablespoon finely minced garlic
2 teaspoons grated ginger
ground black pepper to taste

Combine all ingredients. Marinate meats 3 to 4 hours, covered, or overnight in the refrigerator. Grill or broil meat as desired; serve with steamed rice, dipping sauce, and spinach (cooked, squeezed dry, and dressed with sesame oil and a touch of vinegar) and kimchee. This amount of marinade will cover about 2 pounds of sirloin, flank, or rump roast, and 3–4 pounds or more of short ribs.

BULGOKI DIPPING SAUCE

1/4 cup soy sauce
2 teaspoons sesame oil
1 teaspoon Chinese bean paste or red miso paste (optional)
1/4 cup mirin, sake, or dry sherry
1 teaspoon roasted ground sesame seeds
1 tablespoon finely chopped spring onion
1 heaping tablespoon honey or sugar
1 teaspoon grated fresh ginger
1 teaspoon crushed dried red chilies, chili paste,
or pepper sauce (or more to taste)
1 clove garlic, minced (or more to taste)
salt to taste

Combine first 9 ingredients (if using honey). "Cream" garlic with salt and (if you are using it) sugar into a smooth paste and mix into sauce. Serve in individual bowls.

"QUICK" KIMCHEE

1 large head Chinese or celery cabbage

3 cloves garlic

1 dried red chili, crushed (more for second variation),
or 2 teaspoons hot pepper sauce

1 tablespoon soy sauce

2 teaspoons grated ginger

2 tablespoons sea salt or coarse kosher salt (more for second variation)

2 teaspoons seasoned rice vinegar

1 tablespoon sugar

For "instant" kimchee, simply chop the cabbage into small pieces, crush the garlic, blend with remaining ingredients, and let stand at room temperature until ready to serve (refrigerate if you will be waiting more than 3 or 4 hours).

For a slightly more powerful and somewhat more traditional version, begin a week or 10 days before the day of entertaining. Cut the bottom off the cabbage, slice lengthwise into 5 or 6 sections, and let dry (in the sun, to be really authentic) for 3 or 4 hours. Then coarsely chop and layer in a crock, interspersed with generous coverings of salt and red pepper. Top with a wooden tray or plate small enough to fit inside the dish, weight it down with a large stone or iron, and let it sit for up to a week (allowing another 4 days before serving). Then rinse thoroughly under cold water (and wash the crock as well); squeeze out as much moisture as possible; and return to the crock, this time layering with the combined remaining ingredients. Add water or light stock to cover cabbage. Cover with wax paper or slightly loose plastic wrap, replace top, and refrigerate until serving.

PART VI

THE AMERICAS

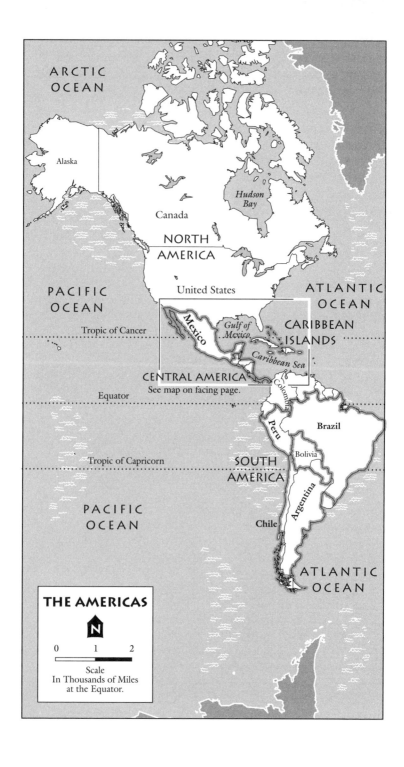

ARCTIC
OCEAN

Alaska

Canada

Hudson
Bay

NORTH
AMERICA

PACIFIC
OCEAN

United States

ATLANTIC
OCEAN

Tropic of Cancer

Mexico

Gulf of
Mexico

CARIBBEAN
ISLANDS

Caribbean Sea

CENTRAL AMERICA
See map on facing page.

Colombia

Equator

Peru

Brazil

Bolivia

Tropic of Capricorn

SOUTH
AMERICA

PACIFIC
OCEAN

Argentina

Chile

ATLANTIC
OCEAN

THE AMERICAS

N

0   1   2

Scale
In Thousands of Miles
at the Equator.

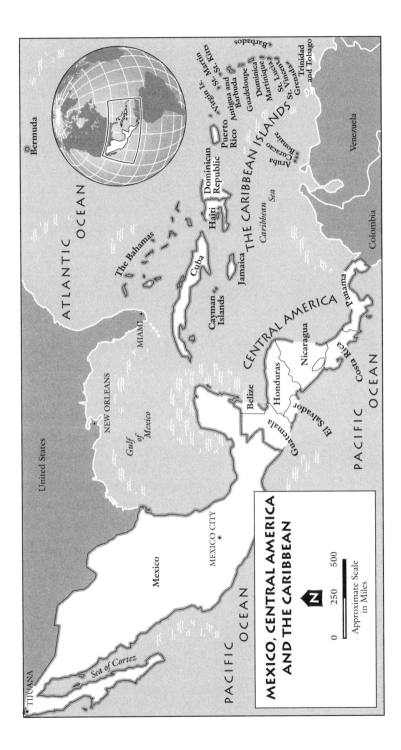

MEXICO, CENTRAL AMERICA AND THE CARIBBEAN

N

0   250   500

Approximate Scale
in Miles

MEXICO, CENTRAL AMERICA, AND CUBA

BASIC CUISINE

DINNER FOR TWO:
Gazpacho, quesadilla, pork adobado, snapper veracruzano

DINNER FOR FOUR:
Ceviche, avocado soup, crab chowder, shrimp, cabrito, chicken mole, paella

GROUP DISH:
Parilladas

STYLE:
Starchy, earthy, spicy

KEY FLAVORS:
Tomato, chili, corn

EATING UTENSILS:
Forks and knives, fingers

DISTINCTIVE FOODS:
Beans, tortillas, pupusas, salsa

UNIFORMITY OF MENUS:
Fair

NUTRITIONAL INDEX:
High carbohydrate, medium sodium, high fat

COST:
Inexpensive to moderate

"THANK YOU:"
"Gracias" (Spanish)

Perhaps the most astonishing thing about Central America, Mexico, and Cuba is how thoroughly we have confused language with culture. The terms "Hispanic" and "Latino" both refer to the Spanish language, paying lip service to the conquistadors rather than the natives, even though the Indians still dominate the population. ("Indians" itself is a misnomer, since Columbus was nowhere near the East Indies.)

"Latino" or not, more than a million Mexicans speak only Indian languages. El Salvador is 80 percent *mestizos*—people of mixed Indian, European, and African blood. Guatemala is evenly divided between mestizos and Indians; Honduras and Nicaragua have only small white minorities. And despite the importance of beef, chicken, and rice, which were introduced by the Spanish, the cuisines of Mexico and Central America are still heavily dependent on the Indian staples: chilies, tomatoes, beans and, most important, corn, which they have been cultivating for 7,000 years.

Moreover, while it may be a poor substitute for revenge, the foods of the New World revolutionized the cuisines of the Old World: Mexico was the source for "French" vanilla, "Italian" tomatoes and, from the cocoa that the Aztecs reserved for their priestly class, "Swiss" chocolate. The "gran turco" of sixteenth-century Venice, which they called the "Turkish grain," was actually Mexican cornmeal that came to the Mediterranean via Middle Eastern trade routes. Native Americans were making whiskey long before Columbus arrived; and though the Europeans swept agricultural concern aside in their quest for American gold, the chilies, peanuts, and particularly the chocolate and tobacco they sent back eventually provided greater wealth than Ferdinand and Isabella could ever have imagined.

THE HISTORY

Central and southern Mexico and Central America were the site of a series of great native civilizations going back four millenia. The Mayans' writing system, calendars, astronomical calculations, and conceptually dazzling mathematical system were fully developed by about 1500 B.C. At its peak, about the eighth century A.D., the Mayan Empire ruled an estimated 14 million people; about 2 million ethnic Mayans still live in the Yucatan and in Guatemala and Honduras. They were gradually dominated by a series of increasingly aggressive tribes, leading up to the Toltec (the "master builders" of pyramids) and finally the Aztecs—Mexicos, as they called themselves—who under their last king, Montezuma, made the fatal error of welcoming the Spanish conquistadors as celestial visitors.

Mexico and Central America, which form the left parenthesis of the Caribbean bracket, are mountainous and thickly jungled, susceptible to hurricanes, earthquakes, and volcanic eruptions. Ironically, considering the country's cornucopia-shaped land mass, only 15 percent of Mexico's land is arable.

Cuba, which was visited by Columbus on his first voyage in 1492, was strategically positioned to become the base of Spanish operations in the New World, because it stretches out across the mouth of the Gulf of Mexico and offers access to both the Caribbean and the Atlantic. Not surprisingly, it was equally attractive to French, British, Dutch, and Carib marauders. It was also an early mainstay of the slave trade: The gentle Arawaks, beset by disease, enforced labor, and punitive living conditions, were all but wiped out within decades of the Spanish land-ings and were replaced by African and other Indian captives. Today the population is an ethnic mix of black, European, and transplants from other Latin countries, along with a trace of Indian.

One of Spain's earliest cash cows, Cuba was thickly planted with the sugarcane that was used for making molasses (and more profitably, rum); even today, two-thirds of its arable land is given over to cane and another large chunk to tobacco. On what remains, subsistence farmers raise rice, corn, beans, citrus fruits, squash, sweet potatoes, and yucca, but they depend heavily on livestock, particularly chicken and pigs, and on fish and seafood.

THE CUISINES

Real Mexican food used to be an oxymoron in the United States, but things have changed tremendously, partly because of the improved eco-nomic position of Mexican-Americans and partly thanks to the interest of modern Mexican, Southwest, and Texan chefs. Mexican cuisine goes far beyond the refried beans and other internally confounding dishes found in the frozen-dinner and fast-food lanes (burritos, in fact, are an American invention), and showcases seafood, chicken, red meat, and dis-tinctly nonmushy vegetables. Tortillas (or rolls), rice, and beans are almost invariably served with the main dish.

In fact, authentic Mexican cuisine would seem very modern today. The Aztecs drank chocolate (probably in a bitter form) and created *mole* (pronounced "MO-lay"), the distinctive chocolate-chili sauce that is the pride of Mexican cooking. Chilies were an ancient preservative, preferred to salt; chilies were believed to be medicinal and healthful as well, and modern nutritionists agree. Smoking was another fairly common preser-vative method. Drying was essential for vegetables; the Native Americans were cooking with sun-dried tomatoes centuries ago.

It was also a fairly healthful diet, high in carbohydrates and protein and low in fat, at least until the Spanish arrived. They introduced pork, beef, and one of the region's less nutritious habits, frying in lard. And black and Creole slaves, French, British, and Portuguese traders, and Chinese and Indian laborers provided a few flourishes, but only a few: One of the scant traces of the brief French occupation is a fondness for crepes and crisp bread.

Geography is the most obvious factor affecting regional cooking: The northerly regions and large cities, such as Mexico City and Veracruz, tend to show the strongest Spanish influence. The plateau-dwellers, particularly Indians, lean to the precolonial staples of their ancestors—tortillas, beans, tomatoes, cheese and other dairy products, and hot chilies. The tropical lowlands and coastal areas are more reliant on fruits, nuts, vegetables, seafood, and poultry. (For more on *norteño* or Tex-Mex cooking, see the Appendix A on regional cuisines of the United States.)

However, one of the greatest distinctions between Mexican cooking and the cuisine of its Caribbean neighbors is in the preliminary handling of seasonings: The roasting or toasting of chilies, onions, garlic, and tomatoes before cooking is a hallmark of authentic Mexican food. In fact, the three-legged stone *molcajetes* in which salsa is traditionally mixed is enjoying a sort of revival among culinary trend-watchers.

Most dishes are either grilled or stewed or braised in clay pots. Soft dishes, such as rice and beans or meat stews, are eaten with a fork, but thick beans or sausage dishes are often wrapped in tortillas and eaten by hand. (Again, this may have something to do with the geography of the region: The poorest Indians, many of whom were field laborers or live-stock herders, packed along foods that required the fewest utensils or containers; the coastal dwellers, whose more tropical foods were picked fresh and spoiled quickly, preferred pots for combining ingredients.)

THE MAIN INGREDIENTS

To grasp just how "American" these cuisines are, consider the list of foods unknown to Europeans until the sixteenth century: tomatoes, coriander, chilies, cocoa, avocados, bananas, beans, corn, potatoes, yams, vanilla, turkey and various other game birds, pine nuts, pecans, peanuts, squash, and tobacco. What the Europeans did bring was significant—rice and wheat, olive oil, beef, mutton, and pork, and the techniques of making wine and vinegar and transforming milk into cheese—but their contributions, while absorbed into the New World cuisine, did not transform it.

FRUITS The Mexican coastal regions and the Central American countries are rich in citrus, bananas and plantains, squash, and maguay, the plant from which the tequilalike mescal is derived. The farther south one goes, the more "Caribbean" the landscape: Coconuts and coconut milk, avocados, dates, figs, watermelon, mangoes, pineapple, turkey, sweet peppers, chayote, and other tropical fruits begin to make appearances.

VEGETABLES   Many people think vegetable dishes begin and end with beans, but in fact Mexico produces many squashes and pumpkins (along with the now-trendy squash blossoms), a wide variety of fine mushrooms, the fresh-sour tomatillos, and avocados, as well as the beans, potatoes, rice (often subtly flavored with saffron, tomatoes and onions, or nuts), and the versatile yucca. Plantains are employed with great imagination: used as dough or as "omelets," (when green) fried into chips, and (when ripe) sautéed. Mexican chefs interested in older Indian dishes have also revived a variety of alternative grains, such as quinoa and wheat berries.

MEAT   Ever since the Spanish introduced pork, it has been a mainstay of the diet; but goat, which is much leaner, is almost equally popular. Lamb appears frequently in the more upscale restaurants, and some of the most ambitious establishments in the United States and in the wealthier tourist areas, such as Acapulco, even offer court dishes of venison.

POULTRY AND DAIRY PRODUCTS   Although chicken and their eggs represent one of the major sources of protein in the area, smaller, more strongly flavored birds—quail, squab, and turkey in particular—are preferred when available. Cheese is widely used throughout the region, but despite the ubiquitous presence of sour cream on U.S. fast-foot menus (along with the Americanized "tortilla" chips and sweet salsa), other dairy products are not major ingredients.

FISH AND SHELLFISH   Few countries enjoy the variety of fresh seafood that Mexico does: marlin, black bass, tuna, trout, sailfish, swordfish, dogfish shark, amberjack, grouper, pompano, sole, break, skate, shrimp, mussels, squid, crabs, even sea turtle. So-called chocolate clams (*almejas chocolates*), far from being dark brown, are rimmed with a coral-red like the color of a typical lipstick.

SEASONINGS   Among the most popular flavorings in Mexican cuisine are *chipotle*, a smoky pepper (dried jalapeño); cilantro, the lemony parsley also known as coriander; cinnamon; cloves; mole sauce, a blend of chocolate and chilies and sometimes ground nuts and spices; ground seeds, particularly pumpkin; *adobado*, a garlic-based chili marinade or rub that underlies the Spanish *adobo*, or stew; ground nuts such as walnuts and peanuts; and dozens of chilies, both fresh and dried, ranging from mild ones to the notoriously fiery habañeros and jalapeños, though sweet peppers are just as common. *Chile colorado* is a red sauce, the salsa most Americans are familiar with, while *chile verde* is a green sauce that is usually not as hot.

The southerly cuisines lean less to chilies and the bitterer spices—the Indian cinnamon, cloves, and nuts—and more to vinegary, citrusy flavors to play against meats and beans. *Aji* is used to denote both pepper itself and a South and Central American condiment or dipping sauce, and *recado* is a garlicky chili paste, particularly common in the Yucatan and Tabasco, but both are considered more as table flavorings than ingredients.

Cuban food is often highly seasoned, but it is not spicy in the way Jamaican or even Mexican food is. Unlike their more tropical neighbors, Cubans are not so heavily accustomed to mixing fruit (or fruit salsas) into their meals; instead, they tend to begin with a fresh fruit appetizer or juice before the main course.

"STREET FOOD"

There are basically two kinds of meals in this region—indoor and outdoor; roughly, "street food" and sit-down food.

Mexicans like what they call *antojitos*, or "little whims," which they pick up from street vendors and grilling stalls and consume at long wooden communal tables. These antojitos—the originals of the tacos, burritos, and such that are now mass-produced in inferior form by "Mexican" chain restaurants—are a perfect example of what we described in the preface as "first-generation food"—quick and cheap market dishes, not sit-down cuisine.

TORTILLAS   In Mexican markets, the street cooks have a variety of grilled meats, barbecue, fish, shrimp, and even organ meats, which they chop with a cleaver, toss into a tortilla, and top with salsa or onions to suit your taste. This is pretty much the sort of food found in cheapeats diners called *cochinas economicas* or in restaurants with the sign *comida casera*—"home cooking." (Mom-and-pop Central American restaurants that dish out blue-plate-special, working-class meals—beans, rice, and a bit of meat—are called *comefores*.) Tortillas, incidentally, are soft pancakelike disks, not the hard, crumbly version common in the States. Those are closer to tostadas, but even tostadas can be so light and puffy they'd make the Doritos company blush.

Central American *mercados*, or markets, are also dotted with stalls and vendors serving *comidas corrientes*—roughly, "the local stuff." Frequently, street vendors just place a sheet of metal across a simple fire and fry tortillas on them.

TAMALES Mexican tamales tend to be a little coarse, but Central American *tamals* are softer, and the Nicaraguan *nacatamal* is served with a generous stuffing of braised pork, raisins, sweet and sometimes hot peppers, yucca or potatoes, and rice. *Chimichangas* are a double-cooked version—tortillas stuffed with chicken, cheese, or beef, and then fried. *Panvidos* are fried tortillas stuffed with turkey, black beans, and cheese; and *sopes* are cornmeal cups or scoops, fried and then filled with stew. Guatemalans particularly enjoy *chili rellenos:* Whole peppers are used as the "wrapping" for chicken and vegetables or cheese and are then fried.

DUMPLINGS Salvadoran pupusas are extremely popular; the "pat, pat, pat" sound of a pupusa maker is as familiar and telling to Central Americans as the "clap-slap" of sushi makers is to the Japanese. Pupusas are made from the inside out: A ground corn dough is patted around the meat, bean, or cheese filling and then grilled. They are traditionally served with pickled cabbage, called *curtido* or *repollo*,

Virtually every meal in Mexico, even the more formal dinners of several courses, will include some finger food. The French say "A meal without wine is like a day without sunshine," but Mexicans would substitute the word "tortilla" for "wine." Most mercado or vendor food can be eaten by hand, wrapped in tortillas. Similarly, any restaurant dish that is thick enough can be turned into tortilla stuffing—the meats from the thicker stews, organ meats, and even some seafood: Oyster tamales are popular in Veracruz.

Stuffed chilies, grilled meats on the bone, and tortas sandwiches are all, likewise, finger food. (Incidentally, most tortas include beans, which may surprise first-timers.) Meats that involve bones—such as goat birria, which in some places you can order by cut (shoulder, rib, leg)—can be eaten by hand as well. Tamales are wrapped in corn husks or sometimes banana leaves before steaming; these wrappings are not edible but should pull away cleanly from the tamale if it has been cooked long enough.

If you live near a large Central American community and want to try eating at a street vendor or cochina, it's likely to be a fairly healthful meal, because the meats are grilled (although you should beware the grease on some grills). Otherwise it can be hard to judge how much fat or oil is in your dinner; even dishes that haven't been visibly fried often include ingredients that were fried before being combined. The best bets are seafoods (except the sautéed shrimp, which are usually swimming in butter), goat (which is usually roasted and is naturally lean), and the mixed grills.

In general, corn (*masa*) tortillas are somewhat more healthful than the wheat (flour) versions, because while the corn meal is mixed only with water and salt, the wheat tortillas require fat or shortening to bind the dough. Unfortunately, Tex-Mex kitchens usually serve wheat tortillas. Tamales also require lard.

which is ladled onto the split-open pupusa to taste. *Pastelitos* are also ground corn dumplings filled with seasoned minced meat. (The word *pastes* is derived from the "pasties" or meat pies that British silver miners used to make.)

MEXICAN SPECIALTIES

Although many of the dishes listed here originated in Mexico, many have spread throughout the region and are apt to appear on any Central or even South American menu. More Cuban and Central American dishes are described below.

SOUPS   Black bean is probably the most famous, followed by chicken and rice, but regional soups also include *albondigas* (meatballs in broth); corn and/or crab chowders; avocado purées; the cold coconut soup that is a speciality of Jalisco, the beach resort region; citrus and chili-spiked broths with strips of tortilla or rice; creamy shrimp soups (Mexican *crema* is more like crème fraîche than American heavy cream); and squash and potato soups with cheese. *Sopa de pan*, or bread soup, is more like a layered appetizer casserole of bread, onion, tomato, plantain, beans, and hard-boiled eggs, soaked in broth and baked.

STEWS   *Cocido* (also called *puchero* in some areas) is a hearty soup, closer to a beef stew, that sometimes serves as a main course; in the chunkiest versions, the meat is spooned into tortillas, dashed with salsa, and eaten by hand. *Caldillo* or *cazuela* is close to what Americans generally mean by "chili"—ground beef cooked in tomatoes, chilies, onions, and beef broth. *Caldo* is a rich seafood soup; it is sometimes called *caldo siete mares*, which means "seven seas soup." *Sopa de* *mariscos* is a lighter, broth-based seafood soup. The tripe stew or soup called *menudo* is the Mexican "hair of the dog," legendarily consumed as a hangover cure. (The Central American name for it is *mondongo*.) *Pozole* is sometimes used to mean cornmeal mush, but it is also applied to a pork and hominy stew.

APPETIZERS Among first courses, the most famous are *ceviche* (also spelled cebiche or seviche), raw seafood and fish "cooked" in the acid of fresh lime juice and chilies; meat-filled quesadillas (flat tortillas filled or layered and grilled); and *camarones*, or shrimp, most often sautéed in butter and garlic. A popular appetizer, and one with more flavor than its Americanized version, is *queso fundito*, melted cheese with chilies and sometimes chorizo.

SEAFOOD Fish may be grilled, deep-fried, stuffed with crab or shrimp, rubbed with a garlic paste, or pan-stewed with tomatoes and onions (known as *veracruzana*, or Veracruz-style). *Pescado envuelto* is usually a whole fish such as black bass dashed with olive oil, cilantro, and lemon, then wrapped in corn husks and steamed or poached. Shrimp is frequently baked in Veracruz sauce or grilled, sometimes as part of a mixed seafood platter, and sometimes pops up inside quesadillas or "shredded" (chopped) in empanadas. Newer-style Mexican restaurants also offer grilled and/or marinated squid, octopus, swordfish, or salmon steaks, and some bake fish and seafood *al espanole*—in the Spanish or Mediterranean style—with olives and capers.

MEATS Goat, particularly kid (*cabrito*), is almost always either braised for birria or roasted; pork may be roasted, marinated, rotisserie-

> ## Watch Your Mouth
>
> It is important to note that the nomenclature of Mexican, Central American, and Cuban dishes is not uniform, and in this case it is not merely a matter of spelling. A Cuban tortilla is an omelet, not a flat corn pancake; a Mexican *torta* is a sandwich, not a sweet. A Central American *empanada* may be made of a mashed plantain dough and may have a sweet filling instead of pork or cheese; a Mexican or South American empanada is a wheat turnover stuffed with meat. A Central American *quesadilla* is a dessert, not a cheese-stuffed soft tortilla, and a real Mexican quesadilla is a stuffed cornmeal turnover related to the papusa. (Again, see the appendix on American regional cuisines.) Cuts of meat are also rather loosely translated, and Cuban "ham" is frequently unsmoked. If you can't tell from the menu, you may want to ask.

grilled, stewed with prunes, dressed with green chili sauce or with vine-gar (*pibil*-style), or wrapped in banana leaves and steamed or braised. (Birria and other stews are eaten with either tortillas or the French-style rolls called *bolillos*; see "How to Eat Like a Native," page 327.) Sometimes pork is first braised in a seasoned broth and then pan-fried to crispness. The word *carne* simply means "meat," but *carnitas* are usually chunks of fried pork. A raisin and almond-stuffed boneless pork loin basted in a sweet-hot sauce is a popular holiday or banquet dish. It may also be done in an almost North African manner—stewed with green olives, raisins, almonds, cumin, and garlic and turned into mini–pot pies with masa dough crusts.

Lamb is stewed or braised, and beef is usually stewed or braised as well, although sometimes it may be fried. *Tinga* is a braised seasoned beef stewed with hot chilies. *Parilladas* are mixed grills, sometimes cooked on tabletop braziers; they may include spare ribs, flank steak, chicken, chorizo, blood sausage (*morcilla*), sweetbreads (*mollejas*), tongue (*lengua*), pork chops, seafood, fish, and even vegetables or plantains.

POULTRY Chicken is frequently grilled and then sauced with ground nuts and spices or tomatoes and onions. Chicken is particularly well suited to the sweet-hot mole sauces and may be either stewed with the mole or grilled and then sauced. Chicken is also frequently stewed with earthy vegetables such as pumpkin and turnips, carrots, yucca, or sweet potatoes; or, especially in the southern Gulf regions, it may even be flavored with citrus and cilantro and coconut milk. Squab, turkey, and quail are also popular, often marinated in olive oil and wine vinegar before grilling.

BEVERAGES The most popular nonalcoholic drinks in the region are milk and fruit shakes, called *batidos* in Cuba and *lucuados* in Mexico. *Orchata* or *horchata* is a rice and milk version, something like rice pudding in a glass, flavored with vanilla, almond, or cinnamon. *Atole* is more corn, a sort of masa milkshake that sometimes comes with chocolate added. Beer, tequila (and its relatives mescal and *pulque*), and coffee are ubiquitous, and after-dinner liqueurs are also popular. Finer restaurants may serve coconut brandy and a surprising tequila "chaser" called *sangrita*, which is not to be confused with the more familiar wine-and-fruit punch called "sangria"; sangrita is a mix of orange juice, grena-dine, salt, and ground pequin chili.

DAIRY PRODUCTS   Eggs are an important source of nutrition, most often seen in the hearty *huevos rancheros*—eggs fried sunnyside up and topped with tomatoes and salsa—or with the shredded meat called *machaca*. Eggs also pop up hard-boiled and chopped inside tortillas. Mexicans are also fond of cheese, but not the bland orangy stuff used here; *cotija* is like a Parmesan, *queso ranchero* is a mild but fresh-tasting white cheese, and *manchengo* is a ripe, full-bodied cheese used for smooth melting.

CUBAN SPECIALTIES

Cuba's unofficial national dish is black beans and rice, known as *moros y cristianos*, or "Moors and Christians," a name that goes back to the early days of the Spanish conquest, when the liberation of Spain from the Muslims was still a fresh memory. But in general, like the Puerto Ricans, Cubans have acquired the Spanish habit of preferring meat and seafood proteins to beans.

MEATS AND POULTRY   Called *puerco asado* or sometimes *lechon asado*, roast pork marinated in citrus and garlic is a Cuban favorite (and no cooks seem to have more patience in slow-cooking onions to a caramel perfection than they). It is so commonly a Sunday dinner sort of dish that in many restaurants it may be available even if it is not listed on the menu. Pork is also frequently cut into chunks and fried, or smoked into hams to be cooked with the black beans or with rice. *Chorizo*, the spicy sausage, is another pork specialty, and one habit-forming (though not exactly low-cal) Cuban appetizer is a quesadilla topped with sliced chorizo, then covered with melted cheese.

Ropa viejo (literally, "old clothes") is a seasoned beef stew cooked till it falls into shreds; *tasajo* is a dry-cured seasoned beef that originated in Brazil and the Caribbean but is also popular here. *Bolicha* is a pot roast or braised brisket. Cubans are expert at lamb and goat as well, although these meats are not quite so common in the United States; in the most authentic spots in established Cuban neighborhoods (Miami or Los Angeles, for example), you may even find organ stews such as tripe and brains.

Chicken may be quick-fried (called *chicharron*) or stewed in tomatoes and wine as well as roasted, and rabbit (which, just as promised, tastes very much like chicken) is not infrequently offered in similar dishes.

SEAFOOD   Cuban shellfish, although perhaps not as famous as the country's meat dishes, is delicious; *mariscos* means "seafood" and is often written on the outside of a Cuban or Mexican restaurant to demonstrate that fresh seafood is prepared inside. Spanish-style *paella*, the shellfish- and ham-studded rice casserole, is very popular, along with garlicky sautéed shrimp, Caribbean-style salt cod stews, and pan-fried whole fish, such as red snapper. *Choros* are steamed mussels, usually with lots of broth to sop up. *Calamares*, or squid, is usually braised in tomatoes or wine and served over rice; as an appetizer, squid is occasionally fried.

CENTRAL AMERICAN SPECIALTIES
Central Americans have traditionally migrated among nations, and although there are regional specialties—tripe in Honduras, stuffed pupusas in El Salvador—the food, particularly as prepared in the United States, is fairly uniform.

ONE-POT DISHES   Common dishes include *pipian* (or *pepian*), spiced stews thickened with ground nuts or sometimes rice or tortilla bits; *picadillos*, meat stews flavored with tomatoes and raisins; and the mixture of shredded beef and corn flour called *indio viejo* (meaning "the old Indian," which may refer to the age of the recipe or the fact that it was a way of using older ground-up corn). *Carne deshilachada* is a sort of skillet hash of minced or chopped beef, eggs, tomatoes, onions, and peppers all fried together.

MEATS   *Vigaron* is a Nicaraguan specialty of fried and chopped pork, shredded cabbage, and yucca, with a tangy dressing. *Hilachas* is stew made with braised then shredded beef; *revolcado* is a Guatemalan pork-organ stew, usually featuring brains, tripe, and all. *Caballo bayo* is marinated grilled beef, the Nicaraguan fajita. (Interestingly, a number of Central American restaurants in the United States have begun offering what used to be considered "South American"–style grilled meats like those in Argentinian *churrascierras*.)

VEGETABLES   Unlike Mexicans, Central Americans do frequently start and end the veggie list with beans. The Central American version of beans and rice usually uses red beans (as in the Nicaraguan *gallo pinto*), but white beans are popular in vinegar-flavored "salads" and in other, softer dishes, such as *frijol blanco*, a Guatemalan dish flavored with pork. Cabbage and heavier squashes do make rare appearances.

SWEETS   The whole region is fond of sweetened breads, both for breakfast (the Guatemalan *campechadas*, the Mexican *pan dulce*) and for dessert (the Caribbean-influenced ginger bun and the tropical coconut *coco* roll). A particular version, flavored with orange and orange-blossom extract, is called *pan de muerto*—"bread of the dead"— and is traditionally served on November 1 and 2, All Saints' and All Souls' days.

Other sweets include *marquesote*, either a spongecake or a custard cake, and *rodojas*, the orange-flavored version; *arroz con leche*, rice pudding; and *capirotada*, bread pudding. *Flan de horchata* is, as it sounds, a custard made with horchata instead of plain milk. In El Salvador particularly, a pineapple torte called *La Semita* is popular. Cheesecakes and ricottalike flavored cheese custards are popular, particularly in Mexico. Fresh fruits—pineapple, coconut, or mango—are also frequently served for dessert.

HOW TO ORDER AND EAT LIKE A NATIVE

Most of the more formal restaurants in the United States are Mexican or Cuban; the Central American (or combined Mexican–Central American) tend to be more family-style cantinas. Main courses are generally eaten with the common utensils, but almost any entree may be placed into a roll or tortilla and eaten by hand.

The main meal in Mexico is a midday dinner that may last from 2 until 5:30, and that is where the more substantial dishes will be found. Between the big dinner and the last supper, about 9 or 10 P.M., comes a sort of "high tea," featuring only coffee or hot chocolate and as likely to mean tamales as pastry. In the United States, however, restaurants have adapted to the traditional time schedule.

The general order of dinner is appetizers, soup, the first entree (probably fish or vegetable), the *platido fuerte* (the main course, or "heavy plate") or meat, the salad and, finally, the dessert. Two people in a good Mexican restaurant will probably find soup, a quesadilla, one fish dish and one meat (preferably pork adobado) plenty to eat. A party of four might order ceviche and two soups (avocado and crab), a shrimp dish, roast kid, chicken mole, and paella. If Cuban black bean soup is offered, be sure to get that, too.

More formal restaurants—those that specialize in Spanish-influenced dishes—may offer tapas, Spain's small, appetizer-size dishes; they range from $4 or $5 up to $15 for mini-paellas, but this option allows you to taste as many dishes as you can hold. In such a restaurant, you should try some of the fine Spanish sherry varieties, especially the nuttier and drier styles, such as palo cortada and amantillado.

A few restaurants with special interest in traditional Indian cuisine serve *atole*, the clove- or almond-flavored corn drink that comes with a platter of finger foods such as fried tortillas or yucca; the idea is to alternate bites of the sweetish appetizers with sips of the spicy atole.

In Central American restaurants, particularly the informal ones, so many side dishes come with the entree—for instance, an order of enchiladas is usually served with rice, beans, lettuce and tomato, guacamole, and picante sauce—that moderation is advisable in the beginning: Just order an entree apiece. But they're extremely inexpensive; only rarely—and usually just for fancier seafood dishes—do they reach $12 per person.

COOKING AT HOME

Central American and Mexican cooking is sometimes labor-intensive, but it is not terribly complex; and now that there are so many markets from which to buy fresh tamales and tortillas, entertaining at home is relatively simple. Most foods are either grilled or stewed; the only important thing to remember is that acidic foods such as salsas and chilies should be prepared in nonreactive ceramic, glass, clay, or enamel-coated cookware. Similarly, wooden utensils are best. Use heavy, patio-style glassware and plates rather than china; this is working people's food.

QUINOA WITH SUN-DRIED TOMATOES

1 cup quinoa
1 scant tablespoon olive oil
2 green or spring onions, white and tender greens chopped
6–8 dry-packed, sun-dried tomatoes
1 small chili, chopped (optional)
1 clove garlic, minced (optional)
2 cups stock, water, or mixture
3 tablespoons chopped cilantro

Rinse quinoa under warm running water and drain. Meanwhile, heat oil in heavy saucepan and sauté onions, tomatoes, chili, and garlic until soft but not brown. Add stock and bring to a boil. Stir in quinoa, return the mixture to a boil, then reduce heat and simmer, covered, until liquid is absorbed (about 30 minutes). Let sit 5 minutes, fluff with fork, and season with cilantro. Makes 4 to 6 side servings.

STEWED BLACK BEANS CUBANO

1/2 pound dried black beans
1/3 cup olive oil
1/2 cup chopped onion
1 sweet bell pepper, seeded and cut into large chunks
1 garlic clove, pressed or minced
2 large mild chilies (such as poblanos), seeded and chopped
1 bay leaf
pinch of sugar
1 teaspoon vinegar or wine or sherry
oregano, cumin, and salt to taste

Soak beans overnight, or bring to boil and allow to sit in boiling liquid for 1 hour. Drain, cover with fresh water, and cook until tender. Pour off some of the water, leaving about an inch covering the beans.

In a small skillet over low heat, sauté onion, pepper, garlic, and all seasonings except vinegar until softened but not browned. Add to cooked black beans. Bring to boil and add vinegar. Reduce heat, cover partially, and simmer 15 to 20 minutes, or until somewhat thickened. If it remains runny, remove about 1/2 cup of the beans, mash or purée them, and stir them back into the pot. Serve with white rice. Serves 6.

CHICKEN FRICASSEE

3 pounds chicken, cut into frying pieces
1 tablespoon coarse salt
4 garlic cloves, minced
1/4 teaspoon ground black pepper
1/4 teaspoon ground oregano
1 tablespoon olive oil
1 teaspoon vinegar or cooking wine

1/2 cup diced ham
1 small onion, chopped
1 tomato, skinned, seeded, and chopped
1 small bell pepper, chopped
2 mild chilies, seeded and diced
1/2 cup tomato sauce
6–8 pitted green olives
1 teaspoon capers (optional)
1/4 cup stock or water
3 medium potatoes, peeled and cut into chunks
1/2 cup canned or thawed frozen peas
oil for frying

Rinse chicken pieces and pat dry; rub with salt, garlic, ground pepper, oregano, and oil. Place in a nonreactive dish, sprinkle with vinegar, and marinate at least 30 minutes. Then heat 1/2 inch of oil in heavy skillet, brown chicken, and set aside. Reserve 2 tablespoons oil and heat in a heavy enamal-coated casserole or Dutch oven. Sauté ham, onion, garlic, and pepper and chili peppers for 5 minutes; add tomato sauce, olives, and capers and sauté 5 minutes more. Add chicken pieces and 1/4 cup stock and bring to simmer; add the rest of the stock and the potatoes and raise heat slightly to maintain simmer; cook until chicken is tender.

RED SNAPPER VERACRUZANO

4 large white or red onions
2 heads garlic, peeled
6 large ripe tomatoes
1 1/2 cups olive oil
1 cup pimento-stuffed green olives, chopped
10 bay leaves, dried
12 tablespoons dried oregano
4 teaspoons thyme
salt and pepper to taste
10 dry-packed, sun-dried tomatoes
3 cup fish stock or mixed clam juice and water
3–4 hot chili peppers
1/4 cup sherry or balsamic vinegar or red wine

1/2 cup lime juice
1 4- to 5-pound fresh red snapper
1/2 tablespoon chopped fresh cilantro

For the tomato sauce, chop 2 onions and mince 4 cloves of garlic; peel, seed, and chop fresh tomatoes. Heat 1/2 cup olive oil in frying pan and add 4 whole cloves garlic; fry until browned, then discard. Add the minced garlic and onion and brown lightly; add tomatoes, olives, 4 bay leaves, 1/2 tablespoon oregano, 2 teaspoons thyme, and salt and pepper. Simmer until thick, stirring occasionally (about 2 1/2 hours). Set aside.

For the chili sauce, roughly chop dried tomatoes (see note below). Cut remaining onions in quarters. In a food processor, combine tomatoes, onion, 3 cloves garlic, and fish stock. Heat 1/2 cup olive oil in a frying pan and add blended mixture. Add 1 teaspoon oregano, remaining thyme, and half the chilies. Simmer 1 hour. Add tomato sauce and vinegar or wine and simmer another 30 minutes.

Rinse out processor bowl and add lime juice, remaining garlic, bay leaves, oregano, remaining olive oil, and a dash of salt. Blend and pour over fish in baking dish. Marinate 1–2 hours in refrigerator. Remove from marinade, pat dry and place into larger dish.

Preheat oven to 350°. Moisten fish with a small amount of sauce and bake 90 minutes, basting a couple of times early on. Serve covered with sauce (rewarmed), and put remaining sauce in dish to pass. Garnish with chilies, jalapeños, and cilantro. Serve with rice. Serves 6.

Note: To roast tomatoes, broil either on baking sheet or on griddle over flame, until they turn brown but not black on each side. You can also substitute tomatoes baked until dried or sun-dried tomatoes soaked in warm water and squeezed partly dry.

THE CARIBBEAN ISLANDS

BASIC CUISINE

DINNER FOR TWO:
Bakes, jerk chicken
wings, goat curry,
escabeche red snapper

DINNER FOR FOUR:
Shrimp beignets, jerk
chicken, callaloo, goat
curry, red snapper,
peanut butter stew

STYLE:
Spicy, starchy, rooty,
sweet-sour

KEY FLAVORS:
Pepper, allspice,
coconut, salted and
smoked fish, vinegar,
brown sugar

EATING UTENSILS:
Fingers, forks

DISTINCTIVE FOODS:
"Jerk" barbecue, cod
fritters, goat curry

NUTRITIONAL INDEX:
High starch and protein,
medium sodium and fat

UNIFORMITY OF MENUS:
Good

COST:
Inexpensive

The Caribbean Sea has been called the "American Mediterranean," partly because of its clear and fertile water but also because it was first colonized by the Mediterranean rivals— Spain, Portugal, and France—before the Netherlands and England followed them in. It might also have to do with the great pirate fleets: Henry Morgan, Blackbeard, Jean Lafitte, and Sir Francis Drake all made and lost fortunes trading spices and rum in the American waters.

But as strong a place as it has in our romantic topography, the Caribbean has barely begun to take shape on our culinary map—outside, perhaps, of Miami. In fact, its greatest contribution to the American diet—barbecue—isn't generally recognized as Caribbean at all. The great majority of "Caribbean" restaurants in the United States are Jamaican, which has produced interesting cultural sidelights: Many Jamaican immigrants who had previously sought assimilation have found new ethnic pride in the youth market's embrace of reggae music and Rasta slang and fashions. The Rastafarian prohibition on eating meat dovetails with the increasing interest in vegetarian establishments, and the traditional spicy-style "jerk" dishes fit the boom in peppery cuisines.

And, like the West African restaurants, Jamaican restaurants—particularly those that feature Creole specialties—recall the islands' ethnic ties to American black culture, a fact that has made them "politically correct" in many urban areas and has contributed to their growing numbers. (Although Cuba is geographically a Caribbean island, its cuisine is far more traditionally Indian and Spanish; see the chapter on Mexican, Central American, and Cuban restaurants.)

THE COUNTRIES

There are hundreds of islands included in the sweeping phrase "Caribbean," the vast majority of them small and virtually unknown except to fishermen and scuba divers. The largest land masses—Cuba, Jamaica, Hispaniola (Haiti and the Dominican Republic), and Puerto Rico—form a short, thick line called the Greater Antilles, which juts out from the mouth of the Gulf of Mexico like a rude tongue. The Bahamas mark a long, slightly flattened curve from offshore southeast Florida to near Haiti; the Lesser Antilles, including Trinidad and Tobago, Curaçao, Barbados, Aruba, St. Martin, Guadaloupe, St. Lucia, and so forth, bulge out again and touch down near Venezuela. In fact, the cuisines and cultures of much of northern South America, particularly, Guyana, Suriname, and French Guiana, are more closely related to the Caribbean islands than to the rest of the continent.

Within this great crescent, framed by the curve of Mexico and the Yucatan peninsula, the Caribbean Sea flows in a warming, counterclockwise direction, brushing the Gulf of Mexico and opening via straits and canals to both the Atlantic and the Pacific. Despite frequent volcanic eruptions and violent storms and hurricanes, the region has a benevolent climate; temperatures rarely stray outside the 70° to 85° range. The water is always warm and is less salty than the Atlantic as well, almost pollution-free and famously filled with exotic plants and animal life.

Traditionally, the great plantation crop has been sugarcane, used for making molasses and, even more profitably in the beginning, rum. The other cash crops are coffee (particularly in Jamaica, where the Blue Mountain beans are a premium export), tobacco (which gave the island of Tobago its name), bananas, cocoa, and spiny lobsters. Subsistence farmers, meanwhile, depend heavily on plantains and yams, breadfruit, cassava, sorghum, rice, and corn, along with a wide variety of citrus and tropical fruits and beans. Spice is legion here, seafood is plentiful, and goat is the most popular meat—particularly since the mountainous terrain makes grazing sheep and cattle problematical. (*Haiti* means "land of mountains" in the indigenous Arawak.) The exception is the prosperous and appropriately named Puerto Rico—the "rich port" of the Spanish colonists—where livestock cultivation runs a close second to sugarcane.

THE HISTORY

The islands are naturally fertile and hospitable. The original inhabitants, the Arawaks, were a pacific people who scarcely even needed to cultivate land; they lived comfortably on the available fruits and vegetables, primarily cassava, yams, papayas, and pineapples—and caught fish and the odd iguana or boar for meat. However, a closely related tribe, the Carib, were extremely aggressive and ritually sacrificial—their name, corrupted by the Spanish to *Galibi*, is the source of the word "cannibal"—and they easily overran the Arawak, scavenging freely among the islands. So many Carib warriors took Arawak women as wives (or slaves) that it became customary for all women to speak Arawak, the subservient tongue, and men to speak Carib.

It was in the islands that a physician among Columbus's second expeditionary force first recognized that the chilies the natives used as preservatives not only aided in the digestion but also packed a powerful gustatory punch. And since this was only a few years after Vasco de Gama's tour around the toe of Africa had launched an inflationary market for Eastern spices, the pepperlike chilies the Spanish fleet carried back eventually proved to be of immense value.

Not so, apparently, the natives, who suffered violently from the combined onslaught of European pestilence, slavery, and enforced conversion. The indigenous populations were virtually wiped out by the end of the sixteenth century, only 100 years after the Europeans arrived; and to replace their labor, the colonists soon began importing slaves—not just West Africans but also North American and Mexican Indians taken by the Spanish and French, as well as a few indentured Europeans hoping to escape poverty at home. The Caribbean became one vital point of a merchant triangle that exchanged African slaves for Jamaican rum and the rum for tea and European textiles.

After the banning of slavery by Great Britain in 1838, Indian and Chinese laborers were imported to work the plantations. Even the fledgling Americans had a part in the Caribbean melting pot, particularly after the discovery of gold in California made the Panama passage so important.

Today, the descendants of Africans are the dominant ethnic group in all but the Spanish-colonized islands. The intermixing of black, European, and Indian blood ironically produced the very thing the Eurocentric caste system was designed to prevent—the Creole, a new and inescapably New World creature.

THE CUISINE

Like the people themselves, the cuisine of the Caribbean is a little this, a little that, part native, part imported, and part synthesized and new. Although the obvious culinary influences are African, French, and Spanish, there are strong Middle Eastern and Indonesian elements that recall the Dutch, Portuguese, and British trade empires (notably tamarind, ginger, coconut milk, eggplant, olives, and nutmeg and its side-product, mace). The overwhelming popularity of curry spices, along with rice and *roti* (wheat-flour crepes), recalls the Indian immigration.

The British installed the custom of high tea, along with Yorkshire pudding and other doughy reminders of the empire—Irish stew, hot cross buns, and fish and chips; the working-class staple called a Cornish pastie, dough stuffed with ground meat, is now an island favorite called a pasty. Residents of Curaçao, a longtime Dutch stronghold (and home of the citrus-spiked liqueur that bears its name), are addicted to a dish called *keshy yena*—Edam cheese stuffed with meat. And one of the most famous elements of Jamaican cuisine, "jerk" spices, is probably a memento of the fiercely resistant Maroons—black slaves who fled into the mountains in the mid-seventeenth century, when Britain wrested the island away from the Spanish, and remained there for nearly a century until being guaranteed independence.

The most visible influence is the West African, and many ingredients and recipes of the islands directly replicate those of Gambia and the Ivory Coast area: The Africans introduced yams and the fermented cassava dough called *gari*. They also "returned" the peanuts, black-eyed peas, okra, and plantains that early Portuguese traders had discovered in South America and taken to Africa.

From Spain came the olives, capers, pork, garlic, and cilantro that characterize Dominican and Puerto Rican dishes; the Spanish also established the practice of raising chickens, for meat as well as eggs; the Indians had relied on waterfowl and the occasional nest raid. French colonies, such as Guadaloupe and Martinique, had a very strong relationship with the mother country, particularly in the lavish mid-eighteenth century—Napoleon's Josephine was born in Martinique, and her rather loose morals were often blamed on the tropical climate—

BBQ Bonanza
Barbecue, that great American favorite, is not Texan or Southern, though both areas claim it; instead, it is Indian. The Arawaks preserved their meat by smoking it over green wood, a method that the Spanish later disseminated into Mexico (i.e., Texas) and Florida. The Arawak word for the smoking pit was *brabacot*, which the Spanish corrupted to *barbacao*. Its similarity to *barbe a queue*, meaning "whiskers to tail," is strictly coincidental, but it makes a great pun.

and their cuisine still features cream sauces and green herbs. In the mid-nineteenth century, the Chinese and Indian laborers radically expanded the regional diet by introducing tofu, rice, wheat flour, mangoes, and curry spices; a technique for boiling coconut milk down into a cream base; and the wok, used to stir-fry vegetables.

Puerto Rico, at the eastern gate of the Caribbean, was among the first islands settled and, despite the repeated attempts of the French, British, and Dutch to acquire it, remained staunchly Spanish, at least in the north. In the south, facing South America and the other islands, it was a busy contraband market. It is the most populous of the islands, having been the most prosperous; and it still has one of the densest populations in the world.

Puerto Rican cuisine is noticeably more meat-heavy than some of its neighbors, and its otherwise fairly straightforward dishes are primarily distinguished by their Spanish, rather than curry- or jerk-style, mixtures of spices. Adobo, a chili-spice barbecue that the Spanish developed in Puerto Rico, turned out to be so addictive that they carried it through Mexico and westward to the Philippines, where it is now the national dish. In return the Puerto Ricans adopted paella, and they still serve an elaborate version. In Puerto Rico's "better" restaurants there are also strong reminders of the Italians, Germans, and French, who began vacationing and trading there in the nineteenth century, but little of that has moved to the United States.

THE MAIN INGREDIENTS

FRUITS   Thanks to the generous climate, the region offers both sweet and citrus fruits: mangoes, pineapple, passionfruit, coconuts, guava, bananas, and plantains, plus oranges, lemons, limes, and grapefruit. So-called jelly coconuts are unripe coconuts whose meat has a jellylike consistency. Tamarinds are sold in markets as pulp as well as a seasoning juice. *Carambola*, also known here as star fruit or star apple, is a starfish-shaped citrusy fruit that slices into stars. Another exotic fruit is *chirimoya*, sometimes called the custard apple; the fruit is halved and its soft, creamy flesh is eaten with a spoon.

Papayas, called "paw-paws" in the American South, are rosy-colored and quite large; they contain a natural tenderizer (which is now being synthesized), and meats are traditionally wrapped in papaya leaves overnight. The sorrel is a bright red fruit with a green pit and sweet-tart flavor. The soursop, also known as the corossol or guana-bana, is a shiny, dark-green fruit that vaguely resembles an artichoke outside but has a cottony or creamy white flesh inside.

STARCHES   The staples are breadfruit, cassava, rice, and sweet potatoes and yams (which are actually different species, though in the American South the "yam" is a sweet potato). Breadfruit, the notorious diet of the *H.M.S. Bounty*, was imported from Tahiti and is used much as potatoes are—fried, roasted, or sliced into chips. (It doesn't look like bread, incidentally, but like a dimpled beachball or overripe melon.) Cornmeal is often referred to by its Indian name, *masa harina*, if it is ground particularly fine. Cassava root is variously known as yucca and manioc and is the source of tapioca flour as well; sometimes it's ground and fried into a mealcake called *bammy*. *Gari* is roasted, rough-ground, and fermented cassava flour. Wheat flour, introduced by the Indian laborers, is used for a variety of (primarily flat) breads.

VEGETABLES   Beans and peas—including, red, black, pink, kidney, and turtle beans, and black-eyed peas—are a reliable source of protein. The most common squashes include pumpkins (or *calabaza*, a corruption of "calabash"), butternut, and hubbard, along with the chayote or christophene, which has become a supermarket staple. *Callaloo* refers to greens, but broadly—it can be either of two plants, one called taro or *choux Caribe*, among other names, and the other known as Indian kale or Chinese spinach. (In some islands callaloo is a stew; see "Soups," page 340.) *Dasheen* is a root vegetable with purple flesh.

SEASONINGS   The most popular flavorings are chilies, ginger, allspice (both berries and leaves), cane vinegar (slightly sweetened with molasses), curry mixes, grated coconut (coconut oil is the cooking medium of choice), nutmeg, peppers, and *cassareep*, a thick blend of boiled-down cassava juice, cinnamon, cloves, brown sugar, and other flavorings. Of these, the chilies are the most obvious; some of the world's hottest chilies originate in the Caribbean, including the notorious Scotch bonnet (*habañero*), fierce bird peppers, and the evocativly named *piment negresse*—whole allspice. One of the oldest condiments in the islands, *piment negresse* is essential for traditional pepperpot stew. Rum, of course, is also a flavoring, along with molasses. And since curries are so popular, Indian-style chutneys—particularly light, fresh versions that mix peppers and fruits or herbs—are common condiments for both fish and meat.

The distinctive *ackee* is served almost exclusively in Jamaica. The red pod of an ornamental tree, ackee can be deadly if picked before it ripens. (When the pod splits to reveal the edible yellow flesh within, natives says the fruit is "smiling.") It looks like scrambled eggs but has a lemony flavor.

FISH AND SHELLFISH   Obviously, seafood is abundant in the islands, including conch, shrimp, crayfish, grouper, mullet, sunfish, spiny lobsters (actually a variety of crawfish, with two large meat-filled "antennae" instead of enlarged front claws), crabs, flying fish (so abundant that Barbados is nicknamed "Land of the Flying Fish"), codfish, snapper, and jackfish. A spiny mollusk roe is eaten much as sea urchin roe is. The Iberian occupation ensured the adoption of salt cod into the diet; West African–style smoked fish is also quite common.

MEATS AND POULTRY   Goat and kid are prized meats, but pork and mutton and the occasional game, venison, or boar are also popular. Beef as steak is primarily tourist-resort fare, but the lesser cuts, particularly ground beef, are fairly common.

POULTRY AND DAIRY Both chicken and ducks are widely raised, and some islands have some game birds available; turkey is becoming more standard. Eggs were not a traditional element in Indian cooking, and since cattle were unknown until the Spanish conquest, milk, cream, cheese, and butter have limited roles as well.

THE MAIN DISHES

APPETIZERS Jerked chicken wings or "drumettes," miniature-sized beef pasties, and codfish balls are common first courses. Bakes are peppery biscuits or fried beignets that can be plain or stuffed with shark or swordfish or some other fish; crab may be fried into cornmeal fritters. Conch needs to be tenderized through pounding or scoring and is most commonly turned into fritters or chowders. Many restaurants also offer smoked fish or fish-and-cornmeal crackers. Chinese-style barbecued or sweet-and-sour ribs and egg rolls are common in some areas.

SOUPS Whether as a first course or as a whole meal, Caribbean soups tend to be hearty and filling. Fish and/or meat is often added to a broth that is thickened with starch, either cornmeal (*fufu*) or ground rice. Peanut soups with either chicken or dried shrimp are popular, and pumpkin soups are quite common. Callaloo is both a vegetable and a Creole soup, sometimes identified as pepperpot soup; although there is no standard recipe, it generally includes the spinachlike callaloo leaf, crabmeat, okra, and coconut milk.

ONE-POT DISHES Puerto Ricans are fond of what they call *asopaos*, rice-based stews with either chicken or seafood. Another Puerto Rican favorite is *mofongo*, a sort of skillet torte with a mashed plantain "dough" and grilled or fried meat on top. Almost every Caribbean restaurant has some version of "hopping john," that African-American staple of rice and beans (black-eyed peas, red or pigeon beans, etc.), sometimes cooked with coconut milk. *Cou-cou* is not cous-cous, though it looks similar; it is actually derived from the Gambian way of mixing fufu, or cornmeal, with okra. *Pelaus* are flavored rice dishes derived from Indian pilaus and, before that, from Persian pilafs.

Metagee is a sort of layered casserole, with root vegetables on the bottom, followed by okra or greens, potatoes, and pumpkin and then fish or shellfish on top. It is most popular in the southern islands and South American coast and is sometimes called *sancoch*.

MEATS AND POULTRY Caribbean recipes are defined more by style than by main ingredient. Jerk can be applied to almost any meat, though chicken and goat are the most common. Curry is probably the second most common type of recipe. Goat is the most popular curry, but the dish is also made with shrimp, mutton, lamb, or whole fish, and frequently with vegetables or tofu. *Roti*, a split wheat or pea-flour pancake, is often rolled around conch or chicken or vegetable curry.

Chicken is also stewed with peanut butter, as in West Africa; mixed with coconut and orange juice, as in Malaysia; and smothered in tomatoes and olives, as in Spain.

SEAFOOD Another characteristic treatment for seafood is a vinegary chutney called *escabeche* (or escho-vishe, escoveitche, or caveach), which can refer either to a cooking sauce itself or to a sauce-"cured" raw seafood, like a Caribbean ceviche. Whole fresh fish, particularly snapper, may be stewed in a tomato and onion sauce, curried, or even jerked. Catfish appears stuffed with crab and shrimp and sauced with bearnaise in a classic French Creole dish you'd expect to see in New Orleans. On the other hand, the Chinese influence shows up when fish are steamed with ginger and garlic; and tamarind, an Indonesian flavor, is popular in Trinidad. Fish is sometimes smoked as well, particularly for use in West African–style stews featuring peanut butter. The more modern or international kitchens, particularly in the resort areas, have taken to jerk-rubbing tuna and just searing it into a cross between sashimi and Cajun blackened fish.

Salt cod is often chopped into patties and fried into the island quick-snack called "stamp and go." Whether that phrase refers to stamping out the cakes or stamping your foot in impatience isn't clear. Salt fish is also essential for "rundown," which is a sort of curry or stew using simmered-down coconut milk.

BEVERAGES The Caribbean islands may be as well known for their drinks as for their cuisine. Rum comes in hundreds of varieties and

---

Do the Jerk

Probably the most famous Jamaican style of cooking is called "jerk," which refers to a type of hot spice-rubbed and pit-barbecued meat or chicken that probably originated with the Maroons; they used a combination of salt and chilies to preserve the meat, and in the United States their invention has become an immensely popular method of cooking chicken—the original "hot wings."

flavors and is mixed with any and all fruit juices. (Juices themselves are available in dizzying supply: passionfruit, guava, guana, mango, papaya, pineapple, coconut milk, etc.) "Irish moss" is a sort of seaweed brewed into a very soothing creamy shake. Ginger is the source of several popular drinks, not only the original ginger ale but also ginger wine (a currant wine steeped in ginger) and ginger beer, which is not alcoholic. Other "real" beers are also brewed locally—the most famous example is Red Stripe—and a Guinness factory in Jamaica keeps the islands supplied with stout.

DESSERTS Among the most popular desserts are banana puddings, bread and rum puddings (along with some rather bland and doughy puddings that recall the dimmer facets of the British Empire), mixed fruit salads, fried plantains, coconut custard, ginger cakes and cookies, and plain preserved ginger. "Tie-me-up" is a cornmeal mush "tied up" or wrapped in a banana leaf for steaming; it can be either sweet or savory. Sweet punches are often served in lieu of desserts.

HOW TO ORDER AND EAT LIKE A NATIVE

Ordering in a Caribbean restaurant is fairly easy, since most menus are divided American-style into appetizers and entrees, and their names are quite uniform (except for that pesky escabeche). In fact, however, the best way to become familiar with the food may be to order as many appetizers as are appealing, two at a time, and then perhaps try a goat curry or escabeche. (It is also wise to go slow, because "appetizers," like most street foods, sometimes show up in large portions.) Many of these are finger foods, ideal for conversation: crab fritters, "shark bites," cod fritters, jerk chicken wings, etc. Two people should try one fried-seafood dumpling or bakes and some jerk chicken wings, then share a curry, preferably goat or vegetable, and a whole fish either baked or escabeche-style. For four add a soup—callaloo if available—and a peanut butter and chicken stew or okra gumbo.

When it comes to curries and stews (or any dish that comes sided with red beans and rice, revealing its Spanish origins), you may use a fork, although many Caribbean residents continue to eat African-based and Indian dishes with their fingers.

COOKING AT HOME

Most Caribbean cooking is done outside, either on grills or in large pots. However, unless you feel up to digging a real smoke pit, most island foods can be reproduced using pots or an outdoor grill; even the broiler will do. Like curry powders, jerk rubs are individualized and can be customized to taste. There are a fair number of hot sauces and jerk rubs available in specialty groceries in the United States, but it's fun to develop your own version. Here's a starter—and, incidentally, a little goes a long way.

JERK RUB

1 onion, finely chopped
2/3 cup scallions, finely chopped
2 teaspoons fresh thyme
1 1/2 teaspoons salt
1 teaspoon ground allspice
1/4 teaspoon ground nutmeg
2 teaspoons ground cinnamon
2–4 hot chilies such as habanero, jalapeño, or serrano, chopped
1 1/2 teaspoons ground black pepper
1 tablespoon dark rum or molasses (optional)

Mix ingredients in food processor or blender to make paste; rub well into uncooked meat or poultry. Store rub in jar or tightly covered container for up to a month. Makes approximately 1 cup.

JAMAICAN JERK CHICKEN BREASTS

1 tablespoon Jerk Rub (see recipe above)
4 large chicken breast halves, skinned, bone in

Smear chickens with thin coating of jerk rub (or to taste) and place in lightly oiled glass dish; cover and marinate in refrigerator 2 to 3 hours. Preheat oven to 275°; bake, covered, about 25 minutes or until nearly done, then finish under broiler. (Note: If crispier finished is desired, leave skin on.)

CODFISH FRITTERS

1/2 pound codfish fillet, skinned
1/4 cup grated coconut
1/4 cup spring onion, finely chopped
1 egg, lightly beaten
2 tablespoons bread crumbs
1 clove garlic, minced
1 teaspoon Worcestershire sauce
2 tablespoons fresh cilantro or parsley, chopped
2 teaspoons jerk mix (see above) or curry mix
Oil for frying

Puree fish in food processor, combine with other ingredients, and shape into patties; fry until deep golden, about 1 minute on each side; drain on paper towels. Serve with chutney, salsa, or any fresh fruit chopped with mint and lime juice.

SOUTH AMERICA: BRAZIL, PERU, AND ARGENTINA

BASIC CUISINE

DINNER FOR TWO:
Black bean soup, ceviche, smothered whole fish, cabrito

DINNER FOR FOUR:
Antichucos, crab chupes, potatoes huancaina, escabeche fish, roast pork, grilled chicken

GROUP DISH:
Feijoada

STYLE:
Spicy, tropical, nutty

KEY FLAVORS:
Chilies, coconut and palm oil, corn, tomatoes, beef

DISTINCTIVE FOODS:
Feijoada, empanadas, churrasco

EATING UTENSILS:
Forks and knives, fingers

NUTRITIONAL INDEX:
Starchy, high fiber (north); high fat, creamy (Brazil); high cholesterol (south)

UNIFORMITY OF MENUS:
Good

COST:
Inexpensive to moderate

"THANK YOU":
"Gracias" (Spanish), "Obrigado" or "Obrigada" (Portuguese, masculine or feminine)

South American cuisine is as yet little known in most parts of the United States, although that is likely to change quickly. Many supposedly Central American establishments are actually Peruvian, Ecuadorian, etc. The prime per-pound beef of Argentina was just beginning to appear in fancy American cities as the role of red meat in our diets began to shrink; however, with the renewed popularity of so-called Australian and Japanese steakhouses, Argentine *churrascarias* cannot be far behind. In addition, a growing number of Brazilian restaurants are moving in behind the craze for Caribbean island foods and rum punches (and such suspect "native" Rio dances as the lambada and commercialized samba).

THE COUNTRIES

The ice cream cone–shaped continent is the fourth largest, though not one of the more populous. Although South America is so large— 4,750 miles top to bottom and 3,300 miles at the widest—it is sharply marked by the high spine of the Andes Mountains, which run north

In many ways, the regional cuisines mirror those of North America; if you folded the two continents at about the middle of Central America, the Guianas and Brazilian coast would meet the Caribbean and Florida Keys, Peru would overlie Mexico, and the cattle ranges and sheep ranches of Argentina would come close to matching the old Texas-Montana cattle trails. Even the long stretch of Chile, with its pockets of temperate-to-wet mountainside and lightly acidic soil, would follow the wine-growing west coast from California to Washington.

to south and separate the deserts from the well-watered territory; the highlands of the northeast and upper Brazil, wedged apart by the the equatorial Amazon River basin; and the long continental slope into the flat pampas of the south. The continent has limited natural ports or arable land; it is part tropical, part alpine, part desert, and only rarely temperate.

The northeast curve of the continent shoulders up into the curve of the Caribbean Sea and enjoys its warm climate and abundant seafood. Below that is the broad bulge of Brazil, with the vast Amazon basin and rainforests covering the upper third; the fertile southeast "belly" of the Bahia region and Rio de Janeiro; and the plains tapering toward the pampas in the south. On the Pacific coast, the Andes slice right down the continent, from just west of the Central American isthmus to the tip of Chile. A large percentage of the coastal region is desert, and although the Peruvian portion of the Andean ranges are wide and relatively fertile, in Chile they are steep and arid. To the east the mountains stretch away into great pasturelands and plains.

The population of the northwestern Andes, Peru, Ecuador, Colombia, and Bolivia, is overwhelmingly Indian and mestizo; Chile is also primarily mestizo, with small but distinct German, French, British, Italian, and even Yugoslavian communities.

Argentina, on the other hand, is predominantly European—Italian and Spanish, but also French, German, Swiss and Eastern European—except for some mestizo villages in the northwest, near Peru. Southeastern Brazil, the most populous region, is truly Creole—a mixture of Indian, African, and European that its citizens boast of as "a new race." The Amazon rainforest is inhabited almost entirely by natives.

THE HISTORY

Like North and Central America, South America has seen much of its native civilization obscured, if not erased, by the European colonial empires. However, the great Quechua empire of Peru (ruled by the Inca, whose title is often applied to the entire nation) had developed highly sophisticated techniques of irrigation and selective breeding thousands of years before the Spanish and Portuguese arrived at the turn of the sixteenth century. By about 3,000 B.C. they had domesticated the remarkably intelligent and willing llama—an animal whose virtues are gradually becoming known in the United States—which supplied not only transportation but also food, clothing, and fuel. They had several ways of preserving food and built silos or warehouses throughout the empire to guard against times of drought or extended winter cold.

The Quechua empire, though centered in Peru, included modern-day Colombia, Ecuador, and Bolivia and reached into Brazil and down into Chile and Argentina. They constructed highways the Romans would have envied: Two extended the 2500-mile length of the empire, one down the coast and another actually through the Andes. They also established a remarkably sophisticated system of aqueducts that carried water up the mountains to the terraced farms, where quinoa, maize, barley, potatoes, sweet potatoes, and beans were cultivated. It was an orderly empire, with prohibitions against murder and theft that made the Quechuas all too susceptible to the warlike Spanish. Because they refused to serve as slaves, even after Pizarro's conquest of Cuzco and the assassination of the Inca, more Quechuas actually died by mass execution than by the epidemic diseases brought by the Europeans.

Thanks to the Treaty of Tordesillas, which may have preceded the actual discovery of Brazil, the Portuguese were "given" Brazil and the Spanish received the rest of South America; hence the Brazilians speak Portuguese, while in most of the other countries, the official language is Spanish (see the chapter on Spain and Portugal). In the northeastern nations (the Guianas), Dutch, English, and French are spoken.

THE CUISINES

Although there are more than a dozen countries on the continent, three regional cuisines dominate both the other South American countries and South American restaurants in the United States: Brazilian, with its mixed Portuguese, African, and West Indian influences; Peruvian, based (like Mexican and Central American) on the foods of its pre-Columbian natives; and the European-influenced food of the southern "cone," particularly Argentina and, to a lesser degree, Chile. (The northeastern countries, which are near neighbors and climactic cousins of the Caribbean islands, have Caribbean-style cuisines; see the chapter on the Caribbean region.)

Brazilian food is the most truly Creole, partly because it was a Portuguese rather than Spanish colony, and the Portuguese were heavily involved in West Indian trading; partly because a large number of West African slaves were imported to work the sugar plantations; and partly because its tropical climate not only provides it with abundant seafood but is hospitable to more fresh fruits and flavorings. The eastern and southeastern part of the country, particularly along the coast between Salvador and Rio de Janeiro, is the most populous region, with many excellent harbors that historically attracted the attention of other European fleets as well: The Dutch actually held Bahia for about 30 years in the middle of the seventeenth century, contributing more Indonesian spices and a taste for cheese; and the Italian sailors found the climate so homelike that thousands never went home—hence the surprising number of Italian restaurants in both Brazil and Argentina.

Before the arrival of the Europeans, the few indigenous Indians of Brazil—mostly Quechuas, in the west—depended primarily on manioc, from which they made a flour called *farinha* (and from that the toasted, nutty thickener/flavoring called *farofa*); Mexican maize, from which they made both tamale meal and mush; greens such as collards and kale; beans; citrus fruits; and fish. The restless Portuguese immediately established in Brazil, as they did everywhere, their beloved salt cod (bacalao) and fried shrimp (the same "tempura" they later introduced to the Japanese), garlic, wine, the sugar that became the first great plantation crop, and the use of egg yolks to emulsify and bind sauces. They also taught the Indians, who traditionally slow-cooked meats whole in pits lined with heated stones, to stew meats and vegetables together.

The Africans introduced yams, okra, dried shrimp, bananas, palm nuts and palm oil, and coconut and coconut oil; although the peanut was native to North America, the Africans had quickly mastered its potential and carried it back and forth to the Caribbean and Brazil. The slaves were also the first to create what might be considered a "culture" of cuisine in Brazil, by infusing the practice of cooking with mystical and religious elements that made recipes (and respected cooks) far more respected institutions.

Brazilian Creole cooking is best known for a flavoring combination of coconut milk (squeezed from freshly grated coconut meat), dried shrimp, and hot malagueta peppers, along with rich avocado and ground nuts. Its other most obvious element is dende oil, the West African palm oil that lends not only a unique flavor but also a characteristic yellow-orange color to dishes and is thus sometimes confused with saffron. This visibly hybrid cuisine, which is increasingly popular in the United States, is also referred to as "Bahia" cuisine, after the port of Bahia (also called Salvador) on the east coast of Brazil, just below the lip.

Brazil is also home to a number of West Indian and Chinese immigrants; and curry spices, lamb dishes, stir-fries, lentil and vegetable stews, tamarind sauces, and chutney and rice dishes show these influences.

Peruvian cuisine is, like that of Mexico and Central America, still heavily influenced by the indigenous foods, though cen-

Ethnic Imports

Despite its great land mass, South America is populated primarily at the edges; virtually everyone, with the exception of some deep-Amazon tribes, lives within 200 miles of the coast. Most of the major cities are along the coast, too; and the many European immigrants have established tight communities and restaurants to feed them. Italian immigrants have outnumbered all others in the last century; hence, a surprising number of the restaurants in Rio de Janeiro are Italian, and most Argentine kitchens, even the steakhouses, offer pastas as the alternative. It's not uncommon to find German dumplings and strudels in Chile and Venezuela, Dutch/Indonesian rijsttafel in Guyana, even Scotch haggis in Brazil. Chinese, Japanese, and Greek restaurants, with their flair for seafood, are increasingly common up and down the eastern coastal resorts.

tral elements have been borrowed from the Spanish. (One could consider the foods of the Andean villages, where the Quechuas retreated as the Europeans advanced, the only "authentic" South American cooking.) The Quechua raised some 80 varieties of potatoes, of which more than 30 are still eaten, including the newly trendy purple, golden, and "transparent" varieties; potatoes in a variety of chili-spiced, cheesy, and chicken-flavored dishes are still prominent on Peruvian menus. Although the Quechuas were first given corn by their neighbors to the north in Mexico and Central America, they themselves eventually isolated hundreds of varieties of corn; one, called *callemote*, has kernels the size of popped corn that are peeled and eaten as a snack. They also turned corn into a beer, called *chicha*.

The Quechua employed a variety of preservation techniques: air-drying, freeze-drying, salting, and sun-drying. They were the ones who first air-dried potatoes and powdered them into the cornstarch we still use in cooking and cosmetics today. The primary meat, although it was wisely limited, came from the llamas and vicuñas that were domesticated millennia earlier; air-dried llama meat is called *charqui*— the original "jerky." Chickens were by some accounts already present, though they were not raised as livestock until the arrival of the Europeans.

The Spanish introduced beef, sheep, goats, and hogs to the Indians, thereby not only increasing the proportion of meat in the diet but also vastly upping the fat quotient; instead of baking or boiling, the Indians were now frying, and dairy products such as cream and cheese also became common. They brought wine, and introduced the planting of vines, along with the eggplants, rice, coffee, almonds, and spices they had adopted from the Moors. They also brought olives, though here, as in Mexico, they prevented the Indians from raising their own and challenging their market monopoly.

Among the seafood Peruvians love most are anchovies, which are grilled fresh or salt-cured or marinated as a seasoning; shrimp (the heads of which are also used as flavoring); mussels and scallops; trout; and red snapper. Bolivia, which is landlocked, has almost identical cuisine except for the seafood; instead, they have giant frogs and fine freshwater fish, including trout and smelt, from Lake Titicaca. They also use somewhat more chilies and spices in their dishes.

Argentina was only lightly populated before the Europeans arrived, and consequently has almost no indigenous cuisine. Its greatest influences are topographical rather than historical—the interior plains and the rich northeast seacoast.

The pampas, the 400-mile-wide grasslands, are the breadbasket of the region, supplying wheat, alfalfa, and corn and also pastureland for the cattle, sheep, and dairy cows. Cattle-ranching has much the same mystique in Argentina as it has in the American West, and the gaucho, the cowboy of the Argentina plains, is similarly a figure of legend. (Many of them were actually black or mestizo Brazilian slaves who fled the sugar plantations and signed on to cattle drives.) Beef was introduced into the area in the mid-sixteenth century, and by the eighteenth century cattle were running wild. Today Argentine beef is among the world's most prized. Along the eastern coast and in the oases of the western desert, farmers cultivate fruit, including wine grapes, corn, and some sugarcane.

Chile offers a rather daunting vista on a map—265 miles at the widest and squeezed between the Andes on the east and the desert seacoast on the west—but it has a hospitable, Mediterranean region in the center that allows for the cultivation of oats, potatoes, wheat, corn, vegetables, and fruits, including wine grapes. Cattle and pigs are raised in the north, sheep and cattle in the south. And the thin, cold-current ocean supplies unexpected luxuries: the conger eels called *congrios*, giant sea urchins (*erizos*), crabs, shrimp, abalone, mussels, oysters, and many oily-fleshed fish.

THE MAIN INGREDIENTS

SEASONINGS The strongest indigenous spices are, of course, the chili peppers, followed by the *achiote* or annatto, a reddish spice something like nutmeg with a punch, and chocolate—used, in the Aztec manner, to flavor some stews. The other major flavors are coconut, rums and fortified wines, the Indonesian spices (turmeric, ginger, mace, cinnamon, cumin, allspice, coriander), Spanish cayenne, Turkish paprika, garlic, vanilla, flavored vinegar, olives and olive oil, palm oil (dende), cilantro, lime, lemon, thyme, dill, mint, sage, and rosemary. Marinated anchovies are often used as a flavoring, too, and the toasted farofa, called farina, is indispensable in Brazilian cooking; it is almost always served in a bowl on the table, as Americans would have sugar.

VEGETABLES As we mentioned above, the Quechuas cultivated some 80 varieties of potatoes, and perhaps three dozen types are still fairly common. Beans (kidney, black, red, yellow, white, garbanzo, string, and lima), peas, and lentils provide crucial proteins; greens (lettuce, watercress, mache, kale, cabbage, chard, spinach), root vegetables (turnips, carrots, fennel, celeriac), squashes and pumpkin, jicama, avocado,

Imported Fat

South American cuisine employs an unusual variety of cooking fats, most of them imported: rendered duck and goose fat, lard, butter, clarified butter, sesame oil, palm oil, coconut oil, rendered bacon and ham fat, olive oil, and corn oil. Unfortunately, the last two, which are the most healthful, are the least common. In some areas, particularly in the cities, American vegetable shortening has become popular, apparently because many people believe it (from its appearance) to be lard. So remember, most fried or sautéed foods—and that includes most with precooked sauces—pack a double whammy. Try to stick to grilled, roasted, steamed, or escabeche-style dishes whenever possible.

broccoli, tomatoes, onions, and olives are also common. Brazilians also have access to a variety of ferns and funghi.

GRAINS AND DOUGHS Corn is, of course, the most important, and is used as hominy, as whole-grain meals, as finer meals (*masa harina*), fermented, and as mush; when dried, it produces a very fine starch. Quinoa is a highly nutritious, nutty-flavored grain; barley, rice, and some wheat and wheat flour are also used. Yucca and cassava flour are very common, particularly toward the north. Doughs for empanadas may include extra butter (some are virtually puff pastries), lard, or potato, yucca, or plantain mashes as well.

FRUITS AND NUTS The South American *limon* tastes more like a lime (they call the North American type "sweet lemons"). Pineapple, quince, mango, plantain, figs, dates, prunes, oranges, custard apples, papaya, breadfruit, grapes and raisins, pears, apples, and coconut are the most common, but a few areas, particularly in the north, also grow peaches and berries. Some nuts grew wild in South America, such as pecans, Brazil nuts, and walnuts, but the Spanish brought along a lot of the Middle Eastern nuts and spices the Moors had brought to them, particularly almonds, cashews, hazelnuts, and walnuts, and pignolis from their North American territories; the Africans passed along peanuts.

FISH AND SEAFOOD Chile, Argentina, and Brazil, with their long coastlines, and the northern states adjoining the Caribbean islands enjoy a huge variety of fresh fish, including anchovies, abalone, bonita, tuna, swordfish, flounder, sole, trout, bass, sardines, a rainbow of snappers, shrimp in all sizes, shellfish (mussels, clams, scallops, crabs), squid, octopus, lobsters, and crabs. In Bolivia, which is landlocked but opens onto Lake Titicaca, giant frogs and river shrimp or crayfish are special-ties. And in Chile, conger eels are highly prized.

POULTRY AND WILDFOWL The chicken may have reached South America before Columbus arrived (it is one of the possible bits of evidence of a very early Chinese trade), but it was considered a poor alternative to turkey, wild turkey, squab, duck, quail, grouse, pheasant, and partridge. Argentina even has a kind of ostrich, the emu, the huge legs of which are considered delicacies.

EGG AND DAIRY PRODUCTS Since the arrival of the Europeans, eggs have become a fairly important ingredient in soups, emulsions, and sauces; but they are often now used as meals in them-selves: scrambled, fried, as omelets, etc. The Portuguese-influenced Brazilians, in particular, use a lot of egg yolks. Cheeses, both goat and cow, are extremely popular, though cream is rarely seen.

MEATS Although pork wasn't known until the conquest, it has become the most popular meat in South America, followed closely by beef and goat; however, the traditional favorites include rabbit (which is usually treated as poultry) and the huge Argentine hare called a *viscacha;* venison; boar and peccary; lamb and mutton; and the cuy, a guinea pig the size of a small dog. Llama meat is still popular, particularly in Peru, where it is often air-dried (the charqui mentioned above). Organ meats are extremely popular, particularly kidneys, liver, sweetbreads, heart, and tripe (*modongo*). Even offal, such as snouts, pig's ears, tails, and hocks, are used in stews and sausages, especially the Brazilian national dish, *fei-joada*. Calves feet are also much admired.

Sausages reflect a variety of influences, including German, Spanish, and Italian. *Morcilla* (blood sausage), the spicy chorizo, and the lightly smoked *paio* are among the most common.

THE MAIN DISHES

APPETIZERS As in Central America, many of the finger foods—empanadas, tamales, fritters, etc.—that are listed as hors d'oeuvre on menus in South American restaurants in the United States are really light meals or snacks. In Brazilian restaurants they are sometimes referred to as *salgadinhos*—literally, salty things such as designed to go with drinks—and these are often taken right off the Portuguese ship: salamilike sausages, batter-fried shrimp, pickles, raw cured hams, tuna,

Known variously as empanadas, empadas, empanaditas (an affectionate diminutive), pasteles, or *salteñas*, stuffed pastries are as ubiquitous in South America as they are in Central America. They may be made of pastry dough, bread dough, or corn, yucca, or plantain dough; fried or baked, sweet or savory; shaped as triangles, half-moons, rounds, or squares. Fillings can be meat, seafood, vegetable, poultry, cheese, or even fruit. In Chile, where the stuffing is often slowly simmered in a rich stock and spiced with raisins, they are called *caldudas*, from the stockpot, *caldo*.

Tamales, too, have a variety of Indian names—*hallaca, bollo, juanes, pamonhas*—to go with the Spanish one we know. They can be made from corn, wheat, yucca, rice, potato, plantain, or quinoa doughs; and filled with chicken, duck, pork, seafood, veal, vegetables, or even curry. In Venezuela, there is a Mexican-influenced version that combines chicken and potatoes with a tomato sauce. There are two debates among tamale cooks: Should they be wrapped in banana leaves or corn husks? and should they be steamed or simmered?

or sardines. However, some are genuinely native first courses: fried smelts, potato tortillas, black-eyed pea fritters, shrimp or crab cakes, and fried fish cubes.

In the Italian and grill-happy Argentine restaurants, chargrilled sweetbreads or kidneys, "mixed fries" of organ meats or seafood, fried marinated fish cubes or grilled sweet peppers or eggplant are common. In some Peruvian kitchens, the cheesy potato dish called *huancaina* is served as an appetizer as well as entree. *Fiambre* means the dish is cold, but that may include meat and seafood dishes as well as vegetables or salad. *Carne seca*, a pickled and then dried meat (also called *xarque*), is a popular Brazilian snack.

SOUPS AND STEWS South American cuisine is particularly rich in seafood soups and vegetable purees, often called "cream" soups but with no dairy product in sight. Among the most popular are black bean soup; a Chinese-inspired hot broth with beaten raw eggs stirred in; calves' foot consommé; chicken with rice; dumpling soups; chowders of clam, crabmeat, or shrimp with corn (called *chupes*); beef and dried-potato soups; and soups with greens, squash, or pumpkin. Fruit soups are particularly characteristic of Brazilian menus, as are soups flavored with coconut milk or ground nuts.

Migas here are not bread salads but stews or thick soups with bread crumbs, often shellfish-flavored. *Mariscadas* are South American bouillabaisses that mix fish and shellfish. *Seco* denotes a (relatively) dry stew, generally a meat or red-meat fowl dish.

ONE-POT MEALS *Feijoada*, or more formally *feijoada completa*, the national dish of Brazil, is a casserole of variety meats (usually pork), greens, black beans, and some powdered cassava and usually flavored with palm oil. Argentines like a *carbonada*, a Moorish-sounding beef stew that mixes pumpkin meat and dried or fresh fruits and is served in the pumpkin shell.

Cochido is a general word for stew, but it's not to be confused with Brazilian *cozido*, a combination of sun-dried beef, pork, and plantains (which distinguish it from its Portuguese ancestors). A stew called, variously, *sancochado*, *sancocho*, *hervido*, or *cazuela puchero* is something like the New England boiled dinner—a mixture of meats and vegetables cooked in water or stock. The most vivid version of this is called, affectionately, *olla podrida*, or "rancid casserole," and combines various cuts of beef (usually starting with a brisket), chicken, pork (hams, hocks, and bacon), and veal with a couple of types of sausages as well as chickpeas, limas, and perhaps potatoes or yams. The nickname may refer either to the well-hung (i.e., green) bacons of South America or to the fact that traditionally such stews were never emptied, just refueled.

RICE AND GRAIN DISHES There are a number of rice, quinoa, and even barley dishes that feature meats and poultry simmered into the cooking grains. Among the most popular are *arroz con pollo* (rice with chicken), *arroz de cuxa* (rice with dried shrimp and vinegar), barley with quail, orzo with rabbit or duck, and quinoa with chopped clams. Brazilians often flavor rice with tomatoes (the original version of what cafeterias used to call "Spanish rice"), and West Indian-style pilaus, flavored with spices and nuts, are also common.

Brazilian *farofa* is a cornmeal sautéed in butter and often mixed with scrambled eggs. *Locro*, a whole grain wheat stew flavored with meat and vegetables, is derived from the couscous that Spanish-Arab settlers remembered.

SEAFOOD One of the greatest contributions of New World cuisine is *ceviche*, the combination of fresh fish and seafood "cooked" in hot chilies, lime or lemon, and onion. The most popular ingredients of ceviche (also spelled seviche or cebiche) are flounder, sole, trout, snapper, shrimp, crab, lobster, prawns, mussels, clams, octopus, and squid. Ceviche is served any time of day, as appetizer, snack, or light meal; a whole dinner of ceviche is called a *cebichada*. It is also considered a hangover remedy, and the booths that dispense fresh-out-of-the-water ceviche at dawn are called *cebicherias*. Escabeche, that vinegar-based Caribbean marinade, is also popular in South America.

In general, fish is steamed, fried, braised in banana leaves, baked, smothered in hot chilies and onions, stewed with sausage or chicken, topped with coconut, mustard, or peanut butter sauce, or stuffed with crab meat or flavored bread crumbs. Squid is often stuffed with ground pork (an Indonesian import) or stewed in its own ink (Chinese). Crabcakes, sea turtle soup, and okra gumbos with shrimp and mollusks (called *caruru* in Brazil) are popular. Stuffed crabs with coriander, tomatoes, and even coconut are a favorite, particularly in Brazil. The Portuguese salt cod and marinated or salted anchovies are used in hashes, fritters, stews, and stuffings.

POULTRY AND RABBIT   South American cooks staunchly maintain that the only way to eat wild pigeon, pheasant, and grouse is grilled rare, to keep the red meat from drying out; wild duck and most wildfowl should also be treated lightly. Turkey is the favorite, and richly fed toms are stuffed with walnuts and corn both before and after stewing. The Moorish tradition lives on in such recipes as duck with olives or figs, the Portuguese in quail braised in sweetened fortified wines such as sherry, madeira, or brandy. One popular Bahia version is chicken with shrimp and almonds. Whether or not the chicken was known to the Quechuas before the Spanish arrived, the Peruvians have perfected the lemon-marinated and charcoal-grilled chicken so popular in the United States today; Brazilians often cut up chicken or smaller birds such as quail and quick-fry them with the bones still in. Poultry is also stir-fried in a number of Chinese-influenced sauces. *Aji* and *picante* mean that the dishes are chili-hot; *aji de gallina* is a very popular chicken dish flavored with ground nuts, coconut milk and chilies.

Rabbit is fried, coated with mustard or coconut (French and Indonesian), stewed with honey and fruit (also Moorish), or flavored Mexican mole–style, with bitter chocolate.

MEATS   Grilling and braising are the two most common methods of cooking meat. Venison in particular is usually grilled or roasted; pork is roasted (particularly with garlic, as the Portuguese preferred) or stewed, or its chops are used in mixed grills with sausages, sweetbreads, and beef. Veal is usually roasted or shank-braised, except in the Italian restaurants of Buenos Aires, where scallopini turn up piccata, parmigiana, and any other classic way.

Goat is grilled, particularly kid (*cabrito*), or curried; lamb is roasted, rubbed with garlic and anchovies, and butterflied or used on mixed grills. (The Brazilians, who pronounce the letter *X* as "*sb*," have a wonderful Gaelic casserole they call *airixtu*—phonetically, "Irish stew.") Among the Argentine steakhouses, the most popular cuts of beef are the flank steak, which is the cut usually meant by *bistek*, and the skirt steak, or *churrasco*. Almost any meat, pork, beef, lamb, or goat, can be ground into meatballs

Great Grills

In Argentina, where the muscular skirt steak called *churrasco* is so popular, all-grill restaurants are called *churrascarias*; they skewer such organ meats as kidneys, livers, hearts, and sweetbreads; pork and lamb chops; beef short ribs; tenderloins; chorizo and blood sausages; and sometimes chicken or veal loin, and serve them as mixed grills. Other churrascarias spit-roast whole quarters of mutton, kid, beef, and pork and then carry them from table to table, slicing off meats to order—a point-and-eat style that is becoming trendy in the United States.

(*abondigas*). *Ropa viejo*, meaning "old clothes," is a mixture of shredded marinated beef and cabbage. *Antichucos*, marinated and grilled beef heart, is a Peruvian specialty. *Lomos saltados* is marinated beef strips cooked with onions and peppers—the Peruvian Philly steak. Argentines also frequently stuff and braise rolled steaks in the Italian manner.

BEVERAGES In Brazil, the most popular alcoholic spirit is *cachaca*, which is 100 proof and related to rum; it is most commonly served in a lime and sugar cocktail called *caipirinha*, which is (not surprisingly) popular in restaurants in the United States. The Peruvian *pisco* sour, often compared to a margarita, is actually closer to a brandy punch and includes sugar and egg whites. *Yerba mate* is a sort of bitter herb tea of the grasslands; in most urban areas, coffee is a staple. Beer is also popular, and many good brands, such as the Brazilian "black beer" Xinhua, are now being imported more broadly.

DESSERTS In general, fresh fruit is eaten after meals, and sweets, such as coconut cakes, cookies, and meringues, are considered either late-morning, coffee-break snacks or afternoon delights.

HOW TO ORDER AND EAT LIKE A NATIVE

The European influence ensures that almost every meal is served in courses, although some Peruvian restaurants may serve everything at once. In general, Peruvian restaurants are quite inexpensive, and Brazilian establishments are moderate; Argentine restaurants, because of the meat, may be somewhat more expensive but are still relatively reasonable.

Where feijoada is served in the traditional manner, the various meats—tongue, bacon, sausage, spareribs, beef chunks, etc.—and greens are served on one platter with the tongue in the center; the beans, white rice, and toasted farofa arrive in their own tureens. Take some rice on your plate, arrange a pile of meats alongside, then top the whole thing with beans and the bean liquor and sprinkle farinha over the top.

In a Brazilian restaurant, two people should start with a soup—either chicken and rice or black bean—and then have smothered or grilled whole fish and cabrito; for four, add ceviche and feijoada. However, feijoada is often prepared only on certain days, or with prior notice; it may also be a group dish, in which case you should look for a seafood/sausage stew or *carne del sol*, air-dried roast beef. For two, a Peruvian menu may offer antichucos on skewers, seviche, escabeche-flavored fish, and roast pork; four people can add a shrimp or crab chowder, potatoes huancaina, and a seafood or goat stew. Argentine restaurants often serve empanadas or delicate organ meats, such as sweetbreads, as appetizers; share a grilled sausage plate or mixed grill and a stuffed flank steak with green chimichurri sauce. Four people should try a squash or pumpkin stew, if possible, and grilled shrimp.

COOKING AT HOME

There is, of course, no "official" recipe for feijoada; one authority says it should be pork, another says beef and pork, a third adds greens. You may want to add or subtract cuts of meat or even substitute lamb or goat; but jerked meat, available at Hispanic groceries and frequently in convenience stores, adds a characteristic tang to the stew. In a pinch, plain dried beef can be substituted, but not the super-thin variety. Serve cold beer or, if you can find cachaca, caipirinhas. (The closest substitute would be a good homemade daiquiri.)

FEIJOADA COMPLETA

1 pound dried black beans
1/2 pound jerked beef in cubes or slices
2 ham hocks, cut into cubes
1/4 pound smoked tongue
1 bay leaf
4 slices bacon, cut in eighths
2 cloves garlic, finely chopped
2 hot chili peppers, finely chopped
2 green onions, chopped
1/4 cup dry or medium-dry sherry, port or madeira
1/2 pound pork sausage
1/2 pound blood sausage
1 1/2 cups orange juice (optional)
8 ounces fresh kale, mustard greens, collards, or spinach, coarsely chopped
2 tablespoons palm oil (optional)
toasted farinha
orange slices for garnish

Pick over dried beans for gravel and soak overnight; also soak jerked beef. The next day, drain beans, cover with 3 1/2 cups fresh water and simmer until done (about 1 1/2 to 2 hours); drain, and reserve liquid. Meanwhile, in a stockpot, cover jerked beef, ham hocks, and tongue with water and add bay leaf; bring to boil and simmer 1 1/2 hours, skimming foam as it rises. Remove beef, tongue, and hocks and cut meat off bones into chunks; set meat aside, return scraps to stock, and continue simmering 30 minutes. Strain and set aside.

In a Dutch oven or casserole, cook bacon until rendered and sauté garlic, chilie peppers and onions until golden; add sherry and bring back to simmer, then add reserved stock, beef, tongue, hocks, sausages, black bean liquid, and orange juice (if you are using it). Cook for about 10 minutes, stir in greens, and simmer until wilted. Add black beans and simmer another 20 to 30 minutes, adding palm oil if desired, or a little more water if the stew seems dry.

Serve feijoada with white rice, toasted farinha (available at specialty groceries), and pumpkin or squash.

SMOTHERED TUNA

4–6 tuna (or swordfish) steaks, about 1/2 pound each
2 cloves garlic, peeled
2 teaspoons salt
1 tablespoon fresh ginger root, peeled
1 teaspoon lime zest, minced
1 teaspoon orange zest, minced
1 tablespoon dry sherry
2 teaspoons lime juice
2 tablespoons palm, coconut or olive oil
1 large onion, sliced
1 large bell pepper, sliced
2 ounces pancetta, bacon, or ham
2 hot chilies, thinly sliced
3 large tomatoes, chopped and drained
3 tablespoons parsley

Skin and pat dry fish steaks; set aside. Combine next seven ingredients in mini-processor or pestle and make into a paste; add 1 tablespoon oil and combine again. Rub fish with paste and let it marinate while grill or broiler heats.

Meanwhile, sauté pancetta or bacon in remaining oil; sauté onion and pepper until they have given up liquid and nearly dried out; add tomatoes and cook until liquid is again nearly drawn out.

If you are broiling the steaks, cook them a few minutes on either side until browned but still raw in the center; stir vegetables in, moving sauce under and alongside the steaks, and place the pan back under the broiler for a couple of minutes more, until hot through but still pink. If you are grilling the steaks, grill them until done and serve with sauce and top with parsley.

AMERICAN REGIONAL CUISINE

The United States is a huge country, encompassing more than 3,750,000 square miles—larger even than China. Italy, with its many regional cuisines, is only two-thirds the size of the state of California, France three-quarters the size of Texas. In the continental mass alone, the topography includes prairie, mountain, forest, pastureland, marsh, river valley, coastal lowland, and desert. Yet the United States may well be the most homogenized country in the world when it comes to food. The culture of the supermarket, the chain restaurant, and the national fast-food commercial encourages an expectation of conformity, from "home cooking" to the steakhouse to the canned escargot at the continental joint—Chez What? The fact that the latest trendy menu description is "New American" only adds to the confusion, since it pops up in New York, Washington, Charleston, Houston, Santa Fe, Boston, Los Angeles, Miami—everywhere and anywhere, and on menus that otherwise bear little resemblance to one another.

There is that one word that links them all—"American"—and it holds out the first hope of a revolution in restaurant cuisine. After decades of imitating the Old World masters, American chefs are finally taking their places as stars in their own right. Not merely "cooks" in the traditional sense, often not even formally trained, they are adventurers, culinary explorers in search of their roots—even, as in the case of New Southwest proponent Mark Miller, anthropologists.

Jacques Pepin has tried to recreate the real spirit of French country cooking by stripping off those pompous layers of sauce. Pierre Franey, longtime New York restaurant chef and author, has spent the last several years leading TV audiences around such uniquely American scenes as the kitchens of Disney World, a bayou cookout, a cattle ranch. Some chefs even use their restaurants for ethnic or social agendas, hoping to turn the spotlight on soul food or on vegetarian or organic or feminist or boycott-correct menus. California icon Wolfgang Puck, in an effort to persuade Congress to tighten labeling of fresh poultry, "bowled" a frozen chicken down the hallway.

If there is any common philosophy among all these self-described New American cooks, the serious and the showboating, it would be their interest in integrating native ingredients into their work. Many chefs prefer the term "modern," as in modern American or modern Southwestern cooking, to suggest an evolution or progression of traditional cuisine, rather than "new," which implies invention. There is renewed affection for the old favorites—variously called soul food, family-style, mom's cooking, and comfort food—only made up fresh, with local flavors and fewer brand-name recipes. American chevre, caviar, chicory, pâté, wild mushrooms, and wines now command the respect that used to be reserved for imports.

And with that increasing confidence, our melting pot has come to an appetizing simmer. American recipes are being reconsidered in the light of Asian cooking techniques, European sauces are being tailored to native ingredients, and so forth. The emphasis has shifted from imported groceries to local produce, regional game and fish, free-range and additive-free livestock, native vegetables, and even wild greens and herbs. American chefs have a broader array of methods to choose from than ever, thanks not only to the many other cuisines and ingredients but also to a plethora of time-saving utensils and appliances. And with more time to reflect, they are rediscovering the various ethnic and historical influences that make regional cuisine vital.

Not all "new" cuisine is particularly authentic. California cuisine is really more a philosophy than a specific style. European and Asian ingredients are used in traditional recipes, and American ingredients are given classic treatments. Because California was in the forefront of the body-conscious culture, restaurateurs on the West Coast were also early proponents of cuisine minceur (now renamed, less punitively, "spa cuisine").

What is beginning to be called "Pacific Rim food" mixes ingredients and techniques from Indonesia, Southeast Asia, Japan, and other Asian nations with California and Northwest specialties. New Southern cuisine isn't so much new as remodeled by a little more seasoning, a little less fat, and a shorter cooking time. (For a little background on soul food, see the chapters on West African and Caribbean cooking.)

Many cities—especially those on the coasts, which naturally absorb the most immigrant traffic—have successfully exploited their culinary inheritances, and with fascinating results: Boston, with its blend of New England seafood and Mediterranean flavors, suggests some street-theater version of *Captains Courageous* featuring the spoiled American rich kid, the African cook, and the Portuguese hero. And Seattle, with its large Japanese and transplanted Californian communities, is developing a reputation for innovative seafood dishes.

But only a few regions have established such distinct culinary styles that you might find their cooking in other parts of the country. Those "exportable" styles include what is variably called South Florida, new Miami, or Florida Keys cuisine; modern Southwestern, which includes Santa Fe and Tex-Mex; and the New Orleans siblings, Cajun and Creole. That these are all themselves related is not so surprising when you remember that the two great colonial powers, Spain and France, and the Africans they imported worked their way into the North American continent primarily via the Gulf and the Caribbean.

Although they may not be "ethnic" in exactly the way the foreign cuisines covered in this book are, these three regional styles are more and more popular and deserve at least a quick description.

MIAMI, SOUTH FLORIDA, AND THE KEYS

Despite its rich and varied influences—Spanish, Mexican, Afro-Caribbean, French, Greek, Indian, and Chinese—the food in the chic new Florida restaurants is light, bright, and bracing. The most characteristic elements are seafood, citrus fruits, and chilies, with avocado, tomatoes, and rum or brown sugar close behind. Color is more of a consideration in this cuisine than in any other; in fact, this is the only region where "hot pastel" is both a visual description and a recipe. Pink grapefruit, grass-green key limes, golden mangoes, black beans, scarlet tomatoes, honeydew melons, orange yams, deep-green cilantro, and purple onions are matched to fish of every hue, from red snapper to silvery mackerel.

Florida cooking has many Caribbean echos, from bacalao, the Spanish salt cod, to barbacao, the Indians' smoked meat. Escabeches, ceviches, okra gumbos, black-eyed peas, coconut, yucca chips, fried plantains, cornmeal, and hominy are common; so are French cream sauces, seafood mousses and bouillabaisses, Greek fried calamari and oregano- and feta-flavored fish, and Jamaican jerk spices.

The wealth of fish includes pompano, grouper, red and yellowtail snapper, redfish, tilefish, trout, mullet, flounder, yellowfin and bluefin tuna, swordfish, mackerel, amberjack, wahoo, and dolphin fish (also known as mahi-mahi or dorado to distinguish it from the mammal dolphin). Other seafood includes blue and stone crabs, shrimp of all sizes, spiny lobsters, oysters, squid, alligator, sea turtle (now politically incorrect), conch, and scallops. Small birds, lightly grilled or smoked, are a regional tradition; they include squab, quail, rail, duck, doves, and so on. (Seafood is fried, but poultry rarely is.) Pork is the most common meat.

Sometimes a restaurant refers to "Gulf Coast cuisine," which can be South Floridian but can also be Texas Gulf Coast–style; that tends to be meatier (with particularly emphasis on roasts, pan-fries, and barbecues), favor more fried dishes, and feature more thick, flour-based west Louisiana sauces. "Gulf Coast" can even refer to dishes from Veracruz or Tabasco.

NEW OR MODERN SOUTHWESTERN

This category lumps together several cuisines frequently served up in combination: The extremely trendy Santa Fe style, Tex-Mex or *norteño* cuisine (which generally includes dishes from the Sonora and Chihuahua regions of Mexico and Arizona as well as Texas), and even some premissionary Native American dishes that show up on New Southwest menus.

The hottest, and hautest, variety is Sante Fe. Over the last decade, the boom in New Mexican cuisine has influenced nearly all other regional styles with its emphasis on smoking, low-fat cooking techniques and, above all, chilies, which are suddenly one of the most popular foods in the United States. Anywhere in the Southwest, you can find a restaurant that serves either shredded meat chili, ground meat chili, red tomato chili, green chili, chicken chili, venison chili, boar chili, or even black bean chili, and probably several at a time; but only in New Mexico could you order a chili dish of pure chilies, roasted, peel, pureed, simmered, even "seasoned." Whole magazines, gourmet catalogs, and accessory stores are devoted to salsas, chili sauces, and seeds, and scores of species—yellow, green, orange, red, purple, and even black—are jealously cultivated. A few years ago, sales of prepared salsas in this country passed sales of catsup.

In Santa Fe, a city that is nearing the end of its fourth century, the cuisine combines Native American, Spanish, and Mexican dishes with some bits of Louisiana and railroad Anglo flavoring. Santa Fe cooks were among the first to use mesquite wood smoking for meats and poultry, and they "rediscovered" such indigenous ingredients as sun-dried tomatoes, piñon nuts, blue cornmeal, cilantro, pumpkin seeds, wild oregano, cumin, and Mexican-style chocolate flavored with nuts and vanilla. Prickly pears and their fruit, also called cactus pears, are another characteristic ingredients. Turkey, which ran wild here, was a staple of the Pueblo Indian diet, along with game (venison, bison, rabbit), prairie dogs, beaver, and other large rodents; traditionally, the Indians spitted and roasted meat, but after the introduction of the iron pot by the Spanish, they began stewing beans and meat with green chilies, nuts, and seeds. The Spanish also brought sheep and cattle (and dairy products), pork (and the lard that is still many cooks' favorite fat), and planted olive trees, orchard fruits, potatoes, greens, and vineyards. Since the Moors had just been evicted from Spain as Columbus was landing in the New World, their culinary influence was still strong when Santa Fe was founded. Hence the presence of raisins and almonds along with the sherry, garlic, and olive oil. ("Texas toast," after all, is transplanted bruschetta—grilled bread spread with olive oil and lots of garlic.) Spanish-style sausages and hams are also fairly common.

The territories of Sonora and Chihuahua, which border Arizona and Texas, were transformed by Spanish wheat and cattle into huge ranges, so Tex-Mex or norteño cuisine started out as, in effect, cowboy food. Much of it was originally limited to what simple outdoor fires and minimal utensils could create (hence quesadillas, which started out as fried turnovers, wound up as the flat cheese and tortilla "sandwiches" we know in the United States). It also meant that although maize and corn-meal were available, wheat-flour tortillas became the standard. El Paso, the quintessential border town, has long claimed credit for inventing the nacho, which is, after all, a way of eating a whole dinner without a fork—or without getting out of the saddle. It may also be responsible for the burrito, or stuffed flour tortilla. It is believed that charcoal grilling began here, where it is called simply *al carbon,* and the flavor of char smoke is characteristic of Chihuahuan food. Chihuahua was also the site of a large Mennonite settlement and traditionally produces a lot of mild and easily melted cheese and *crema,* a cultured thick cream like crème fraîche. *Queso fundito,* the melted cheese eaten with fried tortillas that has evolved into a bar staple in the United States, is a Sonoran tradition; refried beans with cheese is Chihuahuan.

In the larger ranches, hacienda cooks began to mix traditional Mexican tortillas and enchiladas, beans, chilies (red and green), and salsas with prime meat and game, cheese and sour cream, wine and olives, and to recreate Spanish dishes for their homesick employers. Menudo, the tripe stew recommended as a hangover remedy, and adobo, the chili paste that so captivated the Spanish that they carried it around the world, are specialities of this region.

Barbecue, the Indians' spicy pit-smoked meat (which may or may not have been served with tomatoes), gradually worked its way from the Yucatan and coastal Mexico into Texas, picking up Spanish vinegar, Jamaican molasses, and various other refinements along the way. Both beef and pork are given serious attention in Tex-Mex cuisine; more recently, goat, venison, bison (or farmed buffalo), and game birds, particularly quail, rabbit, doves, and squab, are enjoying a revival of respect.

NEW ORLEANS

It's not surprising that so many people are confused about the distinction between Cajun and Creole cooking. For one thing, they share similar influences and similar ingredients; they're both associated with Mardi Gras and crawfish and oysters and New Orleans music (Dixieland, Cajun and zydeco bands have all become increasingly popular outside their home state); and in fact the styles are beginning to merge—so much so that many people are starting to refer to them jointly as New

Orleans cuisine. Etouffées, jambalayas, and gumbos seem to be popular on both sides.

However, there are a few differences, and history helps explain them. Cajun is a mixture of French, Spanish, African, coastal Mexican, and Choctaw and other southern Indian cooking; it's also a working-class cuisine, largely dependent on subsistence crops and hunting and with relatively few intricate techniques. (Because food was often tough and utensils few, long-cooked one-pot meals are the most common). Creole food is upper-class European at heart, and while it also has African and Indian strains, it's a more elaborate style, developed by the cooks—some of them professionally trained and imported—who worked for the wealthier residents and colonial rulers. It involves more sauces (it's hard to imagine a New Orleans brunch without eggs Benedict and hollandaise) and shorter cooking times.

"Cajun" is a corruption of the word "Acadian," and the Cajuns are descended from southern French farmers who moved to Nova Scotia in the early seventeenth century. When Canada fell to the British a century later, they were exiled and began the long trek south (memorialized in Longfellow's "Evangeline") to what was left of French territory—namely, Louisiana. They settled in and around the bayous, where they found abundant fish and shellfish and game. The local Indians showed them how to powder sassafras leaf into a thickening and flavoring agent and how to barbecue meat and make cornmeal; they may also have been the first to "cook" flour into a *roux* ("red"), the basis for gumbos, fricassees, and so forth. The West African slaves brought with them okra, which in one dialect was called *gombo*, leading to the name "gumbo" for an okra-thickened stew. (The word "jambalaya" is variously said to derive from an African dish of stacked, simmered fish, called *jomba*, or to a combination of *jambon*, the French word for ham, and *ya*, an African name for rice.)

Though the word has come to mean ethnically mixed, the original Creoles were French nationals born in Louisiana. They maintained a "first families" roster within the city well into this century and spoke French as a first language. (The Cajuns do too, though their dialect is somewhat different and they have had a more difficult time defending their ethnic heritage.)

Cajun cooking depends more heavily on spices: filé, onions, celery, hot and bell peppers, green onions, garlic and, especially, hot peppers. Cajun chefs often speak of "the three peppers," meaning black, white, and Tabasco; and spicy "blackened" seafood is a typical Cajun dish. The more classic Creole cuisine emphasizes marjoram, sage, fennel, leeks, mustard, and so on. Cajun spices are more commonly cooked into the dish, either in the stew or in the roux, while Creole seasonings are often included in the sauce.

Cajuns lived upriver and used more freshwater fish (particularly crawfish), turtle, water birds, and squirrel; Creole dishes emphasized saltwater fish, venison, beef, geese, shrimp, and so forth. Cajun cooks are more prone to fry fish or even meats and vegetables; Creole chefs prefer to sauce them, stuff them, or sauté them in butter. The Cajuns traditionally cook with lard and eat more fatty meats, particularly sausages; but during the cooking process, they frequently pour off excess oil or fat or deglaze the pan. Creole cooks, who use much more butter and cream and olive oil, do not remove fat and in fact often "finish" sauces with more butter or cream, so while Cajun food may be starchier, Creole food is often higher-fat in a subtle way.

Both eat a great deal of rice, the southern staple, but the Cajun diet features cornmeal and hominy, while the Creole diet includes more breads and rolls. And finally, because they were richer, the Creoles were more likely to expect sweets and desserts and to get them.

THE LAST WORD

Now, if this armchair voyage has piqued your curiosity or your appetite, we urge you to go out and explore these cuisines yourself. Show both your interest and your appreciation to the chefs and staff who serve you. Maybe you won't always like everything, but you will find many dishes, and people, to enjoy. We wish you many fine meals and many new friends. As the great and hilarious Julia Child would say, "Bon appetit!"

Suggested Ethnic Restaurants

To help you along on your culinary odyssey, we have developed a list of recommended ethnic restaurants. The restaurants selected are representative of the cuisine and offer a good introduction to its signature dishes. All of the restaurants were selected solely on the quality of their food, and thus vary considerably in terms of cost, atmosphere, formality, and service. Expressed differently, they are not necessarily the same restaurants that the convention bureau or your concierge would recommend. You will notice in many cities that there are no recommendations for certain ethnicities. This does not necessarily mean that the cuisine is unavailable, but rather that the local restaurants do not (in our opinion) serve particularly authentic or representative fare. In a similar vein, we do not generally list chain restaurants.

Albuquerque, NM

Chinese
　　Malaysian Bay
　　1826 Eubank
　　(505) 293-5597

French
　　Le Crepe Michel
　　4400 San Phillipe
　　(505) 242-1251

German
　　Michelle's Old World Cafe
　　6205 A Montgomery, NE
　　(505) 884-7938

Greek
　　Olympia Cafe
　　2210 Central, SE
　　(505) 266-5222

Albuquerque, NM (continued)

Indian
Shalimar
8405 Montgomery, NE
(505) 275-7949

Italian
Scalo
3500 Central Avenue, SE, Nob
Hill Plaza
(505) 255-8781

Japanese
Minato
10721 Montgomery, NE
(505) 293-2929

Spanish
Broadway Cafe
606 Broadway
(505) 842-9998

Thai
Bangkok Cafe
5901 Central Avenue, NE
(505) 255-5036

ATLANTA, GA

Burmese
Mandalay
5945 Jimmy Carter Boulevard
Norcross
(404) 368-8368

Chinese
Little Szechuan
5091-C Buford Highway
(404) 451-0192

Cuban
Mambo Restaurante Cubano
1402 North Highland Avenue
(404) 876-2626

French Bistro
Anis Bistro
2974 Grandview Avenue
(404) 233-9889

French Classic
Brasserie Le Coze
3393 Peachtree Road
Lenox Square Mall
(404) 226-1440

Greek
Cafe Dimitri
3714 Roswell Road
(404) 842-0101

Indian
Moghul Salute
114 East Trinity Place,
Downtown
Decatur
(404) 371-9554

Italian
La Grotta Ristorante
2637 Peachtree Road
(404) 231-1368

Japanese
Kamogawa Restaurant
3300 Peachtree Road, Hotel
Nikko
(404) 841-0314

Korean
Garam Korean Restaurant
5881 Buford Highway
Doraville
(404) 454-9198

Mexican
Sundown Cafe
2165 Cheshire Bridge Road,
near La Vista Road
(404) 321-1118

Mediterranean
    Oasis Cafe
    752 Ponce de Leon Avenue
    (404) 881-0815

Middle Eastern
    Lawrence's Cafe and Restaurant
    2888 Buford Highway, near
        North David Hills
    (404) 320-7756

North African
    Imperial Fez
    2285 Peachtree Road,
        Peachtree Battle
        Condominium
    (404) 351-0870

Persian
    Pars Persian Restaurant
    215 Copeland Road, NW
    (404) 851-9566

Romanian
    Romanian Restaurant and Cafe
    3081 East Shadowlawn
    (404) 365-8220

Thai
    Zab-E-Lee
    4835 Old National Highway
    College Park
    (404) 768-2705

Vietnamese
    Bien Thuy
    5095-F Buford Highway
    Northwoods Plaza
    Doraville
    (404) 454-9046

BALTIMORE, MD

Afghani
    The Helmand
    806 North Charles Street
    (410) 752-0311

Brazilian
    Rio Lisboa
    4700 Eastern Avenue
    (410) 522-5092

Chinese
    Tony Chen's Szechuan
    801 North Charles Street
    (410) 539-6666

Ethiopian
    Liza's
    739 West Pratt Street
    (410) 385-1448

French Bistro
    Cafe Manet
    1020 South Charles Street
    (410) 837-7006

French Classic
    M. Gettier
    505 South Broadway
    (410) 732-1151

German
    Josef's Country Inn
    2410 Pleasantville Road
        (Route 152)
    Fallston
    (410) 877-7800

Greek
    Ikaros
    4805 Eastern Avenue
    (410) 633-3750

Indian
>Bombay Grill
>2 East Madison Street
>(410) 837-2973

Italian
>Boccaccio
>925 Eastern Avenue
>(410) 234-1322

Japanese
>Kawasaki
>413 North Charles Street
>(410) 659-7600

Korean
>New No Da Ji
>2501 North Charles Street
>(410) 235-4846

Persian
>Orchard Cafe
>8815 Orchard Tree Lane
>Towson
>(410) 339-7700

Spanish
>Tio Pepe
>12 East Franklin Street
>(410) 539-4675

Thai
>Thai
>3316-18 Greenmount Avenue
>(410) 889-7303

Vietnamese
>CoChin
>800 North Charles Street
>(410) 332-0332

BIRMINGHAM, AL

Chinese
>Ming's Cuisine
>514 Cahaba Park Circle
>(205) 991-3803

German
>Klingler's European Bakery &
>Deli
>621 Montgomery Highway
>(205) 823-4560

Indian
>Taj India
>2226 Highland Avenue South
>(205) 939-3805

Italian
>Bottega
>2240 Highland Avenue South
>(205) 939-1000

Japanese
>Asahi
>444 Cahaba Park Circle
>(205) 991-5542

Mexican
>La Paz
>99 Euclid Avenue
>(205) 879-2225

Middle Eastern
>Ali Baba Persian Restaurant
>110 Centre at Riverchase
>(205) 823-2222

BOSTON, MA

Brazilian
>Pampas
>928 Massachusetts Avenue
>Cambridge
>(617) 661-6613

Cambodian
Elephant Walk
70 Union Square
Somerville
(617) 623-9939

Caribbean
Green Street Grill
280 Green Street
Cambridge
(617) 876-1655

Chinese
Eastern Ocean City
27 Beach Street
(617) 542-2504

Ethiopian
Addis Red Sea
544 Tremont Street
(617) 426-8727

French Classic
Julien
250 Franklin Street, Hotel
Meridien
(617) 451-1900

French Provençal
Hamersley's Bistro
553 Tremont Street
(617) 423-2700

German
Jacob Wirth
31 Stuart Street (Tremont
Street)
(617) 338-8586

Greek
Omonia
75 South Charles Street (Stuart
Street)
(617) 426-4310

Hungarian
Cafe Budapest
90 Exeter Street, Copley Hotel
(617) 266-1979

Indian
Bombay Club
57 JFK Street, Galleria Mall
Cambridge
(617) 661-8100

Italian
Ristorante Toscano
41 Charles Street
(617) 723-4090

Japanese
Gyuhama
827 Boylston Street
(617) 437-0188

Mexican
Taqueria Mexico
139 Prospect Street
Waltham
(617) 647-0166

Middle Eastern
Kareem's
600 Mt. Auburn Street,
Coolidge Square
Watertown
(617) 926-1867

Portuguese
Sunset Cafe
851 Cambridge Street
Cambridge
(617) 547-2938

Spanish
    Dali
    415 Washington Street
    Somerville
    (617) 661-3254

Swiss
    Cafe Suisse
    1 Avenue de Lafayette,
        Lafayette Swissotel
    (617) 451-2600

Thai
    Siam Cuisine
    961 Commonwealth Avenue
    Allston
    (617) 254-4335

CHAPEL HILL, NC

Chinese
    Dragon's Garden
    407 West Franklin Street
    (919) 929-8143

Eastern European
    Cracovia
    Corner of Rosemary and
        Church
    (919) 929-9162

French Bistro
    Henri's Bistro
    403 West Rosemary Street
    (919) 967-4720

French Classic
    La Residence
    202 West Rosemary Street
    (919) 967-2506

Indian
    India Palace
    508 West Franklin Street
    (919) 942-8201

Italian
    Il Palio
    1505 East Franklin Street,
        Sienna Hotel
    (919) 929-4000

Mexican
    Papagayo
    137 East Franklin Street
    (919) 967-7145

CHARLESTON, SC

Caribbean
    Blossom Cafe
    171 East Bay Street
    (803) 722-9200

Chinese
    Emperor's Garden
    874 Orleans Road
    (803) 556-7212

Cuban
    Vickery's
    15 Beaufain Street
    (803) 577-5300

French
    Marianne
    235 Meeting Street
    (803) 722-7196

Greek
    Acropolis
    1179 Sam Rittenberg
        Boulevard
    (803) 766-2640

Indian
    Taste of India
    273 King Street
    (803) 723-8132

Italian
    Bocci's
    158 Church Street
    (803) 720-2121

Japanese
    Sushi Hiro of Kyoto
    298 King Street
    (803) 723-3628

Mexican
    Mesa Grill
    35 North Market Street
    (803) 723-3770

Vietnamese
    Binh Minh Restaurant
    7685 Northwoods Boulevard
    (803) 569-2844

CHARLOTTE, NC

Caribbean
    Anntony's Caribbean Cafe
    2001 East 7th Street
    (704) 342-0749

Chinese
    Baoding
    4722 Sharon Road, Suite F
    (704) 552-8899

French
    Chez Daniel
    1742 Lombardy Circle
    (704) 332-3224

German
    The Rheinland Haus
    2418 Park Road
    (704) 376-3836

Indian
    India Palace
    6140 East Independence
    (704) 568-7176

Italian
    Italian Restaurant and Bar
    8418 Park Road
    (704) 556-0914

Japanese
    Restaurant Tokyo
    4603 South Boulevard
    (704) 527-8787

Mexican
    El Cancun
    5234 South Boulevard
    (704) 525-5075

Spanish
    Olé Olé
    709 South Kings Drive
    (704) 358-1102

Thai
    Thai Orchid
    4223 Providence Road,
        Strawberry Hill Shopping
        Center
    (704) 364-1134

Vietnamese
    Saigon Dreaming
    6127 Albermarle Road
    (704) 567-0222

CHICAGO, IL

Afghani
> The Helmand
> 3201 North Halsted Street
> (312) 935-2447

Chinese
> Dragon Inn North
> 1650 Waukegan Road
> Glenview
> (708) 729-8383

Ethiopian
> Addis Abeba
> Clark Street
> (312) 929-9383

French Bistro
> Kiki's Bistro
> 900 North Franklin Street
> (312) 335-5454

French Classic
> Le Français
> 269 South Milwaukee Avenue
> Wheeling
> (708) 541-7471

German
> The Golden Ox
> 1578 Clybourn Avenue
> (312) 664-0780

Greek
> Parthenon
> 314 South Halsted Street
> (312) 726-2407

Indian
> Klay Oven
> 414 North Orleans Street
> (312) 527-3999

Italian
> Vivere
> 71 West Monroe Street
> (312) 332-4040

Japanese
> Hatsuhana
> 160 East Ontario Street
> (312) 280-8287

Korean
> Shilla
> 5930 North Lincoln Avenue
> (312) 275-5930

Lebanese
> Uncle Tannous
> 2626 North Halsted Street
> (312) 929-1333

Mexican
> Frontera Grill
> 445 North Clark Street
> (312) 661-1434

Moroccan
> L'Olive
> 3915 North Sheridan Road
> (312) 472-2400

Polish
> Pierogi Inn
> 5318 West Lawrence Avenue
> (312) 725-2818

Romanian
> Little Bucharest
> 3001 North Ashland Avenue
> (312) 929-8640

Scandinavian
> Ann Sather
> 929 West Belmont Avenue
> (312) 348-2378

5207 North Clark Street
(312) 271-6677

Serbian
Skadarlija
4024 North Kedzie Avenue
(312) 463-5600

Spanish
Emilio's
4100 West Roosevelt Road
Hillside
(708) 547-7177

Thai
Thai Touch
3200 West Lawrence Avenue
(312) 539-5700

Vietnamese
Lac Vien
1129 West Argyle Street
(312) 275-1112

CINCINNATI, OH

Chinese
China Gourmet
3340 Erie Avenue
Hyde Park
(513) 871-6612

Cuban
El Morro
724 Madison Avenue
Covington, KY
(606) 491-4792

French
La Petite France
3177 Glendale-Milford Road
Evendale
(513) 733-8383

German / Hungarian
Lenhardt's Restaurant
151 West McMillan Street
Clifton Heights
(513) 281-3600

Indian
Tandoor India
8702 Market Place Lane
Montgomery, OH
(513) 793-7484

Italian
Barresi's
4111 Webster Avenue
Deer Park
(513) 793-2540

Japanese
Osaka
11481 Chester Road
Sharonville
(513) 771-4488

Korean
Happy Teriyaki
1240 B State Highway 28
Milford
(513) 575-0808

Middle Eastern
Floyd's
129 Calhoun Street
Clifton
(513) 221-2434

Spanish
Mallorca
124 East Sixth Street
(513) 723-9506

Cincinnati, OH (continued)

Thai

Ban Thai
792 Eastgate South Drive
Summerside
(513) 752-3200

Vietnamese

Song Long
1737 Section Road
Roselawn
(513) 351-7631

CLEVELAND, OH

Chinese

Pearl of the Orient
20121 Van Aken Boulevard
Shaker Heights
(216) 751-8181

Czech

Old Prague Restaurant
12405 Mayfield Road
(216) 967-7182

Ethiopian

Empress Taytu
6125 St. Clair Avenue
(216) 391-9400

French

La Pomme
10427 Clifton Boulevard
(216) 651-0001

Greek

Greek Isles
500 West St. Clair Avenue
(216) 861-1919

Hungarian

Balaton
12521 Buckeye Road
(216) 921-9691

Indian

Cafe Tandoor
2096 South Taylor Road
Cleveland Heights
(216) 371-8500

Italian

Giovanni's
25500 Chagrin Boulevard
Beachwood
(216) 831-8625

Japanese

New Sakura
26225 Great Northern
  Shopping Center
North Olmsted
(216) 777-4666

Mediterranean

Sans Souci
24 Public Square, Stouffer
  Tower City Plaza Hotel
(216) 696-5600

Mexican

Fandango Cocina Mexicana
2797 Euclid Heights
  Boulevard, Coventryard
Cleveland Heights
(216) 371-2111

Thai

A Taste of Thailand
5136 Mayfield Road
Lyndhurst
(216) 461-8266

Vietnamese
Minh-Anh Restaurant
5428 Detroit Avenue
(216) 961-9671

COLUMBUS, OH

Chinese
Lai Lai
5125 East Main Street
(614) 759-6868

Caribbean / South American
Tapatio
491 North Park Street
(614) 221-1085

French Bistro
Alex's Bistro
4681 Reed Road
(614) 457-8887

French Classic
The Refectory
1092 Bethel Road
(614) 451-9774

Indian / Pakistani
Delhi Palace
2361 North High Street
(OSU campus)
(614) 421-2323

Italian
Moretti's Italian Cafe
1447 Grandview Avenue
(614) 488-2104

Cranston Center,
5849 Sawmill Road, Dublin
(614) 793-1196

10121 Riverside Drive, Powell
(614) 766-2433

Japanese
Restaurant Japan
1140 Kenny Square Mall (Old
Henderson & Kenny Roads)
(614) 451-5411

Korean
Restaurant Silla
1802 West Henderson Road
(614) 459-5990

Mexican
El Vaquero
2195 Riverside Drive
(614) 486-4547

50 South Young Street (downtown)
(614) 224-7330

3234 Olentangy River Road
(614) 261-0900

Middle Eastern
Firdous Café
1538 North High Street
(OSU campus)
(614) 299-1844

Russian
Matreoshka Russian Tea Room
680 North High Street
(614) 461-7755

Spanish / Basque
Spain Restaurant
3777 Sullivant Avenue
(614) 272-6363

Swiss
Old Swiss House
961 South High Street
(614) 444-0131

Thai

Thai Orchid
7654 Sawmill Road
(614) 792-1112

Vietnamese

Saigon Palace
114 North Front Street
(614) 464-3325

DALLAS, TX

Austrian

The Chimney
9739 North Central
  Expressway (Walnut Hill
  Lane exit, west)
(214) 369-6466

Caribbean

Carib-B
2012 Greenville Avenue
(214) 824-3395

Chinese

Cafe Panda
7979 Inwood at Lovers
(214) 902-9500

Ethiopian

Queen of Sheba
3527 McKinney Avenue
(214) 521-0491

French Bistro

Chez Gerard
4444 McKinney Avenue
  (south of Knox Street)
(214) 522-6865

French Classic

L'Ancestral
4514 Travis Street
(214) 528-1081

French Provençal

Juniper
2917 Fairmount Street
(214) 855-0700

German

Kuby's Sausage House
6601 Snider Plaza (1 block
  west of Hillcrest Road)
(214) 363-2231

Greek

Greek Isles
3309 North Central at Parker,
  Ruisseau Village
Plano
(214) 423-7778

Guatemalan

Gloria's
600 West Davis
(214) 948-3672

Indian

India Palace
12817 Preston Road, Suite 105
(214) 392-0190

Italian

Ruggeri's Ristorante
2911 Routh Street
(214) 871-7377

Japanese

Mr. Sushi
4860 Belt Line Road
Addison
(214) 385-0168

Mexican
> La Calle Doce
> 415 West 12th Street
> Oak Cliff
> (214) 941-4304

Romanian
> Cafe Athenée
> 5365 Spring Valley Road,
> Suite 150
> (214) 239-8060

Spanish
> Cafe Madrid
> 4501 Travis Street
> (214) 528-1731

Thai
> Thai Soon
> 2018 Greenville Avenue
> (214) 821-7666

Vietnamese
> Mai's
> 4812 Bryan Street
> (214) 826-9887

DENVER, CO

Brazilian
> Cafe Brazil
> 3611 Navajo Street
> (303) 480-1877

Chinese
> Imperial Chinese
> One Broadway
> (303) 698-2800

Ethiopian
> Queen of Sheba
> 7225 East Colfax Avenue
> (303) 399-9442

French Bistro
> Le Central
> 112 East 8th Avenue
> (303) 863-8094

German / Austrian
> The Copperdale Inn
> Highway 72 West
> Coal Creek Canyon
> (303) 642-9994

Greek
> Central 1
> 300 South Pearl Street
> (303) 778-6675

Hungarian
> Pine Creek Cookhouse
> 11399 Castle Creed Road
> Ashcroft
> (303) 925-1044

Indian
> India's
> 3333 South Tamarac Drive
> (303) 755-4284

Italian
> O Sole Mio
> 5501 East Colfax Avenue
> (303) 329-6139

Japanese
> Mori
> 2019 Market Street
> (303) 298-1864

Korean
> Seoul Food
> 701 East 6th Avenue
> (303) 837-1460

Denver, CO (continued)

Mexican
>La Cueva
>9742 East Colfax Avenue
>Aurora
>(303) 367-1422

Moroccan / North African
>Mataam Fez
>4609 East Colfax Avenue
>Aurora
>(303) 399-9282

Russian
>Little Russian Cafe
>1424 Larimer Square
>(303) 595-8600

Scandinavian
>Tivoli Deer
>26295 Hilltop Drive
>Kittredge
>(303) 670-0941

South American
>Sabor Latino
>3464 West 32nd Avenue
>(303) 455-8664

Spanish
>Don Quijote
>35 North Federal Boulevard
>(303) 934-9753

Syrian
>Damascus
>2276 South Colorado
>Boulevard
>(303) 757-3515

Thai
>J's Noodles
>945 South Federal Boulevard
>(303) 922-5495

Vietnamese
>New Saigon
>630 South Federal Boulevard
>(303) 936-4954

DETROIT, MI

Chinese
>Mon Jin Lau
>1515 Maple Road
>Troy
>(810) 689-2332

French
>Chez Pierre
>543 North Main
>Rochester
>(810) 650-1390

Greek
>Cyprus Taverna
>579 Monroe
>(313) 961-1550

Guatemalan
>El Comal
>1414 Junction
>(313) 841-7753

Hungarian
>The Rhapsody
>14315 Northline
>Southgate
>(313) 283-9622

Indian
>Passage to India
>3354 West 12 Mile Road
>Berkley
>(810) 541-2119

Italian
Chianti
28565 Northwestern Highway
Southfield
(810) 350-0130

Japanese
Cherry Blossom
43588 West Oaks Drive
Novi
(810) 380-9160

Korean
New Seoul Garden
27566 Northwestern Highway
Southfield
(810) 827-1600

Mexican
El Zocalo
3400 Bagley
(313) 841-3700

Middle Eastern
Waleed's
32425 Northwestern Highway
Farmington Hills
(810) 932-2540

Polish
Polish Village
2990 Yemans
Hamtramck
(313) 874-5726

Thai
Bangkok Cuisine
2240 Sixteen Mile Road at
Dequindre
Sterling Heights
(810) 977-0130

Vietnamese
The Mini Restaurant
475 University West
Windsor, Ontario
(519) 254-2221

HARTFORD, CT

Afghani
Shish Kebab House of
Afghanistan
360 Franklin Avenue
(203) 296-0301

Chinese
China Pan
16000 Southeast Road
Farmington
(203) 674-1311

French
Le Petite Cafe
225 Montowese Street
Branford
(203) 483-9791

German
Edelweiss
980 Farmington Avenue
West Hartford
(203) 236-3096

Greek
Tapas
1150 New Britian Avenue
West Hartford
(203) 521-4609

Indian
Bombay's Authentic Indian
89 Arch Street (Main Street)
(203) 724-4282

Hartford, CT (continued)

Italian
> Alforno Ristorante
> 78 LaSalle Road
> West Hartford
> (203) 523-4448

Japanese
> Osaka
> 962 A Farmington Avenue
> West Hartford
> (203) 233-1877

Mexican
> Aqui Me Quedo
> 259 Franklin Avenue
> (203) 522-1717

Polish
> Fatherland
> 450 South Main Street
> New Britian
> (203) 224-3345

Portuguese
> Ferro Velho
> 1841 Park Street
> (203) 233-4693

Spanish
> Costa Del Sol
> 901 Wethersfield Avenue 1-91,
>   Monte Carlo Plaza
> (203) 296-1714

Thai
> Bangkok Cuisine
> 2477 Albany Avenue
> (203) 236-8142

Vietnamese
> Truc Orient Express
> 735 Wethersfield Avenue
> (203) 296-2818

HOUSTON, TX

Argentine
> Lalo's Cafe
> 5355 West Bellfort
> (713) 668-2255

Armenian
> Phoenicia Deli
> 12116 Westheimer
> (713) 558-0416

Caribbean
> Calypso
> 5555 Morningside Drive,
>   Rice Village
> (713) 524-8571

Chinese
> Dong Ting
> 611 Stuart
> (713) 527-0005

Ethiopian
> Queen Of Sheba
> 5710 Bellaire
> Chimney Rock
> (713) 665-3009

French
> La Reserve
> 4 Riverway, Omni Houston
>   Hotel
> (713) 871-8177
>
> Chez Georges
> 11920 Westheimer
> (713) 497-1122

French Bistro
> La Madeleine
> 4002 Westheimer, Highland
>   Village
> (713) 623-0644

German

Rudi Lechner's
2503 South Gessner
(713) 782-1180

Greek

The Great Greek
80 Woodlake Square (Corner
  of Gessner and Westheimer)
(713) 783-5100

Indian

India's
5704 Richmond
(713) 266-0131

Khyber
2510 Richmond
(713) 942-9424

Indonesian

Indonesian Garden
10600 Bellaire
(713) 495-2833

Iranian

Yildlizar
3419 Kirby
(713) 524-7735

Darband Kabobi
5670 Hillcroft
(713) 975-8350

Italian

Anthony's
4611 Montrose
(713) 961-0552

La Mora (Tuscan)
912 Lovett
(713) 522-7412

Japanese

Ginza Japanese
5868 San Felipe
(713) 785-0332

Korean

Korea Garden
9501 Long Point
(713) 468-2800

Lebanese

Sammy's
5825 Richmond
(713) 780-0065

DiMassi's
5064 Richmond
(713) 439-7481

Mexican

Guadalajara Bar & Grill
210 Town and Country Village
(713) 461-5300

Persian

Garson
2926 Hillcroft
(713) 781-0400

South American

Churrascos
9788 Bissonnet (Beltway 8)
(713) 541-2100

Spanish

Mediterranean
2425 West Holcombe
(713) 662-8302

Swiss

Quail Hollow Inn
214 Morton Street
Richmond
(713) 341-6733

Houston, TX (continued)

Thai
>Thai Cafe
>10928 Westheimer
>(713) 780-3096
>
>Chatchawal's Bay Thai
>1101 Second Street
>Seabrook
>(713) 474-4248

Vietnamese
>Kim Son
>8200 Wilcrest
>(713) 498-7841

INDIANAPOLIS, IN

German
>Cafe Europa
>4709 North Shadeland Avenue
>(317) 547-4474

Greek
>Greek Islands Restaurant
>906 South Meridian
>(317) 636-0700

Italian
>Salvatore's Ristorante
>1268 West 86th Street
>(317) 844-9144

Japanese
>Sakura
>7201 North Keystone Avenue
>(317) 259-4171

Middle Eastern
>Aesop Table
>600 Massachusetts Avenue
>(317) 631-0055

Russian
>Russia House
>4075 West 86th Street
>(317) 876-7990

KANSAS CITY, MO

Chinese
>Bo Ling's
>4800 Main, Board of Trade
>Building
>(816) 753-1718

French
>La Mediterranee
>9058-B Metcalf (Glenwood
>Plaza Center)
>Overland Park, KS
>(913) 341-9595

German
>Rheinland Restaurant
>208 North Main Street
>(off Truman Road)
>Independence, MO
>(816) 461-5383

Indian
>Mother India
>9036 Metcalf,
>Glenwood Plaza Center
>Overland Park, KS
>(913) 341-0415

Italian
>Macaluso's
>1403 West 39th Street
>(816) 561-0100

Japanese
>Jun's Authentic Japanese
>Restaurant
>7660 State Line
>(913) 341-4924

Mediterranean
    Cafe Mediterraneo
    5444 Wesport Road at Mill
        Street
    (816) 531-7221

Mexican
    Rudy's Tenampo Tacqueria
    1611 Westport Road
    (816) 931-9700

Middle Eastern
    Jerusalem Cafe
    431 Westport Road
    (816) 756-2770

Persian
    Kabob House
    8950 Wornall
    (816) 333-2744

South American
    Juanchito
    12112 West 87th Street at
        Quivira
    Lenexa, KS
    (913) 599-5222

Swiss
    Andre's Confiserie Suisse
        (lunch only)
    5018 Main Street
    (816) 561-3440

Thai
    Thai Orchid
    6504 Martway
    Mission, KS
    (913) 384-2800

Vietnamese
    Saigon 39
    1806 West 39th Street
    (816) 531-4447

LAS VEGAS, NV

Brazilian
    Yolie's
    3900 Paradise Road
    (702) 794-0700

Chinese
    Chin's
    3200 Las Vegas Boulevard,
        South, Fashion Show Mall
    (702) 733-8899

French
    Pamplemousse
    400 East Sahara Avenue
    (702) 733-2066

Greek
    Olympic Cafe
    4023 Spring Mountain Road
    (702) 876-7900

Indian
    Shalimar
    3900 Paradise Road
    (702) 796-0302

Italian
    Stefano's
    129 East Fremont Street,
        Golden Nugget Hotel
    (702) 385-7111

Japanese
    Hakase
    3900 Paradise Road
    (702) 796-1234

Korean
    Seoul BBQ
    953 East Sahara Avenue
    (702) 369-4123

Las Vegas, NV (continued)

Mexican
> Lindo Michoacan
> 2655 Desert Inn Road
> (702) 735-6828

Moroccan
> Mamounia
> 4632 South Maryland Parkway
> (702) 597-0092

Thai
> Lotus of Siam
> 953 East Sahara Avenue,
>   Commercial Center
> (702) 735-4477

Vietnamese
> Saigon
> 4251 West Sahara Avenue
> (702) 362-9978

LITTLE ROCK, AR

African
> Calabash
> 1318 South Main
> (501) 372-6858

Chinese
> Hunan
> 2924 South University
> (501) 562-4320

French
> Alouette's/La Casse Croute
> 11401 North Rodney Parham
> (501) 225-4152

Greek
> Leo's Greek Castle
> 2925 Kavanaugh
> (501) 666-7414

Indian
> Star Of India
> 301 North Shackleford
> (501) 227-9900

Italian
> Bruno's Little Italy
> 315 North Bowman Road
> (501) 224-4700

Japanese
> Mt. Fuji
> 10301 North Rodney Parham
> (501) 227-6498

Mexican
> Juanita's
> 1300 South Main
> (501) 221-7777

Middle Eastern
> The Terrace
> 10700 North Rodney
> Parham
> (501) 224-1677

Spanish
> Tapas
> 10301 North Rodney Parham
> (501) 224-7707

LOS ANGELES, CA

Albanian
> Ajetis Albania
> 425 Pier Avenue
> Hermosa Beach
> (310) 379-9012

Brazilian
> Cafe Brazil
> 10831 Venice Boulevard
> West LA
> (310) 837-8957

Chilean

Rincon Chileno Deli
435456 Melrose Avenue
(213) 666-6077

Chinese

Wei Fun
708 East Las Tunas Drive #4
San Gabriel
(818) 286-6152

Colombian

La Fonda Antioquena
4903 Melrose Avenue
(213) 957-5164

Cuban

Versailles
17410 Ventura Boulevard
Encino
(818) 906-0756

Ecuadorean

Ecuatoriano No. 2
1512 South Vermont Avenue
(213) 380-7928

Ethiopian

Rosalind's
44 South Fairfax Avenue
(213) 936-2486

Filipino

Barrio Fiesta
3821 West 6th Street
(213) 383-9762

French

L'Orangerie
903 North La Cienega
   Boulevard
West Hollywood
(310) 652-9770

French Bistro

Pinot Bistro
12969 Ventura Boulevard
Studio City
(818) 990-0500

German

Knoll's Black Forest Inn
2454 Wilshire Boulevard
Santa Monica
(310) 395-2212

Greek

Le Petit Greek
Beverly Connection
100 North La Cienega
   Boulevard
(310) 657-5932

Guatemalan

Guatelinda
2220 West 7th Street
(213) 385-7420

Hungarian

Hungarian Budapest
7986 Sunset Boulevard
(213) 654-3744

Indian

Sabra's
18189 South Pioneer
   Boulevard
Artesia South
(310) 924-4948

Indonesian

Bali Place
2530 Overland Avenue
West LA
(310) 204-4341

Los Angeles, CA (continued)

Israeli
>Tempo
>16610 Ventura Boulevard
>Encino
>(818) 905-5855

Italian
>Bellapasta
>825 West Ninth Street
>(213) 488-0400

Japanese
>Issenjoki
>333 South Alameda #301
>Little Tokyo
>(213) 680-1703

Korean
>Nam Kang
>3055 West 7th Street
>Koreatown
>(213) 380-6606

Lebanese
>Al Amir
>5750 Wilshire Boulevard
>(213) 931-8740

Mexican
>Maria'a Ramada
>1064 North Kingsley Drive
>(213) 660-4436

Moroccan
>Dar Maghreb
>7651 Sunset Boulevard
>Hollywood
>(213) 876-7651

Nicaraguan
>Casa El Pulgarecito
>1007 North Alvarado Street
>(213) 413-1877

Persian
>Javan Restaurant
>11628 Santa Monica Boulevard
>#9
>West LA
>(310) 207-5555

Polish
>Warszawa
>1414 Lincoln Boulevard
>Santa Monica
>(310) 393-8831

Romanian
>Mignon
>1253 North Vine Street #11
>Hollywood
>(213) 461-4192

Russian
>Little Russia
>1132 East Broadway
>Glendale
>(818) 243-4787

Salvadoran
>Papaturro
>4109 West Beverly Boulevard
>(213) 660-4363

Spanish
>Tasca
>6266 1/2 Sunset Boulevard
>Hollywood
>(213) 654-1746

Thai
>Jitlada Restaurant
>5233 1/2 Sunset Boulevard
>(213) 667-9809

Tunisian
Moun of Tunis
7445 1/2 Sunset Boulevard
Hollywood
(213) 874-3333

Vietnamese
Thien Thanh No. 1
5423 West 1st Street
Santa Ana
(714) 554-7260

Yugoslavian
Beograd
10540 Magnolia Boulevard
North Hollywood
(818) 766-8689

LOUISVILLE, KY

Chinese
Asian Pearl
2060 South Hurstbourne Lane
(502) 495-6800

French
Le Relais
Bowman Field
(502) 451-9020

German
Gasthaus
4812 Brownsboro Road
(502) 899-7177

Indian
Shalimar
3315 Bardstown Road
(502) 493-8899

Italian
Bravo's
600 West Main Street
(502) 568-2222

Japanese
Sachicoma
744 Baxter Avenue
(502) 583-0304

Korean
Koreana
5009 Preston Highway
(502) 966-2900

Middle Eastern / Greek
Grape Leaf
2217 Frankfort Avenue
(502) 897-1774

Spanish
De La Torre's
1606 Bardstown Road
(502) 456-4955

Thai
Thai Siam
3002 1/2 Bardstown Road
(502) 458-6871

Vietnamese
Vietnam Kitchen
5339 Mitschner Avenue
(502) 363-5154

MEMPHIS, TN

Caribbean
Automatic Slim's
83 South Second
(901) 525-7948

Chinese
China Grill
2089 Madison
(901) 725-9888

Memphis, TN (continued)

French
Aubergine
5007 Black Road
(901) 767-7840

German
Erika's
52 South Second
(901) 526-5522

Greek
Le Caveau Grec
933 Carling Avenue
(613) 722-8601

Indian
Delhi Palace
6110 Macon
(901) 386-3600

Italian
The Original Grisanti's
1489 Airways
(901) 458-2648

Japanese
Sekisui of Japan
50 Humphrey's Boulevard
(901) 747-0001

Mediterranean
Marena's
1545 Overton Park
(901) 278-9774

Russian
Cafe Samovar
83 Union Avenue
(901) 529-9607

Thai
Golden Dragon
153 North Cleveland
(901) 725-9447

Vietnamese
Saigon Le
51 North Cleveland
(901) 276-5326

MIAMI, FL

Argentine
Zuperpollo
1247 SW 22nd Street
Coral Way
(305) 477-6556

Austrian
Mozart Stube
325 Alcazar Avenue
Coral Gables
(305) 446-1600

Brazilian
Rodeo Grill
2121 Ponce de Leon Boulevard
Coral Gables
(305) 447-6336

Caribbean
Mark's Place
2286 NE 123rd Street
(305) 893-6888

Chinese
Tropical Chinese Restaurant
799 SW 48th Street
Miami West Dade
(305) 262-7576

Cuban

    Victor's Cafe
    2348 SW 32nd Avenue
    (305) 445-1313

Danish

    Fleming
    8511 SW 136th Street, US 1
    (305) 232-6444

French

    Dominique
    5225 Collins Avenue,
      Alexander Hotel
    (305) 861-5252

French Bistro

    Brasserie Le Coze
    2981 Florida Avenue
    Coconut Grove
    (305) 444-9697

German

    Bavarian Village
    1401 North Federal Highway
    Hollywood
    (305) 922-7321

Indian

    Darbar
    276 Alhambra Circle
    Coral Gables
    (305) 448-9691

Italian

    Il Tupliano
    11052 Biscayne Boulevard
    (305) 893-4811

Japanese

    Tani Guchi's Place
    2224 NE 123rd Street, San
      Souci Place
    (305) 892-6744

Mediterranean

    Brickell Club
    1221 Brickell Avenue, 27th
      floor
    (305) 536-9000

Nicaraguan

    El Novillo
    Bird and 67th
    (305) 284-8417

Spanish

    Casa Juancho
    3436 SW 8th Avenue
    (305) 642-2452

Swiss

    La Paloma
    10999 Biscayne Boulevard
    (305) 891-0505

Thai

    Thai Toni
    890 Washington Avenue
    (305) 538-8424

Vietnamese

    Hy Vong
    3458 SW 8th Street
    (305) 446-3674

MILWAUKEE, WI

African

    African Garden
    4124 West Capitol Drive
    (414) 444-4171

Chinese

    Oriental Coast
    1230 East Brady Street
    (414) 278-8680

Milwaukee, WI (continued)

German
Karl Ratzsch's
320 East Mason Street
(414) 276-2720

Greek
Dionysus
770 North Jefferson
(414) 224-6001

Italian
Maniaci's
6904 North Santa Monica
Fox Point
(414) 352-5757

Japanese
Izumi's
2178 North Prospect Avenue
(414) 271-5278

Latin American
Palomas
611 West National Avenue
(414) 649-2565

Mexican
Atotonilco
1100 South 11th Street
(414) 384-2678

Middle Eastern
Au Bon Appetit
1016 East Brady
(414) 278-1233

Persian
Persepolis
730 West Mitchell
(414) 384-9590

Polish
Polonez
2316 South 6th Street
(414) 384-8766

Serbian
The Three Brothers
2414 South St. Clair Street
(414) 481-7530

Thai
Thai Royal
629 North Broadway
(414) 224-8424

Vietnamese
West Bank Cafe
732 East Burleigh
(414) 562-5555

MINNEAPOLIS / ST. PAUL, MN

Afghani
Caravan Serai
2175 Ford Parkway
St. Paul
(612) 690-1935

Austrian
Mitterhauser's
2640 Lyndale Avenue South
Minneapolis
(612) 872-4808

Caribbean
Chez Bananas
129 4th Street, Textile Building
Minneapolis
(612) 340-0032

Chinese

Leeann Chin Chinese Cuisine
900 Second Avenue South,
International Center
Minneapolis
(612) 338-8488

214 East 4th Street, Union
Depot
St. Paul
(612) 224-8814

Bonaventure, 1571 South
Plymouth Road
Minnetonka
(612) 545-3600

East African

Odaa
408 Cedar Avenue
Minneapolis
(612) 338-4459

Ethiopian

Blue Nile
Lake Street and Lyndale
Avenue South
Minneapolis
(612) 823-8029

French Classic

Brasserie
1400 Nicollet Avenue
Minneapolis
(612) 874-7285

German

Gasthof Zur Gemutlichkeit
2300 University Avenue, NE
Minneapolis
(612) 781-3860

Greek

Christos
2632 Nicollet Avenue
Minneapolis
(612) 871-2111

Italian

Ristorante Luci
470 Cleveland Avenue
St. Paul
(612) 699-8258

Buca Little Italy
11 South 12th Street
Minneapolis
(612) 638-2225

Japanese

Kabuki Japanese Restaurant
6534 Flying Cloud Drive
Eden Prairie
(612) 941-5115

Korean

Mirror Of Korea
761 Snelling Avenue North
St. Paul
(612) 647-9004

Lebanese

Emily's Lebanese Deli
641 University Avenue NE
Minneapolis
(612) 379-4069

Mexican

La Cucaracha Restaurante
Corner of Dale and Grand
St. Paul
(612) 221-9682

Minneapolis / St. Paul, MN
(continued)

Peruvian
Machu Picchu
2940 Lyndale Avenue South
Minneapolis
(612) 822-2125

Polish
Nye's Polanaise Room
112 Hennepin Avenue East
Minneapolis
(612) 379-2021

Thai
Royal Orchid
1835 Nicollet Avenue
Minneapolis
(612) 872-1938

Vietnamese
White Lily
758 Grand Avenue, Crocus
Center Mall
St. Paul
(612) 293-9124

Nashville, TN

Caribbean
Calypso Cafe
2424 Elliston Place
(615) 321-3878

Chinese
Peking Duck
1923 Division Street
(615) 327-2020

German
Old Heidelberg
423 Union Street
(615) 256-9147

Greek
Kebab Gyros
210 4th Avenue
(615) 256-4871

Italian
Lorenzo's
2823 Nolensville Road
(615) 254-9888

Japanese
Ichiban
109 2nd Avenue North
(615) 254-7185

Mexican
Blanca's
174 2nd Avenue North
(615) 254-0444

Thai
Siam Cafe
316 McCall Street
(615) 834-3181

New Orleans, LA

Caribbean
Palmer's
135 North Carrollton Avenue
(504) 482-3658

Chinese
Trey Yuen
600 North Causeway
Boulevard (Hwy. 150)
Mandeville
(504) 626-4476

Croatian
Drago's
3232 North Arnoult Street
(17th Street)
Metairie
(504) 888-9254

French

L'Economie
325 Girod Street at Commerce
Street
(504) 524-7405

Greek

The Little Greek
2051 Metairie Road
(504) 831-9470

Indian

Taj Mahal
923 Metairie Road (Rosa
Avenue)
Metairie
(504) 836-6859

Italian

Pascal's Manale Restaurant
1838 Napolean Avenue
(Dryades Street)
(504) 895-4877

Japanese

Little Tokyo
1521 North Causeway
Boulevard
Metairie
(504) 831-6788

Korean

Genghis Khan
4053 Tulane Avenue
(504) 482-4044

Mexican

Gustavo's
3515 Williams Boulevard
(W. Esplanade Avenue)
Kenner
(504) 443-2260

Middle Eastern

Mona's
3901 Banks Street
(beside South Carrollton
Avenue & Scott Street)
(504) 482-0661

Thai

Bangkok Cuisine
4137 South Carrollton Avenue
(504) 482-3606

Vietnamese

Don Phuong
14207 Chef Menteur Highway
(504) 254-0296

NEW YORK, NY

Belgian

Cafe de Bruxelles
118 Greenwich Avenue
(West 13th Street)
(212) 206-1830

Caribbean

Flying Fish
395 West Street
(West 10th Street)
(212) 924-5050

Chinese

Shun Lee Palace
155 East 55th Street
(between Lexington & 3rd)
(212) 371-8844

French

La Caravelle
33 West 55th
(212) 586-4252

New York, NY (continued)

German
Roettelle A. G.
126 East 7th Street
(212) 674-4140

Greek
Periyali
35 West 20th Street (between
5th & 6th Avenues)
(212) 463-7891

Hungarian
Red Tulip
439 East 75th Street
(212) 734-4893

Indian
Gandhi
345 East 6th Street (between
1st & 2nd Avenues)
(212) 614-9718

Japanese
Sushisay
38 East 51st Street (between
Madison & Park)
(212) 755-1780

Korean
Kom Tang Soot Bul House
32 West 32nd Street
(between 5th & Broadway)
(212) 947-8482

Mexican
Zarela
953 Second Avenue
(212) 644-6740

Middle Eastern
Afghan Kebab House
764 9th Avenue (between 51st
& 52nd Streets)
(212) 307-1662

Moroccan
Moroccan Star
205 Atlantic Avenue
Brooklyn
(718) 643-0800

Polish
Little Poland
200 Second Avenue (between
12th & 13th Streets)
(212) 777-9728

Russian
Petrossian
182 West 58th Street (7th
Avenue)
(212) 245-2214

Scandinavian
Aquavit
13 West 54th Street (between
5th & 6th Avenues)
(212) 307-7311

South American
Boca Chica
13 First Avenue
(212) 473-0108

Spanish
The Ballroom
253 West 28th Street (between
7th & 8th Avenues)
(212) 244-3005

Thai
> Thailand Restaurant
> 106 Bayard Street
> (Baxter Street)
> (212) 349-3132

Ukrainian
> Veselka
> 144 Second Avenue
> (9th Street)
> (212) 228-9682

Vietnamese
> New Viet Huong
> 77 Mulberry Street (between
> Canal & Bayard Streets)
> (212) 233-8988

ORLANDO, FL

Brazilian
> Brazilian Pavilion
> 140 West Fairbanks Avenue
> Winter Park
> (407) 740-7440

Chinese
> Ming Court
> 9188 International Drive
> (407) 351-9988

Cuban
> Rolando's Cuban Restaurant
> 870 Semoran Boulevard
> Casselberry
> (407) 767-9677

French Bistro
> Le Provence
> 50 East Pine Street
> (407) 843-1320

French Classic
> La Normandie
> 2021 East Colonial Drive
> (407) 896-9976

French Provençal
> Le Coq au Vin
> 4800 South Orange Avenue
> (407) 851-6980

German
> Bauern-Stube
> 5607 South Orange Avenue
> (407) 857-8404

Greek
> Olympia
> 8505 East Colonial Drive
> (407) 273-7836

Indian
> Passage to India
> 5532 International Drive
> (407) 351-3456

Italian
> Capriccio
> Peabody Orlando
> 9801 International Drive
> (407) 352-4000

Japanese
> Ichiban
> 19 South Orange Avenue
> (407) 423-2688

Korean
> Korea House
> 977 West State Road 434
> Longwood
> (407) 767-5918

Orlando, FL (continued)

Middle Eastern
Phoenician
7600 Dr. Phillips Boulevard
(407) 345-1001

Norwegian
Akershus Restaurant
Norway: EPCOT Center, Walt
 Disney World
(407) 560-5178

Thai
Siam Orchid
7575 Republic Drive
(407) 351-0821

Vietnamese
Ha Long
120 North Orange Avenue
(407) 648-1555

OTTAWA, CANADA

Afghani
Silk Roads
300 Sparks Street
(613) 236-4352

Chinese
Mandarin Ogilvie Dining
 Lounge
1137 Ogilvie Road
(613) 749-8838

Ethiopian
Addis Cafe
1093 Wellington Street
(613) 725-5127

French Bistro
Le Pied de Cochon
242 Montcalm Street
Hull
(613) 777-5808

French Classic
Le Jardin
127 York Street
(613) 241-1424

German
Lindenhof
965 Richmond Road
(613) 725-3481

Greek
Le Caveau Grec
933 Carling Avenue
(613) 722-8601

Indian
Mukut
610 Rideau Street
(613) 789-2220

Italian
Romano's Ristorante
309 Richmond Road
(613) 722-6772

Japanese
Festival Japan
149 Kent Street
(613) 234-1224

Malaysian
Chahaya Malaysia
749 Bank Street
(613) 237-4304

Mexican
Feleena's Comida Mexicana
742 Bank Street
(613) 233-2010

Spanish
>Restaurante Costa Brava
>486 Albert Street
>(613) 741-4045

Thai
>Coriander Thai Cuisine
>282 Kent Street
>(613) 233-2828

Vietnamese
>Good Morning Vietnam
>323 Rideau Street
>(613) 789-4080

PHILADELPHIA, PA

Afghani
>Kabul
>106 Chestnut Street
>(215) 922-3676

Belgian
>Brigid's
>726 North 24th Street
>(215) 232-3232

Brazilian
>Brasil's
>112 Chestnut Street
>(215) 413-1700

Burmese
>Rangoon
>145 North 9th Street
>(215) 829-8939

Chinese Hong Kong
>Golden Pond
>1006 Race Street
>(215) 923-0303

Chinese Taiwanese
>Ray's Coffee Shop
>141 North 9th Street
>(215) 922-5122

Ethiopian
>Dahlak
>4708 Baltimore Avenue
>(215) 726-6464

French Bistro
>Alisa Cafe
>109 Fairfield Avenue
>Upper Darby
>(610) 352-4402

French Classic
>Le Bec-Fin
>1523 Walnut Street
>(215) 567-1000

German
>Otto's Brauhaus & Beer
> Garden
>233 Easton Road
>Horsham
>(215) 675-1864

Greek
>Cafe Theodore
>1100 South Columbus
> Boulevard, Riverview Plaza
>(215) 271-6800

Indian
>Passage to India
>1320 Walnut Street
>(215) 732-7300

Israeli
>Kinneret
>4248 Spruce Street
>(215) 382-7701

Philadelphia, PA (continued)

Italian Classic
Mr. Martino's Trattoria
1646 East Passyunk Avenue
(215) 755-0663

Italian Roman Jewish
Tira Misu Ristorante
528 South 5th Street
(215) 925-3335

Japanese
Sagami
37 Crescent Boulevard
Collingswood, NJ
(609) 854-9773

Korean
Korea House
117 South 18th Street
(215) 567-3739

Lebanese
Cedars
616 South 2nd Street
(215) 925-4950

Mediterranean
Dmitri's
795 South 3rd Street
(215) 625-0556

Mexican
Zocalo
36th and Lancaster Avenue
(215) 895-0139

Moroccan
Marrakesh
517 South Leithgow Street
(215) 925-5929

Persian
Persian Grill
637 Germantown Pike
Lafayette Hill
(610) 566-4110

Polish
Warsaw Cafe
306 South 16th Street
(215) 546-0204

Portuguese
Berlengas Islands Restaurant
4926 North 5th Street
(215) 324-3240

Spanish
Tapas Restaurant
1176 North 3rd Street
(215) 922-2376

Thai
Thai Garden East
101 North 11th Street
(215) 629-9939

Vietnamese
Vietnam Palace
222 North 11th Street
(215) 592-9596

PHOENIX, AZ

Chinese
Gourmet House of Hong Kong
1438 East McDowell Road
(602) 253-4859

Cuban
Havana Cafe
4225 East Camelback Road
(602) 952-1991

French Bistro
Marche Gourmet
4121 North Marshall Way
Scottsdale
(602) 994-4568

French Classic
Voltaire
8340 East McDonald Drive
Scottsdale
(602) 948-1005

German
Bavarian Point
4815 East Main Street
Mesa
(602) 830-0999

Greek
Greekfest
1940 East Camelback Road
(602) 265-2990

Indian
Taste of India
1609 East Bell Road
(602) 788-3190

Italian
Ianuzzi
34505 North Scottsdale
(el Pedregal)
Carefree
(602) 488-4141

Japanese
Yamakasa
9301 East Shea Boulevard
Scottsdale
(602) 860-5605

Korean
Korean Restaurant
1414 North Scottsdale Road
Scottsdale
(602) 994-5995

Mexican
Macayo Mexican Restaurant
4001 North Central
(602) 264-6141

Middle Eastern
Mediterrean House
1588 East Bethany Home Road
(602) 248-8460

Salvadoran
Eliana's
1627 North 24th Street
(602) 225-2925

Swiss
Le Gourmand
12345 West Indian School
Road
Litchfield Park
(602) 935-1515

Thai
Malee's on Main
7131 East Main Street
Scottsdale
(602) 947-6042

PITTSBURGH, PA

Cambodian
Phnom Penh
410 First Avenue
(412) 261-4166

Pittsburgh, PA (continued)

Caribbean
    Jamaica Jamaica
    1430 Fifth Avenue
    (412) 281-3726

Chinese
    China Palace
    210 Forbes Avenue
    (412) 263-2566

Filipino
    La Filipiniana
    5321 Butler Street
    (412) 781-8724

French Classic
    Chez Gerard
    Route 40 East
    Hopewood
    (412) 437-9001

French Provençal
    Le Pommier
    2104 East Carson Street
    (412) 431-1901

German
    Kleiner Deutschmann
    643 Pittsburgh Street
    Springdale
    (412) 274-5022

Greek
    Suzi's
    130 6th Street
    (412) 261-6443

    1704 Shady Avenue
    (412) 422-8066

Indian
    India Garden
    328 Atwood Street
    (412) 682-3000

Indonesian
    Bacchri's
    3821 Willow Avenue
    (412) 343-2213

Italian
    Davio
    2100 Broadway Avenue
    (412) 531-7422

Japanese
    Sushi Too
    5432 Walnut Street
    (412) 687-8744

Korean
    Sushi Kim
    1241 Penn Avenue
    (412) 281-9956

Mexican
    The Fajita Grill
    580 Old Clarton Road
    (412) 653-7230

Middle Eastern
    Ali Baba
    404 South Craig Street
    (412) 682-2829

Russian
    Moscow Nights
    1722 Murray Avenue
    (412) 521-5005

South American
    La Feria
    5527 Walnut Street
    (412) 682-4501

Spanish
Mallorca
2228 East Carson Street
(412) 488-1818

Thai
Rama Restaurant
346 Atwood Street
(412) 687-8424

Vietnamese
Kim's Coffee Shop
5447 Penn Avenue
(412) 362-7019

PORTLAND, OR

Chinese
Fong Chong
301 NW Fourth Avenue
(503) 220-0235

Ethiopian
Jarra's
1435 SE Hawthorne Boulevard
(503) 230-8990

French
L'Auberge
2601 NW Vaughn Street
(503) 223-3302

French Bistro
Cafe Des Amis
1987 NW Kearney Street
(503) 295-6487

Greek
Alexis
215 West Burnside Street
(503) 224-8577

Indian
Swagat
4325 SW 109th Avenue
Beaverton
(503) 626-3000

Italian
Genoa
2832 SE Belmont Street
(503) 238-1464

Japanese
Fuji
2878 SE Gladstone
(503) 233-0577

Korean
Han Kuk Kwan
5021 SE Powell Boulevard
(503) 771-3041

Lebanese
Al Amir
223 SW Stark Street
(503) 274-0010

Mediterranean
Zefiro
500 NW 21st Avenue
(503) 226-3394

Spanish
La Catalana
2821 SE Stark Street
(503) 232-0948

Thai
Lemongrass
5832 NE Glisan Street
(503) 231-5780

Vietnamese
New Saigon
630 South Federal Boulevard
(303) 936-4954

RALEIGH / DURHAM, NC

Chinese
Canton Cafe
408 Hillsboro Street
Raleigh
(919) 832-7867

Neo-China
4015 University Drive
Durham
(919) 489-2828

Greek
Nikos Taverna
905 West Main Street
Brightleaf Square
Durham
(919) 682-0043

Indian
India Mahal
3212 Hillsboro Street
Raleigh
(919) 836-9742

Suman's
912 West Main Street
Durham
(919) 956-7523

Italian
Piccola Italia
423 Woodburn Road,
Cameron Village
Raleigh
(919) 833-6888

Japanese
Kashin
Raleigh
(919) 851-7101

Yamazushi's
4711 Hope Valley Road
Durham
(919) 493-7748

Mexican
Eldorado
2811 Brentwood Road
Raleigh
(919) 872-8440

El Rodeo
905 West Main Street
Brightleaf Square
Durham
(919) 683-2417

Middle Eastern
Neomonde Deli
3817 Beryl Road
Raleigh
(919) 828-1628

Ambrosia
4711 Hope Valley Road
Durham
(919) 490-5770

Thai
Thai Garden
1408 Hardimont Road
Raleigh
(919) 872-6811

SAINT LOUIS, MO

Chinese
China Royal
5911 North Lindbergh
Hazelwood
(314) 731-1313

Ethiopian
Red Sea
6511 Delmar Boulevard
University City
(314) 863-0099

Filipino
Cafe de Manila
3161 South Grand Boulevard
(314) 772-8222

French Bistro
Cafe Provençal
40 North Central Avenue
Clayton
(314) 725-2755

French Classic
Cafe de France
410 Olive Street
(314) 231-2204

German
Bevo Mill
4749 Gravois Avenue
(314) 481-2626

Greek
Spiro's
3122 Watson Road
(314) 645-8383

Indian
India Palace
4534 North Lindbergh
(314) 731-3333

Italian
Tony's
410 Market Street
(314) 231-7007

Japanese
Seki
6335 Delmar Boulevard
University City
(314) 726-6477

Mexican
Pueblo Nuevo
7401 North Lindbergh
Boulevard, Elm Grove
Shopping Center
Hazelwood
(314) 831-6885

Middle Eastern
Saleem's
6501 Delmar Boulevard
University City
(314) 721-7947

Pakistani
Koh-i-Noor
608 Eastgate
University City
(314) 721-3796

Persian
Cafe Natasha
6623 Delmar Boulevard
University City
(314) 727-0419

Russian
Alexander The Russian Tea
Room
Gold Tower/West Port Plaza
(Page Avenue)
Maryland Heights
(314) 434-1800

Saint Louis, MO (continued)

Thai
> Thai Cafe
> 6170 Delmar Boulevard
> University City
> (314) 862-6868

Vietnamese
> Mekong
> 3131 South Grand Boulevard
> (314) 773-3100

SALT LAKE CITY, UT

Chinese
> Golden Phoenix
> 1084 South State Street
> (801) 539-1122

French
> L'Hermitage
> 1615 South Foothill Drive
>   (2300 East)
> (801) 583-5339

French Bistro
> Le Parisian
> 417 South 300 East
> (801) 364-5223

German
> Marianne's Deli
> 149 West 200 South
> (801) 364-0513

Greek
> The Hungry I
> 1440 South Foothill Drive
> (801) 582-8600

Indian
> Star Of India
> 177 East 200 South
> (801) 363-7555

Japanese
> Kyoto
> 1080 East 1300 South
> (801) 487-3525

Italian
> Fresco Italian Cafe
> 1513 South 1500 East
> (801) 486-1300

Mexican
> Red Iguana
> 736 West, North Temple
> (801) 322-1489

Middle Eastern
> Cedars of Lebanon
> 152 East 2nd Street South
> (801) 364-4097

Thai
> Bangkok Thai
> 1400 South Foothill Boulevard,
>   Foothill Village
> (801) 583-7840

Vietnamese
> Cafe Trang
> 818 South Main Street
> (801) 539-1638

SAN ANTONIO, TX

Caribbean
> El Caribe
> 2611 Wagon Wheel
> (210) 826-8818

Chinese
> Ding How
> 4531 NW Loop 410
> (210) 340-7944

French
Chez Ardid
1919 San Pedro at Woodlawn
(210) 732-3203

Greek
Demo's
7115 Blanco
(210) 342-2772

German
Edelweiss
4400 Rittiman Road
(210) 829-5552

Indian
Simi's Indian Cuisine
4535 Fredericksburg Road
(210) 737-3166

Italian
Boccones
1776 Blanco Road
(210) 492-2996

Japanese
Koi Kawa
4051 Broadway
(210) 805-8111

Mexican
La Calesa
2103 East Hildebrand
(210) 822-4475

Spanish
Barcelona's Cafe
4901 Broadway
(210) 822-6129

Thai
Dang's Thai
1146 Austin Highway
(210) 829-7345

Vietnamese
Vietnam Restaurant
3244 Broadway
(210) 822-7461

SAN DIEGO, CA

Afghani
Khyber Pass
4647 Convoy Street
(619) 571-3749

Caribbean
Alizé
777 Front Street
(619) 234-0411

Chinese
Chang
8670 Genesee
(619) 558-2288

5500 Grossmont Center Drive
La Mesa
(619) 464-2288

Cuban
Andres'
1235 Morena Boulevard
(619) 275-4114

French
Mille Fleurs
6009 Paseo Delicias
Rancho Santa Fe
(619) 756-3085

French Provençal
Marius
2000 Second Street,
Le Meridien Hotel
Coronado
(619) 435-3000

San Diego, CA (continued)

German

    Kaiserhof Restaurant
    2253 Sunset Cliffs Boulevard
    (619) 224-0606

Greek

    Athens Market & Taverna
    109 West F Street
    (619) 234-1955

Indian

    Taj Mahal
    13035 Pomerado Road
    Poway
    (619) 748-4845

Italian

    Prego
    1370 Frazee Road
    (Mission Valley)
    (619) 294-4700

Japanese

    Kiyo's
    531 F Street
    (619) 238-1726

Mexican

    El Tecolote
    6110 Friars Road
    (619) 295-2087

Middle Eastern

    Aladdin
    5420 Clairemont Mesa
     Boulevard
    (619) 573-0000

Portuguese

    Cafe Bravo
    895 4th Avenue
    (619) 234-8888

Scandinavian

    Dansk Restaurant
    8425 La Mesa Boulevard
    (619) 463-0640

Spanish

    Cafe Sevilla
    555 4th Avenue
    (619) 233-5979

Thai

    Five Star Thai Cuisine
    816 Broadway
    (619) 231-4408

SAN FRANCISCO, CA

Afghani

    Helmand
    430 Broadway
    (415) 362-0641

Brazilian

    Bahia
    41 Franklin Street
    (415) 626-3306

Burmese

    Mandalay
    4348 California Street
    (415) 386-3895

Cambodian

    Angkor Borei
    3471 Mission Street
    (415) 550-8417

Caribbean

    Cha Cha Cha's
    1801 Haight Street
    (415) 386-5758

Chinese
House of Nanking
919 Kearney Street
(415) 421-1429

Cuban
El Nueva Frutilandia
3077 24th Street
(415) 648-2958

Ethiopian
Rasselas Ethiopian Cuisine
2801 California Street
(415) 567-5010

Filipino
Barrio Fiesta
909 Antoinette Lane
South San Francisco
(415) 871-8703

French Classic
Fleur de Lys
777 Sutter Street
(415) 673-7779

German
Speckmann's
1550 Church Street
(415) 282-6850

Greek
Stoyanof's Café
1240 9th Avenue
(415) 664-3664

Indian
North India Restaurant
3131 Webster Street
(415) 931-1556

Indonesian
Rice Table
1617 4th Street
San Rafael
(415) 456-1808

Italian
Buca Giovanni
800 Greenwich Street
(415) 776-7766

Japanese
Kabuto Sushi
5116 Geary Boulevard
(415) 752-5652

Korean
Seoul Garden
22 Peace Plaza, Japan Center
  Building
  (east wing, 2nd floor)
(415) 563-7664

Mexican
La Taqueria
2889 Mission Street
(415) 285-7117

Middle Eastern
La Mediterranee
2210 Fillmore Street
(415) 921-2956

288 Noe Street
(415) 431-7210

Moroccan
Mamounia
4411 Balboa Street
(415) 752-6566

Peruvian
Fina Estampa
2374 Mission Street
(415) 824-4437

Spanish
Patio Español
2850 Alemany Boulevard
(415) 587-5117

San Francisco, CA *(continued)*

Swiss
> The Matterhorn Swiss
> Restaurant
> 2323 Van Ness Avenue
> (415) 885-6116

Thai
> Thep Phanom
> 400 Waller Street
> (415) 431-2526

Vietnamese
> Golden Turtle
> 2211 Van Ness Avenue
> (415) 441-4419

SANTA FE, NM

Chinese
> Chow's Contemporary Chinese
> Food
> 720 St. Michael's Drive
> (505) 471-7120

French
> Encore Provence
> 548 Agua Fria
> (505) 983-7470

Indian
> India Palace
> 227 Don Gaspar Avenue
> (505) 986-5859

Italian
> Babbo Ganzo Trattoria
> 130 Lincoln Avenue
> (505) 986-3835

Japanese
> Shohko-Cafe
> 321 Johnson Street
> (505) 983-7288

Korean
> Chopsticks
> 238 North Guadalupe
> (505) 820-2126

Mexican
> Old Mexico Grill
> 2434 Cerrillos Road
> (505) 473-0338

Middle Eastern
> Whistling Moon Cafe
> 402 North Guadalupe
> (505) 983-3093

Thai
> Restaurant Thao
> 322 Garfield Street
> (505) 988-9562

SEATTLE, WA

Afghani
> Kabul
> 2301 North 45th Street
> (206) 545-9000

Central / South American
> Cafe Los Gatos
> 6411 Latona NE (65th Street)
> (206) 527-9765

Chinese
> Judy Fu's Snappy Dragon
> 8917 Roosevelt Way NE
> (206) 528-5575

Czech
> Labuznik
> 1924 First Avenue
> (Virginia Street)
> (206) 441-8899

French
Campagne
86 Pine Street
(206) 728-2800

French Bistro
Gerard's Relais de Lyon
17121 Bothell Way NE
Bothell
(206) 485-7600

German
Reiner's
1106 8th Street
(206) 624-2222

Greek
Lakeside Cafe
7419 Greenwood Avenue
North
(206) 783-6945

Indian
Raga
555 108th Avenue NE
Bellevue
(206) 450-0336

Italian
Saleh al Lago
6804 East Greenlake Way
(206) 524-4044

Japanese
Kaizuka Teppanyaki and
Sushi Bar
1306 South King Street
(206) 860-1556

Korean
Han II
409 Maynard Avenue South
(206) 587-0464

Mediterranean
Adriatica
1107 Dexter Avenue North
(206) 285-5000

Mexican
El Puerco Lloron
1501 Western Avenue
(206) 624-0541

Moroccan
Mamounia
1556 East Olive Street
(206) 329-3886

Persian
Shamshiri
6409 Roosevelt Way NE
(206) 525-3950

Russian / Former Soviet Republics
Pirosmani
2220 Queen Anne Avenue
North
(206) 285-3360

Southeast Asian
Wild Ginger
1400 Western Avenue
(206) 623-4450

Thai
Ayutthaya
727 East Pike Street
(206) 324-8833

Vietnamese
Huong Binh
1207 South Jackson Street
(206) 720-4907

Tampa, FL

Caribbean
Saffron's
1700 Park Street
St. Petersburg
(813) 522-1234

Cuban
La Teresita
3246 West Columbus Drive
(813) 879-4909

Ethiopian
Ibex
1005 North MacDill Avenue
(813) 876-3890

French
Le Bordeaux
1502 South Howard Avenue
(813) 254-4387

German
Rumpelmayer's
4812 East Busch Boulevard
(813) 989-9563

Hungarian
Good Times
1130 Pinellas Bay Way
Tierra Verde
(813) 867-0774

Indian
Taj
2734-B East Fowler Avenue
(813) 971-8483

Italian
Lauro
3915 Henderson Boulevard
(813) 281-2100

Japanese
Joto
310 South Dale Mabry
(813) 875-4842

Korean
Sam Oh Jung
602 North Dale Mabry
  Highway
(813) 871-3233

Mexican
Consuelo's
3814 Neptune Drive
(813) 253-5965

Middle Eastern
The Garden
217 Central Avenue
St. Petersburg
(813) 896-3800

Spanish
Columbia
2117 East 7th Avenue
(813) 248-4961

Thai
Jasmine Thai
13248 North Dale Mabry
(813) 968-1501

Vietnamese
Lemongrass
2373 East Fowler Avenue
(813) 971-0854

Toronto, Canada

Austrian
Griffith's on Queen
2086 Queen Street East
(416) 690-4022

Caribbean
> The Real Jerk Pit
> 709 Queen Street East
> (416) 463-6906

Chinese
> Chinatown Cuisine
> 39 Baldwin Street
> (416) 618-8238

French
> Truffles
> 21 Avenue Road,
>   Four Seasons Hotel
> (416) 928-7331

Hungarian
> Duna Corzo
> 456 Bloor Street West
> (416) 532-2557

Indian
> Garam Masala
> 100 Adelaide Street West
> (416) 368-6658

Indonesian
> Indonesia Restaurant
> 678 Yonge Street
> (416) 967-0697

Italian
> Biagio
> 155 King Street East
> (416) 366-4040

Japanese
> Ah-So Gardens
> 614 Jarvis Street (at Bloor)
> (416) 920-4333

Portuguese
> Lisbon By Night
> 802 A Dundas Street West
> (416) 368-6522

Spanish
> El Rancho
> 430 College Street
> (416) 921-2752

Thai
> Bangkok Garden
> 18 Elm Street
> (416) 977-6748

TUCSON, AZ

Chinese
> Lotus Garden
> 5975 East Speedway
> (602) 298-3351

French
> Le Rendez-vous
> 3844 East Ft. Lowell Road
> (602) 323-7373

Greek
> Olive Tree
> 7000 East Tanque Verde
> (602) 298-1845

Italian
> Daniel's
> 4310 North Campbell Avenue
> (602) 742-3200

Mexican
> El Charro
> 311 North Court Avenue
> (602) 622-1922

TULSA, OK

Chinese
> Chinatown Restaurant
> 3711 South Harvard Avenue
> (918) 747-4753

Tulsa, OK *(continued)*

German
Margaret's
5107 South Sheridan Road
(918) 622-3747

Indian
Darbar
7133-C South Yale Avenue
(918) 488-0016

Italian
Ti Amo
8151 East 21st Street
(918) 665-1939

Japanese
Fuji
8226 East 71st Street
(918) 250-1821

Lebanese
Halim and Mimi's Deli
2615 East 11th Street
(918) 599-9623

Mexican
Casa Laredo
1411 East 41st Street
(918) 743-3744

South / Central American
Aristi Latin Grill
6728 East 41st Street
(918) 622-9522

Thai
Thai-Siam
6380-M East 31st Street
(918) 622-7667

Vietnamese
Kim's Saigon
3807-E South Peoria Avenue
(918) 742-4033

VAIL, CO

French
Left Bank
Sitzmark Hotel
183 Gore Creek
(303) 476-3696

Mirabel's
Beaver Creek
(303) 949-7728

German
Ludwig's
Sonnenalp Resort
20 Vail Road
(303) 479-5429

Japanese
Nozawa
West Vail Lodge
(303) 476-9355

Mexican
Jackalope
2161 North Frontage Road
West
(303) 476-4314

Swiss / Austrian
Alpenrose
100 East Meadow Drive
(303) 476-3194

Thai
Siamese Orchid
12 South Frontage Road
(303) 476-9417

VANCOUVER, B.C.

Chinese
Szechuan Chongqing
2808 Commercial Drive
(604) 254-7434

French
Le Crocodile
100-909 Burrard Street
(604) 669-4298

French Bistro
Cafe de Paris
751 Denman Street
(604) 687-1418

Greek
Stephos
1124 Davie Street
(Thurlow Street)
(604) 683-2555

Hungarian
Bandi's
1427 Howe Street
(604) 685-3391

Indian
Ashiana Tandoor Restaurant
1440 Kingsway
(604) 874-5060

Italian
Caffe De Medici
1025 Robson Street
(604) 669-9322

Japanese
Tojo's
777 West Broadway, Suite 202
(604) 872-8050

Mediterranean
Cin Cin
1154 Robson Street
(604) 688-7338

Southeast Asian
Tea & Silk
2767 Commercial Drive
(604) 872-1688

Thai
Chili Club
1000 Beach Avenue
(604) 681-6000

Vietnamese
Phnom Penh Restaurant
244 East George Street
(604) 682-5777

WASHINGTON, D.C.

Afghani
Panjshir
924 West Broad Street
Falls Church
(703) 536-4566

224 Maple Avenue West
Vienna
(703) 281-4183

Argentine
Argentine Grill
2433 18th Street, NW
(202) 234-1818

Brazilian
Grill from Ipanema
1858 Columbia Road, NW
(202) 986-0757

Burmese
Burma
740 6th Street, NW (upstairs)
(202) 638-1280

Caribbean
Hibiscus Cafe
3401 K Street, NW
Georgetown
(202) 338-0408

Washington, D.C. (continued)

Chinese
    Seven Seas
    1776 East Jefferson Street,
      1776 Plaza Shopping Center
    Rockville
    (301) 770-5020

Ethiopian
    Meskerem
    2434 18th Street, NW
    (202) 462-4100

French
    Jean Louis / Palladin
    2650 Virginia Avenue, NW,
      Watergate Hotel
    (202) 298-4488 (Jean Louis)
    (202) 298-4455 (Palladin)

German
    Wurzburg Haus
    7236 Muncaster Mill Road,
      Red Mill Shopping Center
    Rockville
    (301) 330-0402

Greek
    Mykonos
    1910 K Street, NW
    (202) 331-0370

Indian
    Bombay Club
    815 Connecticut Avenue, NW
    (202) 659-3727

Indonesian
    Sarinah Satay House
    1338 Wisconsin Avenue, NW
    (202) 337-2955

Italian
    Galileo
    1110 21st Street, NW
    (202) 293-7191

Japanese
    Tako Grill
    7756 Wisconsin Avenue
    Bethesda
    (301) 652-7030

Korean
    Woo Lae Oak
    1500 South Joyce Street
    Arlington
    (703) 521-3706

Lebanese
    Lebanese Taverna
    2641 Connecticut Avenue,
      NW
    (202) 265-8681

    5900 Washington Boulevard
    Arlington
    (703) 241-8681

Mexican
    Tia Queta
    8009 Norfolk Avenue
    Bethesda
    (301) 654-4443

Moroccan
    Fes
    4917 Elm Street
    Bethesda
    (301) 718-1777

Russian
    State of the Union
    1357 U Street, NW
    (202) 588-8810

Spanish

    Taberna del Alabardero

    1776 I Street, NW

      (entrance on 18th Street)

    (202) 429-2200

Thai

    Busara

    2340 Wisconsin Avenue, NW

    (202) 337-2340

Turkish

    Nizam

    523 Maple Avenue West

    Vienna

    (703) 938-8948

Vietnamese

    Cafe Saigon

    1135 North Highland Street

    Arlington

    (703) 243-6522;

    (703) 276-7110

West African

    Bukom

    2442 18th Street, NW

    (202) 265-4600